HINDUISM

ITS HISTORICAL DEVELOPMENT

Troy Wilson Organ

Distinguished Professor of Philosophy
Ohio University
Athens, Ohio

Barron's Educational Series, Inc.
Woodbury, New York

All inquiries should be addressed to:
Barron's Educational Series, Inc.
113 Crossways Park Drive
Woodbury, New York 11797

Library of Congress Catalog Card No. 73–10676

Paper Edition
International Standard Book No. 0–8120–0500–7

2 3 4 5 6

Table of Contents

Introduction

The Sanskrit terms have been transliterated without using diacritical marks, except in the case of "Brahmā" which is necessary to distinguish the God of Creation from "Brahma," an alternative for "Brahman." The diacritical marks are indicated in the Index, and should be referred to for correct pronunciation. In general, consonants are pronounced as in English and vowels as in German. The following key may be helpful:

a	as in *A*merican	s'	as in *sh*ell
$\bar{a}$	an in f*a*ther	$ṣ$	as in *sh*un (a sibilant, i.e., *sh* with the tongue turned backward)
e	as in pr*e*y		
i	as in f*i*t		
$\bar{\imath}$	as in pol*i*ce	$ṭ$,	*ṭh*, *ḍ*, *ḍh*, *ṇ* (cerebrals, i.e., pronounced with the tongue turned up and against the roof of the mouth)
o	as in g*o*		
u	as in p*u*ll		
$\bar{u}$	as in f*oo*l		
ai	as in *ai*sle	t,	*th*, *d*, *dh*, *n* (dentals, i.e., pronounced with the tongue against the back of the upper front teeth)
au	as in h*ou*se		
s	as in *s*un		

CHAPTER 1

Problems in
Understanding Hinduism

Hinduism belongs in a series of volumes on the religions of the world, yet Hinduism is not *a world religion*. The word "a" misrepresents Hinduism in suggesting a singularity whereas Hinduism is a multiplicity; the word "world" misrepresents Hinduism because Hinduism is largely limited to India; and the word "religion" misrepresents Hinduism because Hinduism is too broad to be confined within any of the usual definitions of religion. Hinduism is a spectrum of beliefs and practices ranging from the veneration of trees, stones, and snakes in villages scarcely out of the Stone Age to the abstract metaphysical speculations of sophisticated urban intellectuals whose attainments have been recognized by British knighthoods, Nobel prizes, and entrance into international learned societies. Although "Hindu" and "Indian" are derived from the same word—the name of the river which the Indo-Europeans called Sindhu, the Iranians Hindu, the Greeks Indos, and the English Indus—the leaders of the modern nation of India are quick to remind

1

foreigners that not all Indians are Hindus. Modern India's desire to be known as a secular state in contrast to the religious state of Pakistan prompts the reminder and rebuke that 15 to 20 per cent of the citizens of India are not Hindus. But there are no criteria for determining who is and who is not Hindu. There are no hierarchies of priests, no rolls of congregations, no uniformly accepted sacraments, no creedal statements to be agreed to, no initiatory rites universally accepted by Hindus, and no practices which always distinguish the Hindu from the non-Hindu. Being a Hindu appears to be a matter of individual decision, yet few Hindus have chosen to be Hindu. A Hindu has been described as anyone who does not say no when asked, "Are you a Hindu?" For example, Govinda-Dasa writes that "any and every one is a Hindu who does not repudiate that designation" and who "accepts any of the many beliefs, and follows any of the many practices that are anywhere regarded as Hindu." [1] But Govinda-Dasa does not name the beliefs and practices. Instead he offers a list of items which he says have been thought by some to be essential to the Hindu, whereas in fact none is necessary: birth from Hindu parents, birth in geographical limits of India, belief in the Vedas, practice of the caste system, belief in the sanctity of the cow, belief in God, leaving the scalp lock (*shikha*), wearing the sacred thread, observing special rules concerning diet, belief in *karma* and reincarnation, belief in incarnations of gods, belief in the sacredness of *Brahmin* priests, holding to restrictions of race and color, and practice of Hindu law! This list seems extreme, as we shall indicate in the next chapter, but it does serve to call attention to the scarcity of universally accepted beliefs and practices among Hindus. In India today it is not unusual to find a person who denies he is a Hindu but who acts in a manner which others associate with Hinduism. I recall an occasion in India in which a dinner companion who, after assuring me he had completely deserted Hinduism, carefully removed a fly from his glass of water, placed it on the floor, and then observed, "I think it will be all right now." I could not refrain from reminding my friend that his act revealed more about his religion than his words.

Native versus Western Studies

Indological studies were inaugurated by Westerners. The Asiatic Society of Bengal is the oldest and one of the most highly regarded of the many organizations for the study of things Indian. It was founded in 1784. Early scholars of this society were Sir William Jones, H. T. Colebrooke, and H. H. Wilson. Other pioneers were A. E. Gough, F. Max Müller, Paul Deussen, and Richard Garbe. All were Europeans. Most of the Western scholars who studied Indian thought were of the idealistic schools of Western philosophy, and, not surprisingly, when in the 1920s Indian intellectuals like S. Radhakrishnan, S. K. Belvalkar, R. D. Ranade, S. N. Dasgupta, M. Hiriyanna, S. C. Vidyabusana, and K. C. Bhattacharyya published works on their own culture, they made Indian philosophy look as if it might have come from the pens of men like Kant, Hegel, Fichte, Bosanquet, Bradley, and Green. The political independence movement in India changed the direction toward which Indian scholars look. Many have discovered the eye of Shiva, the eye that looks within. For example, R. C. Majumdar and A. D. Pusalkar, the editors of the monumental series of books entitled *The History and Culture of the Indian People*, announce as one of their intentions the correction of the errors consciously or unconsciously contained in British histories such as *The Cambridge History of India*. One might argue that especially in the area of religion the practitioner is a more competent expounder than the objective student. That is the argument Kenneth W. Morgan gives for the studies incorporated in a book entitled *The Religion of the Hindus*: "The religious, social, and speculative patterns of India have been built on assumptions and beliefs so different from ours that it is difficult for a Westerner to describe them without distortion." [2] One cannot disagree with this observation, and yet this does not exhaust the problem, for the assumptions and beliefs of the Westerner are so different from those of the Hindu that it is difficult for the Hindu to communicate his religious, social, and speculative patterns in a manner in which they can be comprehended by the Westerner without distortion. My own experiences in bringing Hindus, Buddhists, and Confucian-Taoists into the classroom to interpret their own religions to Western students have been so unsuccessful that I have given up the practice. Communication of the delicate subject matter known as religion places a high premium on understanding both the religion being presented and the intellectual categories of the audience. The non-Hindu has the advantage of being sufficiently detached that he may be better able to recognize a Hindu belief or act than can a Hindu. If the Westerner is not sympathetic to Hinduism, he may produce a caricature like *Mother India* by Katherine Mayo, and if the Westerner is gullible, he may distort and misrepresent Hinduism by approbating everything in Hinduism. The Theosophists have sometimes been guilty of this. Louis Renou, one of the best students of Hinduism, has warned that "the different theosophical sects, the anthroposophists, traditionalists, and the Western schools of Yoga . . . can be described more justly if one simply mentions and then ignores them. . . . All that these people succeed for the most part in getting out of Hinduism is an artificial vocabulary and arbitrary interpretations chosen haphazardly from the total field. . . . Let us always remember that India is an Eldorado for charlatans." [3] Great harm has been done to intercultural communications between India and the West by both Western detractors and Western sycophants. A Western scholar who studies Hinduism with the desire to understand sympathetically this pattern of life and thought, who is thoroughly familiar with Western thought patterns and fairly comfortable in Western value systems so that he is not looking to the East for "salvation," [4] may be the best interpreter of Hinduism to Western minds. At least such is the hope of the author of this volume.

Problems of Chronology

"The only way to acquire a correct knowledge of Hinduism is to study it in its historical development." [5] But how can we study the historical development of a people who cared nothing for history, who did not write history? "Probably speaking," writes Dhan Gopal

Mukharji, "India has no history. We as a race have no consciousness of it, for our history has been written mostly by foreigners—the Greeks, the Arabs and the Chinese. The consciousness of history as an asset of life and as an expression of our people, does not seem important to us. History is the record of men's relation to time, but the Hindu does not believe in time, and all our life, according to the Hindu's vision, is an illusion and something to be transcended." [6] Mukharji is often extreme in his statements, but this has the ring of truth. The Hindu "has no faith in his power to change history because for him there is no history." [7] Kings and princes did not leave precise records of their own achievements on the monuments they erected. Military leaders did not hire secretaries to record their exploits, and authors did not sign nor date their works. Only one date of Indian history in the years B.C. can be claimed to have become settled: the date of the death of the Buddha, 487 B.C. This lack of interest in dates is not to be attributed to inability of a primitive people to think of any time other than the present. Quite the contrary, the Hindus have been from earliest times much interested in the past. But the interest has been in tradition rather than in what might be called history. The past in which they are interested is that manifested in the present, not the past that is long ago and far away. The past lives in the present. Any event in the last two thousand years may under certain circumstances be "contemporary." "I have never seen such a disregard of time and place as in this God-mad country of ours," says Dhan Gopal Mukharji. [8]

Greece and India have produced two magnificent civilizations, great in literature, art, and philosophy; but at one crucial point they differ: the Greek civilization died. Modern Greece is a nation that does not have its roots in the splendor of ancient Greece, but modern India is in part the manifestation of a civilization five thousand years old. This unbroken tradition is a matter of great pride to contemporary Indians. But while the preservation of a civilization for this length of time is unique except for China, survival is not a value in itself. The chairman of the committee which wrote the Constitution of India once punctured that pride in these words: "That the Hindu Society has been able to stand still while others have died out or disappeared is hardly a matter of congratulation. . . . the foreigner, who conquered the Hindus did not find it necessary to kill them wholesale. There is no honour in mere survival." [9] Antiques are valued as antiques; the utilitarian value of antiques is quite another matter. An old custom may be quaint, but it can also be a fossilized, outmoded form of behavior which should be discarded. The ox-drawn wooden plow used extensively throughout India today is quaint, but the low yield of crops in ground so tilled suggests that there are better ways to cultivate fields. Some of the traditional ways of acting become so out of step with modern aspirations that they must be stopped by law, e.g., Untouchability. Sometimes the death of a civilization mercifully clears the decks for new ways of thinking and acting. India has been described as a land where nothing dies.

Indians are a tradition-minded people, not a history-minded people. These attitudes are changing today. The movement toward Indian Independence, which roughly can be limited to the twentieth century, was marked by sustained efforts to examine India's past in order to determine what her future might be. Jawaharlal Nehru, India's dynamic leader for the first decade and a half after the departure of the British, urged Indians to break with tradition: "India must break with much of her past and not allow it to dominate the present. Our lives are encumbered with the dead wood of this past; all that is dead and has served its purpose has to go." [10] Nehru was uneasy about his own Hindu background, and often said he was an agnostic rather than a Hindu, as though the two were incompatible. Yet Nehru's sentences which follow this clarion call to a break with the past reveal reverence for tradition: "But that does not mean a break with, or a forgetting of, the vital and life-giving in that past. We can never forget the ideals that have moved our race, the dreams of the Indian people through the ages, the wisdom of the ancients, the buoyant energy and love of life and nature of our forefathers, their spirit of curiosity and mental adventure, the daring of their thought, their splendid achievements in literature, art, and culture, their love of truth and beauty and freedom, the basic values that they set up, their understanding of life's mysterious ways, their toleration of other ways than theirs, their capacity to absorb other peoples and their cultural accomplishments, synthesize them and develop a varied and mixed culture; nor can we forget the myriad experiences which have built up our ancient race and lie embedded in our subconscious minds." [11] When one reflects on what Nehru wanted to preserve from the past, one wonders what is left from which he wanted Indian citizens to break.

If the first problem faced by the student who wishes to study the historical development of Hinduism is the absence of dates for events in Indian history, the second is the problem of affixing periods of development. The tendency to divide history into ancient, medieval, and modern seems hard to resist, and the results are odd indeed—e.g., D. S. Sharma suggests an ancient period of 3000 years (2000 B.C.–A.D. 1000), a medieval period of 800 years (1000–1800), and a modern period from 1800.[12] Even as radical a thinker as K. Damodaran uses the traditional Western pattern, although he varies it slightly in his book *Indian Thought: A Critical Survey*, adding a pre-ancient period which he calls "The Dawn" which ends at 150 B.C. The ancient period for him ended with the ascension of the first of the Gupta kings in A.D. 320, and the modern begins, as claim many other historians of India, with the conquest by the British, although they differ as to whether the British conquest dates from the Battle of Plassey (1757) or the Sepoy Mutiny (1857). Although Indian intellectuals sometimes remark sarcastically that the ancient-medieval-modern pattern is impossible because India has not experienced a series of "falls" as has the West, a better appraisal of the situation is that the ancient-medieval-modern pattern implies a progression which does not fit the Indian scene. The Advaita Vedantists are prone to trace such a line of development with respect to Indian religion: from primitive polytheism to an ethical religion, from the religion of morality to monotheism, and from the worship of one personal god to the realization of one's identity with the impersonal Absolute. This line of thought has unfortunately been given support by many philosophers in the West who have been advised that non-dual Vedanta is a true picture and the supreme development of Hinduism. This must be written off as a form of special pleading of a noble and brash form of living Hinduism.

Any theory of progressive development in Hinduism must be restrained and countered by pointing out the fundamental conservation of Hinduism. In India the old and the new are concurrent.

Probably nowhere else do people live in so many centuries simultaneously. Sun worship and atomic research, ox carts and jet airplanes, astrology and theoretical physics, magic and modern medicine, ultramodern multistoried buildings and mud huts—these do mix in India. Many businessmen in New Delhi, Calcutta, Bombay, and Madras wear Western suits during working hours and change to traditional dhotis and lungis at home. Who can say when tradition is an asset and when it is a burden? Civilizations differ in the tenacity with which they hold to the past and also in the quantity of past with which they must cope. The student must keep in mind that Hindus are proud of a living tradition which goes back at least four thousand years.

Such considerations as the above cause us to realize the folly of trying to trace the historical development of Hinduism in the three traditional Western periods. Therefore, we shall study Hinduism in the following four periods:

1. *The Vedic Period* begins at the rather conservative date of 2000 B.C., the time just before the first invasions of the Indo-Europeans. It is the period of the composition of the basic scriptures of Hinduism. The end of the period is the date of the birth of the Buddha, which we shall round off at 600 B.C.

2. *The First Period of Challenge and Reaction* begins with the appearance of Buddhism and Jainism as variants on the Hindu theme, and also with some of the most vigorous attacks of a group of thinkers whom we now refer to as the Materialists. The reaction to the challenges took the form of the writing of the great epics of Hindu religion, especially the *Mahabharata,* which may be regarded as an encyclopedia in the framework of an epic. The year A.D. 300 is the approximate date for the completion of the *Mahabharata.*

3. *The Period of Reformation* runs to the time of the first Muslim emperors, and is marked by efforts to reform Hinduism from within as a result of the first challenges. The assumption of the reformers was that what was needed was a re-examination and alteration of the indigenous products of India, specifically the Vedic literature. The reforms were of two types: an effort to develop philosophical

understanding of Hinduism, and an effort to develop a religion of the heart.

4. *The Second Period of Challenge and Reaction* is a period in which the challenge came from the outside. Islam, Christianity, and Western culture have been disruptive forces in India. Islam and Hinduism are diametrically opposed at many important points. Christian missionaries introduced religious propaganda into India. The Indian experience of Western learning, attitudes, and values has been cathartic and corruptive of Hindu ideas and ideals. While some Indians have adapted Hindu tradition to the attainment of Western goals, others rebel from aping the West and seek to vitalize Hinduism from her own wellsprings. The national goals of modern India have stimulated an examination of the ancient religion, and, while for some the old has been found wanting, for others the result is a new birth of Hinduism. The inclusion of the last eight hundred years as one period of Indian cultural history may seem strange to the Western student, but we must keep in mind that changes take place slowly in India. Hindu culture is loaded with tradition and custom. The central government of India since Independence has been trying to press the Indian people into the Modern Age without their having gone through the Renaissance, the Enlightenment, and the industrial and social revolutions which brought European man from the Dark Ages to modernity. The success of this movement has thus far been modest.

Religion and Culture

Paul Tillich distinguishes three types of culture: the heteronomous, the autonomous, and the theonomous. In heteronomous culture the forms and laws of thinking and acting are subjected to an authoritative criteria, either that of an ecclesiastical religion or a political structure. Western countries have often taken this form. The Christian church, the Jewish synagogue, the Muslim mosque, the Nazi state, and the Communist party are among the authorities by which Western culture has been fashioned and evaluated. In autonomous culture an effort is made to fashion forms of personal and social life with no reference to anything ultimate or unconditional. Man's reason, both theoretical and practical, is the determiner of values and life-styles. Seventeenth-century Europe was an age of reason, when men like Bacon, Galileo, Hobbes, Descartes, Spinoza, and Leibniz argued that knowledge is power and that men could solve all their problems if they would put their minds to the task. Both heteronomous cultures and autonomous cultures introduce a split into the life of man: the former between authoritative agencies speaking in the name of transcendent realities and values and the people who must be subjected to laws and norms from which they are estranged; the latter between the bearers of pure universal reason and those who need to be guided into rationality. A theonomous culture is one in which the superior law is at the same time the innermost law of man himself. The guidelines of human living are not something strange to man but his own spiritual ground. Theonomous culture is therefore distinguished from both heterono-mous and autonomous culture in that the ideal is not superimposed upon the real.

Hinduism is a theonomous culture. Hinduism as a religion and Hinduism as a culture are so intertwined that we can never be sure whether a certain mode of behavior is Hindu or Indian. We can never be sure whether a way of behaving is prescriptively right or descriptively correct, whether it is normative or traditional. Perhaps this is the penalty and the premium of a long unbroken tradition. The customary and the moral, the cultural and the religious, are no longer discernible. Tillich says, "Religion is the substance of culture and culture the form of religion." [13] We are tempted to alter this for our purposes to read: "Hindu religion is the substance of Indian culture and Indian culture the form of Hindu religion." Hinduism, in other words, has been such a pervasive element in the life of the people of South Asia that the disentanglement of religion and culture is a risky undertaking. For example, the caste mentality, which is surely Hindu in origin, has permeated the thinking of all peoples of India. Muslims in India divide themselves into Sayad, Mughal, Sheikh, and Pathan; Zoroastrians distinguish Atharva, Rathaestha, Vastryafshuyan, and Huiti; and Christians and Jews make similar distinctions. Some Christians in Madras state even boast that they hold more firmly to the caste system than do Hindus.[14]

Since Hinduism is not easily divided into the sacred and the profane, a Hindu will have difficulty in interpreting his religion to a Westerner. Sanskrit has no word for religion. Words like "devotion" (*bhakti*), "duty" (*dharma*), and "discipline" (*yoga*) have to suffice. The Hindu will have further complications in explaining Hinduism when the Westerner asks questions like "What does Hinduism believe about . . . ?" and "What is the Hindu practice with regard to . . . ?" His difficulty arises from two counts: because Hinduism is not an independent phenomenon in Indian society, and because it has so many diverse forms. India has been a melting pot of races and religions for more than five thousand years. The melting has not been a smelting but a smoothing of rough edges in order that people of many beliefs and practices could live together. Accommodation, not assimilation, has been the usual sociological pattern in India. Christians, Jews, and Muslims tend to assume that religions are necessarily excluding, that each person is either a Christian or a heathen, a Jew or a gentile, a Muslim or an infidel. How difficult for such people to be convinced that a nonexcluding religion is really a religion! How strange and disturbing to hear a Hindu suggest that perhaps a Christian is a crypto-Hindu! How threatening to discover that Jesus Christ can be listed as one of the many incarnations of God! Hinduism is not altogether amorphous, although it does have a spectrum ranging from primitive magic, superstition, and animism to the world's most subtle and profound forms of idealistic philosophy. One of the early Western students of Hinduism, Alfred C. Lyall, noting "the entire absence of system" described Hinduism as "the wandering beliefs of an intensely superstitious people" and "a conglomerate of rude worship and high liturgies; of superstitions and philosophies, belonging to very different phases of society and mental culture." [15]

Hinduism as Religion and as Philosophy

Religion and philosophy cannot be separated in Hinduism. The reason is quite simple: both are therapies, both are constructed in the pattern of traditional Indian medicine. Siddhartha Gautama, the Hindu genius who came to be known as the Buddha, gave a profound and simple expression of Hinduism as therapy in four questions:

1. What are the symptoms of the illness?
2. Do they denote a real illness?
3. Is the illness curable?
4. What is the cure?

Unfortunately, by this time Hinduism had become so clouded with ancillary metaphysical issues that Gautama's analysis, instead of clarifying the Hindu therapy, inaugurated a break which remains to this day.

Even though Hindu religion and Hindu philosophy are inseparable, efforts are made to disentangle them. Often in a volume on Hinduism, the author, if he is a philosopher, will say, "Hinduism is a philosophy, but it is a *religious* philosophy, that is, it is a way of living as well as a way of thinking." If the author is a student of the history of religions, he will say, "Hinduism is a religion, but it is a *philosophical* religion, that is, it is a way of *thinking* as well as a way of living." Heinrich Zimmer, for example, wrote, "Oriental philosophy is accompanied and supported by the practice of a way of life." [16] Louis Renou said that Hinduism "is not a religion in quite the same sense in which we use the word in the West. . . . On one side it is inseparable from philosophy; on another, from communal and social life." [17] Franklin Edgerton observed, "Philosophy in India has always been practical in its nature. And its practical motive has been what we should call religious." [18] Some Indians talk out of both sides of the mouth; for example, G. R. Malkani of the Indian Philosophical Institute says, "Hinduism . . . is a religion that cannot be divorced from philosophy, and is in fact the highest form of philosophy." [19] Swami Nikhilananda identifies the goals of the two: "The goal of philosophy may be Truth, and the goal of religion, God; but in the final experience God and Truth are one and the same Reality." [20] Nalini Kanta Brahma says in the preface to his book, *Philosophy of Hindu Sadhana*, that it is "a presentation of the practical side of

Hindu Philosophy," [21] but S. Radhakrishnan says in the foreword, "In 'Hindu Sadhana' Dr. Nalini Kanta Brahma contributes a highly interesting and important work to the literature of Hindu Thought and Religion . . . a book which will be invaluable to all students of Religion." [22] T. M. P. Mahadevan has analyzed the problem of Indian philosophy and religion as follows: "It has puzzled many a Western student of Indian thought how and why there has been maintained in India a close alliance between religion and philosophy. Generally speaking, the preacher and the philosopher alike in the West deplore this alliance for quite opposite reasons. To the preacher, it would appear that Hinduism is too philosophical to be a religion. He finds in it a cold intellectualism, not an appeal to life in all its aspects, but an appeal to logic. To the philosopher, Indian philosophy seems to be overweighted on the side of intuition because of its association with religion." [23] A young Indian philosopher, B. K. Matilal, launched in the spring of 1970 a new periodical entitled *Journal of Indian Philosophy*. The announcement of the new journal states, "The field of our contributions will be bound by the limits of rational inquiry: we will avoid questions that lie in the fields of theology and mystical experience. . . . Our aim will be to attract professional philosophers rather than professional internationalists." Matilal continues, "We make this statement not in a spirit of snobbery but out of regret at the long neglect of Indian philosophy by those professionals in the West who might best have put it to creative use." Matilal says the *Upanishads* and the *Gita* are philosophy only in an "etymological sense." I share Matilal's concern, and I agree that the *Upanishads* and the *Gita* are more speculation than philosophical argument, but I contend that when one studies Indian philosophy "without recourse to religion or ontological commitment" (Matilal's words), what one is studying is only that portion of Hinduism which satisfies the Western criterion of philosophy.

Part of the difficulty is that the Indian—be he Hindu, Jain, or Buddhist—does not do philosophy as philosophy is done in the West. For him philosophy is essentially a quest for values. For example, L. C. Gupta in a paper delivered at the 28th Indian Philosophical Congress (1953) said, "A philosophy which is merely an enquiry into the ultimate nature of the spatio-temporal world or the nature of consciousness as such and is thus merely a philosophy of being is a truncated thing. . . . no philosophical theory can be wholly true unless it is based on and shaped by our deepest experiences involving active interaction between ourselves and the objective world. It should be a reflection of the whole of our life and not simply a fraction of it." [24] Whereas philosophy in the West began in wonder and seeks above all to make ideas clear, philosophy in India began as a way to eliminate suffering and to integrate man with his total environment. Even the classical logical treatises, the *Nyaya Sutras*, open with the observation that logic is offered as a means to "supreme felicity."

Rather than trying to classify Hinduism into religious slots like pantheism, henotheism, theism, or atheism or into philosophical slots like monism, dualism, rationalism, intuitionism, naturalism, or idealism, a wiser course would be to recognize it as a unique life-style concerned primarily with developing the candidate for humanity into the paradigmatic self-aware man. Hinduism is *sadhana*. But unfortunately the English language has no word synonymous with *sadhana*. The term comes from the root *sadha* meaning to reach one's goal, to accomplish an aim, to guide aright, to fulfill, to subdue, to gain power over. It is the process of the perfecting of man. It is the liberating of dormant powers, the fulfilling of potentialities. *Sadhana* is not simply the notion of the full development of the individual man; it keeps man in the social context, for man is to be redeemed both in the physical world and in society. He is not saved from matter nor from his interpersonal relationships and obligations, since only in matter and in society can man realize his being. *Sadhana* is the healing of the hiatus between theory and practice. It is a becoming of being, a realizing of what we are, a perfecting of latent perfections. It is the existential achievement-discovery of man's essence.

When Hinduism is interpreted as *sadhana* the student is able to discuss Hindu "religion" and Hindu "philosophy" without the usual constant reminder that religion in Hinduism is not like Western religion, and philosophy in Hinduism is not like Western philosophy. Consider, for example, the plight of Betty Heimann when she wrote in her book, *Facets of Indian Thought*, "Two ways are thus open to Hindu religion and philosophy. The way of concrete cult and contact between the beings in heaven and earth—and the other, the higher way, of abstract speculation on the ever unmanifestable fullness of the Divine." [25] Miss Heimann revealed her problem by referring to the ways of "cult" and "speculation" as two ways of "Hindu religion and philosophy." She was not able to separate the two, yet she undoubtedly knew that they are separable though related. Surely she did not mean that there are four distinct ways: (1) cult in religion, (2) speculation in religion, (3) cult in philosophy, and (4) speculation in philosophy. What she needed was the concept of *sadhana*. Then she could have referred to cult and speculation as the religious and the philosophical aspects of *sadhana*.

Hindu *sadhana* is both goal and means to the goal, truth and way to truth. Hinduism does not leave the devotee to his own devices; rather it offers to him a variety of techniques for implementation. Existentialism did not need to appear in Hinduism, disrupting the ideology of the system, since in Hinduism existence is part of the total pattern. In the words of René Guénon, "In all doctrines that are metaphysically complete, as those of the East, theory is always accompanied or followed by an effective realization, for which it merely provides the necessary basis; no realization can be embarked upon without a sufficient theoretical preparation, but theory is ordained entirely with a view to this realization as the means towards the end, and this point of view is presupposed, or at least tacitly implied, even in the exterior expression of the doctrine." [26] This is why—to use Western categories—Hindu philosophy has not been able to dissociate itself from religious tendencies. Hindu philosophy and Hindu religion are but aspects of the realizing of the highest ends of life. *Sadhana* is the tenor of human life to the attainment of an ideal goal. Although Hinduism has manifested itself in almost every form of religion and philosophy, it is not merely religion nor philosophy. It is a life-style which has been focused essentially and existentially on the fundamental human problem: the problem of being human. Knowing the external world and building the ideal social order have in Hinduism been secondary to actualizing the potentialities of man.

To call Hinduism a *sadhana* is not to assert that Hinduism is a single pattern of life which is to be followed by anyone who identifies himself as a Hindu. The only *sadhana* which realizes the goal is *ishta sadhana* (one's own *sadhana*). One man's eating will not nourish another man's body. In the words of the Buddha, each must work out his own salvation.

The Hindu Way of Thinking

"We know very little about any thought except our own, especially about Indian thought." So wrote Albert Schweitzer in the first line of his controversial book, *Indian Thought and Its Development.* He added that it is difficult to become familiar with Indian thought because "in its very nature [it] is so entirely different from our own." [27] Few Westerners would choose to disagree with Schweitzer, but when he adds that the difference is in Indian "world and life-negation" as contrasted to Western "world and life-affirmation," many would argue that Schweitzer's acquaintance with Indian thought was far too limited. A more salient point would be to indicate that there is a difference in how thought moves in the West and in India. Hinduism is shaped by a way of thinking which seems to be primarily directed to the preservation of insights of the past. It is a living tradition. Progress does not involve destroying the old to make way for the new. We in the West are accustomed to building upon the past, but we also stress the destruction of the past; Copernicus destroys Ptolemy, Newton destroys Copernicus, and Einstein destroys Newton. Not so in India. A Westerner arguing with an Indian may find himself in the strange position of being disproven by a quotation from the *Upanishads.* Truth is eternal. "Nothing ever incorporated in their traditions has completely vanished," writes A. Barth, "and even what has the most modern appearance, we may look to find again some day or other in their most ancient monuments. In very few cases only, are we likewise able to ascertain which of their ideas are ancient or modern, and every attempt at an accurate division in some way lays itself open to objections." [28] Some Indians are unhappy about this feature of their culture. Madan Gopal contends that conservation of traditions is India's chief problem: "The real problem of India is, at its root, the problem of our fixed attitude towards life and its problems. . . .

nowhere is this pattern of life so rigid, nowhere are age-old and meaningless traditions and conventions so deeply ingrained, nowhere is the life of the masses so minutely regulated and, also, nowhere is the freedom of mind so limited as in India." [29] Gopal argues, "The result of all this is that we are a thoroughly melancholic race—you may euphemistically call it mystic. Our sense of humor, if we have any, is very weak. Life is looked upon as an unwelcome burden, never as a privilege." [30] His generalizations are far too sweeping, but he does rightly call attention to the fundamental conservatism of the Hindu style of thinking.

Another indication of the Hindu desire to preserve the past can be noticed in the way thinking moves in the West and in India. We in the West think in distinct independent steps. These are in a logical order such that moving from one to the next is often a deserting of one for the next. Our thinking is linear. If A leads to B, then we drop A upon reaching B; and if B leads to C, we drop B upon reaching C. But in Hinduism thought proceeds by radiations from a productive center: that which is a means of reaching B is treated as a value in itself which must not be lost in the movement of thought. Hindu thinking is nonlinear, clustery, configurative. Starting from A, the Hindu moves to AB, AC, AD, and AE; then he moves from AB to ABW, from AC to ACX, from AD to ADY, and from AE to AEZ; and hence out in wider and wider relationships. Hindu thinking is progressive-conservative. It moves from an original starting point without losing the reality and value of the original. This can also be illustrated from the zero (*bindu*), an Indian invention. *Bindu* is not naught as in Western mathematics; instead it is an unlimited entity. The term *bindu* means seed or semen. It is the productive point of potentiality. Therefore, the Hindu in thinking of the *bindu* continually wanders from the formality of mathematics into the enigma of a reality positioned between generation and destruction, life and death. It is the creative matrix within which all is contained.

Progress in Hindu thought consists in retaining the insights of previous thought and in building upon those insights. There is a profound sense of continuity. Dialogue takes place with little regard to the historical date of the ideas expressed but with great concern to preserve the traditional values and truths into the present and the future. This has been possible because of a stability unknown in the West since the Renaissance. The tolerance which has been a characteristic of Indian culture makes it possible for the Hindu to avoid experiencing a shattering revolution when he is thrust into violent and conflicting relations with the West. Modern India's most unsettling experience—the attempt to become an independent, self-supporting nation among the modern nations of the world—has not swept India away from Hindu moorings. Although Prime Minister Nehru never stressed his nonalignment policy as rooted in Hinduism, the unwillingness to take sides in the cold war is a fitting manifestation of the religious-philosophical tradition of Hinduism. It is a refusal to an either-or attitude toward communism and democracy.

In India change is not a standard way to increase the good. Value lies in sameness, in the repetition of the familiar. A nonclimactic ongoingness is experienced in the monotony of the Indian diet, in the sleepy tending of cattle throughout the dry season, in the dreary sameness of cinema plots, in the repetition of *mantras* in temples, and even in the anticlimactic sexual activity recommended in Tantra. The universe itself is a huge perpetual-motion machine. In fact, Indian mathematicians have often occupied themselves with plans for the creation of perpetual-motion machines, e.g., Aryabhata in the sixth century and Bhaskara in the twelfth. Hollow rims filled with quicksilver was the secret formula.

Intellectual research in Hinduism is chiefly the explication of wisdom already possessed. Thus Swami Dayananda Saraswati, the founder of the Arya Samaj, contended that the Vedas contained all the knowledge possible to mankind. He located the latest discoveries of chemistry and physics and all technological advances in the Vedas, and even hinted of scientific knowledge in the Vedas which future research and experience would discover. Dayananda was stating what had been believed for generations by Hindus. But not all Indians take a charitable attitude toward the Hindu style of thought. Nirad C. Chaudhuri writes, "There is no such thing as thinking properly so called among the Hindus, for it is a faculty of the mind developed only in Greece, and exercised only by the heirs of the Greeks. A very large part of what is called Hindu thinking is woolly speculation or just mush." [31]

Hindu thinking may seem to Westerners to be scholastic, unrealistic, dreamy, and fuzzy. Things do not appear to be presented in sharp focus; rather they seem to blend into each other. The Western mind is tempted to regard this as an Indian inability to see things as they are. But the difference is rooted in different assumptions. In the West we take the law of noncontradiction as fundamental because we view the objects of reality as independent in ontological status. Hindus call this the law of either . . . or, and they reject it because they tend to view reality as a unity. For them the thesis and the antithesis are necessary correlatives of the same thing. Andre Breton has stated it in this fashion: "Everything tends to make us believe that there exists a certain point of the mind at which life and death, the real and the imagined, past and future, the communicable and the incommunicable, high and low, cease to be perceived as contradictions." [32] No one can understand Hinduism until he has entertained the possibility of styles of thinking strikingly different from the exclusively two-valued logic which we Westerners sometimes parochially regard as the thinking of all rational beings.

This consideration of the problems inherent in attempting to understand Hinduism is not intended to discourage the student from undertaking the task, but it is designed to warn him against the facile assumption he can grasp Hinduism on his own terms. The twisting of Eastern ideas and practices until they resemble Western thought and Western values, the demand that everything be as much like us as possible, has been a pattern of even the best intentioned scholars. The pattern is not uncommon among Westernized Indians. They are the ones whom Macaulay desired to create, "a class of persons Indian in blood and colour, but English in tastes, in opinion, in morals and in intellect." The contention of this book is that there is a better way to study Hinduism. We recognize the truth in the somewhat gloomy remark of Surendranath Dasgupta, "No foreigner has ever adequately understood our land," [33] but we contend that the most adequate way to understand Hinduism is to seek to learn about it by trying to study it in its own terms and categories.

CHAPTER 2

The Hindu Motif

Each religion proceeds from a conceptual structure. Each begins with assumptions about the nature of the world, of man, and of man's place in the world both ontologically and axiologically, i.e., both what man is and what he can become, both his reality and his ideality. In the words of A. N. Whitehead, "Our intuitions of righteousness disclose an absoluteness in the nature of things, and so does the taste of a lump of sugar." [1] These intuitions, assumptions, or presuppositions constitute the foundation and framework of religion. They determine the attitude man takes toward his life in his total environment, whether he is a stranger or an integral part, whether he is a disvalue or a value in the universe, whether he is impotent or capable. This conceptual structure has two parts. One part is the implicit, the never stated, the never open to discussion; the part that is never reached by argument. This part is so obvious that the followers may not even be aware of it. An example would be the assumption of the writers of the New Testament that the universe is stacked in three layers—heaven, earth, and hell, that one god, many angels, and countless demons are among the rational beings of the universe, that man lives but one life on earth. The other part is as fundamental to religion as the implicit part, but it is stated, argued for, and defended. For example, the New Testament argues that man is an impotent sinner and that the world process will soon end.

The fundamental conceptual structure of a religion determines and manifests itself in myths, rites, and social organization. But this is not to say that a society first works out its conceptual structure and then creates its myths, rites, and social organization. The priority of the conceptual structure is logical, not chronological. Myths, rites, and social organizations celebrate, actualize, mobilize, clarify, and utilize the conceptual structure. No religion can be understood by cataloging its myths, ceremonies, and social structures. Hinduism especially with its myriad forms is thoroughly confusing unless we first trace its conceptual structure. Without a grasp of its pattern or motif, Hinduism appears to be a confusing jumble of unrelated ideas, rituals, prohibitions, and prescriptions.

Before attempting to state the Hindu motif, we should stress that the conceptual structure of Hinduism must include its dynamics. This is like a refrain or phrase in a musical composition. For example, in Wagnerian music dramas there is a leitmotif, a marked melodic phrase which is associated with some person, idea, situation, or sentiment. Parsifal's reappearance is always announced by the same short passage. In Hinduism, if the sympathetic student, or for that matter the practicing Hindu, is unaware of the Hindu motif, he may regard Hinduism as cow protection, or child marriage, or snake worship, or vegetarianism, or Advaita philosophy. That there is a motif among the varieties of beliefs and practices clustering under the class term "Hinduism," a unity in the diversity of Indian civilization, may be considered as bordering on the miraculous. But there is such—and when it is grasped, one has a tool for understanding the development of Hinduism. We shall state the Hindu motif in ten points:

1. *The universe is real and knowable.* One Western stereotype about India is that the Hindu is a meditative individual resigned to living in a world of illusions. This is a nice example of cultural misunderstanding, as any traveler who has been outsmarted by a Hindu merchant will testify. Perhaps part of the reason for this view is rooted in the fact that one of the first Europeans to study Hinduism was the pessimistic Schopenhauer who read his own philosophy of life into the *Upanishads*. He found them a consolation of death. Albert Schweitzer picked up this theme, characterizing Hinduism as "world and life negation." He wrote, "World and life affirmation consists in this: that man regards existence as he experiences it in

himself and as it has developed in the world as something of value *per se* and accordingly strives to let it reach perfection in himself, whilst within his own sphere of influence he endeavours to preserve and to further it." [2] "World and life negation," according to Schweitzer, "consists in his regarding existence as he experiences it in himself and as it is developed in the world as something meaningless and sorrowful, and he resolves accordingly (a) to bring life to a standstill in himself by mortifying his will-to-live, and (b) to renounce all activity which aims at improvement of the conditions of life in this world." [3] In the course of his analysis Schweitzer backed away from his earlier claims that in Indian thought "world and life negation occupies a predominant position" [4] and indicated that the distinction was made because he believed the development of Indian thought was determined by the conflict between world and life negation and world and life affirmation. [5] This Hegelian methodology might be used in a polar opposition interpretation of the thought of almost any culture, but Schweitzer's thesis has done much harm to Indian studies in that those who have not read his work carefully assume he condemned Indian thought as denying worth and reality to the world. The fact is that Hinduism has never been nihilism. Hindu philosophers do frequently call attention to the appearances within which our lot is cast, and they question perhaps more often than do Western philosophers the reality of time and space, but with the exception of the Charvaka, a school long since extinct, there is an affirmation of a reality behind appearances. The "snake" was illusory—to appeal to an ancient Indian story—but it was a real rope which made the traveler see the "snake." The substructure reveals itself in human experiences of the real, the good, the beautiful, and the true. The ground of beings is also the ground of values. The Sanskrit word *sat* means existing, existent, present, being, real, and actual, but the word blends into the value spectrum, for *sat* also means genuine, right, good, and virtuous. Again Hinduism is not an agnosticism. Words and ideas may be inadequate to grasp reality, and they may only indicate what reality is not, but Hinduism has consistently operated on the assumption that knowledge in some form can be established about the real world, while at the same time admitting honorable points of ignorance.

2. *The universe is orderly.* Even in the early centuries of the formation of Hindu nature gods—whose number was said to be 330,000,000—there was the notion of cosmic order or the regularity of the cosmic processes. This was known as *Rita*. It was manifest in the rising and setting of the sun, in the orderly appearance of the stars, in the regularity of the seasons, in the predictability of the monsoons, in springtime and harvest, and even in the intrinsic rightness of things. "The dawn follows the path of *Rita*, the right path; as if she knew them before. She never oversteps the regions. The sun follows the path of *Rita*." [6] So sang an ancient seer. The gods conformed to this order of things. They were not petitioned to work outside the framework of cosmic order. Miracles, i.e., violations of cosmic law, were not in their power. They were a class of beings within the sovereignty of *Rita*. A corollary of this is that there have been few serious conflicts between science and religion in India, for Hindus do not recognize two orders of explanation: the natural and the divine. We speak, of course, within the context of those who are sufficiently educated to understand modern science. Among the illiterate, especially in the villages, Hinduism sometimes remains at the level of primitive animism, magic, and superstition.

Two phenomena with respect to Hindu gods are puzzling, especially for theistically-minded Westerners. One is that the gods became—and still are in the last analysis—supernumeraries. The universal order was not the order of their will; the universe could function quite well without them. One by one they slipped into limbo as they were perceived to be rooted in human subjectivity. We who approach Hinduism from the West must be careful not to take the gods too seriously, for, as the *Upanishads* remind us, the gods are part of the phenomenal manifold manifested by Totality in categories less than real. The second phenomenon puzzling to Westerners is a tendency of Hinduism to deify almost anything: a stone, a tree, a river, a human, a cow, etc. Near Tinnevelly a granite pillar seven feet high is covered with a greasy coating of clarified butter, the result of Hindu veneration. Yet this pillar is a Muslim relic said to have been brought from Mecca.[7] At least three British citizens have had the embarrassing experience of being worshiped as gods while fulfilling their civic and military duties in India: Tilman Heckell,

James Outram, and John Nicholson.[8] But again there is a cross-cultural confusion, for "god" in Hinduism obviously does not mean what "god" means in Judaism, Christianity, and Islam. To describe something as a god in Hinduism means that it is worthy of respect, honor, even veneration, not that it is an agent who can willfully violate natural law. Hinduism is not a god-oriented religion, at least not in any Western sense of God.

There is another feature of the orderliness of the universe which ought to be mentioned. According to Hinduism, the universe had no absolute beginning and will have no absolute ending. The universe moves in great cycles (*kalpas*) each one of 4,320,000 years as measured by the human calendar. Each *kalpa* is divided into four ages (*yugas*) of diminishing length and of decreasing virtue. One thousand *kalpas* constitute a "Brahmā day" and are followed by a "Brahmā night" of equal length. Thus the orderly sequence continues endlessly. The orderliness of this pattern is obvious; the psychological impact is debatable. A member of the Indian Parliament when asked about the problem of getting Hindus to meet the goals set by India's Five-Year Plans once replied, "I think it is a terrible mistake to give people too much time to do a job." However, we may assume that few Hindus going about their daily tasks are existentially oppressed by the thought of endless *kalpas*.

3. *All life is a unity.* The Sanskrit term for life is *jiva*. Substantially the *jiva* is the soul, and this is a common translation of the term, although *jiva* denotes different aspects of the soul in various schools of Indian thought. For example, sometimes *jiva* means only the principle of vitality, that which distinguishes a living thing from a lifeless thing, and in other contexts the term includes consciousness and/or mentation. *Jiva* considered only as life is held to be shared with all lower animals, and in some cases with all plants and with orders of beings higher than men. "The heart and essence of the Indian experience is to be found in a constant intuition of the unity of life, and the instinctive and ineradicable conviction that the recognition of this unity is the highest good and the uttermost freedom," writes Ananda K. Coomaraswamy.[9] It is this conviction which suggests to the Hindu the ideal of the fellowship of all living

creatures. This means that men must practice the "Golden Rule" in their relationships with all forms of life: "Do naught to others which, if done to thee, would cause thee pain: this is the sum of duty." [10] Thus arose the doctrine of *ahimsa*. *Ahimsa* comes from the root *han* meaning to kill or to damage. By adding the negative prefix it means not to kill. It is a virtue which can be demanded only of man, the self-directing animal. He is expected to get rid of the egoism of his private ego and the class egoism of his species, knowing that the life now being enjoyed in the human body has only a temporary lease on that body. *Ahimsa* has taken many forms in Hinduism. There are at least four varieties of its negative application: vegetarianism, harmlessness, pacifism, and passive resistance. Although vegetarianism means refusal to eat meat, there is an amazing variety of interpretations of what "meat" denotes: for some it means only beef, for others it means also mutton and pork, for others beef, mutton, pork, and fish, and for others beef, mutton, pork, fish, fowl, and all animal products including milk, butter, cheese, and honey! Harmlessness is the pattern of avoiding any violence to any living creature. It is a letting alone policy, not a policy of altruistic endeavors. Pacifism is the view that no human ought to take up arms against another human, and this again has a variety of interpretations. Passive resistance was made well-known by Gandhi. It is the nonviolent use of noncooperation as a technique to coerce a superior to recognize one's own rights and desires. Passive resistance need not mean the abjuration of the use of force; it is the nonviolent rather than the violent use of force. This distinction may be drawn very finely. In addition to these four negative forms of *ahimsa*, there is a positive form which can be called compassion. It holds that actual assistance should be given to any and all living creatures who are in need. This fellowship feeling may take the form of *karuna* (intelligent charity), *maitri* (active good-doing), or *daya* (tender sympathy). Cow protection as a form of *ahimsa* is much publicized and little understood in the West—and, unfortunately, also in India. The arguments for cow protection range from the mythological which ties the cow and the human together in genesis, the practical which calls attention to the services the cow renders to man, and the symbolic which claims that since man cannot pay respect to all animal life as he ought, he has singled out the cow as symbolic of all lower animals and in honoring the cow he is recognizing his relationship to all animals. There are some efforts in Hinduism, and more in Jainism, to express man's fellowship with plants.

Synthesis, not analysis, and sameness, not diversity, run throughout the Hindu motif. This is the vision of the One which marks Hinduism in many ways. Plurality is meaningful in calling attention to the manifold richness of the One.

4. *Each birth is a rebirth.* The self, soul, or vital principle which animates a body is without beginning or end. Each birth into a body has been preceded by an earlier birth. There is no first birth. There is some evidence that the assumption of rebirth was not found in the earliest literature of the Hindus, although this depends upon how passages about the repetition of the birth of the dawn and the "many births" of human beings are to be interpreted.[11] Do the passages refer only to the dawn, or do they also denote analogically the birth and rebirth of humans? Does "many births" mean rebirth?

The notion of rebirth may have resulted from speculation that as life on the earth terminates so life in *svarga* (heaven) comes to an end. This was known as *punarmrityu* (re-death, death after death, death of death, or repeated death), e.g., "Death after death attains he who thinks he sees manifoldness in this world." [12] The death of the post-mortem state could only mean the coming into the opposite state, the state of life. So the death of death is also the re-entry into earthly life again.

The hypothesis of reincarnation has suffered at the hands of both its believers and its disbelievers. One of the serious misunderstandings is that reincarnation must include the continuation of consciousness, whereas the significance of the doctrine is to be found in the area of the conservation of values rather than in the ability to remember previous incarnations. Hinduism as a *sadhana* is a program for self-perfection, not a technique for displaying feats of memory reaching back into earlier embodiments of the human spirit.

5. *Each birth is determined by karma.* One of the early gods of Hinduism was Varuna, the keeper of the cosmic order. As the early inhabitants of India grew out of the animistic and nature worship

period, the ancient gods slipped into oblivion, but the belief that the cosmos is orderly remained. The orderliness Hindus have in mind is both the order of natural law and the inherent order of justice and injustice, right and wrong, good and bad. Order in the moral realm is known as *karma*. It is causality operating in the moral aspects of human life. According to *karma* there are necessary and sufficient causes which account for the events in the total life of the human being. An act is the result of "forces" set in operation by previous acts, and it may also be the cause of future acts. Some of these effects will appear as causes in this incarnation and others in later incarnations. Thus *karma* is closely related to reincarnation or transmigration. *Karma* requires the doctrine of reincarnation to make it intelligible, since gross observation will tell us that not all of the causes initiated by an act come to fruition within the lifetime of the actor.

Karma determines both the fact of another incarnation and the nature of that incarnation. It fixes both the thatness and the whatness of incarnations. "Obtaining the end of his action, whatever he does in this world, he comes again from that world to this world of action." [13] "[The Soul] being overcome by the bright or dark fruits of action, enters a good or an evil womb." [14] Transmigration continues—life after life—as long as the karmic forces are operative. Trips on the wheel of birth and death continue until *karma* is exhausted. One of the aims of the Hindu is to exhaust—"eat up" is the common expression—his *karma*. Although there are differences as to how this can be done, one of the tenets of Hinduism is that each individual is accountable for his own life and that salvation from karmic causes of his embodiment is his own responsibility.

6. *The human condition is misery and opportunity.* Those who find nothing but life-negation in Hinduism are as far from the truth as those who assume from the existence of the *Kama Sutras* and Tantrism that Hinduism is erotic hedonism. According to Hinduism the human condition is misery *and* opportunity. The misery is depicted in many ways: in estrangement from reality, in a feeling of impotence, in a longing for the state of ecstasy with one's god, in recognizing limited attainments in the presence of infinite possibili-

ties, in an overwhelming sense of inadequacy in attaining the vision
of perfection, in a profound sense of sin, etc. The First Noble Truth
of Buddhism—the Noble Truth of Suffering—remains one of the
most insightful analyses of the human condition, but it is only one
aspect. There is also the opportunity to eliminate suffering. Hinduism is a universalism in the sense that no one is denied the
possibility of dealing with the misery of human existence, but the
opportunity is not always possible for everyone within every
incarnation. As we shall see, some cults and branches affirm the
possibility only for the twice-born, i.e., for fewer than half the total
Hindu population, and some affirm the possibility for only males
among the twice-born, but other sects contend that the possibility of
release is open to all regardless of class or sex. The opportunity is
open only to humans, but any *jiva* can ultimately inhabit a human
body. Only the human being can be aware of the misery of
existence, and only the human can cope with it.

One of the surprises in the study of Hinduism is to discover that
the gods are in some respects less significant than men. The gods are
beings that have come to the end of a dead-end street. They are cases
of arrested development. They have reached the end of their
perfection. They are not liberated, and they cannot be liberated. A
god is only a god, but a man can be more than "man." Hence, the
birth of a human is a rare and happy event. Whereas the Orthodox
Jew daily thanks God that he has been born a man rather than a
woman, the orthodox Hindu is grateful that he has been born a
human rather than a god.

7. *Atmansiddhi is the goal of human endeavor.* The telos of the
opportunity offered to man is *atmansiddhi,* the perfecting of the
essential nature of man. Perfectionism is found throughout Hinduism—even the word for Sanskrit (*samskrita*) means perfected,
cultivated, polished. This grew out of an ancient tradition that the
language of the ancient Aryans was a nonsymbolic language; that the
sounds of the words were so harmonious with reality that Sanskrit
words properly spoken could do what the object related to the word
could do; e.g., the word "food" could nourish.

"*Atmansiddhi*" is preferred to other words which might stand for salvation, freedom, liberation, escape, release, realization, illumination, fulfillment, integration, etc. Words like *"mahatma"* or *"mahapurusha"* (great soul), *"uttamapurusha"* (superior person), and *"purushartha"* (person of riches) are inferior to *"atmansiddha"* (the perfected man) as a designation of the one who has attained. Many different interpretations of the goal of human existence have been offered in the development of Hinduism: liberation from the weight of matter, release from *karma,* getting off the wheel of birth and death, loss of illusions, removal of ignorance, getting of positive insight, discovery of one's true identity, realization of latent potentialities, development of talents, union with the Absolute, loving harmony with one's god, etc. In the *Rig Veda* the *atmansiddha* is the pious man, the man faithful in reciting hymns and sacrificing to the gods. The *Brahmanas* mark a change. The ceremonies had become so complicated that the head of the family could no longer perform them. Proper performance required a professional. The *atmansiddha* was the sacerdotal man, the priest who could conduct the ritual without error. In the Upanishadic period knowledge of esoteric doctrines was added to the perfection ideal. The *atmansiddha* was the sage who possessed secret doctrine and was able to transmit it to the pupil who was ready to receive it. In the *Dharma Shastras* the ideal man was the regal man, the man mature enough to assume the duties of the tribal assembly, the man who had undergone the training and had received the instruction requisite for leadership in the community. And in other periods the *atmansiddha* was the *bhakti* man (the man devoted to his chosen deity), or the *dhyana* man (the adept in meditative practices), or the yogic man (the man whose body and mind are fully controlled), or the *sabhya* man (the man who serves in the *sabha* or village assembly). In the *Bhagavad Gita* he is the man of stabilized wisdom (*sthitiprajña*), the man who has overcome the desires of the flesh, who is at peace with himself, who is stoically indifferent to pleasure and pain, who has no selfish aims or personal hopes, and who makes no demands on others. In recent years the *atmansiddha* has been viewed differently—e.g., for Ramakrishna he was the mystic lost in adoration of his deity; for Aurobindo, the yogi proficient in meditation; for Gandhi, the *satyagraha* steadfastly loyal to truth and expressing his loyalty in active participation in social

improvement; for Tagore, the Supreme Man "infinite in his essence
. . . finite in his manifestation";[15] and for Radhakrishnan, the free
spirit.[16] Despite the variety of conceptions two presuppositions
prevail: (1) *atmansiddhi* is a moral conception with emotional,
intellectual, and spiritual overtones, and (2) *atmansiddhi* begins with
man turning inward but it finds fulfillment in turning outward to the
world and the needs of men.

The *atmansiddhi* ideal is central in Hinduism. Therefore, we shall
examine it in some detail. It is open to three misunderstandings. The
first of these is inherent in the problem of putting the state in time
and yet not making it a time-bound state. *Atmansiddhi* is an eternal
condition which may or may not be manifested in time. This is what
is meant by the distinction between *jivanmukti* (perfection before
death) and *videhamukti* (perfection after death). To stress this
distinction is to miss the fact that the *atmansiddha* is indifferent to the
presence or absence of the physical conditions of earthly life. The
quality of a complete value experience does not depend upon its
temporal extension. The limiting conditions of space and time
neither add to nor detract from the highest values.

A second misunderstanding is in making a sharp distinction
between the *atmansiddha* as *jiva* (individual self) and the *atmansiddha*
as *atman* (social self). Much of the language about the *atmansiddha*
suggests that it is the individual who attains the goal, but the Hindu
ideal is not the ideal of an individual isolated from social and cosmic
contexts. In India the individual never stands in splendid isolation; he
is never the *deinos aner,* the all-powerful man of ancient Greece. The
true individuality remains in the *atmansiddha;* the false distinctions
which separate men from each other are seen for what they are. The
Universal Man (*vishvatman*)—to use a term favored by Tagore—
finds himself, knows himself, and fulfills himself. He becomes
humanized. He learns to empathize with others so he respects,
tolerates, aids, and loves others. He becomes homonized. He becomes
the generic man, unable to set himself apart from other men. He
becomes divinized. He sees the godhead in all and embraces
god-in-man. He becomes Brahmanized. The gods fade away as he
intuits the unity of being and value.

A third misunderstanding arises out of translating *"atmansiddhi"* as

"the perfection of man" and *"atmansiddha"* as "the perfected man."
If *atmansiddhi* is the telos of Hindu *sadhana,* it is an ideal which never
seems to be realized, for the literature of Hinduism does not present a
human paradigm. The nonrealization of *atmansiddhi* is an extremely
important fact about Hinduism. The ideal remains an ideal; it never
becomes a reality. It is beyond being, but not beyond imagining.
Man's potentiality exceeds his actuality. He is never all that he can
be. His being *as man* is his eternal becoming. Man is the being that
includes the potentiality of becoming more than his status as mere
man. Man perfected is more than man. As Lord Krishna says to
Arjuna in the *Bhagavad Gita,*

> Rid of passion, fear, and wrath,
> Made of Me, taking refuge in Me,
> Many by the austerity of knowledge
> Purified, have come to my estate.[17]

If there were a concept of *hybris* in Hinduism, it would not be the
overweening pride of man, but the jealousy of gods directed toward
men.

Atmansiddhi is human perfecting, not human perfection. Hinduism is concerned with the melioristic direction of man's life,
individually and generically. "The individual's aim of perfection,"
writes Radhakamal Mukerjee, "is the same as the group's aim of
culture, complete, balanced and practical—the realization of the
Universal Self and the Universal Community." [18] That is to say,
perfecting is to the individual as culturing is to the group, a process of
becoming rather than a state of being. Miss Heimann correctly
analyzes the goal of Hinduism: "This ideal of the final goal of
Perfection is a Western postulate, not an Indian one. The West
thinks on results, believes in facts which ultimately can be reached
and fulfilled. . . . the Western ideal rests in perfection, the
fulfillment of a distinct aim which can be accomplished by limitation
and selection only. The end, ideal, is static and changeless in its
perfected individuality. By contrast, the Indian is never satisfied with
any static end. . . . For him there cannot be a resting-place in a
personal perfection, in a distinct single survival. The end of

development is for all phenomena a final re-flow and in-flow into the general receptacle of the 'Ocean,' the Brahman, the universal reservoir out of which all forms sprang forth and into which all of them, in the end, are reabsorbed." [19]

The goal is a movement. Part of the difficulty Westerners have in understanding Hinduism is rooted in the fact that static categories of Western essentialism miss the dynamic character of Indian thought. Hindu soteriology is progressive. Christianity, having rooted its atonement in a historical event, is constantly puzzling as to whether salvation is a reality already accomplished or an invitation to assist in a saving process. Hinduism, having no one historical soteriological event, has less difficulty in making salvation a process. The life of each person is an evolution, a *pravritti marga* (a path of progress). Man is a *margayayin* (a wayfarer). Tagore once described the good life, "Where tireless striving stretches its arms toward perfection." [20] Schweitzer conceived of ethics as "the maintenance of one's own life at the highest level of becoming more and more in spirit," [21] yet because of his conviction that Indian thought is "world and life negation," he was unable to perceive the degree to which Hinduism approximated his own definition.

Hinduism is a pursuit, an endeavor, a striving. According to the *Mahabharata*, immortality is the "pursuit of Brahman or self-knowledge." [22] The drive to fulfillment is a promise which forever falls short of the goal, but it ought not to generate despair. Mysore Hiriyanna, a twentieth-century Indian philosopher, has said, "Some Indian thinkers admit *jivanmukti*, which means that the goal of life can be reached here on this earth; others do not recognize it and so make it realisable hereafter—in a future existence. If I may conclude by expressing a personal opinion, the question whether the highest value is attainable is not of much consequence. We may grant that it is not finally attained and that man's reach will always exceed his grasp. What really matters is the deliberate choosing of it as the ideal to be pursued, and thereafter making a persistent and continued advance toward it." [23]

The Perfecting Man is a man of forward-looking enthusiasm. Whereas the ancient Greeks advised moderation in all things, the Indians have sought to derive the full worth of each idea, each value, each *marga* by pushing to what Aurobindo has called "a fine excess." [24] Yet this is not the end, for in the extremes the Indian seeks for a rule which will result in a measure of harmony and balance. He thrives on polarities. The Buddha is a classical example of this existential dialectic. According to legends, the young prince lived in three palaces, one for each season of the year. A retinue of servants, mistresses, and a doting father were ready to satisfy his desires. When he turned from this life-style, he wrenched the hair from his head, changed his royal robes with the first beggar he met, and finally, according to the legends, reduced his diet to a few grains of rice a day. After his enlightenment he established the Middle Way, the way which avoided the extremes of pleasure and asceticism. The Indian makes distinctions only to turn upon them and to deny all distinctions. To quote again from Aurobindo: "Balance and rhythm which the Greeks arrived at by self-limitation, India arrived at by a sense of intellectual, ethical and aesthetic order and the synthetic impulses of its mind and life." [25]

Atmansiddhi is a programmatic telos, a direction for moving, not a goal for reaching. The Perfecting Man is the reality to be attained; the Perfected Man is the ideal to be approximated. The aim is progression toward an ever receding goal of perfection. According to the *Aitareya Aranyaka*, "Whatever he [man] reaches, he wishes to go beyond. If he reaches the sky, he wishes to go beyond. If he reaches the heavenly world, he would wish to go beyond." [26] Gandhi expressed the same idea: "The goal ever recedes from us. The greater the progress the greater the recognition of our unworthiness. Satisfaction lies in the effort, not in the attainment. Full effort is full victory." [27] On another occasion Gandhi described man as "a spiritual unit . . . launched on a pilgrimage to perfection." [28] Hinduism glorifies man as the being who is capable of knowing and living in accord with the highest truths and deepest values. Carl R. Rogers says one of the things it means to be a person is "the willingness to be a process." Hinduism agrees. Were man established, he would be god or brute—both are inferior to man. This is the message of the dying Bhishma who in the *Mahabharata* discloses the *upanishad* (secret truth): "This is the secret and supreme doctrine. There is nothing in the universe higher than man." [29]

The disproportionate amount of space given to *atmansiddhi* is justified because of its importance in the Hindu motif and because of the tendency in the West to misconstrue the goal of Hinduism. Hinduism is best understood in terms of its goal and program with respect to the development of man. Hindus and non-Hindus are beginning to realize that "a high sense of life-affirming humanism has been the essence and the running thread of the teachings of religious leaders and philosophers of India." [30] Finally—a delicate point—the emphasis on the humanistic aspects of Hinduism is necessary to right the overemphasis on Vedantism and to indicate the relevance of Hinduism to the modern world. This was excellently stated by A. Chakravarti in the Miller Lectures at the University of Madras more than thirty-five years ago: "Thus we notice that the history of Indian thought is the history of Humanism with a bias toward spirituality. We may say, in short, that Indian philosophy is a running commentary on the text 'Thanks that I am a man.' This Indian Humanism, which had its logical development in Jainism and Buddhism has been pushed to the background by the more dominant school of Vedantists. This dominant but reactionary school of Indian thought has been successful in preventing the re-appearance of the humanistic ideal in modern India, but it is time that leaders of thought in modern India recognize the necessity of reviving and restoring this ideal in order to bring about a social readjustment consistent with modern conditions." [31]

8. *Techniques are provided for the atmansiddha.* The Hindu program for the life of man includes both goals and means. In addition to the goal of *atmansiddhi,* there are secondary goals: hedonic satisfactions, physical possessions, dutiful relationships, and liberation itself. These we shall consider later. Also the ideal life for man is divided into four periods of approximately the same length: the time of study and preparation, the period devoted to home and vocation, a period of gradual releasing of the bonds binding one to family and vocation, and the final period during which full attention is given to the things of the spirit. In addition to these four goals and four periods of life there are four *margas* or paths which the

individual can follow. These are distinguished by whether the emphasis is on thought, works, devotion, or yogic discipline. They are excellently designed to accommodate the different types of human personality: the intellectual, the active, the emotional, and the volitional. Hinduism has developed in such a manner that each person can find his own style within the broad and tolerant *sadhana*. No one need feel cut off or inadequate because he cannot fit the mold of mysticism, or sacerdotalism, or devotionalism, or philosophy. The tolerance of Hinduism is best seen in this provision for all types of experiences and all types of persons. It is because of this broad tolerance of variations on the common theme that we are in this chapter attempting to identify them in order not to lose our way in the study of the ramifications of the Hindu development.

9. *Each person is free to choose his own techniques.* Although *karma* fixes the individual in his position in life, the individual is free to select the means he wishes to follow toward the goal of *atmansiddhi*. Each can do his own thing. This is not to deny that physical and psychological factors are relevant to the selection. A mesomorph would be foolish to select the philosophical path, and an endomorph would probably be unwise not to consider the philosophical path, but if one wishes, he can choose an unlikely path. The choice of *marga* is one's own. It is not at all unusual for an individual to choose a *marga* not appreciated by the other members of his joint family. In general, there is more social pressure to follow the same vocation in a family than to follow the same *marga*. Husband and wife may worship different gods, visit different temples, and identify themselves with different sects and *gurus*. In a large home one room may be set aside for a member of the household who has selected a special god for worship. Friendly banter between husband and wife about their different forms of worship is a frequent form of household amusement. It is not unusual for a member of the Arya Samaj, the Brahmo Samaj, or some other innovative branch of Hinduism to marry a more traditional Hindu. Half-serious and half-humorous conversations about "true Hinduism" may be heard in Hindu households, especially at those times of the year when one member of the household is engaged in activities appropriate to a cult.

10. *Any technique faithfully pursued will realize the goal.* At the close of the *Bhagavad Gita* Krishna advises the warrior prince, "Act as thou thinkest best." [32] The grounds for the advice is not that no act will avail or that all are basically alike, but rather that any act will avail if faithfully pursued. One of the key concepts of all forms of Hinduism is *dharma* (duty). This is why many people have great expectations for democracy in India. In spite of serious problems of extreme poverty and overpopulation India has within its dominant Hindu community a long tradition of duties rather than rights. If India can capitalize on the *dharma* morality rather than imitate the morality of rights associated with democracies in the West, India may develop a citizenry among whom social responsibility is spontaneous rather than one in which the duties and obligations of citizenship are considered to be the price citizens must pay for the rights they enjoy. The Hindu places so much emphasis on *dharma* with its rich connotations of duty, faithfulness, and personal responsibility that he holds the faithfulness with which a *marga* is followed may be more significant than the *marga* itself. This is the rationale for *ishta devata* and *ishta marga,* i.e., one's chosen god and one's chosen way. The individual may worship the god he chooses and may follow the way he chooses—but, having chosen, he must faithfully fulfill the responsibilities associated with that god and that path.

Inherent in the *dharma* concept is an ultimate optimism. Any technique will successfully lead to the goal of *atmansiddhi* providing it is faithfully followed. No Hindu *sadhana* falls into despair. Pluralism, tolerance, diversity, and manifoldness mark the Hindu way of life from the first-millennium B.C. seer who sang, "We all have various thoughts and plans, and diverse are the ways of man," [33] to the nineteenth-century Bengali saint, Ramakrishna, who at various periods of his life lived as a Hindu, as a Buddhist, as a Muslim, and as a Christian to demonstrate his conviction that all ways are ways of salvation.

CHAPTER 3

The Indus Valley Civilization and the Aryans

America was discovered by Europeans looking for a new trade route to India. The short-lived belief that Columbus had reached India is perpetuated in the term "Indian" still applied to the American aborigines. This error is typical of later misconceptions and stereotypes: India is a land of fabulous wealth, a land of abject poverty; the people have no ambitious aspirations, a people still in a state of childlike primitivism, a dreamy people out of touch with reality, a heathen people anxiously waiting for the twin lights of the Christian gospel and European civilization. Two of the better ambassadors from the United States to India felt the need after their service in India to write books designed in part to sort out the differences of opinion between themselves and the United States Department of State: Chester Bowles in *Ambassador's Report* (1954) and John Kenneth Galbraith in *Ambassador's Journal* (1969). To this day Western public opinion about this land tends either to follow the affluent view—Taj Mahal, Maharajahs, tiger hunts, spices, and jewels—or the indigent view—poverty, overpopulation, starvation, beggars, and lepers. We do not suggest that the truth lies somewhere between the extremes, but rather we plead for an unprejudiced open-mindedness before the facts, plus a conscious effort to avoid imposing Western values upon this land and its people. India may yet be discovered by Westerners looking for new ways to understand the business of being human.

The Stone Age in India

Man first appeared in India during the Second Interglacial Period, i.e., between 400,000 and 200,000 B.C. These people followed the receding glaciers over the Australian land-bridge and into South Asia by way of what is now Burma. Neither a human skeleton nor a fragment of a human skeleton has been found from this period. Furthermore, the fact that man could live in the fertile jungles by food gathering rather than by hunting has made the reconstruction of his life more difficult for the paleontologists since vegetable and fruit remains do not survive as do bone piles left by predominately meat-eating peoples. A few cave paintings have been found in India which may be their work, but most of these paintings have been painted over by much later people so that as yet little can be learned from this source. Stone implements are the chief means for studying these paleolithic people. These have been found in scattered sites throughout India and also in the Soan valley of Pakistan. Archeologists distinguish three general types of stone tools: (1) the core tools formed by chipping away from a large block until one of the chips is satisfactory; (2) the flake tools formed by working a chip into a finished tool with corrugated edges; and (3) the polished tools formed by rubbing the chip against an abrasive until a smooth surface has been achieved. The flake tools predominate the finds in India. The nature of these tools indicate a people who were occupied with digging for roots and tubers. They were wanderers who moved about following the monsoons and establishing nothing more permanent than an occasional salt camp. Stone rings have been found which are thought to have been used to weight digging sticks for primitive agriculture. These people controlled fire and possessed cattle. Their numbers, of course, can only be guessed; surely there were not many, perhaps one per ten square miles. Innovative practices seem to have proceeded from the north and moved southward as might be expected from the fact that invading peoples came overland from both the east and the west. There is too little known about these prehistoric Stone Age people to indicate the nature of their religion. The best guesses are that they practiced the same sort of religion found among prehistoric men in any part of the world, e.g., animism, fetishism, nature worship, animal worship, honoring of ancestors, etc. Primitive survivals in Hinduism may be remnants from prehistory, e.g., attitudes toward fire, sun, storm, menstruation, etc. Some regard the contemporary practice in villages of putting red paint or dye on stones as an ancestral memory of human sacrifices. But the religion of these prehistoric peoples may never be established, and the belief that some of the primitive people of India today, such people as the Andamaneans, Kathakari, Dhangars, Birhors, Bhils, Gonds, Todas, Chenchus, Oraons, and Santals, are descendants of the first inhabitants of the subcontinent is without empirical support.

Indus Valley Civilization

The Western world became apprised of the existence of an ancient urban civilization in India on September 20, 1924, when the British archeologist Sir John Marshall gave an account in the *Illustrated London News* of the discoveries made at two sites along the Indus River. These are called Harappa, after the modern town of that name built on the site in the Punjab, and Mohenjo-daro (The City of the Dead), a name given to the ruins in the Sind by the people living nearby. Archeologists had known of their existence for more than a hundred years, and also of an archeological tragedy that had taken place in the area in 1856. In that year two brothers, John and William Brunton, were building the East Indian Railway from Karachi to Lahore. They, needing ballast for the railway line, hit upon the ingenious plan of using ruined cities built of bricks as quarries. They leveled a medieval town named Brahminabad, and then farther north along the line plundered the ruin near Harappa. Stuart Piggott, in anger and disgust, writes that today "the trains rumble over a hundred miles of line laid on a secure foundation of third-millennium brick-bats." [1] Fortunately, Mohenjo-daro escaped intact the Brunton brothers' search for ballast. The ancient Indus valley civilization is now called the Harappa culture. Piggott refers to the cities as "twin capitals of an empire." [2] This has elicited the following comment from an Indian historian: "The two great cities have been regarded by some distinguished British archeologists as the northern and southern capitals of an empire; not only on the analogy of Egypt but perhaps because of the feeling that anything so advanced in India could have resulted only from strong imperial rule (like the British). This opinion needs no further comment." [3] There are more than eighty known sites along the Indus, all the others being village settlements. The twin capital hypothesis is highly conjectural. The area of the Harappa culture is about one-half million square miles in extent. If there was no empire, at least there must have been excellent communication, for the culture was remarkably uniform, e.g., the size and shape of bricks was the same throughout the one-thousand-mile length of the civilization.

The excavations of the "twin capitals" were begun at Harappa in 1920 under the direction of Daya Ram Sahni and at Mohenjo-daro in 1922 under Rakhal Das Banerji. Sir John Marshall was then General-Director of Archeology in India. The work at Mohenjo-daro continued from 1922 to 1931 and was renewed in 1935–1936, while at Harappa the principal work was in 1920–1921 and 1933–1934. Since the partition of India, the Archeological Department of Pakistan has discovered a pre-Harappan culture now known as the Kot Dijian culture. Pre-Harappan artifacts have also been unearthed under a bicycle shop in the center of the model city Chandigarh and have been examined by scholars from the University of the Punjab. Thus far nothing has been found to modify the conclusions reached from the original excavations. Recent radio carbon dating indicates that both Harappa and Mohenjo-daro enjoyed a four-century period of existence, from 2150 to 1750 B.C., and also that they were terminated by a series of catastrophes.[4] The cities were burned and destroyed, and the villages which rose on their ruins were markedly different.

The excavations in the Indus valley have proved to be extremely important in tracing the development of Hinduism. Scholars have recognized two strands within Hinduism, an Aryan and a non-Aryan commonly called Dravidian—e.g., "In the study of our culture, this fact should never be forgotten: Indian culture is the product of Aryo-Dravidian synthesis, ethnic, social, religious and cultural." [5] The synthesis is far from complete, as is indicated by wide differences in vernacular languages, in dress, and in food habits in the north and the south. Some Indologists interpret the cultural history of India in terms of Aryanization: ". . . the Punjab has been Indo-European for about 3000 years, but the Ganges valley was only gradually subdued in the course of the last millennium before Christ, and the attack on the Deccan succeeded only in the west and north of the plateau, and to this day it meets a resistance which has not been overcome." [6] Hinduism can perhaps be defined as civilized Aryanism grafted on primitive Dravidianism. Aspects regarded as subtle, intellectual, or highly developed are Aryan (noble), whereas aspects magical, superstitious, or animistic are Dravidian. This interpretation has been especially tempting to European scholars. Evidence for such conclusions was the assumed appearance of the first urban areas in India during the first millennium B.C., in other words, after the Aryans had settled in northwest India. The city, we should add, is commonly regarded as the sign of that stage of human development known as civilization. The discovery of Harappa and Mohenjo-daro has changed the picture altogether, both in that they flourished two thousand years before Patna, the city formerly regarded as the oldest major city in India—indeed the age of Harappa culture cannot be determined since already in the third millennium B.C. these cities were old and stereotyped—and also in that the quality of the Harappa culture has forced scholars to discount the derogatory epithets employed by the Aryans to characterize the people they found in the river valleys, such terms as *asuras* (demons), *dasas* (blacks), *krishna tvachah* (black people), *anaschs* (people with no noses), *anasa* (without speech), *akarmanah* (without ceremonies), *avratah* (without purpose in life), *ayajvah* (without sacrifices), *adeva* (godless), *anindra* (without Indra), and *pashus* (two-footed beasts). The excavations at Harappa and Mohenjo-daro give new meaning to the admission of the Aryans that the cities they destroyed had "well-built dwellings." [7] Perchance the Aryans were the primitives. The hypothesis that the Dravidian peoples of South India today are the descendants of the Harappan peoples driven out of North India by the Aryans is still not completely established, nor do experts agree to whom to relate the Harappans. While most scholars call attention to the similarity to Mesopotamia and refer to the inhabitants of the Indus valley as Sumero-Dravidians, Sir John Marshall pointed to similarities of the Harappa pottery and that of Memphite Egypt, and Suillarme de Hervey drew comparisons between the ancient civilizations of Harappa and Easter Island.

Each of the cities had a population of between thirty and forty thousand, and each was about one square mile in area. Harappa was on the left bank of the Ravi River; Mohenjo-daro was on the right bank of the Indus River. Each had a "citadel" between city proper and the river built on a platform of brick about thirty feet high. "Citadel" is the term archeologists have given to these structures, but they were poorly designed as fortresses since an outside ramp leading to the top could have been easily climbed by an enemy. The absence of weapons of war other than thin spears, which seem designed more for religious or state ceremonies than for battle, indicate that they were not a military people. Perhaps they did not need weapons of defense before the coming of the Aryans. Some think that the huge structures between city walls and river were places of sacrifice and worship like the ziggurats of Mesopotamia. These divergent interpretations call to mind the observation that whereas the British archeologists find citadels, the Germans find palaces, the French temples, and the Americans kitchens. Also near the rivers were huge granaries and clusters of two-room apartments, presumably for workmen. Work floors with large platforms for the grinding of grain into flour were located beside the granaries. The walls around the city were forty feet wide at the base, rising to a height of thirty-five feet. The lavish use of kiln-dried brick indicates that at that time dense forest must have been near as a source of wood for charcoal for the kilns. The bricks were standardized at three by ten by twenty inches. They were held in place by mud mortar in the walls and by lime and gypsum mortar in the drains. One of the most remarkable features of the cities was the elaborate provision for sewage disposal. There was a sewer system for the cities complete with terra cotta pipes and manholes through which a workman could enter to clean the sewer. The houses were chiefly multistoried with flat roofs. The walls were as much as seven feet thick. Houses were equipped with rubbish shoots ending in trash bins. Outside stairways suggest that the people may have spent hot nights on the roofs of their homes. The houses were fitted with bathrooms and toilets. A public bathhouse one hundred and eight by one hundred and eighty feet has been excavated in Mohenjo-daro. The tank in the center of the bathhouse is about twenty-three by thirty-nine by eight feet deep. The walls of the tank are seven to eight feet thick. The similarity to the *pushkaras* (lotus ponds) which adjoin Hindu temples today suggests that the building was for ritual bathing. Another interesting feature of the two cities was a large "city hall" which may have been a temple. Unfortunately, the one at Harappa was badly destroyed in the ballast-seeking operation and the place where one is presumed to be at Mohenjo-daro cannot be excavated because a ruined Buddhist stupa of the Kushan period stands upon it.

The pottery remains are of good quality but lacking in artistry. The pots were mass produced, utilitarian, and poorly decorated. Piggott thinks the Harappans had discovered assembly-line production. They worked in copper, bronze, lead, silver, ivory, and gold. Bronze knives and ivory combs of good quality have been found. Their luxury items were jewels, pearls, and peacocks. They were a trading people with a sea route to Mesopotamia, where they were known as the Meluhha. Some Indologists think they were the Vikings of Asia, but others think the evidence of sea travel is too limited. It seems strange to suppose that a people living on the banks of a river with twice the flow of the Nile would not become a sailing people. Wheat, barley, peas, and sesamum were grown along the rivers. Cotton was grown and cotton cloth woven two thousand years before cotton appeared in the West. The Harappans used a harrow but no plough, and from this archeologists conclude they farmed by flood irrigation along the banks of the river. No irrigation canals have been found. Their domesticated animals included both the humped and flat-backed cattle, water buffalo, goats, sheep, dogs, camels, and asses. They do not appear to have had horses.

Thus far the discoveries of human skeletal remains have been insignificant. No cemetery of the oldest period has been found. A few later graves show the curious custom of placing a slaughtered goat limb by limb on the human corpse, a custom referred to in *Rig Veda* 10. 16. In this cremation hymn the fire god is petitioned, "Burn him not up, nor quite consume him." The hope is that the fire god will accept the body of the goat in lieu of the human body or in lieu of parts of the human body.

Perhaps the most important finds of the Indus valley civilization have been the more than two thousand engraved soapstone seals of square shape ranging from three-quarters to one and one-quarter inches which seem to have been used to mark property of this commercial people. The scenes carved with great delicacy on the surface of the seals are frequently of animals, both real and mythical, usually shown in profile. But beyond the archeological and artistic value of the seals, each seal also has on it a script which has no direct affinity to any known ancient script. This script is unchanged throughout Harappan history. About four hundred distinct signs have been noticed in this quasi-pictographic script. Some progress has recently been made in decipherment. For example, it is now agreed that the script is read from right to left if there is but one line; but if there is a second line, it is read from left to right. Thus far the script has been found only on the seals and on a few potsherds, indicating that a low value was placed on the written word. Unsuccessful translation efforts thus far have proceeded on the assumption that the language of the Harappans was Indo-European or Dravidian. A new and promising approach was offered in 1969 by the Scandinavian Institute of Asian Studies at Copenhagen. This approach assumes that the language is Proto-Dravidian. Other scholars doubt that the script is related to any language since it is merely a series of signs like potters' marks for the purpose of indicating ownership of property.

The overall impression of the Harappan culture is that it was the creation of an intensely conservative, dull, utilitarian people whose personalities were submerged in public interests. There are no commemoration monuments, stones, or pillars erected to the memory of a citizen or hero. The walls of houses are undecorated; even the doorways have no ornamentation. The houses have no windows facing the street. This must have given the streets the appearance of tunnels. Both Harappa and Mohenjo-daro show urban planning of a most excellent type. The streets range from fourteen to thirty-four feet wide. They are straight, and meet at right angles. Both cities were built over and over again, probably due to the silting from flooded rivers, and in the rebuilding the houses, streets, and walls were built on top of the previous constructions with no significant changes. Nine occupational levels have been uncovered at Mohenjo-daro, six at Harappa. Wells after the digging of the archeologists look like chimneys. The monotony of the life of the people is further indicated in the uniformity of the pottery, the standardization of bricks, the sameness of the houses, and also in a very exact system of weights. The fact that in a seven-hundred-year period there is no perceptible material change indicates more than conservatism—it indicates stagnation. The quality of workmanship revealed in the walls, the houses, the "citadels," the baths, the streets, and the sewers evidences a people that had once been creative, but the sameness suggests that creativity had yielded to unimaginative uniformity. It was a culture which had lost the vitality it once possessed. Mohenjo-daro (The City of the Dead) is an appropriate name.

The same resistance to change can be observed in the neolithic rock paintings of central India and the folk murals commonly used in nearby villages. Unless told, one cannot determine which is neolithic, which contemporary. No wonder Nehru compared Indian culture to a palimpsest. Piggott, describing Harappa arts and crafts as "one of competent dullness," adds, "The secrecy of those blank brick walls, the unadorned architecture of even the citadel buildings, the monotonous regularity of the streets, the stifling weight of dead tradition all combine to make the Harappa civilization one of the least attractive phases of ancient Oriental history. One can grudgingly admire the civil engineering of the Roman army in the Provinces, but with as little real enthusiasm. I can only say there is something in the Harappa civilization that I find repellent." [8] Richard Lannoy says Harappa shows "the most amazing, indeed unprecedented, standardization in prehistory." [9]

There are a few finds which might require a tempering of the condemnation of the Harappa culture as dull commercialism. One is the small bronze statue of a nude dancing girl caught as though pausing in her dance with one arm akimbo and the other resting on her thigh. The artistic balance between the right arm with hand on hip and the left arm heavily covered with armlets, relaxed and extended on the left leg, shows a fine feeling for form and design. The sticklike legs and arms convey the image of a lithe and supple young girl. The second important artistic find is the torso of a young man sculptured in red sandstone. The sculpture is only three and three-quarters inches high. The fullness of the body is in striking contrast to the shapeless body of the dancing girl. The first statue catches movement, the second rest, and each is excellent of its type. If these are products of Harappan artists, perhaps archeologists have been hasty in condemning the culture for its artistic barrenness.

Attempts to delineate the religion of Harappa and Mohenjo-daro have been marked by the widest divergency; e.g., the small rooms in the large public bathhouse have been described as rooms for dressing and rubdowns, for priests' quarters, and for prostitution. Seals which portray bulls with heavy dewlaps, one-horned rhinoceros, elephants, and above all a one-horned beast which has been called a "unicorn" might be indications of a variegated animal worship. Some of the seals give trees a prominent position, which could be interpreted as the origin of the veneration of trees within Hinduism. On other seals cobras are depicted with worshipers kneeling before them. Terra cotta female figures, often shown pregnant or with small children, might link the Harappa culture with the Great Mother cults of Elam, Anatolia, Mesopotamia, and Egypt. The most striking finds which may help determine the religion of these people are those of the frontal view of a male figure seated on a low stool in a half-lotus position with hands resting on his extended knees. His headdress has been fashioned of buffalo horns. Three faces are visible, the front and one on each side. The front face is animal in appearance, perhaps a bit like that of a hound dog. His erect penis indicates fertility. The figure is usually shown surrounded by animals. The best-preserved seal contains an elephant, a tiger, a rhinoceros, and a water buffalo. "Lord of the Animals" or "Lord of the Creatures" are titles frequently given to him by archeologists and historians. The possibility that he represents a prototype of Shiva worship is worthy of consideration.

The most significant clue about the religion of the Indus valley civilization may be not in what has been found but in what has not been found. There is no temple. The finest public buildings were for the citizens, not for the gods. This reveals a great deal about the importance of man among the Harappans.

Kosambi stresses the pacific nature of the Indus valley civilization: ". . . the curiously weak mechanism of violence. . . . Whatever authority controlled the people did so without much force." [10] Piggott contends that uniformity is the chief characteristic of the civilization, and this, he believes, indicates a priest-ridden culture: "A state ruled over by priest-kings, wielding autocratic and absolute power from two main seats of government, and with the main artery of communication between the capital cities provided by a great navigable river, seems then, to be the reasonable deduction from the archaeological evidence of the civilization of Harappa." [11] Some argue that it was a culture stressing female gods, and others think masculine virility was the central emphasis. Obviously not enough has yet been found to establish with any degree of certainty the nature of the religion of these people, although one is tempted to relate the monotonous uniformity of the buildings to the conservatism which is a hallmark of Hinduism throughout its development.

There are evidences of decline before the final violent destruction of the cities. The houses built in the last of the rebuildings were inferior to the earlier houses. The design of the streets was carelessly followed, and for the first time the kilns were built within the city walls. This may be interpreted as a growing sloth of the people or as evidence of attacks by enemies. It could also have been the result of decimations caused by climatic conditions, or by the loss of agricultural land along the rivers because of sand and gravel deposited by the rivers in flood. Flooding was certainly a factor, for the virgin soil at Mohenjo-daro lies thirty-nine feet below the modern plain.

The cities came to an end about 1500 B.C. and the Punjab and the Sind became lands of small villages. Wood and reed displaced brick and mortar, thus giving archeologists a blank period of about one thousand years in Indian history. Fortunately, literary sources are able to supply some of the answers about developing Hinduism between 1500 and 600 B.C.

The Aryans

The peoples who pushed through the mountain passes and down into the valleys of the Indus and its tributaries and who presumably put Mohenjo-daro and Harappa to the torch were part of a series of invading northern tribes into southern lands. By taking a long view of human history, we can say that these are the peoples who followed the melting glaciers northward after the Ice Ages until they ran out of pasture for their flocks and herds. Then they changed their migrations, returning to the lands of greater fertility, bringing with them the vigor associated with northern climates. The Aryans were but one of these groups of nomadic invaders. Will Durant in a witty, yet profound, observation writes, "The Aryans poured down upon the Dravidians, the Achaeans and Dorians upon the Cretans and Aegeans, the Germans upon the Romans, the Lombards upon the Italians, the English upon the world. Forever the north produces rulers and warriors, the south produces artists and saints, and the meek inherit heaven." [12] They called themselves Aryans, the people of noble birth, the free born. *"Arya"* comes from the root *ar* (earth); hence they thought of themselves as autochthonous. The word survives in "Iran" and "Eire." Eire or Ireland is the westernmost land reached by the Indo-European peoples in ancient times. All European languages are Indo-European save the Finnish, the Hungarian, and the Basque. The word "Aryan" was first used by the Mitannians, the first Indo-European people in the Near East, a people who challenged the Egyptians, and whose existence, together with the Hittites, helps the historians trace these early movements from south Russia to northwest India. Although the term does refer to a language group, and specifically to the eastern branch of the Indo-European languages with Sanskrit and Greek as the primary languages, to hold too stringently to this interpretation is to fail to note that the Aryans also prided themselves on racial characteristics, e.g., fair skin and pointed noses, as indicated by their disgust with the dark skin and the flat noses of the people they found in the Indus valley. But to indicate that the Aryans thought of themselves as a race is not in any way to give credence to the Nazi myth of "the Aryan race." The northern home of the Aryans is indicated by the Sanskrit words for common objects; e.g., the Sanskrit word for tree seems to have been the birch tree, and the word for fish was the word for salmon. Moreover Sanskrit and Lithuanian share many common words. Bala Gangadhara Tilak in a book entitled *The Arctic Home in the Vedas*[13] argued from references to heavenly bodies in the *Rig Veda* that the Aryans once lived north of the Arctic Circle. More recently Nirad Chaudhuri has claimed that the Indians are Europeans who have forgotten who they are.[14]

The Aryans were a pastoral and nomadic people. They did not live in cities nor in permanent dwellings. In gypsy fashion they followed their herds, counting their wealth in cattle. The horse was well known. Horses were used to pull chariots, but for heavier cargoes oxcarts were used. When the Aryans stayed in one spot long enough to grow crops, barley was the favored crop. But meat was the principal food in their diet. Beef was supplemented by animals they could hunt with bow and arrow or catch in snares and traps. They did not fish, and they never learned to navigate rivers. They produced no distinctive pottery nor tools, and their craftsmanship was limited largely to weapons of war or implements needed for herding and agriculture, but they did bring iron to India. They were a vigorous, fun-loving people whose amusements were chariot-racing, gambling, and fighting. Storytelling and singing were their chief arts, the arts of entertainment around the campfire.

It was a male society. The tribes were structured on patriarchal lines, the domestic priest was an important member of society, and the gods were overwhelmingly male. The head of the gods was Sky Father (Jupiter, Zeus Pater, Dyaus Pitar). Yet the cow, rather than the bull, was the favored animal; whereas the Harappans, who appeared to honor a Great Mother, favored the bull.

The outstanding characteristic of the Aryan tribes was their mobility. When they pushed into Italy, Greece, Persia, and India they acquired more civilization than they brought, but they always contributed the ingredient of enthusiasm. They broke up closed social systems, demolished stereotypes, devastated cities, and acted as a catalyst. No people were the same after being touched by the Aryans.

The century in which the northern Aryans first turned southward in search of pasture cannot be determined. The eastern Aryan tribes settled in Anatolia between the Black Sea and the Mediterranean before splitting again in order that one group of tribes might push farther east in what proved to be the end of their eastward migrations. Those that stayed in Anatolia were known as the Khatti (Hittite), a term believed to be related to *Kshatriya* (warrior). On the way to India they probably paused for centuries in the area of modern Iran, as is indicated by the sharing of many of the same gods, e.g., Indra, Varuna, Agni, and Mitra—gods that remained among the Medes and Persians until the reformation of Zoroaster. One remarkable difference between the Persian gods and the Aryan gods, however, is that whereas *deva* meant gods and *asuras* meant demons for the Aryans, the meanings were reversed by the Persians. This may be an ancestral memory of serious social conflicts between the two peoples.

The date of the arrival of the Aryans in the Indus valley is open to wide differences of opinion. Some set the first invasions as early as 4000 B.C. If the Aryans were the destroyers of the two cities of the Indus valley, then the middle of the second millennium B.C. would be the date of their presence in large numbers. Moriz Winternitz once gave up trying to fix the date of the invasions, and wrote, perhaps facetiously, "The right date is X to 500 B.C." [15] Others have argued for two invasions, both in the second millennium, one at the opening and the other at the close of the millennium. The first group is believed to have returned to Iran and Anatolia; the second is thought to have settled in the valley of the Indus. There have been some efforts to identify the Harappa people themselves with the Aryans, but this hypothesis runs into many problems. Besides the vast difference in life-styles of the Harappans and the Aryans, one can point to the many minor points of divergence—e.g., the Harappans were familiar with the elephant, but the Aryans revealed their unfamiliarity by calling the elephant "the animal with the hand," and again, while the Harappans did excellent work in silver, the Aryans simply referred to the metal as "white gold."

The most important sources of information about the Aryans are the hymns to their gods which were passed down orally by priestly families, and were finally compiled into the collection known as the *Rig Veda.* The *Rig* reflects a complex society of illiterate people ruled by constantly warring princes and dominated by a priestly class who effectively manipulated the gods in order to secure health, longevity, posterity, wealth, food, and drink. They wanted "a life of a hundred autumns" [16] followed by a similar life in a heaven of unlimited pleasures. The best insight into the character of the Aryans is to look at their favorite god, Indra. Indra was the Aryan projection of himself: a warrior with all the virtues and faults of a man of battles. He was the personification of the exuberance of life, a boastful thunderbolt-throwing god, a slayer of dragons, and a heavy drinker. He released the waters of heaven, separated sky and earth, and fashioned the earth. He drank the highly intoxicating beverage *soma,* not because he enjoyed it or needed it but because he wanted to become drunk. Indra may have been an Aryan culture hero elevated to the status of divinity. He was a paradigm of the human qualities the Aryan most admired: vigor, enthusiasm, strength, courage, success in battle, gluttony, and drunkenness. Indra slew both his brother and his father. He was a *svaraj* (a king by seizure), not a *samraj* (a king by right of inheritance). In other words, Indra was an upstart who gained sovereignty by force. Whereas Varuna ruled by law (*Rita*), Indra ruled because he had subdued his enemies by daring and physical strength. Therefore, Indra was the god of warriors. Without Indra, men do not conquer in battle,[17] but with Indra's aid the dark-colored people (*dasas*) have been "humbled and dispersed." [18] When at last the Aryan catalyst lost its strength, Indra vanished into nothingness and Varuna was assimilated into his own law. But before the demise of Indra over two hundred and fifty hymns were composed to him. A typical hymn celebrating Indra as god of monsoons and battles is contained in *Rig Veda* 1. 32. It should be read not only as a celebration of Indra but also as the Aryan celebration of himself.[19]

I will proclaim the manly deeds of Indra,
The first that he performed, the lightning wielder.
He slew the serpent, then discharged the waters,
And cleft the caverns of the lofty mountains.

He slew the serpent lying on the mountain:
For him the whizzing bolt has Tvashtar fashioned.
Like lowing cows, with rapid current flowing,
The waters to the ocean down have glided.

Impetuous like a bull he chose the Soma,
And drank in threefold vessels of its juices.
The bounteous god grasped lightning for his missile;
He struck down dead that first-born of the serpents.

When thou hadst slain the first-born of the serpents,
And thwarted all the wiles of crafty schemers,
Anon disclosing sun, and dawn, and heaven,
Thou truly foundest not a foe, O Indra.

Indra slew Vritra and one worse than Vritra,
Vyamsa, with lightning, his resistless weapon:
Like trunks of trees, with axes hewn in pieces,
The serpent clinging to the earth lay prostrate.

He like a drunken coward challenged Indra,
The headlong, many-crushing, mighty hero.
He parried not the onset of the weapons:
The foe of Indra, falling, crushed the channels.

Footless and handless he with Indra battled,
Who smote him then upon his back with lightning.
But, impotent, he strove to match the hero:
He lay with scattered limbs in many places.

As thus he lay, like broken reed, the waters,
Now courage taking, surge across his body.
He lies beneath the very feet of rivers
Which Vritra with his might had close encompassed.

The strength began to fail of Vritra's mother,
For Indra had cast down his bolt upon her.
Above the mother was, the son was under;
And like a cow beside her calf lies Danu.

The waters deep have hidden Vritra's body,
Plunged in the midst of never-ceasing torrents

That stand not still, but ever hasten onward:
Indra's fierce foe sank down to lasting darkness.

Enclosed by demons, guarded by a serpent,
The waters stood like cows by Pani captured.
The waters' orifice that was obstructed,
When Vritra he had smitten, Indra opened.

A horse's tail thou didst become, O Indra,
When, on his spear impaled, as god unaided,
The cows, O hero, thou didst win and Soma,
And free the seven streams to flow in torrents.

Him lightning then availed not nor thunder,
Nor mist, nor hailstorm which around he scattered:
When Indra and the serpent fought in battle,
The bounteous god gained victory for ever.

Whom saw'st thou as avenger of the serpent,
As terror seized thy heart when thou hadst slain him,
And thou didst cross the nine and ninety rivers
And air's broad spaces, like a hawk affrighted?

Indra is king of all that's fixed and moving,
Of tame and horned beasts, the thunder-wielder.
He truly rules, as king of busy mortals;
Them he encompasses as spokes the felly.

CHAPTER 4

Vedism

The religions associated with the Aryans and the Harappans are so difficult to reconstruct that the earliest form of Hinduism is not to be identified with their cultures but with the culture resulting from the mixing of Aryans, Harappans, and other peoples of the Indus and Gangetic valleys. The Indo-European name for the principal river was Sindhu, which meant simply river. However, the names which have been utilized to designate the river and the religion and culture of the assimilated peoples—Hindu and Hinduism—conform to the Persian pronunciation. Some scholars prefer to use the term "Hinduism" for the religions which developed after the formation of the great epics, the *Mahabharata* and the *Ramayana*, that is, after A.D. 300, on the grounds that by that time practical agreement had been reached about the fundamental social structure and scriptures. A term like "Brahmanism" is preferred by such scholars as a generic term for the earlier religions of India to which Hindus look back as the source of their religious traditions.[1] Other scholars use "Hinduism" to denote all the religions which have developed in India—for example, Benjamin Walker identifies Pre-Dravidian Hinduism,

Dravidian Hinduism, Medieval Hinduism, Reformed Hinduism, and National Hinduism.[2] The usage in this book is a compromise between these two extreme positions. The term "Hindusim" will here be used to designate the indigenous religious development in India from the time of the Indus valley settlement of the Aryans to the present day. The first form of Hinduism we shall call "Vedism" after the name given to the collection of early sacred lore. Hindus today refer to this early Hinduism as *Sanatana Dharma* (the ancient correct way). The term also means the principle which holds the world together. This term is a twentieth-century device to establish a feeling of long historical continuity, and it flies in the face of the fact that, despite a few reformations such as those associated with the Arya Samaj, Hinduism today has only remote relations with Vedism. The Vedic gods have been forsaken, the Vedic sacrifices are no longer part of the ceremonial ritual, and the Vedic cosmology has been drastically demythologized. Yet Vedism lives on sufficiently in modified form to justify the claim that it is an ancient form of living Hinduism. Not only are portions of the ancient scriptures used at weddings and funerals, but also millions of Hindus begin each day with an ancient Vedic prayer to the sun: "Let us meditate on the excellent glory of Savitar. May he stimulate our prayers."

The difference the excavations of the Indus valley civilization have made in our understanding of the Vedic form of Hinduism can be noted by comparing the following statement by a great American Indologist in 1907 with what we now know because of the Harappan digs: "Vedic tradition is in some respects the most remarkable in recorded history. From the entire Vedic period we have not one single piece of antiquarian or archaeological material, not one bit of real property; not a building, nor a monument; not a coin, jewel, or utensil;—nothing but winged words." [3] Although this is no longer the case, the written records remain a valuable source of information about these people and their way of life.

The Vedas

The Aryans were not an artistic people. At least the pottery and tools which have survived are mediocre and unoriginal in design and ornamentation. Yet there is one area in which they can be said to have been creative and artistic. Like all nomadic pastoral peoples, they loved storytelling and singing. They were a verbal people. They sang their ancient hymns in a poetic-priestly language filled with coined words in which verbs are derived from nouns, e.g., "give battle" rather than "fight," and "cultivate the gods" rather than "be pious." Human speech was even elevated to divine status in Vacaspati (Lord of Speech) and Vac (Goddess of Human Sound). Even before reaching India in the second millennium B.C. they had developed hymns of praise and petition to their gods which they transmitted orally from generation to generation. We assume that priestly families were responsible for the preservation of the hymns. Some of them may have been composed during the European stage of their migrations, e.g., hymns to the sky (Dyaus) and to the dawn (Ushas); others may have been composed while they were living in Iran where they shared such gods as Indra, Varuna, Agni, and Mitra with the peoples of that area; and still others indicate events and gods associated with India. The majority of the hymns (*suktas*) are of the third classification, although, because of many redactions, classification upon the basis of geographical or temporal origin is conjectural. The canon of Vedic *suktas* was fixed by the end of the third century B.C., but oral transmission was so highly prized that as late as the eighth century A.D. writing down the Vedas was regarded as sacrilege.

The word *"veda"* means wisdom, and is related to the English "wit" and the German *"wissen."* Wisdom in this instance means absolute, intuitive, and esoteric wisdom as distinguished from discursive knowledge, either rational or empirical. *"Veda"* is used either to designate the entire early literature of the Hindus or only the earliest collections of hymns, sacrifices, and prayers. We shall use the term only in the latter sense. When we refer to the entire early literature, the terms "Vedic scriptures" or "Vedic writings" will be used. The wisdom presented in the *suktas* is implicit rather than argued or defended. The Vedic writings are said to be *shruti*. This technical term is often translated "revealed," a translation which encourages Western scholars to compare Vedic *shruti* with the doctrine of revelation in Judaism and Christianity. This comparison must be avoided. Revelation in Judaism and Christianity assumes that a divinity has conveyed truths to man which transcend truths man can discover for himself. But *shruti* does not imply a conveyer of truths. The word literally means that which is heard, but this must not be interpreted to mean that which was spoken by someone. The *rishis* (seers) were believed to have heard the eternal truths in states of ecstasy. Perhaps "become aware of" would be better than "heard." That which was heard in this fashion was said to be *shrauta*, i.e., sacred because heard. The *shrauta* nature of the Vedic scriptures is linked with the view of the spoken word as a metaphysical principle. Words were the Vedic *yoga*. They united thought and action, mind and matter. The *shrauta* word is itself the effective cause when properly uttered by the proper person under the proper circumstances at the proper time. *Nada*—primordial sound—is the beginning of all.

When the orthodox Hindu says that the Vedic scriptures are *shruti*, he means that they have no origin either human or divine, that they were before the world came into being, that they have always been, and they will never cease to be. Those Hindus who hold this view of the early literature believe that Vedic wisdom cannot be conveyed from person to person in a mundane pedagogical manner. *Shruti* material cannot be transmitted by the printed page nor by ordinary vocal methods. It can be conveyed only in the living relations of minds, one mind prepared to teach and the other prepared to receive. The criterion of fitness (*adhikaribheda*) applies both to the teacher of such truths and to the pupil, that is, to the *guru* and to the *shishya*. The *guru-shishya* relationship in traditional Hinduism transcends any other relationship because so much is at stake. The selection of a *guru* is more significant than the selection of a spouse.

The *Vedas* consist of four collections (*Samhitas*) known as the *Rig*, the *Sama*, the *Yajur*, and the *Atharva*. The first is the oldest, largest, and most important; indeed, it is so important that it is sometimes known simply as *The Veda*. It contains 1017 original *suktas*, to which eleven apocryphal ones are sometimes added. While all of the 1017 are generally said to be hymns to the gods, closer inspection will reveal that some are magical poems, riddles, and legends. They are not the folklore of a primitive, animistic, and nature-worshiping people, as has sometimes been thought by those who know them largely in abridged editions. They are the work of sophisticated priests seeking riches, success, long life, power, safety, posterity, food, and women for their patrons. The formula is quite simple: praise the god, and then petition the god for benefits. Notice in the following representative hymn to Agni, the god of fire, that the god is praised for his heroic virtues and then petitioned for destruction of enemies and wealth for the patron.

> The man who seeks success and aid approaches
> The son of strength, with feast and newest worship.
> He rends the wood and has a blackened pathway,
> The brightly radiant and divine invoker.
>
> The shining thunderer who dwells in lustre,
> With his unaging, roaring flames, most youthful,
> Refulgent Agni, frequently recurring,
> Goes after many spacious woods and chews them.
>
> Thy flames when driven by the wind, O Agni,
> Disperse, O pure one, pure in all directions;
> And thy divine Navagvas, most destructive,
> Lay low the woods and devastate them boldly.
>
> Thy steeds, the bright, the pure, O radiant Agni,
> Let loose, speed on and shave the ground beneath them.
> Thy whirling flame then widely shines refulgent,
> The highest ridges of earth's surface reaching.
>
> When the bull's tongue darts forward like the missile
> Discharged by him who fights the cows to capture,
> Like hero's onset is the flame of Agni:
> Resistless, dreadful, he consumes the forests.
>
> Thou with the sunbeams of the great impeller,
> Hast boldly overspread the earthly spaces.
> So with they mighty powers drive off all terrors;
> Attack our rivals and burn down our foemen.
>
> Give us, O splendid one of splendid lordship,
> Wealth giving splendour, splendid, life-imparting.
> Bestow bright wealth and vast with many heroes,
> Bright god, with thy bright flames, upon the singer.[4]

Not all the *suktas* seek material blessings. Many of the prayers to Varuna, the god of cosmic and moral order, ask for forgiveness of wrongs, e.g.,

> If we have sinned against the man who loves us,
>   have ever wronged a brother, friend, or comrade,
> The neighbor ever with us, or a stranger, O Varuna,
>   remove from us the trespass.
>
> If we, as gamesters cheat at play, have cheated,
>   done wrong unwittingly or sinned of purpose,
> Cast all these sins away like loosened fetters, and,
>   Varuna, let us be thine own beloved.[5]

The *Rig* is divided into ten books called *mandalas* (circles). The first eight contain for the most part hymns of praise and petition to the gods of ancient India, but the last two are unique: the ninth is a collection of *suktas* celebrating Soma, the god of drink, and the tenth is a miscellany of *suktas* to many of the familiar gods but also to some unusual "gods," for example, to Ka, the unknown god (10. 121), to speech (10. 125), to Indra's two bay horses (10. 96), to the carts which carry the sacrificial materials (10. 13), and to the stones which are used to crush the *soma* plant (10. 76, 95, 175). Something else appears in the tenth *mandala* which indicates that much of the material is late: here are found many *suktas* used as *mantras,* i.e., as word magic to make things happen. The mantric use of the *suktas* of the tenth *mandala* include the following uses: to aid in recovering lost cattle (10. 19), to increase the effectiveness of medicinal plants (10. 97), to improve begging (10. 117), to get rid of a rival wife (10. 145), to avert an abortion (10. 162), to purge phthisis (10. 163), to banish a nightmare (10. 164), and to destroy a rival (10. 166). In addition, the tenth *mandala* contains philosophical *suktas* like 10. 90, which presents Purusha as the primeval man who is the prototype of humanity, and 10. 129, which is a profound cosmogonical speculation.

In addition to the *Rig Veda Samhita* (the collection of the praise wisdom) there is also the *Sama Veda* (the chant wisdom), the *Yajur Veda* (the sacred formula wisdom), and the *Atharva Veda* (the magical charm wisdom). The *Sama* is the songbook of the *Vedas*. Its *suktas* are largely selected from the *Rig* and are arranged according to their use in the sacrificial ceremonies. They are meant to be sung to fixed melodies. The *Yajur* also borrows heavily from the *Rig*. It is a priestly handbook containing both *mantras* and prose directions for the performance of sacrifices. The importance of the *Rig*, the *Sama*, and the *Yajur* is indicated in that they are commonly referred to as the *Trayi Vidya* (Triple Knowledge) of Hinduism. The *Atharva* is late in the development of Vedic literature. It is mainly a book of spells and incantations designed to meet the demand of people possessed with anxious dread of evil spirits. Many of its *suktas* are to be used with magical plants, potions, lotions, and drugs. Here, for example, is a charm to grow hair:

> As a goddess upon the Goddess Earth thou wast born, O plant!
> We dig thee up, O Nitatni, that thou mayst strengthen (the growth) of hair.
>
> Strengthen the old (hair), beget thou new!
> That which has come forth render more luxurious!
>
> That hair of thine which does drop off, and that which is broken root and all,
> Upon it do I sprinkle here the all-healing herb.[6]

The chief significance of the *Atharva Veda* in India today is that it is the basis of the form of medicine known as *Ayurveda*. The classic book of medicine and health is called the *Ayurveda*, and it is added as a supplement to the *Atharva*. As such it is sometimes called "the Fifth Veda."

In addition to the four *Samhitas* three other types of religious-philosophical-poetic materials were composed in ancient India. These are known as *Brahmanas*, *Aranyakas*, and *Upanishads*. The *Brahmanas* are directions for the performances of sacrifices; the *Aranyakas* are interpretations of the sacrifices, usually analogical and allegorical; and the *Upanishads* are metaphysical speculations which go far beyond the assumptions of the hymns and prayers of the *Samhitas*. The creative activity which resulted in these new materials occurred between the eighth and the third centuries B.C. The entire literature —*Samhitas*, *Brahmanas*, *Aranyakas*, and *Upanishads*—constitutes the entirety of the Vedic literature. This is the literature denoted by *shruti*. Through the centuries Hindu scholars have developed a classificatory schema by which each *Brahmana, Aranyaka,* and *Upanishad* is assigned to one of the four *Vedas:*

Samhitas	Brahmanas	Aranyakas	Upanishads
Rig Veda	*Aitareya* *Kaushitaki* (Also called *Shankhayana* or *Ashvalayana*)	*Aitareya* *Kaushitaki*	*Aitareya* *Kaushitaki*
Sama Veda	*Chandogya* *Prauda* (Also called *Pañchavimsha* or *Tandya*) *Shadvimsha* *Samvidhana* *Adbhuta* *Vamsha* *Arsheya* *Jaiminiya* (Also called *Talavakara*)		*Chandogya* *Kena*
Yajur Veda	*Taittiriya* *Shatapatha*	*Taittiriya* *Brihad*	*Taittiriya* *Katha* *Shvetashvatara* *Mahanarayana* *Maitrayani* *Isha* *Brihad-* *Aranyaka*
Atharva Veda	*Gopatha*		*Mundaka* *Prashna* *Mandukya*

The division of the *Yajur* into *Black* and *White* is a traditional division between early and late portions of this work. *Samhitas* and *Brahmanas* are jointly referred to as the *karma-kanda* (works section) of Vedic literature since the stress is on action, i.e., the sacrifices, and *Aranyakas* and *Upanishads* are called the *jñana-kanda* (knowledge section) since they embody an intellectual approach.

The Hindu lawbooks enjoin Vedic study on all males of the twice-born classes, although this study is usually limited to *Brahmins*. According to the *Laws of Manu* a *Brahmin* male who does not study the *Vedas* is a *brahmabandu* (a *Brahmin* only in name). On the other hand, a Hindu not of the twice-born classes who hears the reading of a *Veda* suffers the penalty of having hot wax poured into his ears! Vedic study has taken two forms: memorization and analysis. In either case the *suktas* of the *Samhitas* are the principal subject matter. The goal sought in memorization in traditional Vedic study was absolute accuracy. To insure this a Brahmin boy was sometimes expected to recite a *sukta* backwards as well as forwards. Understanding the meaning was secondary. Also from ancient times there has come another form of Vedic study: a form in which the student was expected to grasp the meaning of the *suktas*. This approach resulted in the rich tradition of Hindu philosophy. *Veda*-memorizing was and is largely a village phenomenon in which the *shishya* studies alone with his *guru*; *Veda*-philosophizing is associated with a school in urban conditions. As might be expected, the memorizer is trained largely for priestly functions, whereas the philosopher graduates to the *Upanishads* and to the commentaries upon the *Upanishads* in learning which might be called general education as contrasted to the vocational training of his village counterpart.

The Vedic Gods

The *Rig Veda* is hopelessly confusing if it is approached as an encyclopedia of information about the earliest form of Hinduism, but if it is examined as a record of the religious experiences, practices, experiments, and thoughts of these early Hindus, it can prove to be immensely valuable. It is "a mythology in the making." [7] "Nowhere in the world is the process of god-making so clear as in the *Rig Veda*." [8] The gods of Vedism are the personalizations and reifications of natural powers—powers in the sky, in the atmosphere, and on the earth. The gods were not postulated as explanatory devices to account for the world of human experience. The Aryans were probably unaware they were explaining anything. They were merely stating the way things behave: the sun shines, the storm howls, fire burns, etc. The absence of gods of an underworld ought not to go unnoticed. Although the gods were benevolent, this should not be taken to mean that it was a light-hearted cult, for there were remnants of an older cult of underworld demons.

The term used in the Vedas for a god is *deva,* and since *deva* means a shining one, the easy conclusion is that the gods in Vedic Hinduism were the heavenly bodies. However, *deva* also means one who gives; a learned person is a *deva* of knowledge, parents are *devas* who give sustenance and guidance to their children, and a guest is a *deva* of pleasure to his hosts. The Vedic *devas* are givers; they are used as the source of the goods of life rather than adored for their intrinsic worth. "Angel" and "archangel" have been suggested as translations of *deva,* but most Indologists fall back on "god" as the best translation. A second but ill-defined group of gods were known as the *asuras.* Although *"asura"* is sometimes translated "devil," this is misleading, for the *asuras* were not devils or demons but rival gods who at one time had challenged the sovereignty of the *devas.* In ancient Iran the superior gods were the *asuras* and the demons were the *devas.* This may indicate that a conflict between *deva*-worshipers and *asura*-worshipers was instrumental in the separation of the Indo-Iranians who stayed and the Indo-Aryans who moved on to India. In Vedism the *asuras* are the anti-gods, the polar opposites of the *devas. Devas* were gods who ruled by reason of conquest—as did the Aryans; *asuras* were gods who ruled by reason of inheritance. Indra was the chief of the *devas;* Varuna may at one time have been the chief of the *asuras.* By the time of the development of Vedism, the *asuras* had ceased to be worshiped.

The gods were conceived anthropomorphically, theriomorphically, and therianthropically, i.e., in human form, in animal form, and in part human and part animal form. The common practice was to indicate the god's special powers by means of extra appendages. Multiple arms, heads, and eyes were common. The personalities of the gods were not as sharply conceived as were those of the Olympians. They were cases of arrested development. The most distinguishing feature of a *deva* was power. *Devas* were kratophanies, i.e., manifestations of power. The powers were conceived functionally rather than substantially. Thus there was not a god of the sun *per se*, but a god of the sun as illuminator, of the sun as stimulator, of the sun as bringer of warmth, of the sun as causer of drought, etc. Most of the gods were masculine, and most had a feminine consort who was known as the god's energy (*shakti*). The *shakti* was a sort of emanation of the god. She brought the power of the god to man, and she was in most instances more approachable than the god himself. Few of the *shaktis* were more than shadowy counterparts of the god; their names were usually nothing more than "*Shakti* of . . ."

Of course the Vedic Indians worshiped many gods; one *rishi* said the number was 330,000,000! The number of gods a devotee might worship during a year depended upon what was needed: fertility of herds, rain for the barley fields, cure of an old man's aches, the birth of a healthy male child, etc. "Polytheism," however, is not the right term to describe the Vedic pantheon because the *devas* were not always clearly distinguishable. They did not retain their identity as distinct and different individual *devas*, nor did they preserve their proper places in the divine hierarchy. There was a certain shifting among the *devas*, a tendency to assume while worshiping one god that he was supreme, or even unique, among the gods, while the other gods diminished or vanished altogether. This tendency was noticed by Max Müller and was given the identifying name kathenotheism (one-by-one theism), which has since been shortened to henotheism and has been described as "opportunistic monotheism" and as "pragmatic polytheism." The term refers to worship patterns rather than to theological beliefs. It may denote either the form of worshiping one god while recognizing the propriety of other persons or tribes worshiping another god or the pattern in which during the act of worship the god that is being adored is regarded either as the only god or as the supreme of all gods. Notice in the following prayer addressed to Varuna the worshiper incorporates Agni into Varuna:

> Present to Varuna the gracious giver
> A hymn, Vasishtha, bright and very pleasant,
> That he may bring to us the lofty, holy
> And mighty steed that grants a thousand bounties.
>
> Now having come to Varuna's full aspect,
> I think his countenance like that of Agni;
> May he, the lord, lead me to see the marvel:
> The light and darkness hidden in the cavern.[9]

In the following *sukta* Indra is addressed as the only god:

> Powerful Indra, be present and favourable
> to the mortal (who adores thee): there is no
> other giver of felicity, Maghavan, than thou;
> hence, Indra, I recite thy praise.[10]

Four chronological layers of gods can be identified. The oldest gods were the arching sky and the conceiving earth, Father Sky and Mother Earth. They must have come from Indo-European times, if we can judge from the similar names given to Father Sky: Jupiter (Latin), Zeus Pater (Greek), and Dyaus Pitar (Sanskrit). By the time of the formation of the *Rig Veda* the descendants of the primordial couple had taken over most of their functions. Dyaus is addressed in no *sukta,* and Prithivi (Earth) in but one:

> Thou bearest truly, Prithivi,
> The burden of the mountains' weight;
> With might, O thou of many streams,
> Thou quickenest, potent one, the soil.
>
> Who steadfast, holdest with thy might,
> The forest-trees upon the ground,
> When, from the lightning of thy cloud,
> The rain-floods of the sky pour down.[11]

Six *suktas* of the *Rig* are addressed to Dyaus Pitar and Prithivi Matar jointly, but by this time they were ancestral memories rather than living gods. Their existence was a mystery to the Vedics.

> Which of the two is earlier, which the later?
> How were they born, ye sages, who discerns it?
> They by themselves support all things existing.
> As with a wheel the day and night roll onward.[12]

The second layer of the gods are those of the Indo-Iranian period. Gods such as Indra, Varuna, Mitra, Agni, and Soma were worshiped by the ancient Iranians. If Dyaus and Prithivi can be compared to Uranos and Gaia of the Greeks, then the gods of the Indo-Iranian period can be compared to the Olympians.

The third chronological layer of the gods are the gods created on Indian soil. Brahmā, Vishnu, and Shiva are examples. They are not Vedic, although they are descendants or outgrowths of the Vedic *devas*.

The fourth layer consists of a number of abstract *devas* indicated by such impersonal identifications as Eka Deva (One God), Tat Ekam (That One), Ka (Who), and Prajapati (Father of Creation). They represent a movement away from theistic entities to an Absolute behind the gods.

The priestly classification of the gods was into celestial, atmospheric, and terrestrial gods. Each of the three spheres (the *tri-loka*) was thought to have its presiding deity; thus the sun (Savitar or Surya) was the chief of the *dyuloka* or celestial sphere, Indra (the god of the monsoon) was the most important god of the *antarikshaloka* or intermediate space, and Agni (fire) was the chief god of the *bhurloka* or terrestrial sphere. Eleven gods were assigned to each sphere. The ancient *deva*, Dyaus Pitar, was listed among the celestials, although by this time he had no sovereignty over the gods. His place had been filled by Varuna. Dyaus had no moral attributes and was represented as a black bull or steed decked with pearls, i.e., the dark sky set with stars. The two daughters of Dyaus were Ratri and Ushas; the former was the goddess of the dark night, the protector from night thieves; the latter was the ever young and colorful goddess of the dawn. Ushas was born anew each day to travel across the sky in a shining chariot drawn by reddish horses or cows. One of the loveliest of the *suktas* of the *Rig* is addressed to Ushas:

> This light has come, of all the lights the fairest:
> The brilliant brightness has been born effulgent.
> Urged onward for god Savitar's uprising,
> Night now has yielded up her place to morning.
>
> Bringing a radiant calf she comes resplendent:
> To her the Black one has given up her mansions.
> Akin, immortal, following each the other,
> Morning and Night fare on, exchanging colours.
>
> The sisters' pathway is the same, unending:
> Taught by the gods alternately they tread it.
> Fair-shaped, of form diverse, yet single-minded,
> Morning and Night clash not, nor do they tarry.
>
> Bright leader of glad sounds she shines effulgent:
> Widely she has unclosed for us her portals.
> Pervading all the world she shows us riches:
> Dawn has awakened every living creature.
>
> Men lying on the ground she wakes to action:
> Some rise to seek enjoyment of great riches,
> Some, seeing little, to behold the distant:
> Dawn has awakened every living creature.
>
> One for dominion, and for fame another;
> Another is aroused for winning greatness;
> Another seeks the goal of varied nurture:
> Dawn has awakened every living creature.
>
> Daughter of Heaven, she has appeared before us,
> A maiden shining in resplendent raiment.
> Thou sovereign lady of all earthly treasure,
> Auspicious Dawn, shine here to-day upon us.[13]

Varuna was the second greatest of the gods in the *Rig*. He was so closely identified with Dyaus Pitar that some scholars believe he is but another name for Dyaus. He was the *deva* of physical order. He was the one who kept rivers within their banks, the seasons in proper rotation, and the stars in their courses. He became the god of moral order. He was the god upon whom oaths were taken, the third party in all contracts. He was often described as holding a rope, the symbol of binding promises. Moral wrongs were violations of Varuna's law; hence most of the prayers to Varuna end with a petition for forgiveness:

> As guilty may we not, O wizard, suffer:
> Do thou, O sage, grant shelter to thy praiser.
> O may we, in these fixed abodes abiding,
> Now from the lap of Aditi find favour.
> May from his noose king Varuna release us.
> Ye gods protect us evermore with blessings.[14]

> May we be free from sin against that Varuna, who has compassion upon him who commits offence.[15]

> Varuna, loosen for me the upper, the middle, the lower band; so, son of Aditi, shall we, through faultlessness in thy worship, become freed from sin.[16]

> Cast off from me, sin, Varuna, as if it were a rope.[17]

> Keep us all our days in the right path, and prolong our lives.[18]

The other celestial gods were functional powers of sunlight. They may have been originally sun gods of various tribes. Mitra was the personification of the beneficent power of the light of the sun. Surya was the sun as the way-finder, the spy of the whole world. He was both brother and husband of Ushas. Savitar was the sun in its role as vivifier and stimulator. At dawn his gold arms extended over the earth in benediction, and it is to him that the first prayer of the day has been addressed among Hindus for more than three thousand years. Pushan was a pastoral solar deity who served as messenger of Surya. He was the guide and patron of travelers, and he also guided the spirits of the dead into the paths of ancestral spirits. Vishnu was a minor sun god in the Vedic religion, a god who was thought to be especially considerate to man. His fortune has been different from that of most Vedic deities; he has waxed to become one of the greatest gods of modern Hinduism. He is today the Preserver in the Trimurti (Three Forms), i.e., Brahmā (Creator), Vishnu (Pre-

server), and Shiva (Destroyer). He was often referred to by the
Vedic seers as the god of the three strides because he was thought to
traverse the regions of earth, air, and heaven. His spanning ability
endeared him to his worshipers because he could take messages to
and from the departed. As the other Vedic gods faded away, Vishnu
rose to become the most beloved of all the gods, the god who returns
in each cosmic cycle to redeem mankind.

The Ashvins and the Adityas were two important clusters of
celestials. The Ashvins were the twin horse-headed sons of Dyaus.
They appeared each morning between dawn and sunrise to dispel
darkness and fear and to restore vigor and sight to all creatures of the
day. They became associated with medicine and with wisdom. For
some reason they did not like *soma,* the stimulating drink of gods and
men, preferring honey instead. The term "Adityas" was used for
various groups of gods of celestial light. Their number ranged from
two to twelve. The mother of the Adityas was called Aditi. The
grouping of the gods was apparently an effort to establish unity in the
Vedic cosmology. Thus in the *Rig* in addition to the Adityas there
were the Vasus (eight natural phenomena: water, pole-star, moon,
earth, wind, fire, dawn, and light), the Vishvamitras (all the gods of
light), and the Vishvadevas (the gods as a whole).

The atmospheric gods were the powers of wind, storm, thunder,
lightning, and rain. The most important and the favorite of the Vedic
peoples as they relived the exciting days of the migrations and
invasions of their Aryan forefathers was Indra, the god of mountain
storms, monsoons, battles, and conquests. He was the personification
of exuberance of life, a *Kshatriya* (warrior) with all military virtues
and defects. Indra was a braggart whose boastfulness may have been
a screen for character defects, for he was able to engage in demon
slaying only when his courage was well fortified with large drafts of
the intoxicating *soma.* The chief myth about Indra is of the genre of
the Hero and the Dragon, e.g., St. George and the Dragon, and
Marduk and Tiamat. According to the myth there once lived a
powerful *brahmin* who disliked Indra. The *brahmin* had a son who
surpassed all men in physical strength and cunning. Indra fought the
son, killing him with a thunderbolt (*vajra*). To avenge the death the
brahmin created the demon Vritra, a demon so huge that his head

reached the sky. Indra and Vritra fought long and hard, but neither won. At last a truce was made in which Indra and Vritra promised that they would not attack by day or by night, they would use no weapon of wood, iron, or stone, and they would not strike with any object wet or dry. Under the protection of the truce Vritra continued in his demonic ways. But when he penned up the heavenly waters so that plants and animals began to die, Indra decided to act. One evening at dusk when it was neither day nor night Indra saw Vritra by the ocean. He seized a column of foam which was not wood, iron, or stone, and which was neither wet nor dry, and with this weapon he slew the demon, split him, and released the waters. The myth, we suspect, is an account of a long drought broken by a fearful storm. There are two hundred and fifty *suktas* addressed to Indra in the *Rig*. The following is typical:

> All our praises magnify Indra, expansive as the ocean, the most valiant of warriors who fight in chariots, the lord of food, the protector of the virtuous.
>
> Supported by thy friendship, Indra cherisher of strength, we have no fear, but glorify thee, the conqueror, the unconquered.
>
> The ancient liberalities of Indra, his protections, will not be wanting to him who presents to the reciters of the hymns, wealth of food and cattle.
>
> Indra was born the destroyer of cities, ever young, ever wise, of unbounded strength, the sustainer of all pious acts, the wielder of the thunderbolt, the many-praised.
>
> The reciters of sacred hymns praise with all their might, Indra, the ruler of the world, whose bounties are computed by thousands, or even more.[19]

Yet, despite the admiration for the exploits of Indra, before the period of *Rig Vedic sukta* composing ended, Indra worship had diminished, prompting a *rishi* to write a hymn celebrating Indra's mighty works and pleading with the people to believe in Indra.

> He who just born as chief god full of spirit
> Went far beyond the other gods in wisdom:

Before whose majesty and mighty manhood
The two worlds trembled: he, O men, is Indra.

Who made the widespread earth when quaking steadfast,
Who set at rest the agitated mountains,
Who measured out air's middle space more widely,
Who gave the sky support: he, men, is Indra.

Who slew the serpent, freed the seven rivers,
Who drove the cattle out from Vala's cavern,
Who fire between two rocks has generated,
A conqueror in fights: he, men, is Indra.

He who has made all earthly things unstable,
Who humbled and dispersed the Dasa colour,
Who, as the player's stake the winning gambler,
The foeman's fortune gains: he, men, is Indra.

Of whom, the terrible, they ask, "Where is he?"
Of him, indeed, they also say, "He is not."
The foeman's wealth, like players' stakes, he lessens.
Believe in him: for he, O men, is Indra.[20]

If Indra was the Aryan god of monsoons, Rudra may be regarded as the Dravidian god of monsoons. Some scholars speculate that he was a composite god made up of earlier native Dravidian gods such as Sarva (the lord of thunderbolts), Bhava (a sky god), and Urga (the ruler of the underworld). Rudra seems to have been a prototype of Shiva. He was celebrated as fierce and destructive, the personification of the dangerous elements of nature. He alone among the Vedic gods was asked to go away rather than to come to the sacrifice and remain nearby.

May Rudra's missile turn aside and pass us,
May the fierce Rudra's great ill-will go by us.
Relax thy rigid bow to save our patrons;
Spare, O thou god of bounty, child and grandchild.

So brown-hued, mighty Rudra, widely famous,
Here to our invocations be attentive,
As not, O god, to rise in wrath and slay us.[21]

The word *"rudra"* means taboo. The name was so feared that in *Aitareya Brahmana* 3. 3. 9–10 it is intentionally mispronounced

Rudriya, in the belief that by saying the name incorrectly one will not bring evil upon oneself. Rudra is the one god among the thirty-three who makes it impossible to say that all the Vedic gods were benevolent.

Most of the other atmospheric gods were of minor significance. The Maruts, whose number according to the *Rig* was both thrice-seven and thrice-sixty, were the noisy wind gods who accompanied Indra. They shook mountains and caused the earth to tremble. They were both fierce and playful. They were feared because of their destructiveness, yet they were praised as the instruments of the eternal renewal of the world. Anyone who has lived a full year in India recalls how the coming monsoon is both longed for and feared. In similar oxymoronic fashion the Maruts were dreaded as somehow tied up with the souls of the dead and enjoyed as the singers of heaven. Other wind gods were Vayu, Vata, and Matarisvan. Apam Napat, an ancient god, lived in deep waters. Apas was the god of the flow of rivers. Prajanya, the god of gentle rain, was easily pushed aside by Indra, Rudra, and the Maruts. Trita was a minor god of lightning.

We have already noted the ancient terrestrial god Prithivi, the broad earth. Several ancient river gods were included among this group of eleven: Sindhu, Vipas, Shutudri, and Saraswati. The latter god became important in post-Vedic times as the goddess of music, scholarship, and speech. She is the wife of Brahmā, and remains one of the loveliest of the gods. But in Vedic times the two chief terrestrial gods were Agni the fire god and Soma the god of drink. Agni was fire in many aspects: the sun, lightning, the sacrifice, and the family hearth. Agni was the god who took the petitions of the devotees to the gods. As hearth deity Agni was protector of the home, the lord of the house. As the devourer of corpses he was a purifier and dispeller of evil spirits. He is described in the *Rig* as butter-backed, flame-haired, with sharp jaws and golden teeth, and with seven tongues designed for licking *ghee* (clarified butter). The nearness of Agni is indicated in the following *sukta:*

> Agni I praise, the household priest,
> God, minister of sacrifice,
> Invoker, best bestowing wealth.

Agni is worthy to be praised,
By present as by seers of old:
May he to us conduct the gods.

Through Agni may we riches gain,
And day by day prosperity
Replete with fame and manly sons.

The worship and the sacrifice,
Guarded by thee on every side,
Go straight, O Agni, to the gods.

May Agni, the invoker, wise
And true, of most resplendent fame,
The god, come hither with the gods.

Whatever good thou wilt bestow,
O Agni, on the pious man,
That gift comes true, O Angiras.

To thee, O Agni, day by day,
O thou illuminer of gloom,
With thought we, bearing homage, come:

To thee the lord of sacrifice,
The radiant guardian of the Law,
That growest in thine own abode.

So, like a father to his son,
Be easy of approach to us:
Agni, for weal abide with us.[22]

Soma, the Vedic Bacchus, is addressed in over two hundred *suktas* of the *Rig*. He is a god with few anthropomorphic aspects. He is described as riding in a celestial cart, as having a bow and one thousand arrows, as a stimulator of the voice, an awakener of thought, a generator of hymns, the lord of plants, and a conveyer of immortality. The descriptions of the effects of *soma* suggest that it was a hallucinogen rather than an intoxicant. It was made from the juice attained by crushing a plant which had been gathered on mountain sides by moonlight. The juice was mixed with milk. Speculation as to what the plant was varies from a mountain rhubarb (*Asclepias Acida*) to the common poisonous mushroom *Amanita*

Muscaria.[23] The recipe for making the drink has been lost, but the description of the effect of its use is explicit.

> I have partaken wisely of the sweet food
> That stirs good thoughts, best banisher of trouble,
> The food round which all deities and mortals,
> Calling it honey-mead, collect together.
>
> We have drunk Soma and become immortal;
> We have attained the light the gods discovered.
> What can hostility now do against us?
> And what, immortal god, the spite of mortals?
>
> Be cheering to our heart when drunk, O Indu,
> Kindly, like a father to his son, O Soma.
> Like friend for friend, far-famed one, wisely
> Prolong our years that we may live, O Soma.
>
> These glorious, freedom-giving drops, when drunk by me,
> Have knit my joints together as do thongs a car.
> May these protect me now from fracturing a limb.
> And may they ever keep me from disease remote.
>
> Like fire produced by friction, make me brilliant;
> Do thou illumine us and make us richer;
> For then I seem in thy carouse, O Soma,
> Enriched. Now enter us for real welfare.
>
> Away have fled those ailments and diseases;
> The powers of darkness have been all affrighted.
> With mighty strength in us has Soma mounted;
> We have arrived where men prolong existence.[24]

The Vedic Rituals

The rituals associated with the *suktas* during the Vedic period of the historical development of Hinduism were relatively simple. The *shrauta* (sacred) ceremonies required no temples and no images. The place of worship was any spot of ground which the patriarch of the clan selected. The boundaries of the place of worship were indicated by freshly cut grass, and when the sacrifice was over the spot was no longer regarded as sacred. Often the ritual place was near a river, but the focal point of worship was the fire not the water. *Ghee* was poured on the wood to increase the flames of Agni as he carried the praises and petitions to the *devas*. *Soma* was poured into a hole in the ground to insure the immortality of the gods, and some was consumed by the worshipers in order to share in the feelings of immortality. The fathers of the clan were the priests in these simple rites, although we may assume that certain men of the clan must have been considered better priests because of their superior ability in chanting the *suktas*. There seemed to be no separation of the duties of fire-tending, *ghee* and *soma* pouring, or chanting of *suktas* in the early ceremonies. There is also no indication that impromptu or extemporaneous praises or petitions were used, but we can assume that in addition to the recitation of the *suktas* there must have been special and specific prayers to the gods. The separation between gods and men was not definite since both gods and men drank the *soma*. The gods were asked to come near, to enjoy *ghee* and *soma,* and sit beside men on the grass at the holy place: "May Varuna, Mitra, and Aryaman, triumphant in riches, sit on our sacrificial grass as they did on Manu's." Later the sacrifices became extremely elaborate and complicated, but in Vedic Hinduism they were simple.

The purposes of the rites were thoroughly practical: to secure happiness, success, health, offspring, long life, and other good things of this world and to continue such blessings into the afterlife. Insofar as we are able to distinguish the early and the late hymns, the former are the instruments of persuasion. They are the means by which the gods as efficient causes could be encouraged to confer favors upon their worshipers. The late hymns are part of the sacrifices themselves; they may be regarded as the sacrifice gone poetical.

The Vedic View of the World

The Vedic Indians believed that the world of their experience was also the world of the *devas*. Natural phenomena were the activities of purposive agents who were at least partially controllable by human beings. Wind, storm, flood, drought, fertility, health, disease, wealth, and happiness were the results of beings with minds, emotions, and wills. Food, drink, and adulation given to these beings could induce them to give to man what he wanted. "You have given us rain," reads one *sukta* to Prajanya; "now stop it!" [25] There was a growing conviction that the sacrifice was more than a form of persuasion; it was a form of compulsion. The next step was the belief that the sacrifice itself accomplished the end. The gods became supernumeraries—but not at the time of the formation of the *Rig*, the *Sama*, and the *Yajur*.

The elements of the world were earth, air, fire, and water. Water seems to have had priority, for it was from water that the others were thought to have evolved. Although Vedic man divided the world into earth, atmosphere, and sky, this was not the entire picture. For example, in *Rig Veda* 2. 12. 1 there is a reference to "the two worlds" which trembled in the presence of Indra. Also in 10. 129 reference is made to the "Non-existent" (*Asat*) and the "Existent" (*Sat*). The universe was imaged as two sacrificial bowls positioned facing each other, one above the other. The upper bowl was at least partially hollow; the nether bowl was filled. The earth is the upper surface of the nether bowl. Atmosphere was thought to be between the bowls, and it was believed to extend partly into the upper bowl. The upper bowl, the space between the bowls, and the surface of the lower bowl was called *Sat* (The Real). This was the region inhabited by men and gods. *Sat* is an ordered realm. *Rita*, the course of things, is directed by Varuna in *Sat*. This is the area in which *shrauta* rites are applicable, because this is the area of the right, the orderly, the predictable. In this realm each god and each man has his individual function (*vrata*). Cosmic Order (*Rita*) is also the Truth (*Satya*). Knowledge is possible in the world of *Sat* because *Rita* rules. But below *Sat* is the nether bowl of which earth is the surface. This is *Asat*, the realm of the Unreal, an unorganized, chaotic chasm. It is the region of the Lie, of *Anrita* (Anti-order). It is inhabited by demons (*asuras*), of which the chief is Vritra. Even today Indian villagers believe that demons hide in the cold dark caverns beneath the surface of the earth to emerge at night to do their fiendish works upon the earth. The night according to the Vedic Hindus was a time of dread, a time of anxious waiting for the return of Ushas and the Ashvins, followed by Savitar and the Adityas—and so it remains for millions of Hindus today.

The most advanced theory of cosmogony in the *Rig* is the "Hymn of Creation" (10. 129). In this *sukta* the unknown *rishi* attempts to push beneath the realities of *Sat* and *Asat*, beyond life and death, behind day and night. He theorizes that it is a darkness hidden by darkness, and he calls it the matrix of all that is. His name for it is Tat Ekam (That One). That which disturbed Tat Ekam was desire, a "creative force" and "fertile power." But at this point the *rishi* restrains himself and asks what are his credentials for such speculations. How can anyone know what was before what is and what is not? The gods, he says, came later than *Sat* and *Asat*, so even gods cannot know the answer to questions about ultimate origins. How then can man know? But Tat Ekam, the One who surveys everything from highest heaven, the One who transcends *Sat* and *Asat*—he knows, or perhaps even he does not know! And with that note of cosmological agnosticism, and perhaps of despair, the *rishi* silences his speculations.

> Non-being then existed not nor being:
> There was no air, nor sky that is beyond it.
> What was concealed? Wherein? In whose protection?
> And was there deep unfathomable water?
>
> Death then existed not nor life immortal;
> Of neither night nor day was any token.
> By its inherent force the One breathed windless:
> No other thing than that beyond existed.
>
> Darkness there was at first by darkness hidden;
> Without distinctive marks, this all was water.
> That which, becoming, by the void was covered,
> That One by force of heat came into being.
>
> Desire entered the One in the beginning:
> It was the earliest seed, of thought the product.
> The sages searching in their hearts with wisdom,
> Found out the bond of being in non-being.

Their ray extended light across the darkness:
But was the One above or was it under?
Creative force was there, and fertile power:
Below was energy, above was impulse.

Who knows for certain? Who shall here declare it?
Whence was it born, and whence came this creation?
The gods were born after this world's creation:
Then who can know from whence it has arisen?

None knoweth whence creation has arisen;
And whether he has or has not produced it:
He who surveys it in the highest heaven,
He only knows, or haply he may know not.[26]

The Vedic View of Man

A human being, according to the *Rig*, is a self or soul (*atman*)
inhabiting a human body. The *atman* is the unborn portion (*ajo
bhaga*) of the human being. "*Atman*" is derived from the root
meaning to breathe, but the term is not used in the *Rig* to indicate
the breath of any beings other than the human. It is the intelligible
principle, the essence of man, but it is not an independent substance.
It must inhabit a body, either in earth or in heaven. The *atman* as
breath is always the breath of a body. While it may be possible to
read transmigration into the *Rig*, there is little support for the claim
that there is a doctrine of transmigration of the *atman* in the *Rig*.

The Vedic Hindu found life to be good. He believed he had
discovered the *modus operandi* of the cosmos: the powers which
controlled the natural environment were the *devas*, the rites
controlled the *devas*, and man controlled the rites. So man could
control his environment—except for death. But, reasoned the Vedic,
death is not the end of all, for Yama, the first to die, has found a way
to a home which cannot be taken away, "the place of our departed
forefathers." The Vedic believed that after dying he would pass
terrible mastiffs with four eyes and huge nostrils before coming to the
palace of Yama. Meanwhile he sought a full life, a life of "a hundred
autumns" on earth, and he looked forward to further life in *svarga*

(paradise) where he would experience eternally the joys he had known in his earthly existence, but then in an undecaying world. *Svarga* was the place "where wishes and desires are, where the region of the sun is, where food and delight are found . . . where there is happiness, pleasures, joy and enjoyment, where the wishes of the wisher are obtained." [27] But if one's acts during earthly life did not merit the joys of heaven, then one would suffer both in this life and in the next. The place of punishment beyond this life was referred to as "unbounded caverns." There the wicked were cast down into "inextricable darkness." It was a place of no happiness; a place where the *soma* stones grind the wicked into pieces; a place where thunderbolts rain upon the victims but without slaying them.

Obviously the conceptions of sin and the sinner were poorly developed by the Vedic *rishis*. Sin was an external accretion which could be removed by the application of prayers and rituals. "It is not our own choice," pleads a *rishi* to Varuna, "that is the cause of our sinning, but it is our condition." [28] The meaning is that man is essentially good, but if perchance he does evil, that is an accidental condition which can be remedied. One *rishi* advised that sometimes what appears to be a man or a woman is in reality a *rakshasa* or a *yatudhana*, i.e., an evil spirit whose particular delight is in taking the form of animals, and especially of human beings. A *real* human being could not be a sinner. The Vedic *rishis* did not plumb the depths of man and his condition, but they did lay the foundation of the views which were extended and developed in the *Upanishads*.

CHAPTER 5

Brahminism

Two tendencies were operative in Vedism: the intellectualistic (*jñana*) and the ritualistic (*dravya*). The intellectualistic surfaced late in the composition of the *Rig Veda* and is most obvious in *sukta* 129 of the tenth *mandala*. The speculation of a reality prior to the separation of the cosmos into *Sat* and *Asat* is the apex of the philosophizing in the *Rig*. This tendency reached its Vedic fulfillment in the *Upanishads*. The ritualistic is prevalent throughout the *Rig* and in the central theme of the *Sama* and the *Yajur*. This tendency had two sides: the theological and the magical. The theological is manifest in the hundreds of hymns and prayers addressed to the Vedic deities. The magical also appears in the *Rig*, e.g., 7. 55. 2–3 is a *mantra* designed to put a dog to sleep so robbers can steal: "White offspring of Sarama [Indra's bitch], with tawney limbs, although barking thou displayest thy teeth against me, bristling like lances in thy gums, nevertheless, go quietly to sleep. Offspring of Sarama . . . why dost thou intimidate us? Go quietly to sleep." But the magical is not the central theme of the *Rig*. It sneaks in, as it were, around the edges and corners of an otherwise dignified *Samhita*. It is the contribution of primitive peoples. India from Vedic times to the present has been a country in which pockets of aboriginals hold out and sometimes make their appearance when and where least expected. To this day urban intellectuals are embarrassed by primitive superstitions and practices of village Hindus—e.g., Manasa, the queen of snakes, is still widely worshiped by rural Bengalis not far from the modern city of Calcutta.

The tradition of the *Atharva* as a Veda is too well established to be reversed now, but even the tolerant and urbane S. Radhakrishnan speaks of the "weird religion that the *Atharva-Veda* represents." [1] The *Atharva* speaks of incantations, spells, charms, and chants. Its world is filled with evil spirits, witches, goblins, and imps. The priest becomes a medicine man. When the Vedic gods appear—often with altered names—they are approached as magical powers rather than as the powers of natural phenomena. The world view of the *Atharva* is animistic. It represents beliefs and practices which antedate the composition of the *suktas* of the *Trayi Vidya*, although its composition as a Veda is much later than that of the other three. The admission of the *Atharva* to Vedic status was not without a struggle, and considerable time must have elapsed before it was given *shruti* standing. Two outstanding intellectuals of the fourth century B.C., Panini, the greatest grammarian of India, and Jaimini, the author of the *Mimamsa Sutras*, observed that the Vedas were three. The *Atharva* with its sorcery and its primitive view of the world was not well received by the established priests. This attitude still prevails among the influential *Brahmins* of South India. Defenders of the *Atharva*, on the one hand, sometimes have retaliated by placing the *Atharva* at the head of the four Vedas. The problem involved in the inclusion or exclusion of the *Atharva* is more significant than that of the classification of ancient literature. The issue is whether Tantrism is to be regarded as integral to Hinduism, e.g., "If one may risk an opinion, it may be said that the *Atharva Veda* represents a current of Indian culture that runs parallel to the current represented by the other Vedas; and that it is the earlier stage of a current that culminated in the Agama and Tantra literature." [2] Many Hindus would be pleased to have Tantrism regarded as an appurtenance.

The previous chapter dealt with theological ritualism; this chapter considers magical ritualism; and the next will examine the intellectual tendency as it appears in the *Upanishads*. The literary sources for the study of this chapter are two: the *Atharva Veda Samhita*, the repository of the magical animism of the masses of people, and the *Brahmanas*, the handbook for priests. Although one is a lay book and the other a collection of books for professional priests, they reflect a common world of opinion. It was a post-*Rig* Vedic age, but not yet an Upanishadic age. For identification purposes we shall name the

religion of this stage in the development of Hinduism "Brahminism."
The root from which so many related terms have been derived in
Hinduism is *brahma* or *brahman,* which means the productive power
in a magical spell. It also means the power in a prayer to accomplish
its intent. From this root the following words have been developed:
brahmin (the professional priest), *Brahmin* (the class of priests and
scholars), *Brahma* or *Brahman* (the Absolute Reality), *Brahmā* (the
creator god), and *Brahmanas* (the expository liturgical books of the
priests). Brahminism, then, is the religion of magical ritualism found
in India located chronologically between the theological ritualism of
Vedism and the intellectual speculations of the Upanishadic seers.

The Atharva Veda

The *Rig* and the *Atharva* are the two most important Vedic
Samhitas. The former is the product of the religion of the upper
classes, of the wealthy and established householders. Its ceremonies
came to require elaborate and expensive materials and the services of
priests who placed a high material value on their services. It was a
cult of decency, constraint, and poise. The latter is the product of the
religion of superstitious peasants and modest householders. Whereas
the *Rig* reveals an enjoyment of nature, the *Atharva* expresses a
dread of spirits. The *Atharva* was addressed to the needs of common
people rather than to the state needs of kings. But even a king sometimes desired to ease a toothache, to drive evil spirits from the royal
chambers, to overcome the resistance of a mistress, and to get rid of a
personal enemy. Even a king sometimes used a charm against a cough.

> Just as the soul with soul-desires
> Swift to a distance flies away,
> So even thou, O cough, fly forth
> Along the soul's quick-darting course.
>
> Just as the arrow, sharpened well,
> Swift to a distance flies away,
> So even thou, O cough, fly forth
> Along the broad expanse of earth.[3]

From earliest times there has existed in addition to the intellectual-istic aspect and the ritualistic aspect of Hinduism certain primitive tribal practices which were not incorporated into either the way of rationality or the way of established ceremonies. These are preserved in the *Atharva Veda*, the Mimamsa philosophical system, and Tantrism. The *Atharva* is the magical formulary of ancient India. It contains the gloomier side of the life of man. In the *Atharva* the demons of *Asat* have as it were come out of the caverns to plague man openly and arrogantly. But demons were banished by impreca-tions:

> Bend round and pass us by, O curse,
> Even as a burning fire a lake.
> Here strike him down that curses us,
> As heaven's lightning smites the tree.[4]

Human foes were met with a curse:

> As, rising in the east, the sun
> The stars' bright lustre takes away,
> So both of women and of men,
> My foes, the strength I take away.[5]

The priests even had curses to bring upon those who were miserly in their support:

> Water with which they bathe the dead,
> And that with which they wet his beard,
> The gods assigned thee as thy share,
> Oppressors of the Brahman priests.[6]

Some of the charms were intended to assist Kama, the god of love with his bow and arrow, in weakening feminine resistance:

> 'Tis winged with longing, barbed with love,
> Its shaft is formed of fixed desire:
> With this his arrow levelled well
> Shall Kama pierce thee to the heart.[7]

Another was to help a gambler:

> O dice, give play that profit brings,
> Like cows that yield abundant milk:
> Attach to me a streak of gain,
> As with string the bow is bound.[8]

The culture which produced the charms, chants, and incantations of the *Atharva* has not been identified. Some of the spells for curing ailments of the body are similar to certain German, Lettic, and Russian magical remedies. This supports the claim that the charms were brought into India by the Aryans from their original home. Other scholars, calling attention to a wizard named Atharvan of Persian ancestry,[9] argue that they show a Mesopotamian influence. Some relate the charms to the work of the ancient Magi of Western Asia. Tilak argued for a Chaldean origin. Others, including Radhakrishnan, say they are Indian, but pre-Aryan and non-Aryan, probably Dravidian, and use the preservation of the *Atharva* as an occasion to praise the invaders for assimilating rather than destroying the barbarians or being overwhelmed by them: "The effect of the Vedic Aryan to educate the uncivilized resulted in the corruption of the ideal which he tried to spread." [10] The charms seem far too primitive to be associated with the Harappan culture. Or do we underestimate the ability of people to hold to the pre-rational and the nonrational? The London editors of *The Times* report that one day a few years ago when the astrology column was inadvertently omitted over fifty thousand telephone calls were received from anxious people who wanted to know what the stars advised for that day.

The *Atharva Veda* is a *Samhita* of 730 *suktas*. About one-sixth of it is prose, and about one-fifth is borrowed from the *Rig*, although the borrowed elements have usually been worked over for sorcerous purposes. The oldest name for the book is *Atharvangirasah*. Atharva and Angirasa appear to have been two priestly families. Since the Atharva family specialized in medical charms and the Angirasa in witchcraft, the book was the volume of "Blessings and Curses." The two families may have suffered ostracism from the *shrauta* ceremonies, for the *Atharva* originally contained few items directly related to Vedic sacrifices. Macdonell has written, "The relation of the *Atharva* to the *shrauta* rites was, however, originally so slight, that it became necessary, in order to establish a direct connection with it, to add the twentieth book, which was compiled from the *Rigveda* for the purposes of the sacrificial ceremonial." [11] This indicates why the *Atharva* was for so long not accepted as a *Veda*.

The *devas* are different in the *Atharva*. Whereas in the *Rig* most of the gods were male, the gods of the *Atharva* are predominantly female. The gods are said to be thirty-three, and many appear with their familiar names, but there are also many with unfamiliar names: Kala (Time), Kama (Desire), Pashupata (Lord of Cattle), Rohita (The Sun), Matarishvan (Wind), Viraj (Cosmic Waters), Uchchhishta (The Remains of the Sacrifice), Endor (Son of Death), Parameshthin (He that is in the Highest), Vidhatri (The Arranger), and Chitraratha (King of Gandharvas, i.e., invading spirits).

Far more important than the introduction of new gods was the beginning of a movement to monism. The sun, water, earth, wind, time, and desire are all said to have been the one thing out of which everything has come. Also there is introduced for the first time a unifying principle, "the principle of identification." The simplest form of this belief is the view that things alike in some respects are alike in other respects. This magical law of similarity is still evident in Durga *puja* in Bengal when an idol is ceremonially bathed by pouring water over its reflection in a mirror, or when a villager attempts to cure a disease by transferring the illness to a clay dummy which is then destroyed. The most significant use of the principle of identification is the doctrine of the Vedanta that the essential nature of man is identical with the Absolute. Monism is anticipated in the *Atharva* in an abstract entity called *Skambha* (Support). *Skambha* is the cohesion which binds the Adityas, the Rudras, and the Vasus. *Skambha* makes firm the earth, the atmosphere, and the sky. From *Skambha* the gods have come.

> In what member of him is Fervour located? In what member of him is Right deposited? In what part of him is Vow, is Faith located? In what

member of him is Truth established? In what member of him does
Agni blaze? From what member of him does Wind blow? From what
member does the moon measure out, in measuring the body of the
mighty *Skambha*? In what member of him is Earth located? From what
member is Atmosphere located? In what member does the Sky remain
set? In what member is located what is above the Sky?

. . . . .

In which the Adityas and the Rudras and the Vasus are fixed together,
in which what has been and what is to be, and all the worlds, are
established; declare that *Skambha*: which one of all, pray, is he?

. . . . .

Skambha made firm both heaven and earth here; *Skambha* made firm
the wide atmosphere; *Skambha* made firm the six wide directions;
Skambha has entered into this entire world.[12]

"Which one of all, pray, is he?" is a remarkable question. The
meaning is that *Skambha* is not a god among gods, not a being among
beings. Rather *Skambha* is the support of being, the ground of
existence. Hence, *Skambha* cannot be numbered among the identifi-
able gods, or as earth, atmosphere, or heaven, or among any class of
things. *Skambha* is that which "presides over what has been and is to
be, and over everything." Again in *Atharva* 2. 1. 1 Vena (about
whose identity there is dispute) saw "that highest that was in secret,
in which this All comes of one form." And in another passage *Atman*
appears for the first time in Hindu literature as the universal Self:
"Desireless, wise, immortal, self-existent, satiated with enjoyment,
not deficient in any respect—he fears not death, who knows this
Atman, which is wise, ageless, eternally young."[13] *Atman* also is
found in 10. 2. 31–33: "The impregnable citadel of the gods has eight
circles, nine doors. In it is a golden treasure-chest, heavenly,
enveloped in light. In this golden treasure-chest, which has three
spokes and is triply based—the prodigy in it which consists of Self
(*Atman*), that verily Brahman-knowers know. Brahman has entered
into this shining, yellow, golden, impregnable citadel, which is all
enveloped in glory."[14]

Among other "firsts" the cow is for the first time declared sacred.
The warning is given that he who kicks a cow will not cast a shadow
any more.[15] The same warning is given in this verse to anyone who

urinates facing the sun. Hell is for the first time given a name—Naraka.[16]

But not all is superstitious and pessimistic in the *Atharva*. What could be lovelier than this hymn of praise to Mother Earth?

> Let your hills, your snowy mountains, your jungleland be pleasant, O earth. The brown, dark, red, many-coloured, firm, broad earth, guarded by Indra, upon this earth I have settled, unconquered, unsmitten, unwounded. Your middle, earth, and your navel, and the nourishments that have sprung up from your body, in them set us; purify yourself for us; earth is my mother, I am earth's son.[17]

Much of the *Atharva* deals with the problems of human illness. In addition to the sections of the *Atharva* which are concerned with such problems, there are auxiliary *Vedas*, the *Upavedas*. The *Upavedas* attached to the *Samhitas* are on topics such as music, architecture, erotics, medicine, and alchemy. The principal *Upaveda* of the *Atharva* is the *Ayurveda*. The word *"Ayurveda,"* which is usually translated "medicine," means life-knowledge, and is concerned with techniques for insuring long life, health, and the curing of diseases. The origins of Indian medicine are both empirical and magical. Some of the medicinal plants were first discovered by watching animals and birds heal themselves by eating certain fruits, seeds, leaves, and roots; others came to be regarded as curative because of magical associations—e.g., the unnatural flush of the fever victim was believed transferable to the natural redness of an animal or bird. Many of the cures operated on the notion of the polarity of hot and cold, wet and dry. Water, earth, minerals, plants, insects, animals, dung, urine, hair, milk, *ghee,* curds, honey, salt, rice, and many other materials were included among the remedies. Word and symbol magic were also part of the therapy. The gods of healing were the Ashvins, Prajapati, Indra, Brihaspati, Vata, and, above all, Surya.

The original *Ayurvedic* classification of diseases was into the supernatural, the physical, and the spiritual. But this gave way to a more elaborate eightfold classification of diseases and cures: (1) major surgery, (2) minor surgery, (3) inner medicine, i.e., constitutional diseases, (4) demonology, i.e., evil influences caused by ghosts, planets, etc., (5) pediatrics, (6) bites and stings of poisonous snakes and insects, (7) tonics and elixirs to preserve and restore youth and vigor, and (8) aphrodisiacs.

Ayurvedic healing was a householder rite which required only one fire and one priest, rather than the three of each for a *shrauta* rite. The priest was of a new order: the domestic priest (*purchita*). The *purchita* is peculiar to the *Atharva*. He, as family priest, stayed close to the thoughts, desires, and needs of the common people. His forte was in the areas of magical charms, the determining of propitious times, and *Ayurveda*. The ingredients of healing were usually simple and easily procured. The cure for a form of jaundice will sufficiently convey the nature of the ancient Hindu art of healing. After the priest had recited selected *mantras* from the *Atharva,* he gave the patient water which had been poured over the back of a red bull. When this had been drunk, an amulet steeped in cow's milk anointed with *ghee* was tied on the patient while sitting on the skin of a bull. Then the patient took milk and porridge made of the plant *haridra*. Some of the porridge was left to anoint the patient. Three yellow birds were then tied to the foot of the bed by their left legs. The patient was bathed, and the bath water was poured over the birds. After another drink of the water, the patient addressed the birds asking them to take his yellowness upon themselves. Finally, an amulet of hairs from the belly of the red bull was covered with gold and tied on the patient. If this treatment did not cure, there was still "extreme unction" in which the priest commanded the dying individual,

> Rise up from hence, O man, and straightway casting
> Death's fetters from thy feet, depart not downward;
> From life upon this earth be not yet sundered,
> Nor from the sight of Agni and the sunlight.[18]

The *Ayurvedic* priest was able—and probably willing for a fee!—both to cure and to cause disease; i.e., his repertoire included both the white magic of healing (*bheshajani*) and the black magic of producing ill luck and bringing curses (*abhichara*). We are not surprised, therefore, to discover that physicians were for centuries not well received in Hindu society. Curses, however, were the specialty of another group, the astrologers. The word *"jyotisha"* meant both astronomy and astrology—which illustrates again the Indian habit of mixing the empirical and the intuitive, the scientific and the magical. A few astronomical-astrological *Upavedas* were affixed to the *Atharva*, but they are so deficient in observational data that they do not merit serious consideration. The astrologers themselves were even less well received than were the physicians, as is evidenced by their exclusion from all funeral rites. Astronomy did not attain full respectability in India until the third century A.D., when Greek astronomy entered India and was accepted so completely that even the Greek terms for the zodiac were adopted. Today in India the astrologer, though feared, has a secure role in society. He is necessary in the preparation of horoscopes of prospective brides and grooms and in the determination of the auspicious days for weddings, business openings, celebrations, and ceremonies of every conceivable sort. In 1966 after the death of Lal Bahadur Shastri two astrologers were flown from Calcutta to New Delhi to aid in the selection of a new Prime Minister. But to assert that therefore astrology is an integral part of Hinduism may be no more accurate than to identify superstitions of the Western world as integral to Judaism and Christianity.

The Brahmanas

After the completion of the Vedic *Samhitas* a new form of literature appeared—the *Brahmanas*. These were priestly handbooks dealing with the proper methods for conducting the sacrifices and the possible explanations of their meaning. They were written by priests for priests. These books are characterized by uncritical assertions, imaginative symbolisms, and contrived interpretations. One translator of the most important of the *Brahmanas* offered as his evaluation of the works: "For wearisome prolexity of exposition, characterized by dogmatic assertion and flimsy symbolism rather than by serious reasoning, these works are perhaps not equalled anywhere." [19] B. K.

Ghosh described the *Brahmanas* as "an arid desert of puerile speculations on religious ceremonies marking the lowest ebb of Vedic culture." [20] Maurice Bloomfield called them "monuments of tediousness and intrinsic stupidity." [21]

The *Brahmanas,* like the *Atharva,* represent an aboriginal more than a Vedic priesthood. Although they are the products of cultural atavism, they are not to be discounted, for they contain valuable insights into the Vedic sacrificial system. They present the first myths in Indian literature of the Deluge and of the original human couple. The myths are, in the words of Bloomfield, as "crisp and clear-cut as a cameo." The "Noah" is Manu Vaivasvata, the son of the sun-god Vivasvat. Manu captured a small fish which promised to save him from the coming flood if he would rear it. When the flood came, the fish guided Manu to the Northern Mountain. After the flood Manu became the progenitor of mankind through his own daughter. The myth of the first couple is translated by Bloomfield as follows: "Yama and Yami are the first man and woman. Yama died. The gods sought to console Yami for the death of Yama. When they asked her she said, 'Today he hath died.' They said, 'In this way she will never forget him. Let us create night!' Day only at that time existed, not night. The gods created night. Then morrow came into being. Then she forgot him. Hence, they say, 'Days and nights make men forget sorrow.' " [22]

The word *"brahmana"* means holy practice as contrasted to *mantra* (holy utterance). The concern for orthopraxy in the *Brahmanas* has induced scholars to refer to these works as the "Hindu Talmud." The times of the composition of the *Brahmanas* were remarkably sterile. Seers no longer experienced revelations. Kings were devouring the people. The priests were charging exorbitant fees. The Vedic rites became more elaborate and more costly. It was a time of class conflict. The lower classes were no longer called the *asuras* (devils). Women began to lose their place of equality with men. Prohibitions against husband and wife dining together appeared: "Whence let him not eat in the presence of his wife; for from him who does not a vigorous son is born; and she in whose presence he does not eat bears a vigorous son." [23] In the *Aitareya Brahmana* the importance of a son is celebrated:

In him a father pays a debt
And reaches immortality,
When he beholds the countenance
Of a son born to him alive.

Food is man's life and clothes afford protection,
Gold gives him beauty, marriages bring cattle;
His wife's a friend, his daughter causes pity;
A son is like a light in highest heaven.[24]

The gods were still thirty-three in number, but they were not the thirty-three of the *Rig,* and they were classified as Vasus, Rudras, and Adityas rather than the gods of earth, atmosphere, and sky. In *Shatapatha Brahmana* 4. 5. 7. 2 the gods are listed as follows: Dyu (Sky), Prithivi (Earth), the eight Vasus (Dhava, Dhruva, Soma, Apa, Anila, Anala, Pratyusha, and Prabhasa), the twelve Adityas (Dhatri, Mitra, Aryaman, Rudra, Varuna, Surya, Bhaga, Vivasvat, Pushan, Savitri, Tvashtri, and Vishnu), and the eleven Rudras. The names of the Rudras are not given in the *Brahmanas,* but in the *Mahabharata* they appear as Mrigavyadha, Sarpa, Nirriti, Ajaikapada, Ahirbudhnya, Pinakin, Dahana, Tryambaka, Kapalin, Sthanu, and Bhaga. This did not exhaust the number nor the classification of the gods; a new kind of god had appeared, a god less controllable than the gods of the *Rig.* The new gods were *deva-manus* (human gods): "Verily, there are two kinds of gods: for, indeed the gods are the gods, and the *brahmins* who have studied and teach sacred lore are the human gods." [25] The Vedic deities were usually associated with the natural world rather than with men, and now they paid a price for their inhumanity. Men—at least priests—were no longer cringing weaklings pleading for forgiveness from Varuna, for mercy from Indra, for rain, for sunlight, for sons, etc. The controls were now in the hands of man. Priests exercised the charismatic power they had formerly assigned to the gods. The "human gods" who controlled the sacrifices were the real agents of control. The sun did not rise because of Ushas; the sun rose because the sacrifice made it rise, and the priest controlled the sacrifice. The Vedic gods were said to offer sacrifices in order to sustain their own existence. The priests were feared and honored more than the gods because the priests could destroy enemies merely by changing the ritual.

The *shrauta* rites of the *Rig* had been simple ceremonies conducted by the father of the family, but the rites in the *Brahmanas* were too complicated for laymen. The emphasis was on the ceremony itself rather than on the *deva* to whom the ceremony was addressed. Whereas in *Rig* Vedic times the holy place was any spot on which grass was piled or a hole lined with grass, now the act of cutting the grass was itself a ritual. After the grass had been cut, a circle was drawn three times with the sickle on the ground around the pile of grass. A formula was then recited three times without error, and a pit was dug. The cut grass was then brushed from the bottom of the pit to the top. The sacrificial tools were placed in the pit when not being used. More grass was then cut with a single stroke while the priests recited another sacred formula, and the grass was tied in bundles as thick as the handle of the sacrificial spoon—or as thick as a thigh-bone, according to another formula.[26] These small bundles were then placed in designated positions in the pit accompanied by prescribed *mantras*. Deviation from any part of the ritual not only would invalidate the ceremony but also would require a purification for the offender more elaborate than the ceremony itself.

The *soma* rituals were at this time giving way to fire rituals which required three altars to represent the three regions of Agni: the hearth fire on earth, lightning in the atmosphere, and the sun in the sky. The altars were known as the *Garhapatya* (fire of the home), *Ahavaniya* (fire of offering), and *Dakshina* (southern fire). The *Garhapatya* was used chiefly to prepare the food for the sacrifice, the *Ahavaniya* was the main altar of offering located east of the preparation altar, and the *Dakshina* was the altar used for appeasing avenging spirits. According to *Shatapatha Brahmana* 2. 1. 1, the fire altars were made of five ingredients: a piece of gold, salty soil, earth dug by a wild rat, gravel, and water. Brick altars were made of bricks of five different shapes. The number of bricks ranged from one thousand to ten thousand eight hundred. Each brick was laid in position with a special *mantra,* and the whole altar was built in a unique shape, e.g., hawk, eagle, heron, chariot, etc. The ceremonies were held in the open air; no temples were a part of Hinduism at this time.

The exactness of altar formation and ceremony performance required the services of professionals. The fathers of the clan could not be trusted with such sacerdotal demands. At first there were three classes of priests: the *hotri* to tend the sacrificial fire, the *adhvaryu* to handle the sacrificial instruments and to measure the quantities of materials for the sacrifices, and the *udgatri* to sing the chants. But now a fourth priest appeared. This was the *brahmin*, whose responsibility was to act as general supervisor, to see that everything was properly timed. The *Brahmanas* inform us that the *brahmin* sat on the north side of the altar, the *hotri* on the east, the *udgatri* on the west, and the *adhvaryu* on the south. We are also told that the *brahmin* was associated with the *Atharva*, the *hotri* with the *Rig*, the *adhvaryu* with the *Yajur*, and the *udgatri* with the *Sama*.

The *shrauta* ceremonies became more elaborate and detailed; e.g., the *Aitereya Brahmana* describes a *soma* rite known as the *guvama-nana* which lasted for three hundred and sixty days, and another known as the *pañchavimsha* was a complex ritual which enabled a non-*Brahmin* to become a *Brahmin*. The coronation of a king (*rajasuya*) was, as might be expected, an elaborate ceremony, but the most elaborate was the horse sacrifice (*ashvamedha*). At the opening of the *ashvamedha* a young white horse was bathed, fed wheat cakes for three days, consecrated with fire, and then released. For one year it was allowed to wander in complete freedom. An escort of princes and an army followed the horse. The territory into which it wandered was claimed as the king's, and it was to be taken by force, if necessary. At the end of the year the horse was returned as the central object in the concluding ceremonies. The king at new moon shaved his head and beard, sat on the lap of the first queen, while the priests chanted *mantras*. After an all-night vigil by the sacred fire, the queens anointed the horse at dawn, decorating it with pearls. Then began an amazing sacrifice of six hundred and nine selected animals, ranging "from the elephant to the bee," including a human being. The horse was then slaughtered, and the first queen lay beside the dead horse. A blanket was thrown over the queen and the horse, and the queen enacted sexual union with the horse accompanied by obscene encouragements from the other queens and the priests. The ceremony ended with the eating of the horse. The *ashvamedha* was reputed to accomplish almost anything the king desired, and one hundred *ashvamedhas* would make a king supreme in the universe. Although no king lived long enough to conduct one hundred *ashvamedhas*, there are records of kings who sacrificed one hundred horses in a single *ashvamedha*.

The incredible number of animals slaughtered in these ancient fire and blood sacrifices (*yajñas*) gives the appearance of a potlatch. The greater the number of animals slain, the more certain would be the attainment of the desired results. Sacrifices dominated the life of the people. The larders of the priests must never have been empty, as part of their fee was the carcass of the animal. Vegetarian Hindus today often are silent about the ancient meat-eating priests of their religion, and all Hindus dislike admitting that human sacrifices were part of the *yajñas*. By the time of the *Shatapatha Brahmana* the sacrifice of a human was a rare event, a rite reserved for making impregnable a fortress or city gate, or making secure a bridge or dam.

What caused the ceremonies to become so complicated at this time? What was the rationale for the sacrifices? The first expression of ritual is found in *Rig Veda* 10. 90, the *Purusha Sukta*, in which "the gods of old" sacrificed *Purusha*, the prototypical man, to form the world. *Purusha* was "all that yet hath been and all that is to be." From him was born the World-Egg, "the creatures of the air, and animals both wild and tame," the *Vedas*, the four classes of man, the moon, the sun, sky, earth, atmosphere, and the gods of the three regions. "Gods, sacrificing, sacrificed the victim: these were the earliest holy ordinances." [27] Since the entire cosmic order came into being as the result of a great sacrifice, the conviction grew that sacrifice was the way of renewal, of power, and of strengthening. Furthermore, if the primordial man was the sacrificial victim from which all came to be, then man himself is the source of all, and the human body is "the impregnable citadel of the gods." [28] A sacrifice, properly performed, exerted the creativity and the power of the primordial sacrifice; and a sacrifice, improperly performed, would bring unspeakable harm to the sponsor and to the priests. The power of the sacrifice was believed to be turned against the one who performed improperly, even though the impropriety was only a misused or mispronounced word. When an error was made, it was

Vishnu who was invoked, for he was the Vedic god associated with grace, love, tenderness, and forgiveness. As the god of the three steps, he could take man's petitions, and finally man himself, to the highest heaven "where even birds dare not fly," [29] The safe refuge from the sorrows of life and death.

The operative cause in the sacrifice was *tapas,* a term which originally meant the heating of gold in order to test it. *Tapas* came to mean heat, pain, torment, and burning. *Tapas* meant the conserving of power in order that it might be expended in desired channels. No doubt one of the reasons why the fire ceremonies displaced the *soma* ceremonies was the association of the heat of the fire with the power of the fire to destroy. *Tapas* also came at this time to be identified with the heat of sexual desire. Asceticism, austerity, withdrawal, mortification, and torment were means for the conservation of the energies of a person in order that they might be expended elsewhere. There was much self-restraint and self-abuse, including the exposing of the body to extreme heat and cold, eating of strange and forbidden foods, assuming painful postures, and inflicting harm upon the body.

A second feature of the expanded sacerdotalism was the emphasis on the power of the ancestral queen of sound, Vac. Whereas in the *Rig* Vac was separated from the power of the ritual, seen for example in the offering of *soma* to gods of ritual power like Indra and of honey (*madhu*) to gods of wisdom like the Ashvins, in the *Atharva* and in the *Brahmanas* the power of the word and the power of ritual were integrated. *Atharva Veda* 8. 10, for example, contains a warning at the ending of almost every line that the ignorant performance of the ceremony is not enough—one must know the esoteric meaning. The ending is "who knows this," and the meaning is that the ritual will accomplish its end only if the performer knows the ritual. Vac denoted both the sounds and the meaning of the sounds, and this difference resulted in different modes of performing the ceremonies. For some *japa* (muttering) was enough, i.e., the repetition of the sacred formula. For example, in *Atharva* 13. 3 the refrain "Against that god in his anger is this an offence; whoever injures a *brahmin* that has such knowledge, do you, Rohita, make him tremble, destroy him; fasten bonds on the oppressor of *brahmins,*" is repeated twenty-five times. But for others *japa* and word magic were not enough. For them, not the word, but the knowledge conveyed by the word, was power. Even this view often contained magical undertones. Part of the difficulty in avoiding the magical grew out of the assumption about the Sanskrit language. These Sanskrit-speaking people believed that Sanskrit was a nonsymbolic language in which the relation between word and referent was one of such identity that the proper speaking of the Sanskrit word not only produced what the word stood for but also that the word was itself the reality. Thus a properly conducted *yajña* with properly chosen and properly pronounced Sanskrit *mantras* made changes in reality because it was itself the reality! But this emphasis on the importance of the semantic and epistemic aspects of the ritual was the death knell of the sacrificial system. It prepared the way for the Upanishadic rejection of the sacrifices just as the emphasis on the sacrifices had displaced the *devas*. The ceremonies were later reinstated in Hinduism in the *Dharma Shastras* but with many modifications.

The *Atharva* and the *Brahmanas* remain as memorials to the dangers of sacerdotalism; but to pass them by as "the *reductio ad absurdum* of the nature-worship of the hymns" [30] might cause the student to miss seeing that Vedic religion was "first and foremost a liturgy, and only secondarily a mythological or speculative system." [31]

6

The Religion
of the Upanishads

Hinduism is an unstable mixture of the primitive and the sophisticated. When we turn from the sacerdotal ritualism of the *Atharva Veda* and the *Brahmanas* to the *Upanishads* we are acutely aware of two strands: one rooted in primitive survivals, the other in lofty speculations superimposed upon the oboriginal elements. Conflicts between the supporters of the magical and the supporters of the rational are found in Hindu literature centuries before the composition of the *Upanishads*. For example, in one of the hymns of the *Rig Veda* the author ridicules the *brahmins,* their schools, and their sacrifices. He compares the endless repetition of *mantras* to frogs croaking to each other and the *brahmins* hovering over bowls of *soma* to frogs around a small pool. He speculates that the largess of frogs is superior to the riches dispensed by priests.

> Resting in silence for a year,
> Like Brahmins practising a vow,
> The frogs have lifted up their voices,
> Excited by Parjanya's call.

> When one repeats the utterance of the other,
> As those who learn the lessons of their teacher,
> All this is like concordant recitation,
> As eloquent ye prate upon the waters.

> One lows like cows, one like a goat is bleating;
> This one is Spotty, one of them is Tawny.

Bearing a common name they're many-coloured,
They variously adorn their voice in speaking.

As Brahmins at the mighty Soma offering
Sit round the large and brimming vessel talking;
So throng ye all around the pool to hallow
This annual day, that, frogs, begins the rain-time.

These *Soma*-pressing Brahmins raise their voices
And offer their recurrent year's devotion;
And these Adhvaryu priests with kettles sweating
Come forth to view, and none of them is hidden.

The twelve months' god-sent order they have guarded,
And never do these men infringe the season.
When in the year the rainy time commences,
Those who were heated milk-pots gain deliverance.

Both Lowing Cow and Bleating Goat have given,
Spotty and Tawny, too, have given riches.
The frogs give kine by hundreds; they for pressings
Of *Soma* thousandfold, prolong existence.[1]

The *Upanishads* pick up the theme of ridicule of the Vedic rituals. In the *Mundaka* the sacrificial forms are characterized as "unsafe boats" which are not likely to convey one to the desired destination, and those who trust in rituals are fools deluded by blind leaders.[2] In the *Chandogya* priests circumvoluting the altar are compared to dogs going around carrion chanting, "Om! Let us eat. Om! Let us drink. Om! May the god Varuna, Prajapati, and Savitri bring food here! O Lord of food, bring food here!—yea, bring it here! Om!" [3] Although it would be a mistake to assume that the *Upanishads* were written by atheists, agnostics, and iconoclasts, we are not wrong in assuming that for the Upanishadic *rishis* the original Vedic intuitions of man's experiences with nature had lost their pristine charm and the sacrificial ceremonies had become stale repetitions of meaningless acts and words. It was a time of examining established ways and of attempting new approaches to the meaning of human existence.

The Upanishads

The collection of ancient books known as the *Aranyakas* and the *Upanishads* constitute the knowledge section of Vedic literature. The *Aranyakas* retain some respect for the ancient ceremonies and provide interpretations of the sacrifices, often of an allegorical nature for those unable or unwilling to perform the rites. They teach that meditation upon the symbolic aspects of the sacrifice is as efficacious as the actual performance. For example, meditation on the dawn as "the head of the horse" and on the sun "as the eye of the horse" was deemed a fitting substitute for the performance of the horse sacrifice. The hold of ritualism was weakening and the way was being prepared for an outburst of abstract speculation, just as the conception of *vac* (word) as a metaphysical entity was preparing the way for the attainment of life goals through the power of knowledge to effect changes upon that which knowledge symbolized.

The term *"Upanishads"* denotes the more than two hundred books of speculation composed between 800 and 300 B.C. Many are pre-Buddhistic, but some reveal familiarity with the Buddhist challenge. The traditional number of the books is one hundred and eight, although only a dozen are of lasting significance. They, like the *Aranyakas*, are known as the forest treatises by reason of their composition by people who had retired to the forests to contemplate the human condition and to formulate therapies for human suffering. The word *"upanishad"* is composed of *upa* (near), *ni* (down), and *shad* (to sit). An *Upanishad* is a secret teaching given by the teacher (*rishi*) to the pupil (*shishya*) when the pupil sits so near that the teaching will not be overheard. This secret teaching seems to have been conveyed, not as part of esoteric initiation rites, but as information either meaningless or dangerous for the person who was not ready to cope with it. Hindu tradition contains many illustrations of the danger of giving information before the pupil was ready. Secret instruction probably had been used earlier as a way to keep the religious rites within priestly families, but the instruction in the *Upanishads* is metaphysical rather than vocational. The *Upanishads* as collections of speculations which span a five-hundred-year period are diverse with ideas of varying degrees of development. There is no effort to be systematic or doctrinaire. While they are often regarded as the fountainhead of the systems of Indian philosophy, they are in fact poetic illuminations rather than philosophical reflections. Although they are an extension of the questioning of the rituals found in the *Aranyakas*, they contain reservations and doubts of the direction in which they move; e.g., in *Brihad-Aranyaka Upanishad* 1. 4. 10 the *rishi* says the gods are displeased with the teachings of the *Upanishads* because when these are applied they deprive the gods of the sacrifices. Perhaps the authors of the *Upanishads* did not intend to terminate the sacrifices, but such was the result.

The *Upanishads* are the last of the *shruti* literature. Hindu scriptures composed after the *Upanishads* are known as *smriti* (remembered) rather than *shruti* (revealed). Much of the material is in the form of dialogues among gods, between gods and men, and among men. The two most important, the earliest, and the longest of the *Upanishads* are the *Brihad-Aranyaka* and the *Chandogya*. The most important *rishi* in the *Brihad-Aranyaka* is Yajñavalkya. Women were not excluded from philosophical speculation; e.g., a woman named Gargi once had a discussion with Yajñavalkya. The *Upanishads* became so thoroughly established in Indian thought that adherence to them was the test of orthodoxy (*astika*, literally "yes-saying"), yet the opinions expressed in the *Upanishads* cover a wide spectrum. As Radhakrishnan has said, "So numerous are their suggestions of truth, so various are their guesses at God, that almost anybody may seek in them what he wants and find what he seeks, and every school of dogmatics may congratulate itself on finding its own doctrine in the sayings of the *Upanishads*." [4] Dasgupta says they are "a melting pot in which all later philosophical ideas were still in a state of fusion." [5]

There is no doubt that the *Upanishads* were of paramount importance in the development of philosophy within India, but their impact on religion is difficult to assess. From the point of view of Vedism, they are to be evaluated as detrimental because they questioned the reality of gods and the efficacy of sacrificial rites. They introduced a new dimension into the religious quest of India, a quest for a knowledge which would make the entire universe understood. This was a quest for a special kind of knowledge. According to *Mundaka Upanishad* 1. 1. 4 there are two forms of knowledge: *apara vidya* (lower knowledge) and *para vidya* (higher knowledge). The lower knowledge is the knowledge of gods and rituals as well as the knowledge of the phenomenal, perishable world gained through sense impressions and reasonings upon these data. Such knowledge is worse than ignorance, for its objects lead away from the objects of true knowledge:

> Into blind darkness enter they
> That worship ignorance;
> Into darkness greater than that, as it were, they
> That delight in knowledge.[6]

Yajñavalkya advised, "Let a *Brahmin* become disgusted with learning and desire to live as a child. When he has become disgusted both with the state of childhood and with learning, then he becomes an ascetic. When he has become disgusted both with the non-ascetic state and with the ascetic state, then he [truly] becomes a *Brahmin*." [7] In order to avoid any misunderstanding about lower knowledge, one *rishi* named the sources of this kind of knowledge: the *Rig*, the *Yajur*, the *Sama*, and the *Atharva*;[8] and, in order to clarify still more, he mentioned six secondary subject matters, the so-called "Limbs of the Vedas": Phonetics, Ritual, Grammar, Etymology, Metrics, and Astrology. Knowledge from such sources and about such topics lead into great darkness. The meaning, we assume, is that the lower knowledge cannot be relied upon to lead one from the unreal to the real, from darkness to light, from death to immortality, and not that such knowledge is worthless in all contexts. The higher knowledge regards theology, ceremony, and all forms of empirical and rational knowledge as but symbols of the Imperishable (*Akshara*). The thrust of the *Upanishads* is to pass from knowables vis-à-vis *apara vidya* to the Absolute which, while it is unknowable by the lower form of knowing, can be adumbrated in *para vidya*. When the teachings of the *Upanishads* are systematized, the result is called the Vedanta, i.e., the end of the Vedas. The Vedanta is end both in time, because the *Upanishads* are chronologically the last of the Vedic scriptures, and also in value, because the Vedanta is the goal of the movement from the earliest *suktas* of the *Rig* to the latest of the *Upanishads*—at least this is the position of the Vedantic philosophers. Objective scholars agree that the *Upanishads,* the commentaries upon the *Upanishads,* and the systems of philosophy developed from the commentaries constitute the apex of the intellectual attainment of the entire Hindu tradition. Although Hindu philosophy is based upon the *Upanishads,* the *Upanishads* themselves are not philosophy since they offer speculations rather than arguments for positions. They, as the products of thought, can appropriately be described as philosophical, but in the form in which we have them they are instructions rather than defenses, records of visions rather than efforts to convince others, professions of believers rather than appeals to nonbelievers. The intellectual progression through the entire body of Vedic literature culminating in the *Upanishads* may be analyzed into three movements: from plurality to unity, from objectivity to subjectivity, and from materiality to spirituality. The result was to change Hinduism from the worship of reified natural forces in order to insure physical goods to a *sadhana* seeking identification with the Absolute manifested in the world of time and space. The centrality of the concept of Brahman in the *Upanishads* justifies naming the religious aspects of Hindu *sadhana* expressed in these words "Brahmanism," but because of the danger of confusing this with "Brahminism," we shall call it "the religion of the *Upanishads.*"

Movement to Unity

The assumption of an underlying unity in the manifoldness of experience and expression gives to the Hindu a feeling of the appropriateness of elements which to Western eyes seem to be discords and contradictions. Again and again Western scholars return to this theme. "India always seeks for the underlying unity within, before, and after all single things and events. This accounts for the fact that all empirical single things are considered as necessarily incomplete and relative." [9] "The Indian mind is constantly seeking hidden correspondences between things which belong to entirely distinct conceptual systems." [10] "Thus throughout the whole course of Indian history, the characteristic Indian endeavour has been to look for the common element in apparently different things, the single reality which underlies the apparently many appearances." [11] "If there is any one intellectual tenet which, explicitly or implicitly, is held by the people of India, furnishing a fundamental presupposition of all their thinking, it is this doctrine of universal immanence, of an intelligent monism." [12] Why this movement has been such a central feature of Indian life, we cannot say. It is not uncommon to find people seeking a single meaning in the flow of events, but no people have sought for oneness with greater determination than have the Hindus. One of the earliest manifestations of this movement to cosmic unity was the effort of the Vedic peoples to consolidate the *devas* into groups. One early grouping was known as the Vasus.[13] They were the personifications of the powers inherent in eight natural phenomena: water, the pole-star, the moon, earth, wind, fire, dawn, and light. They were said to be the "preservers of men" and the "bestowers of rewards." The integration was sometimes extended to include nine or ten *devas*. There were other *devas* treated only in groups, such as the Maruts, the Rudras, and the Ashvins, but the Vasus by the divergence of the natural phenomena they represent show more of the unifying aspect than do the others. References can also be found in the *Rig Veda* to collections of gods identified with the use of *vishva* (universal) as a prefix, e.g., Vishvamitras (all the gods of light) and Vishvadevas (all the gods). In the *Bhagavad Gita* the latter are identified as the Vishvas.

Henotheism was a second way in which integration proceeded. Although it was more ritualistic than philosophical, it was another step in the direction of monism; e.g., in one of the prayers to the fire god the worshiper exclaims, "Thou at thy birth, O Agni, art Varuna; when kindled thou becomest Mitra; in thee, O son of might, all gods are centered; thou art Indra to the worshiper." The henotheistic movement, contrary to what might have been expected, did not end in monotheism.

A third monistic movement was the identifying of a first cause of the universe, or creation itself reified as a god. There are many names in early Vedic literature of this Creator. Sometimes he is Vishvakarman (World Maker). For example, in *Rig Veda* 10. 82 Vishvakarman is described as "the father of the eye," "the wise in spirit," "mighty in mind and power," "maker, disposer, and most lofty presence," "the germ primeval," and "that One wherein abide all things existing." He "created both these worlds submerged in fatness." He "knows all races and all things existing." He is "the deities' name-giver." The other gods "seek him for information." He is indeed worshiped by the other gods. He is "earlier than this earth and heaven, before even the Asuras and gods had being." Knowledge of him seems to be only by the way of negation, for "You will not find him who produced these creatures." According to *Shvetashvatara Upanishad* 4. 17,

> That God, Vishvakarman, the Great Soul,
> Ever seated in the heart of creatures,
> Is framed by the heart, by the thought, by the wind—
> They who know That, become immortal.

In *Rig Veda* 10. 121 the first cause is Hiranyagarbha (Golden Egg): "As Hiranyagarbha he arose in the beginning; when born he was the one Lord of the existent." He is said to have established earth and sky. He is also referred to in *Shvetashvatara* 3. 4 and 4. 12. In *Rig Veda* 10. 72. 2 Brahmanaspati (Lord of Prayer) is said to have produced the world "with blast and smelting, like a smith." This term does not appear in the *Upanishads*, but in the *Laws of Manu* the creator Brahmā after living for a year in the Golden Egg split it and from the two shells formed the heaven and the earth. Prajapati (Lord of Creation) according to *Rig* 10. 121 is the "king of the world" and the "generator of the earth." He "arose in the beginning." Earth and sky are sustained by his aid; he gives breath and strength to everything. "O Prajapati, none other has encompassed all these created things."

Sometimes a *deva* named Aditi (Free or Boundless), signifying the unlimited sky as contrasted to the limited earth, was singled out as the one above all others. Aditi was regarded as the *deva-matri* (mother of gods). In the *Yajur Veda* she is addressed as "supporter of the heavens, sustainer of the earth, sovereign of this world, wife of Vishnu." In the *Mahabharata* and the *Ramayana* she is the mother of Vishnu. In the *Rig* she is the mother of the Adityas, a collection of celestial deities whose number varies from six to seven to twelve.

In some passages the many *devas* are said to be but a priestly pluralization of the basic One, e.g., "The wise seers through their praise make into many forms the bird [the sun] which is only one." [14]

A fourth movement to oneness was in the conception of *Rita*, which meant literally the regular course of things. At first *Rita* meant the correct order of the performance of the sacrifice; then it meant the order of the natural world; and later it was expanded to include the moral order, i.e., cause and effect in the realm of good and evil. *Rita* was sometimes personalized as "the father of all." As cosmic order *Rita* was a principle which even the gods could not transgress: "The dawn follows the path of *Rita*, the right path; as if she knew them before. She never oversteps the regions. The sun follows the path of *Rita*." [15]

The fifth movement to the conception of a one behind the gods was a variety of names used to designate an impersonal reality from which experienced plurality has come. Beings such as Tat (That), Tat Ekam (That One), Eka Deva (The One God), Vac (The Word), Sat (Being), and Ka (Who) are found in Vedic literature. *Rig Veda* 10. 121 is perhaps the most remarkable of all the hymns which contain monistic tendencies. Max Müller called it "The Hymn to the Unknown God." In this hymn Ka is described as "present at the beginning," "the sole lord of created beings," the one who "upheld this earth and heaven," "the giver of soul," "the giver of strength," the one "whose command all beings, even the gods, obey," "whose shadow is immortality," "the sole king of the breathing and seeing world," the one "who rules over this aggregate of two-footed and four-footed beings," the one "by whom the sky was made profound and the earth solid," the one "by whom the heaven and the solar sphere were fixed," "the measure of the water in the firmament," and "the one supreme god among the gods."

In the *Upanishads* the question of the number of the gods is raised with the seriousness appropriate to detachment. Ordinarily one does not raise theological questions while engaged in acts of devotion, but when religious ceremonies have lost their hold, questions about religion seem very fitting. "How many gods are there?" a pupil asked Yajñavalkya.[16] "As many as are mentioned in the introduction to the hymn of the Vishvadevas, namely, three hundred and three, and three thousand and three [i.e., 3306]," replied Yajñavalkya. "Yes, but how many gods are there really?" pressed the pupil. "Thirty-three," replied Yajñavalkya. "Yes, but how many gods are there really?" "Six." "Yes, but how many really?" "Three." "But how many really?" "Two." "How many really?" "One and a half." "And how many really?" "One." The truth of the matter was that Yajñavalkya no more believed in one god than he believed in 3306 gods. Hindus at this time were falling out of touch with the great gods of the *Samhitas* and the *Brahmanas*. The Vedic *devas* were becoming names without denotation. But the movement from many to one was important, and the One as a unitary principle became the cornerstone of the dominant philosophy of India. However, the philosophical system which developed first, the Samkhya, selected the dualistic passages of the *Upanishads*. This which was the minority opinion of the *rishis* remains to this day the philosophy of the loyal opposition. As we proceed to examine the attempts to identify the nature of the One, we must remember that there are passages in the *Upanishads* which suggest a dualism of *purusha* (passive spirit) and *prakriti* (active matter).

The speculations as to the nature of the One in the *Upanishads* are of three orders: (1) those which make the One personal, (2) those which make the One impersonal but not abstract, and (3) those which make the One impersonal and abstract. A good example of the One as personal is given in *Brihad-Aranyaka* 1. 4. 1: "In the beginning this world was *Atman* alone in the form of a Person. Looking around, he saw nothing else than himself. He said first, 'I am.'" The person, designated as "He," being lonely, divided himself into male and female fragments. The male and female parts of the One then sexually brought into being the entire living creation including man, the gods, and the heavenly bodies. "I, indeed, am this creation, for I emitted it all from myself," proclaimed the primordial person, and the worshipers were encouraged to respond, "He is himself all the gods." [17]

The One as an impersonal but not abstract principle can be noted in *Brihad-Aranyaka* 5. 5. 1: "In the beginning this world was Water. That water produced the real." Also in *Chandogya* 7. 10. 1: "It is just water solidified that is this earth, that is the atmosphere, that is the sky, that is gods and men, beasts and birds, grass and trees, animals together with worms, flies, and ants; all these are just water solidified. So reverence water." [18] The element earth, symbolized often by the Sanskrit word for food, is also presented as the first cause, e.g.,

> From earth, verily, creatures are produced,
> Whatsoever dwell on the earth (the planet).
> Moreover by earth (as food), in truth, they live.
> Moreover into it also they finally pass.[19]

Elsewhere the cause of all is "the universal fire." [20] But the element which is most often defended as the one creative principle is breath (wind or air). For example, Yajñavalkya in a conversation about the number of the gods is finally pushed by his persistent pupil into the disclosure that the one god is breath. In four *Upanishads—Brihad-Aranyaka* 6. 1. 7–13; *Chandogya* 5. 1. 6–15; *Kaushitaki* 3. 3; *Prashna* 2. 1–4—a contest is reported between the various bodily functions— speech, sight, hearing, reasoning, reproducing, and breathing—and breathing is declared superior. In the *Brihad-Aranyaka* version of the contest each of the functions other than breath departs for a year, and upon returning is informed that, while it was missed, the others have been able to function during its absence. But when breath prepares to leave for its year's absence, the others cry, "Sir, do not go off. We shall not be able to live without you." And they thereupon declare breath to be supreme.

The One as impersonal and abstract is expressed in such speculations as: "In the beginning this world was merely non-being." [21] "In the beginning this world was non-being, and from being was produced." [22] " 'To what does this world go back?' 'To space,' he said. 'Verily, all things here arise out of space. They disappear back into space, for space alone is greater than these: space is the final goal.' " [23] In *Chandogya* 6. 3. 2 the *rishi* Uddalaka, observing that some have said, "In the beginning this world was just non-being," asks, "How from non-being could being be produced? On the contrary, in the beginning this world was just being, one only, without a second." The One without a second is that which when known makes all things known, for it is the unitary principle of reality. The word "Brahman" is given to it. "Brahman" originally meant the power of the prayer to accomplish the intent of the worshiper, but by this time the word had been expanded to mean the power inherent in and supportive of the cosmos. Thus metaphysical significance was added to the original devotional connotations. Brahman is the answer to the question of the identity of the "Unknown God" of *Rig Veda* 10. 129. Of all the names for deity in the Vedic literature the most abstract is "Brahman." *Kena Upanishad* 14–28 contains a delightful story in which the Vedic gods Agni, Vayu, and Indra became aware of a presence in their midst which they could identify only as "It." They desired to know who It was and whether It was a threat to their own power. The three approached It and identified themselves. Agni contended he could burn anything on earth, and Vayu contended he could blow anything away. But when It put a straw before them, Agni could not burn the straw and Vayu could not move it. When Indra approached, the unknown presence vanished. Uma (Knowledge) then informed Indra that the mysterious It was Brahman.

Brahman in the *Upanishads* is the Ultimate Principle, the Absolute, Totality, the One beyond which there is nothing, the One which makes all things known. Brahman as the unity of existence includes all objects—men, gods, the physical universe, space, everything. Brahman, therefore, is not a god, not even the God of gods. Brahman is One, but not a numerical one, not one in contrast to two but one as opposed to plurality. Brahman is One without limit. Brahman is not a this one as contrasted to that one, but a Unity such that all pluralities are inherent in the One. Brahman is not an object of worship, for that would require the existence of a non-Brahman as worshiper. By the same token Brahman cannot be an object of knowledge as that would require a non-Brahman to be the knower; and Brahman cannot be the knowing subject as that would require an epistemological object in order for there to be a knowing subject. To try to know Brahman would be like trying to see the eye with the eye, or, to state this in a better metaphor, seeking to know Brahman is like a man seeking to know himself, forgetting that the self he seeks to know is the self that is doing the seeking.

The Brahman concept was far too obtuse for even the forest *rishis*. Therefore, they fell back upon the distinction between the lower knowledge (*apara vidya*) and higher knowledge (*para vidya*) mentioned previously. Just as the pattern of Vedic philosophical training passed from formal study, i.e., knowledge by acquaintance, through reflection or conviction to a direct grasp of the truth, so knowledge itself was thought to proceed from the knowledge of the objective, phenomenal, and perishable world to an experience of immediacy such that the object and the subject cannot be separated. Although the custom seems to have been to refer to two species of knowledge—the lower and the higher—they are far too diverse to be regarded as two forms of knowledge. Knowledge objectifies. Separation between the epistemological subject and the epistemological object is the essence of knowledge. Mystical union and poetic esthesis are not forms of knowing. Water as H_2O is not water as rain on the face. The distinction can be indicated by referring to *apara vidya* and to *para "vidya."*

The *apara-para* distinction is the ground for Shankara's Brahman-as-qualified and Brahman-as-unqualified. The distinction, however, to be noted within the *Upanishads* themselves is a difference in interpretation of the nature of Brahman arising out of the difference between the point of view of metaphysical speculation and the point of view of religious worship. *Brihad-Aranyaka Upanishad* 2. 3 refers to two forms of Brahman: the formed and the formless. The former is described as that which is different from the wind and the atmosphere; the latter is that which is identical with the wind and the atmosphere. In religious categories the former is theistic, and the latter is pantheistic (or better, panentheistic); in philosophical categories the former is transcendent, the latter is in part immanent. The panentheistic Brahman is an all-pervading, inscrutable, integrative principle: "It is conceived of by him by whom It is not conceived of. He by whom It is conceived of, knows It not. It is not understood

by those who say they understand It. It is understood by those who
say they understand It not." [24] It cannot be apprehended by senses,
nor stated by speech. It is beyond all understanding. The only way
to think and to speak of the formless Brahman is the way of
negativity (*neti, neti*), the way of denial of affirmations, of denial of
negations, of denial of both affirmations and negations, and of denial
of neither affirmations nor negations. In other words, Brahman as the
all-encompassing foundation of existence must possess all qualities,
and must, therefore, embrace all contradictions. The name "Brahman" is the word we use to refer to the Absolute Unity of the
cosmos. Brahman is not a being but the ground of being—and also
the ground of nonbeing. In the words of *Rig Veda* 10. 129. 1
Brahman is that which is behind, before, and beyond *Sat* and *Asat*.
No relationships can be established epistemologically, ontologically,
or axiologically with the formless Brahman, for It is what makes
relationships possible. No being has relationships with the principle of
relationships. Yet Brahman is that which makes existence, knowledge, and value possible. The formed Brahman is Brahman as the
Supreme Being. Whereas the formless Brahman is designated as It,
the formed Brahman is He. He is man's "best support" and "supreme
support." [25] He is "all-knowing, all-wise." [26] He is "worthy of being
worshiped day by day." [27] He "grants desires" of men.[28] He is man's
shelter, liberator, and eternal home:

> As the flowing rivers in the ocean
> Disappear, quitting name and form,
> So the knower, being liberated from name and form,
> Goes unto the Heavenly Person, higher than the high.
>
> He verily, who knows that supreme Brahman,
>   becomes very Brahman . . .
> He crosses over sorrow.
> He crosses over sin.
> Liberated from the knots of the heart,
>   he becomes immortal.[29]

The fact that the passages on the formed Brahman are found
largely in the later *Upanishads* may indicate the *rishis* withdrew from

their earlier abstractions regarding the nature of Brahman as the primary ontological principle to Brahman as an object of worship because of their realization that the heart has reasons the mind knows not of, or it may have been an effort to offer a viable alternative to Buddhism.

Movement to Subjectivity

The second movement in Vedic literature is from objectivity to subjectivity, from the reification of natural powers of the external world to the discovery and cultivation of the powers within the human being. Psychology replaced cosmology. The reality sought was the reality within. "What is It?" was replaced by "Who am I?" However, the answer to both questions was the same: "It is I, and I am It." In other words, the quest for the nature of the self turned out to be an extension and a clarification of the quest for the unifying principle of the universe, for the conclusion was that the Self is Brahman. Hindu thought in the *Upanishads* became increasingly anthropocentric. Abstract thought for its own sake is incomprehensible to Hindus. All thought is for use, specifically for the salvation of the self. The *Upanishads* are the watershed of Hindu thought. In them Hindu thought turned in upon itself—and it did not like what it saw. The heyday of the "life of one hundred autumns" was over because a franker view of the human condition revealed anxiety and temporality. Indian thought became, and remains, existential.

The identification of the human self and the cosmos began early in Vedic thought. In a cremation hymn in the *Rig* the petition is offered: "Let the eye repair to the sun; the breath (*atman*) to the wind; go thou to the heaven or to the earth, according to thy merit; or go to the waters if it suits thee to be there, or abide with thy members in the plants." [30] The *Purusha* Hymn (*Rig* 10. 90) may also be interpreted as an expression of the assumed correspondence between man and the cosmos.

Brihad-Aranyaka 2. 1 is the earliest passage in the *Upanishads* which teaches the subjectivity of the Brahman. Driptabalaki of a tribe named Gargya comes to Ajatashatru, King of Banaras, and offers to give him instruction about Brahman so he may become a Janaka, i.e., a very learned king. Ajatashatru agrees that such teaching would be worth a thousand cows. But the teaching is that Brahman is to be worshiped as sun, moon, lightning, space, wind, fire, water, etc. In other words, the Brahman that Driptabalaki knows is the external Brahman manifested in external objects. When he has finished, Ajatashatru observes, "Is that all? With that much Brahman—the formless Brahman—is not known." Then Driptabalaki, although a *Brahmin,* requests to be taught by the King of Banaras, who is a *Kshatriya.* No mention is made of payment. Ajatashatru by appeal to the example of a sleeping man teaches that while awake man is subject to the distractions and constraints of voice, eye, ear, breath, and mind, but while in deep sleep all worlds are his. The unconditioned Brahman is within. Brahman is the inner core of the self. "As a spider might come out from his thread, as small sparks come forth from the fire, even so from this Self comes forth all vital energies, all worlds, all gods, all beings." This is the Real, the Brahman within. The point of the story is that Brahman is to be found both in the external world of natural objects and also in the inner world of the self. The reality of cosmic phenomena and the reality of the mental phenomena of the human being is the same Reality. The individual human self *(jiva)* is a microcosm of the macrocosm. From this analogy the next step in the speculation seems to have been to consider the macrocosm itself a macro-*jiva,* and as such it was called *"Atman."* The words *"jiva"* and *"Atman"* have many denotations and connotations in Indian thought. *Jiva* is the principle of life; but when applied to man, it includes sensing and thinking as well as living. The *jiva* is the individual and mortal self; the *Atman* is the universal and immortal Self. *Atman* originally meant breath, but it became extended to denote the soul or self. In the *Upanishads* and in *astika* writings in general *"atman"* with lower case "a" denotes the undying soul in the individual, and *"Atman"* with upper case "A" denotes the Universal Soul, the Brahman conceived subjectively. The *atman* is the miniature of the *Atman.* In an interesting metaphor the two selves are imaged as two birds perched in the same tree (the body):

> Two birds, fast bound companions,
> Clasp close the self-same tree.
> Of these two, the one eats sweet fruit;
> The other looks on without eating.[31]

To eat means to identify one's self with. The *jiva* identifies itself with the body, and therefore is caught up with the life of the body, migrating from incarnation to incarnation; but the *atman* is a witnessing self, watching the life of the *jiva* in the body without partaking in the joys and sorrows of the embodied life.

A further development in the movement to subjectivity is the teaching of *Chandogya* 5. 18 that the human must realize the *atman* in himself before he can comprehend the cosmic *Atman*. The expression is that the individual must live as if (*iva*) the *Atman* were separate and individual. The meaning here is that the individual must see himself as though he were *Atman*, for such he is in a sense. Subjectivity here becomes the methodology by which the nature of the *Atman* may be apprehended. By knowing one's self as a microcosm one may be able to grasp in a measure what is the nature of the macrocosm: "He who meditates on the Universal Self as of the measure of the span or as identical with the self, eats food in all worlds, in all beings, in all selves." [32] In other words, he no longer makes distinctions between himself and other selves, between himself and other beings, between himself and other worlds.

The final development in the movement to subjectivity is the identification of the *Atman* and the Brahman, the two world-grounds, the two aspects of Total Reality. The best illustration of this is the account of the return of Shvetaketu to his home after twelve years of study with his *guru*. His father, Uddalaka, wishes to know if he learned from his *guru* "that teaching whereby what has not been heard of becomes heard of, what has not been thought of becomes thought of, what has not been understood becomes understood?" [33] But Shvetaketu does not even understand the question! So Uddalaka explains that just as clay is the first principle of all that is made of clay, so there is a first principle of the entire world. Has he learned of it? Shvetaketu has not. So his father offers the instruction by pointing out to his son that all classes of objects in the phenomenal world have as their soul that which is the finest essence: "That is Reality. That is *Atman*." And he adds, "*Tat tvam asi*, Shvetaketu." That you are! The first principle of all that is external is exactly the same as the first principle of all that is internal. He who knows what he is essentially knows the nature of everything. *Atman* is Brahman. *Tat tvam asi* also appears as *aham Brahman asmi* (I am Brahman).

"*Atman* is Brahman" appears to be a statement describing the nature of the world. If it is, then it can be examined as can any statement of fact. The question to be asked first is about the meaning of the connective "is." The word "is" has at least five logically discernible meanings: (1) predication, e.g., "This apple is green"; (2) class inclusion, e.g., "Fido is a dog"; (3) class membership, e.g., "Brown pelicans are vanishing"; (4) equality, e.g., "Two and two is four"; (5) identity, e.g., "IV is [equivalent to] 4." "*Atman* is Brahman" seems to be a form of identity or equivalence. There are many classes of identity: (1) absolute physical identity, e.g., "A is identical with A"; (2) relative physical identity, e.g., identical twins; (3) same entity at various stages of development, e.g., Joe Doakes as boy and J. D. as man; (4) same species, e.g., Harry Truman as man and Herbert Hoover as man; (5) same being in different contexts, e.g., Jane as mother and Jane as wife; (6) whole and part, e.g., a cup of water dipped from the Atlantic Ocean and the Atlantic Ocean; (7) appearance and reality, e.g., a photograph and the person of whom it is a photograph; (8) the same object considered from different perspectives, e.g., the duck-rabbit example of perception. Probably the last subclass of identity is the identity of *Atman* and Brahman: *Atman* is Totality viewed internally; Brahman is Totality viewed externally.

Another possibility is that "*Atman* is Brahman" is not a metaphysical statement but a soteriological statement. It is not intended to state anything about the nature of *Atman* or Brahman, but rather it states the experience of the man who is liberated. Rudolf Otto has written, "The word 'is' in the mystical formula of identification [*Atman* is Brahman] has a significance which it does not contain in logic. It is no copula as in the sentence: S is P; it is no sign of equality in a reversible equation. It is not the 'is' of a normal assertion of identity." In order to suggest what the statement is attempting to express, Otto adds, "For instance one might say instead of 'I am Brahman,' 'I am "existed" by Brahman' or 'essenced' by Brahman, or 'Brahman exists me.' " [34]

"*Atman* is Brahman" is the reduction of all the correspondences the Hindu mind had been seeking for centuries. The principle of identification had at last completed its work.

Movement to Spirituality

The third movement of the Vedic period was the movement from materiality to spirituality. The *Rig* was the product of a period of well-being. Life was good. The earth was home. Man desired to live upon the earth for one hundred years, and then to live an afterlife where the joys and satisfactions of earthly life would continue endlessly. The *Upanishads* mark the end of this period of happy hopes and expectations. The earth was no longer attractive. Pessimism and illusionism now possessed and obsessed the minds of men. This movement from materiality to spirituality, from optimism to pessimism, can be traced within the *Upanishads* themselves. Whereas in the early *Upanishads* Brahman was said to be the same as physical space[35] and *maya* was the magical power of the gods to create the physical world man enjoyed,[36] in the later *Upanishads* Brahman became the maker of illusions and *maya* was the power to conceal rather than the power to create: "This whole world the illusion-maker projects out of this Brahman. It is by illusion (*maya*) the other (the *jiva*) is confined. One should know that Nature is illusion (*maya*), and that the Mighty Lord is the illusion-maker." [37] The first meaning of *maya* was a distinction between the manifested and the manifesting. That which is manifested does not exhaust the manifesting, and perhaps never can. If the manifesting is thought to be always more than the manifested, then it is understandable that the next step would be to believe that the manifested misrepresents the manifesting. Man's experiences are not trustworthy. In *Prashna Upanishad* 1. 16 *maya* is associated with crookedness and falsehood. *Maitri Upanishad* 6. 35 affirms that the Brahman transcends all fragmentary manifestations, and that only a portion of the Real is real to us: "Of the bright power that pervades the sky it is only a portion which is, as it were, in the midst of the sun, in the eye, and in fire. That is Brahman. That is the Immortal. That is Splendor. That is the Eternal Real." The belief that Reality is hidden and that everything man experiences by means of his unaided faculties is unreal is expressed in the ancient purificatory prayer: "Lead me from the unreal to the real."

There were two sides to the growing sense of unreality of the world in the *Upanishads*. One was a loss of confidence in man as knower. The "self-wise, thinking themselves learned, running hither and thither, go around deluded, like blind men led by one who is himself blind." [38] The knowledge offered in the *Upanishads* was a secret knowledge, a knowledge which could not be attained by reasoning upon ordinary experience. Instead it was a knowledge which had to be conveyed by *rishis* to pupils prepared to receive it. The other side of the sense of unreality was believed to be rooted in the nature of things. The word "*iva*" (as it were) was used over and over again when referring to the world of common experience. The *rishis* reminded their pupils that motion is an appearance, thought is an appearance, all objectifying is an appearance, i.e., all efforts to distinguish one's self as observer from the things one observes. [39] "Now, as it were, enjoying pleasure with women; now, as it were, laughing, and even beholding fearful sights." [40] Shankara, the formulater of the nondualistic system of philosophy over one thousand years later, seized upon these and other passages using the innocent-appearing word "*iva*" to develop a full doctrine of *maya*, but in the *Upanishads* only the germ of the idea of the unreality of the phenomenal world is found. The *Upanishads* grant that men may be, and often are, deceived, but they do not declare the world to be only a play of shadows, an illusion, an unreality; rather it is an unreliable manifestation of Reality. The conclusion of the *Upanishads* is that if one is to get to the Real, he must turn from the external to the internal. Objectivity is the way of *maya;* subjectivity is the way of Reality.

The earliest and one of the clearest teachings of subjectivity is found in two recessions of the *Brihad-Aranyaka Upanishad,* i.e., 2. 4 and 4. 5. This is the story of the great Yajñavalkya preparing to leave the life of a householder and to enter upon the retirement stage of life. He desired to make a financial settlement with his two wives so they would not suffer hardship when he left the family. One of his wives, Katyayani, having "just a woman's knowledge in that matter," was willing to accept the financial settlement. But the other wife, Maitreyi, was "a discourser on sacred knowledge." She, therefore, would not accept merely monetary security. She asked, "If this whole world filled with wealth were mine, would I by reason of this be immortal?" Yajñavalkya admitted that there is no hope for immortality through wealth. Then Maitreyi asked, "What should I do with that through which I may not be immortal?" Yajñavalkya praised Maitreyi, "Though you were previously dear to me, you are dearer now." Yet, he continued, one must keep value priorities in proper hierarchical order. A wife is dear not because the husband loves his wife; rather a wife is dear because of the prior value the husband places on *Atman*—and the same is true for all that one holds dear: husband, sons, wealth, cattle, social class, worlds, gods, and even the Vedas. Only the *Atman* has intrinsic value.

> Lo, verily, not for love of the beings are beings dear, but for love of the *Atman* beings are dear.
> Lo, verily, not for love of all is all dear, but for love of the *Atman* all is dear.
> Lo, verily, it is the *Atman* that should be seen, that should be harkened to, that should be thought on, that should be pondered on, O Maitreyi.

Yajñavalkya ran through the list again, this time warning that all that one holds dear will desert the person who fails to give priority in being and value to the *Atman*:

> Brahmanhood deserts him who knows Brahmanhood in aught else than the *Atman*. Kshatriyahood deserts him who knows Kshatriyahood in aught else than the *Atman*. The worlds desert him who knows the worlds in aught else than the *Atman*. The Vedas desert him who knows the Vedas in aught else than the *Atman*. Beings desert him who knows everything in aught else than the *Atman*. Everything deserts him who knows everything in aught else than the *Atman*.

The *Atman* is the manifesting Reality; all else is manifested. The relationship of manifesting-manifested must not be confused with two beings in the same order of reality. The manifesting is known by *para vidya*; the manifested by *apara vidya*. And again we are informed that the *Rig, Yajur, Sama,* and *Atharva* and also the secondary subject matters—this time listed as legend, ancient lore, sciences, mystic doctrines, verses, aphorisms, explanations, commentaries, sacrifices, oblations, food, drink, this world and the others, and all beings—"have been breathed forth" from the *Atman.* The person who is not existentially aware of the distinction between the manifesting *Atman* and the manifested reality is misled into the error of assigning to all "realities" equal ontological status. He cannot distinguish reality and Reality, *jiva* and *Atman,* gods and Brahman. But for the one who has the secret knowledge (*upanishad*) the duality is *iva* (as it were). For him "everything has become just one's own self." He does not make the error of confusing the *Atman* with that which the *Atman* manifests. He knows that the *Atman* is not this and not that (*neti, neti*), because he knows the *Atman* is no thing. The *Atman* is unseizable, indestructible, unattached, and unbound. *Atman* is Brahman.

We noted above that the *Upanishads* are the foundation for Hindu philosophizing, but they are not in themselves philosophy. They are speculations rather than arguments for position. Now we can indicate their striking philosopical deficiency: they contend that the world is pluralistic, objective, and material in its appearance whereas it is unity, subjectivity, and spirituality in its Reality, but they do not argue why the world appears to man in this manner nor why it is other than the way it appears.

Karma and Samsara

Karma may have developed out of the magical efficacy of the sacrifices. The belief that the sacrifices were reliable means for securing what an individual wanted was a primitive form of the cause-effect relationship. According to the doctrine of *karma* there are necessary and sufficient conditions which account for the fortunes and misfortunes in the life of every living being. The individual reaps only that which he sows, no more and no less. Every act is both the result of forces set in operation by previous acts and the cause of forces which will come to fruition in future acts. *Karma* is the law of the deed. The idea first appears in *Shatapatha Brahmana* 6. 2. 2. 27: "Every man is born in the world fashioned by himself." There are many references to *karma* in the *Upanishads*: "One becomes good by good action, bad by bad action." [41] "According as one acts, according as one behaves, so does he become. The doer of good becomes good, the doer of evil becomes evil. One becomes virtuous by virtuous action, and bad by bad action." [42] "[The soul] being overcome by the bright or dark fruits of action . . ." [43]

Karma may be thought of as *Rita* operative in the moral realm. Had the Upanishadic *rishis* been philosophers, they would have argued over the problem of freedom in a deterministic world; but they were not philosophers, and therefore, while believing in *karma*, they also believed in a less than completely karmic world, for they asked their pupils to take voluntary attitudes and to engage in voluntary acts which would have been impossible in a world of complete determinism. The *Bhagavad Gita*, as we shall see, is constructed on the theme that the warrior can choose to fight or not to fight. The doctrine of fate is often expressed in the *Mahabharata*, e.g., "No creature is able to avert fate. Indeed destiny, I think, is certain to take its course; individual exertion is futile." [44] But despite any illogicality of the position, the assumption in the *Upanishads* and throughout Hindu literature is that man is able to make free choices. The *rishis* could have argued convincingly that freedom of choice has meaning only in a *Rita* world, i.e., in a world of natural and moral order.

Meanwhile another idea was developing which was related to *karma*, and which was to have a profound effect on the development of Hinduism. This was the concept of *samsara*, the impermanent and changing aspects of the physical universe. Since *samsara* is most obvious to man in his own experience of birth and death, the term came to stand for the theory of reincarnation or transmigration of the vital principle from one physical body to another. So it was used in its first appearance in the *Upanishads*:

He, however, who has not understanding,
Who is unmindful and ever impure,
Reaches not the goal,
But goes on to reincarnation.[45]

The idea of reincarnation was much earlier, having been expressed in the *Brihad-Aranyaka*: "As a goldsmith, taking a piece of gold, reduces it to another newer and more beautiful form, just so this soul, striking down this body and dispelling its ignorance, makes for itself another newer and more beautiful form." [46] The body of the next incarnation might be a human, an animal, a plant, or even the mystical bodies of orders of beings beyond the human.

The doctrine of reincarnation also arose from another line of thinking. In the *Brahmanas* are found references to the fear of what is called "re-death" or "death beyond death" (*punarmrityu*). This was the fear that as life ends so the afterlife may end. "Death of death" could only mean the thrusting of the individual into the opposite of death which is life. So earthly birth came to be viewed as the death of the afterlife even as earthly death had been assumed to be the beginning of the afterlife. Birth and death were two aspects of the same event. The resulting cycle was not greeted with enthusiasm: "In this sort of cycle of existence what is the good of enjoyment of desires, when after a man has fed on them there is seen repeatedly his return here to earth? . . . In this cycle of existence I am like a frog in a waterless well." [47]

In the *Upanishads* the two conceptions—*karma* and *punarmrityu*—were brought together to form the full notion of reincarnation. The afterlife was a return to this life in another body; it was another trip on the wheel of birth and death. The doctrine of reincarnation helped solve some of the difficulties inherent in the doctrine of *karma*. The *rishis* recognized that some of the fruits of a life did not appear to be the harvest of seed sown within a particular incarnation, and some of the karmic seed sown in an incarnation did not appear to reach fruition within the incarnation. But when *karma* was linked with *samsara*, then the karmic seeds and the karmic fruits could be considered to be distributed over many incarnations.

Karma has a two-fold mode of operation: it determines that there will be another incarnation, and it determines the nature of that incarnation. The *jiva*, the carrier of *karma*, may take any living form, human or nonhuman. Some Hindus have claimed there are 8,400,000 species of bodies which can carry *karma* and into which the *jiva* may migrate; and others have speculated on the hierarchy of plants, insects, fish, birds, and mammals through which the migrating *jivas* must move before they have the opportunity of inhabiting a human body.

Karma and *samsara* are considered as inseparable in many passages in the *Upanishads*, e.g.,

> Whatever he does in this world,
> He comes again from that world
> Because of his action.[48]

> Accordingly, those who are of pleasant conduct here—the prospect is, indeed, that they will enter a pleasant womb, either the womb of a *Brahmin*, or the womb of a *Kshatriya*, or the womb of a *Vaishya*. But those who are of stinking conduct here—the prospect is, indeed, that they will enter a stinking womb, either the womb of a dog, or the womb of a swine, or the womb of an outcaste.[49]

> Some go into a womb
> For the embodiment of a corporeal being,
> Others go into a stationary thing
> According to their deeds, according to their knowledge.[50]

> The individual self roams about according to its deeds.[51]

The doctrine of *karma* and its ramifications have become so important in Hinduism that one Indologist has suggested the essentials of Hinduism could be entirely covered merely by analyzing *karma*.[52] *Karma* eliminated the hope of a heaven which would terminate the tribulations of the earthly pilgrimage and replaced it with the expectation of one weary incarnation after another until all *karma* is exhausted. The end desired was a liberation, a release, an escape. The goal was freedom from death and rebirth, from the unreal, from sorrow, from the body and its problems, from the "knots of the heart" (the empathetic pain for loved ones), and from *anrita* (falsehood and sin). Yet the goal was not entirely negative.

The liberated ones "cross over to the other side of sorrow," [53] find "the further shore of darkness," [54] and "cross over sorrow." [55] The truth is that the goal attained by the elimination of *karma* was not very attractive. The general tone of the evaluations of this life and the expectations for future lives was not optimistic. Many post-Upanishadic leaders of Hindu thought felt obligated to offer something more desirable than absorption into the Absolute. "What is the worth of salvation if it means absorption, the mixing of water with water?" asked Ramprasad Sen, an eighteenth-century poet. "Sugar I love to eat, but I have no wish to become sugar!"

Jñana Marga

The religion of the *Upanishads* is a discipline to create the "knowledge" that the external Brahman and the internal *Atman* are one and the same. This "knowledge" is neither *para vidya* nor *apara vidya* for the reason that *vidya* is an intellectualistic conception of knowledge, and there is no salvation in mere learning. *Vidya* is knowledge which can be capsuled in books and journals. *Jñana* is liberating "knowledge." It is the fruit of the life of the spirit, not of the mind. It can never be taught. *Jñana* is the Enlightenment which opens the life of the individual. It is the wisdom gained from life deeply lived. It cannot be communicated by voice or pen. "The *Atman* is not to be obtained by instruction, nor by intellect, nor by much learning." [56] In the strictest sense, *jñana* is not knowing but being. One of the best insights into *jñana* as a *marga* is to be found in the *Mandukya Upanishad*. According to the *rishi* of this *Upanishad* the self has four states: (1) the waking state is the state of outward cognition, of separation between knower and known; (2) the dreaming state is one of inward cognition, i.e., one in which the dreamer is both the fashioner and the knower of the objects in his dream; (3) the dreamless or deep-sleep state is the fully unified state, i.e., the state of knowing nothing within nor without; and (4) a state which has no name. It has no name because to name it would objectify it. The *rishi* very wisely shifted at this point to the negative, and wrote what the state is not: "Not inwardly cognitive, not outwardly cognitive, not both-wise cognitive, not a cognitive-mass, not cognitive, not non-cognitive, unseen, with which there can be no dealing, ungraspable, having no distinctive mark, non-thinkable, that cannot be designated, the essence of the assurance of which is the state of being one with the Self." [57] He then demonstrated by appeal to the *mantra* AUM. The waking state, the common-to-all-men state is the letter A; the sleeping state is the letter U; the deep-sleep state is the letter M; and the fourth state is "symbolized" by the nonsymbol, the unheard sound, the unseen letter: "The fourth is without an element, with which there can be no dealing, the cessation of development, benign, without a second. This AUM is the *Atman* indeed. He who knows this, with his self enters the Self." [58] The fourth is the unified AUM. The *Atman* is the nonsymbolizable Totality "known" by the "knowledge" which is a "knowing" from no point of view, which, of course, is nonknowing since all knowing is from a point of view.

Hindu literature is full of stories which try to convey the meaning of *jñana*. Swami Vivekananda liked to tell the story of a tiger cub which had been adopted by a flock of sheep. The cub grew up as a sheep, bleating and eating grass. One day a tiger killed a sheep from the flock, and then, noticing the cub, asked, "Who are you?" "I'm a sheep," bleated the tiger cub. "Come with me," commanded the tiger as he led the cub to a water hole. "Look in the water and tell me what you see." "I see that we look alike," responded the cub. Then the tiger forced the cub to thrust his jaws into the bloody carcass of a freshly slain sheep; and the cub realized he was a tiger. To say that he now "knew" he was a tiger would be weak indeed. He now was a tiger. The religion of the *Upanishads* leads to the culminating "I am Brahman." This is the "secret knowledge" which opens the doors to Reality. According to the *Taittiriya Upanishad* there are five sheaths (*koshas*) of the Self which make the self manifest as the *jiva*. These are matter (*prakriti*), life (*prana*), consciousness (*manas*), intelligence (*vijñana*), and bliss (*ananda*). The five *koshas* hide the Self. Only when they are taken away can the Self be realized in its pure state. When the *koshas* fall, the *Atman* stands alone. The individual-as-*jiva* cannot say, "I am *Atman*," for there is no "I" to speak, no "I" to know or to be known, and no "I" to be distinguished from *Atman*—not "I am *Atman*" but "*Atman*."

> He is not grasped by the eye nor even by speech nor by other sense-organs, nor by austerity, nor by work, but when one's (intellectual) nature is purified by the light of knowledge then alone he, by meditation, sees Him who is without parts.[59]

CHAPTER 7

Materialism, Jainism, Buddhism

In the first part of this book, we have followed the development of Hinduism from the Vedas through the *Brahmanas* and the *Upanishads*. The movement can be described as one from poets to priests to philosophers. The place of these developments was the valleys of the Indus and its tributaries and the headwaters of the Ganges and the Jumna. The period was one of conflict between priests and seers. For the most part it was a development and explication of the insights of the Vedic *rishis* plus infiltrations from non-Aryan sources. The sacerdotal system had been challenged by the Upanishadic seers, but nothing which can be called a revolt had appeared. With the sixth century, however, there arose upon the Hindu scene the first period of challenge. The *Upanishads*, despite their obvious brilliance of conception and expression, had failed to appeal to the masses. The average man could not hope to attain the lofty liberating knowledge set forth as the ideal in the *Upanishads*. The sacrificial system had been taken from him and he had received in return that which was beyond his intellectual powers and which did not satisfy his

125

emotional needs. Furthermore, some of the intellectuals had not found the new religions fully acceptable, for the Upanishadic *rishis* rather than giving convincing arguments for their doctrines merely recorded their own intuitions and asked their hearers to accept on faith the truth and value of the insights.

By the sixth century three types of challenges were being made against the *Upanishads*. The first was the materialistic challenge. According to the materialists, the *rishis* not only were giving the wrong answers but also were raising the wrong questions. The problem, they said, was not how to liberate man from the miserable conditions of this life, but how to enjoy to the full this earthly life. The second challenge was that of the Jains and the Buddhists who, accepting the doctrines of *karma* and *samsara,* offered ethical and psychological means of liberation rather than appeals to the realization of the identity of the self and the Absolute. These two challenges originated at the east end of the Gangetic watershed. The materialistic challenge was a revolt; the Jaina and the Buddhistic bordered on revolt. Meanwhile the third challenge was developing at the west end of the watershed. It grew out of the needs of common people for a religion of love and devotion, a religion which warmed the heart rather than one which stimulated the mind. This protest against intellectualism was centered in the vicinity of Mathura where several tribes had developed their own forms of devotion. The first two challenges will be considered in this chapter; the third is the subject of the next chapter.

Historical Background

The early part of the Vedic period was a time of conflict between the invading Aryans and the peoples of the Indus valley, but the latter part was a time of accommodation, assimilation, and adjustment. The Aryans ceased to be nomads. The village displaced the tribe as the unit of society, thus setting a pattern of villages, which remains to this day the predominant political unit in India despite the claims of the central government of modern India. The vast majority of Indians still feel stronger ties to their village than to the nation. Priests, poets, philosophers, craftsmen, herdsmen, and farmers have their niches within the villages. By the sixth century B.C. a new class of people had appeared: the class of free peasants and land-owning farmers. Property ceased to be owned solely by the tribe. Private property brought in traders, merchants, landlords, and moneylenders. Wealth was no longer measured in cattle. The head of the village was likely to be the wealthiest man. He was dominant during times of war, but during times of peace the priest who conducted the sacrifices was likely to be more influential. There were also village assemblies to advise the king and, possibly, to restrain the priest.

Since the Indians were such poor keepers of records, we are forced to depend largely upon the unreliable references to events in the religious literature, supplemented by the documents of their more history-conscious neighbors. We know that Vedic culture developed in "the land of the seven rivers" and moved slowly southward and eastward down the wide valley of the Ganges. The focal point of developing Hinduism moved out of the Indus valley permanently. Northern India at this time was divided into sixteen kingdoms. The Kurus of Kurukshetra near the present city of Delhi with their capital city of Asandivat (the Hastinapura of the epics) and the Panchalas close by were the "first families." They displaced the Bharatas, the prominent tribe in the *Rig*, the tribe from which the ancient name for India—Bharata—is derived. The Kashis were situated on the banks of the Ganges near Banaras, although this city at that time was known as Kashi or Varanasi. Other peoples were the Vasas, Usinaras, Srinjayas, Kosalas, Videhas, Magadhas, and Angas. The kingdom of Magadha was destined to surpass them all, but at this time it was of minor importance.

The life of one of the early kings has been constructed from the religious literature. This is King Parikshit, the founder of the first strong dynasty in India, and one with whom are associated many important events in the history of Hinduism. According to legend, although he was still-born, Krishna gave him life and blessing. As the grandnephew of Yudhishthira, he succeeded to the throne at Hastinapura. His accession marks the beginning of the Kali Yuga. During his reign he extended the kingdom as far north as Taxila. He is praised for having performed the horse sacrifice, although the motive for the performance was less praiseworthy: he sought to absolve himself from the guilt of having killed *brahmins*. There are many stories about Parikshit. One story is that Parakshit once lost his way in a dense forest, and coming upon a holy man in meditation, asked directions of him. But the priest did not break his meditation to answer. In anger at the silence of the holy man, Parikshit threw a dead snake at him. For this impious act Parikshit was himself bitten by a poisonous snake. His son, Janamejaya, removed the taint of his father's act by performing an elaborate rite known as the serpent sacrifice, but, like his father, he also slew *brahmins* and had to perform the horse sacrifice. As part of the ritual the entire text of the *Mahabharata* is reputed to have been recited for the first time. The dynasty collapsed, but the fame of Kurukshetra lives on because there was fought the battle which is the framework of the *Mahabharata* and the *Bhagavad Gita*.

In the sixth century B.C. invaders again appeared in the Punjab. A Persian explorer sailed down the Indus River and returned along the coast. Afterwards the Persians seized the Punjab and made it a province of the Achaemenian empire. This province, known as Gandhara, survived for centuries, not by reason of strength, but by willingness to recognize the existence of other kingdoms; e.g., it sent an embassy to Bimbisara, King of Magadha, in the fifth century. The latter had grown so that it was able to claim suzerainty over northern India as far west as Mathura before it collapsed. During the heyday of the Magadha kings, intrigue, corruption, and murder were the favorite instruments of persuasion and rule. Magadha united the many kingdoms of the Ganges and founded the city of Pataliputra, the city which for centuries was the political center of India. The Magadha empire prepared the way for the Maurya empire.

The valley of the Indus had seen two Western invasions—the Aryan and the Persian—and in the fourth century it experienced the third, the Greek. Alexander the Great was a man who possessed a curious mixture of emotions. He wished to integrate cultures by contacts and intermarriages; he sought adventure and riches; he loved to dominate; and he wished to spread the benefits of Greek culture. After defeating the Persians and occupying Persepolis, he moved on to subjugate the eastern provinces of the empire. Upon reaching the tributaries of the Indus, his appetite was whetted to move against the kingdoms of the Ganges, but in 324 B.C. after three years of fighting in India, his army was unwilling to advance farther into India, and Alexander returned to Babylon, where he died the following year. From the point of view of the historian, the great contribution of Alexander was the accurate account he kept of his adventures, thus leaving a legacy of reliable information about ancient India. But, unfortunately, his records are of little consequence for our purposes in tracing the development of Hinduism because by this time the most significant events in the growth of Hinduism were taking place at the eastern end of the valley of the Ganges. In the west in the Kuru and Panchala kingdoms conservative priests were in control, the ancient fire and blood sacrifices and adoration of gods remained as the dominant forms of religions, and the language was Sanskrit; but in the east in the kingdoms of Kashi, Kosala, Videha, and Magadha the ruling and warring class was strong, animal sacrifices were discouraged, and the languages were the Prakrits, i.e., the popularized forms of Sanskrit. Vedic sacerdotalism and Upanishadic speculation had not been firmly established in the east. Whereas the west accepted *Brahmin* lore, the east argued against it. The east was a *Kshatriya* stronghold, not because *Kshatriyas* were regarded as superior to *Brahmins* but because wealth rather than scholarship was the determiner of social status—and the *Kshatriyas* were wealthy.

When Alexander was forced by his generals to abandon his plans to conquer all of India, he left only a few Macedonians to rule the upper portions of the Indus valley. These were easily overthrown shortly after the death of Alexander. Chandragupta Maurya, an upstart with some claim to royalty, was the leader of the Indian forces which drove the Macedonians back across the Indus. He then proceeded to conquer all northern India, and thus the Mauryan empire was established. By the beginning of the third century the quarrels among Alexander's generals had been settled. Seleucus Nikator was in command of the eastern wing of the Macedonian empire, and he and Chandragupta Maurya had resolved their boundary disputes. Nikator withdrew west of the Hindu Kush, thus giving Chandragupta a natural boundary. Nikator sent an ambassador named Megasthenes to the royal court at Pataliputra. This proved to be a happy choice, for Megasthenes compiled an elaborate account of his life in court which gives us a reliable external source of information about India in the early third century B.C. Of special interest is his report that the people were divided into seven classes. The highest class was the king's ministers, who ruled directly under the monarch. The second class consisted of inspectors who secretly spied upon the people and reported their findings to the king. The next class, whom Megasthenes called the gymnosophists, were the custodians of learning and the performers of both private and public ceremonial rites. Their advice to the king, when good, was rewarded with exemption from taxation. Megasthenes said of the gymnosophists' manner of life, "They live in a simple style, and lie on beds of rushes or skins. They abstain from animal food and sexual pleasures, and spend their time in listening to serious discourse and in imparting their knowledge to such as will listen to them." The fourth class was the large group of agriculturalists who annually gave one-fourth of the produce of the land to the king. Herdsmen and hunters constituted the fifth class. Traders, merchants, and craftsmen were the sixth class, and the soldiers were the last class.

The Maurya empire was extended southward by Bindusara, the son and successor of Chandragupta. Bindusara's son, Ashoka, inherited a vast empire stretching across northern India from the Hindu Kush mountains to the Bay of Bengal. Cordial lines of communication between the Seleucids and the Mauryas were maintained, as is indicated by a letter from Bindusara asking the Macedonian emperor to purchase for him some Greek wine, figs, and one Sophist. The reply was that the wine and figs were being sent, but Greek philosophers were not for sale! Ashoka made animal sacrifices illegal in the empire, promoted vegetarianism by forbidding the serving of meat at the royal table, propagandized peace and nonviolence on memorial columns erected throughout his empire, became a Buddhist, and finally, according to some accounts, took the vows of a Buddhist monk. He may have been the savior of Buddhism, for it was he who turned Buddhism into a worldwide religion by sending missionaries of Buddhism outside the Indian mainland.

Materialism

The intellectual, religious, and social leaders of kingdoms at the west end of the Gangetic watershed had remained throughout the Vedic period completely orthodox. The Sanskirt word is *"astika"* (yes-sayer); i.e., they accepted the Vedas as the supreme authority, which meant also that they acknowledged a Reality higher than the realities of the sensed-perceived world. For them the Vedas were *shruti.* At the eastern end of the Ganges heterodoxy had developed. Some of the intellectuals were radically anti-Vedic. *Nastika* (no-sayer) was the term used to identify them. They rejected the Vedas and all teaching which suggested that there might be a reality other than that discovered by the senses. These were the materialists and those Buddhists who were most adamant in their denial of the self. The heterodoxy of the Jains was more restrained. Such terms as *"avaidika"* (non-Vedist) and *"shramana"* (magician) are more appropriate as descriptions of their position.

The materialists were so out of step with developing Hinduism that all their early works were destroyed by their Vedic opponents. The delicate manner in which twentieth-century Indian philosophers refer to this episode in Indian intellectual history is amusing. Radhakrishnan says the original materialistic texts are "not available." [1] Dakshinaranjan Bhattacharya says they are "now lost to us." [2] On the other hand, a Western Indologist who describes the materialistic challenge as "one of the finest chapters in the history of Hindu and Buddhist speculation," adds, "Indian materialism and rationalism, as exemplified in the theories of *nastika* thinkers appears to have played a great and liberating part in the development of Indian thought, a fact which has been immensely neglected by students of Hindu philosophy." [3]

Very little can be discovered about the materialists themselves. We do not even know where they lived, although from the fact that much of the material about them is in Buddhist texts, and also from what we know about the eastern end of the Ganges valley as contrasted to the western end, we can confidently place the scene of their activities in the same geographic regions as those of the Jains and the Buddhists. This was the area of intellectual ferment in the sixth century B.C.

The traditional founder of the movement was a man named Brihaspati who is thought to have composed his *sutras* (aphorisms) in the sixth century. But we know no more about him. We know a bit more about a materialist named Ajita. According to Buddhist literature the Buddha identified six teachers as heretical with respect to the Vedas: Purana Kassapa, Pakudha Kaccayana, Makkhali Gosala, Ajita Keshakambalin, Sanjaya Belatthiputta, and Nigantha Nataputta. Ajita lived in the late sixth and early fifth centuries B.C. He was given the nickname Keshakambalin (hair-blanket) because he and his disciples for some unknown reason wore blankets made of human hair. His materialism was thoroughgoing. Everything in the universe, including man himself, he said, is composed of the four primary elements: earth, air, fire, and water. The difference among things is solely the result of the different proportions of the elements. At death the human being without remainder is dissolved back into the primary elements. There is no afterlife and no reincarnation. "Soul" and "god" are words—and only words. Sacrifices and good works confer no merit; sins and evil works bring no punishment. There is no pain nor pleasure. These opinions of Ajita are credited with having been the source and justification for the horrible brutalities practiced by the Magadhan rulers who murdered freely in their efforts to enlarge their empire by destroying all other kingdoms in northern India. Knowledge was believed by Ajita to be only sensation, and any reasoning beyond sense experience was declared invalid. The so-called knowledge offered in the Vedic literature was described by Ajita as "the vomit of *brahmins*."

The materialistic philosophies as a group—for there were many types—were called either Lokayata or Charvaka. The term "Lokayata" comes from *loka* (this world, or the world of things). It seems to have been used in the sense of people of the world or the people who deal with things. The term "Charvaka" is derived from *charu* (sweet) and *vac* (word). There is a difference of opinion as to whether "Charvaka" was the name of an early leader of the movement—a Mr. Sweet Tongue!—or whether it was a name for the school itself insofar as it held to a hedonic ethic.

The Charvaka philosophers operated in two directions: negatively they sought to destroy confidence in *shruti,* and positively they sought to offer an alternative to brahminic teachings. Their favorite weapon of destruction was ridicule. If the sacrificial animals ascend to heaven as the *brahmins* say, they asked, then why do not sacrificers offer their own parents and children? The Vedas themselves were authored by "buffoons, knaves, and demons," and they are tainted with "untruths, self-contradictions, and tautologies." The Vedas, those "incoherent rhapsodies," are but cheats, and the priests who perform the sacrifices, read the Vedas, conduct penances, and rub their bodies with ashes are ignorant men with no manliness nor sense who have discovered that the value of the ceremonies is a means of self-support—the ceremonies have no other fruit.

According to the Charvakas the only realities are physical objects, i.e., objects which can be sensed. Whereas other philosophers recognized five primary elements—earth, air, fire, water, and ether—the Charvakas held that only the first four exist; the latter is unperceivable, therefore unreal. From such a simple physicalism they concluded that all inference is impossible for the obvious reason that all inferences must include at least one universal, and universals are not physical—e.g., "This is B, because this is A, and all cases of A are cases of B (the universal)." Somehow they did not note that their argument against inference was itself an inference involving a universal. They also used their physicalism to reject the existence of a soul.

The Charvaka philosophers rejected the concept of causality, and in its place introduced the concept of *svabhava* (ownness). According to this subtle theory the determining factor in the production of anything is not a cluster of causes but its own unique matter. There are no ultimate causes, no natural law, no uniformity which makes prediction possible. For example, a particular egg develops into a duck or into a chicken depending upon its *svabhava,* and one cannot predict which with any degree of certainty because the egg in question may be a chicken egg which happens to look like a duck egg. The doctrine of *svabhava* becomes particularly interesting when applied to humans, for it means that each is a law unto himself: each man is the measure of all things. Values and reals are completely relative to each individual. A completely *svabhava* world is a solipsistic world. This notion has had an interesting history in India in such doctrines as Jaina relativism, the religious notion of the right of chosen deity, and even Gandhi's opinions about self-rule and self-sufficiency.

The Charvakas rejected not only the concept of efficient cause but also the concept of first cause. The only "god" is "the earthly monarch whose existence is proved by all the world's eyesight." [4] Hell is physical pain, e.g., stepping on a thorn, and heaven is "eating delicious food, keeping company of young women, using fine clothes, perfumes, garlands, sandal paste, etc." [5] Religion in all its forms is foolishness. Only the fool wears himself out in penances and fasts. The construction of temples is good, because it gives a place for travelers to rest. But the allurements of religion are only for stupid fools who cannot see that all the promises of *brahmins* are lies.

The only proper goal for humans is the enjoyment of sensual pleasures. Therefore, men ought never to shun a visible pleasure. What, asked the Charvakas, can compare to "the ravishing embraces of women with large eyes, whose prominent breasts are compressed with one's arms?" [6] The materialists were not so foolish in their hedonism as to suppose all of life could be song and dance: "It is our wisdom to enjoy the pure pleasure as far as we can, and to avoid the pain which inevitably accompanies it. . . . The berries of paddy, rich with the finest white grains, what man, seeking his true interest, would fling away because covered with husk and dust." [7] Only fools think one ought to throw away the pleasures of life because they are mixed with pain. The evils of the world must be accepted in their reality and avoided as far as possible, but they are not to be denied, nor can they be entirely eliminated.

How effective were the materialists in combating the *shrauta* rites and the Upanishadic *sadhana* of knowledge? They must have had a following which endangered the *shruti* tradition, for, otherwise, why would their writings have been destroyed? If they were ineffectual, we can suppose that they would have been allowed to die a natural death. But they were destroyed, and today in reconstructing the Charvaka philosophy we are largely limited to the writings of their enemies. The Charvakas offered a challenge to the religion of the *Upanishads* and to Vedism which appears to have prompted an immediate and vigorous reaction. They purported to offer an optimistic alternative to the life-style of the *Upanishads,* but it was a life-style without hope, and that is the Achilles' heel of any life pattern for the rational animal.

Jainism

Jainism is an Indian anomaly. It is a non-Vedic offshoot of Vedism which radically objected to Vedic traditions only to become so rigid in its own traditions that no changes have been made in its basic ideology in the more than two thousand years of its existence. It originated among the warring class, but its followers are the most pacific of all people. Although the founder was an aristocrat, it won its followers from the middle class. Jainism rejects the world and advises voluntary starvation as the proper mode for departing from the world; yet even during the lifetime of its founder it became so well organized that the forces which drove Buddhism from India could not eradicate Jainism. It is an ascetic cult, yet today the Jains are the wealthiest people in India.

Both Jainism and Buddhism offer an innovation in Hindu tradition: a religious movement inaugurated by a historical person. Jainism is associated with Vardhamana, who was born in a village twenty-seven miles north of Patna. His father and mother were the descendants of kings, and his father was a royal governor. Vardhamana was given the education appropriate for a prince and was married at an early age, but after the deaths of his parents he deserted the householder life and turned to the most vigorous asceticism. During the next twelve years he was often the target of ridicule, derision, and even physical abuse, but at last he found enlightenment. He was thereafter known as Mahavira (The Great Souled One). The remainder of his life was spent in teaching and in organizing his order of ascetics. His success in winning followers was phenomenal.

His organization at the time of his death was reputed to consist of 14,000 monks, 36,000 nuns, 159,000 laymen, and 358,000 laywomen. The strength of Jainism, unlike that of Buddhism, was in its laity and its women. The laymen and laywomen, whom he called *shravakas* (hearers), earned merit by supporting the clerics with alms.

Mahavira's movement was a challenge to the *yajña marga* of the *Samhitas* and the *Brahmanas* and to the *jñana marga* of the *Upanishads*. He accepted the doctrines of *karma* and *samsara*, and he wanted to do something practical about the problem of liberation from continuous reincarnations. He appealed to those who were impatient to do something concrete and tangible about the human condition. Salvation by acts upon one's person was more immediate in its effects than the ceremonial slaying of animals, more obvious than attaining a new conception of the nature of reality. His formula appealed to the pragmatic people of northern India, who, like pragmatic people everywhere, found philosophical speculations too abstract and obtuse to claim their loyalties.

The term "Jainism" comes from *ji* (to conquer). The *jina* ideal is one who has controlled his emotional and volitional life so he is indifferent to pain or pleasure. Mahavira was more than a conqueror; he was, according to Jaina tradition, a *tirthankara*, which may be characterized as the Jaina equivalent to the Hindu *avatara* and the Buddhist *arhat*. The term *"tirthankara"* means a ford-crosser, i.e., one who has successfully crossed the river of life. Mahavira was believed to be the twenty-fourth and last of the *tirthankaras* who have appeared in the present world period of evolution and growth before the coming world period of decay and dissolution, the two great divisions of each complete cosmic cycle of time. Whereas a *jina* represents the self-salvation aspect of Jaina soteriology, a *tirthankara* is concerned for the salvation of others. A *tirthankara* is a pointer to the way of enlightenment and liberation.

Jainism as a protest movement appears to have been originally and consistently opposed to the entire sacrificial system. Unlike Confucius who when asked about the blood sacrifices replied that he cared more for the ceremony than for the animal victims, the Jains cared very much for the victims, and were therefore adamantly against the Vedas and the priests insofar as these required and supported rituals which included the slaughter of animals. The metaphysical foundation for the Jaina rebellion was the doctrine of *jiva-ajiva*. According to this dualistic doctrine all entities (*dravyas*) in the universe are either conscious (*chetana*) or unconscious (*achetana*). The *chetana dravyas* are known as *jivas*, the *achetana dravyas* as *ajivas*. The *ajivas* are *pudgala* (the material principle which makes it possible for anything to be perceptible to touch), *dharma* (the principle of resistance which makes motion possible), *adharma* (the principle of rest), *akasha* (the principle of space), and *kala* (the principle of time). *Pudgala* differs from the other *ajivas* in being *rupi* (with form) rather than *arupi* (formless). The form which *pudgala* takes is that of the atom (*paramanu*). Atoms are the basic realities, the fundamental building blocks of the physical universe. Jainism thus repudiated the monism of the *Upanishads* in its affirmation of both dualism and pluralism. Although there are different classes of *jivas*, they are equal in that each *jiva*, no matter how simple, is actor, knower, and enjoyer. Each *jiva* determines its own destiny. All *jivas* are living beings, and the destruction of life is always unqualifiedly wrong. The taking of life is the act which builds *karma* and makes incarnations necessary; the refraining from taking life is an act which does not build *karma*, which does not make incarnations necessary, and which is therefore the way of liberation from the cycles of births and deaths. Jainism is a *karma marga*, a way of liberation by action, or, more sharply stated, a way of liberation eschewing certain modes of acting.

There are five classes of *jivas*. Each class is determined by the number of senses the *jiva* has. *Jivas* possessing only the sense of touch are earth things, e.g., stones, clay, and chalk; wet things, e.g., water, rain, dew, and fog; fire things, e.g., sparks, fire, and electricity; wind things, e.g., breezes, whirlwinds, and tornadoes; and plant things, e.g., vegetables, grass, and trees. Therefore, according to Jainism one can say either "I touched the tree" or "The tree touched me." Two-sensed *jivas* have the senses of touch and taste. These include the simpler insects. The *jivas* of three senses have the senses of touch, taste, and smell. These are the more complex insects such as ants and moths. The four-sensed *jivas* are the living beings which lack only hearing. Gnats, flies, and mosquitoes are listed in this group. And the five-sensed *jivas* include animals, man, *devas* (divine beings), and *narakas* (hellish beings). But *jivas* of every class are equal in the sense that the destruction of a *jiva* can only be described as murder.

The Jain is therefore confronted with a terrible situation: he must live in such a manner as not to kill any *jiva*, yet this is impossible. There seems to be no way in which he can avoid eating plants, stepping on insects, and injuring air and stones. Jain monks have at various times ceremonially swept the path in front of them in order not to crush insects, strained water through a sieve to remove all living bodies, worn a cloth mask to avoid squeezing the air painfully, and even refrained from clapping their hands, but complete noninjury (*ahimsa*) is impossible. Therefore, compensation by a starvation death has been recommended, and is frequently practiced. *Ahimsa* is the religion of the Jains, but the sad fact is that complete *ahimsa* is an ideal that can be approximated but never realized. The situation is somewhat relieved through the possibility of doing acts resulting in merit (*punya*). This can be accomplished by giving food to the hungry, by providing shelter for travelers, by speaking without hurting another's feelings, and even by thinking well of others. Jainism tends to become a form of keeping accounts, of insuring that one's merits exceed one's sins (*papas*). The sins are catalogued with *himsa* (injury) at the top of the list. The most revealing of the sins is the sin of becoming overfond of anything or any person. One Jaina scripture advises, "Man! You are your only friend! Why wish for any friend other than yourself?"

Mahavira made his movement and his *marga* understandable by formulating vows for the laity and for the ascetics. The twelve vows for laymen and laywomen were: (1) Never intentionally to destroy a *jiva* of more than one sense. (2) Never to speak great falsehoods. (3) Never to steal. (4) Never to be unfaithful in marriage nor unchaste outside marriage. (5) Never to possess more than a specified amount of money—the amount to be agreed upon by the individual. (6) Never to travel beyond geographical limits set by the individual. (7) Never to possess more than what one needs. (8) Never to think evil of others. (9) A vow to sit in meditation a certain number of times. (10) A vow to limit activities to certain agreed-upon areas. (11) A vow to spend some time as a temporary monk or nun. (12) A vow to support the community of ascetics.

The vows of monks and nuns were similar, although more rigorous, e.g., an agreement not to destroy any living thing, and an agreement not to speak any untruth. The monk also vowed to limit his food to thirty-two mouthfuls a day. The vow of chastity made Jainism the first to introduce celibacy as a religious ideal into India. The overriding concern of Jainism is the notion of setting restraints and limits on the life of the individual, and the interesting point is that the concern is limitation for limitation's sake rather than a concern for just what those limits are. There is also the curious unexpressed idea that while it is better to do good than to do evil, the doing of good is so fraught with possibilities of evil that the best course may be to do nothing! Jainism as a great do-it-yourself religion rejected gods as agents of salvation and placed man in full control of his own life. It rejected the notion that *brahmins* are superior as a class, although it did seem to hold that a person by his own individual effort could become superior to others. The notion of the balancing of merits and sins opened the door to extreme forms of bodily punishment (*tapas*). It was this in part which split Jainism about five hundred years after Mahavira into two sects, viz., the Digambaras, who held that the monks could not wear any clothes but must become indifferent to the cold of winter and the heat of summer, and the Shvetambaras, who held that monks could wear clothes. The Digambaras also countermanded Mahavira's original liberal attitude toward women by decreeing no woman can attain liberation.

Jainism not only opposed monism with dualism and pluralism but also spirituality with materiality. The Jaina conception of *karma* is a case in point. *Karma*, according to the Jains, is a sticky stuff which clings to the *jiva*, weighing it down so the *jiva* must be reincarnated rather than ascend to the top of the universe to dwell eternally in Isatpragbhara.

Jainism had many spinoffs. One of the most extreme was that known as Ajivika (the living). Its founder was Makkhali Goshala, who at one time was a disciple of Mahavira. Goshala broke from

Mahavira after a very simple incident. One day when Mahavira and Goshala were walking together, Mahavira called attention to a sesamum plant by the roadside and said that when they returned later that day the plant would have seven flowers. Goshala, in an effort to discredit his master, secretly pulled up the plant, but when they returned it had rerooted itself and had seven flowers. This convinced Goshala of the inevitability of destiny (*niyati*). He decided that if everything is destined then the effort to attain liberation as prescribed by Mahavira was without foundation. He left Mahavira, abandoned all speech, engaged in the most rigorous *tapas,* and practiced black magic. He is reputed to have attained such magical powers as a result of sitting for six months facing the sun with his arms over his head that he was able to burn down whole villages with his curses. One day he angrily returned to Mahavira to denounce him with the curse that he would die in six months, but Mahavira turned the curse back upon Goshala with the prediction that Goshala would die in seven days—which he did.

The asceticism of the Ajivikas was extreme. The monks went completely nude throughout the year. They begged for their food, and were not allowed to carry even a begging bowl. The drinking of cow urine was obligatory. Initiation rites included the plucking of the hairs of the head one by one by the members of the order while the initiate stood in a pit, the holding of hot metal in the hands, and the breaking of a bone or the cutting of a muscle. Consequently, many of the Ajivika monks were cripples. One ceremony required the severing of a finger in order to attain flowing blood for the increase of psychic power. Lying on beds of thorns, living in earthen vessels, and swinging upside down from trees were other methods for augmenting magical powers. As roving bards they used to dance and sing on special occasions. A natural death was disparaged; suicide was a requirement.

Ajivika died out in the fourteenth century, but Jainism survives in India, and today it has about two million adherents including some of India's wealthiest and most influential families. Jainism remains a rigid religion, refusing to adapt to changing times. Its doctrine of *ahimsa* continues to have a meliorative effect on all Indians.

Buddhism

The third organized protest against the *brahmins,* their sacrifices and their teachings, was Buddhism, and it also appeared in the *Kshatriya-*dominated eastern end of the Ganges valley. The many similarities between the lives of Vardhamana and the Buddha once caused Indologists to speculate that one borrowed from the other, but there are few who support this view today. Although similar in some respects, Buddhism and Jainism are considered to be separate challenges to the religion of the *Samhitas,* the *Brahmanas,* the *Aranyakas,* and the *Upanishads.*

That a man who came to be called "The Buddha" lived at the eastern end of the Ganges valley in the sixth century B.C. has been established beyond reasonable doubt, but how he lived and what he taught are beyond reconstruction. The Buddhists have lovingly woven so many legends and myths around him and have prefaced so many of their ideas with "The Buddha said . . ." that it is folly to separate fact and fiction. For example, he is said to have been the son of a rajah so wealthy that he was able to provide three palaces for the young prince, one for each season of the year, but this may be only the devotees' way of saying that he was the son of a laborer so poor that he followed the monsoon in order to work in the fields and that he could provide no home other than the laborers' huts. But we cannot demythologize the stories until we have more external evidence, so we must repeat what the devoted minds and hearts of his followers have recounted.

He was born Siddhartha Gautama in the city of Kapilavastu in what is now southern Nepal about one hundred miles from Banaras. His father was a rajah. His mother—appropriately named Maha-Maya (Great Illusion)—died seven days after his birth. Although the conception and the birth were attended by miracles, it is interesting to note that the stories of his childhood, unlike those of Krishna, are relatively free from the preternatural. This is in keeping with the common insistence of Buddhists that it is the teachings, not the life, of the Buddha which should be honored and followed. According to the scriptures he was a precocious child, asking questions far exceeding what was expected from a boy of his age. When he began to show signs that he was not planning to follow his father as rajah of the small kingdom, the father attempted to revive his zest for living by securing a beautiful wife for him and by ensuring that the young prince never see an aged person, an ill person, a corpse, or a monk, on the hypothesis that if he never saw these limitations of human joy he would be unaware of the conditions of mortal existence. Of course the plot failed, and at age twenty-eight or twenty-nine Siddhartha broke from the householder life, assumed the life of a homeless wanderer, and began a six-year quest for the meaning of human existence. He tried the way of *Brahmin* knowledge and the way of *tapas*. He abused his body without mercy. His diet of a few grains of rice a day reduced him until, as he reported, "When I placed my hand on my stomach, I had my backbone in my hand." When he realized he was making no progress in either method, he took food and quietly thought his way through to a solution.

The solution to which Siddhartha came was regarded by him and by his followers as more than a reasoned conclusion—it was a revelation, an enlightenment, a *bodhi*. Hence, he was called the Enlightened One, the Buddha. The Buddha, unlike the mystics of most cultures who contend that the content of their vision is esoteric, made his enlightenment public in his Deer Park Sermon at Banaras. He devoted the remaining forty-five years of his life to instructing others in his Four Noble Truths. The Buddha as a teacher was a genius. Whether his enlightenment came to him in the systematic manner in which he taught is open to question, but the manner in which he taught made his challenge to the Vedic tradition clear and persuasive. Buddhists have never departed from the fundamentals of the Four Noble Truths and the Eight-fold Noble Path.

The pattern of the presentation of the Four-fold Truth took the form of the Indian medical diagnosis which we have already noted. The First Noble Truth is the sickness of the human life, a sickness which men feel but find difficult to express in words. The Buddha found the word for it—and the word is *"duhkha."* Although *"duhkha"* is often translated as "suffering," words like "impermanence," "transitoriness," and "incompleteness" express more of its flavor. *Duhkha* is the frustration rooted in the existential awareness of the temporal, unfinished, and imperfect nature of all human experiences. We look in vain for the permanent, the fully satisfying. The cause of this universal human frustration is *upadana*, the clinging to objects of desire. It is not wrong to desire good food and drink, fine clothes, pleasant stimulation of the senses, human companionship, and sex, but it is morally wrong and psychologically destructive to cling to these satisfactions of normal desire. This clinging or grasping is the meaning of *upadana*. This is the Second Noble Truth. The Third Noble Truth is that since *upadana* is a natural cause and *duhkha* a natural effect, there must be a natural way of dealing with the cause and thus eliminating the effect. The Fourth Noble Truth outlines the practical method of dealing with the *upadana* of life, and thereby curtailing or eliminating the *duhkha* of life insofar as this is humanly possible. In original Buddhism man was advised to expect no assistance from any external source. There were no gods or transhuman agents to help. Each human being was to work out his own salvation. The way of liberation from *duhkha* was outlined as an Eightfold Noble Way: proper understanding, proper attitude, proper speech, proper action, proper vocation, proper efforts, proper reflection, and proper meditation.

Proper understanding is the recognition that there is no unchanging reality beneath or behind the changes man experiences. The external world is *anicca*; i.e., it has no duration or permanence. There is no *sat* (being); all is becoming. The internal world is *anatman* (no self); there is no substance which can be called a person. "Person" or "self" are names given to modes of behavior associated with an individual body. In place of *sat* (being), *chit* (consciousness), and *ananda* (bliss), the Buddha substituted *anicca* (no duration), *anatman* (no self), and *duhkha* (no bliss). Whereas the Upanishadic *rishis* taught that the real world is a fixed reality which appears as changing, the Buddha taught that the real world is perpetual change which appears as fixed. One of the favorite examples of Buddhist teachers is that of a firebrand which when twirled rapidly gives the appearance of a ring of fire. Proper understanding is knowing that the ring of fire is the apparently stable but in fact illusory appearance of the changing reality. This theory of reality when applied to the self became the crucial problem for Buddhism; for if the goal of Buddhist endeavor is *nirvana*, i.e., the state of emancipation from incarnation, then what is it that is set free if "self" is only a name for a phenomenal functioning of the body?

Proper attitude means that the individual must discipline himself so thoroughly and so completely that he finds it impossible to wish that things be other than they are. After long and intensive training he will no longer have even the slightest wish for a substratum behind the fleeting expressions. He will not wish for a god, a priest, or a sacrifice upon which to depend for help. He is to become fully determined to pursue his own liberation and to allow no obstacles to stand in his way.

The first two Noble Truths constitute the wisdom portion of the Eight-fold Noble Way. They link together thought and volition. The Buddha as philosopher did not ignore human animality, and as psychologist did not ignore human rationality.

The next three items in the Eight-fold Noble Way deal with the moral dimension. The Buddhist on the way to *nirvana* must guard his speech, since words lead to action. In his action the Buddhist refrains from injury to living things, from stealing, from sexual immorality, from lying, and from "liquors which engender slothfulness." The third of this group is the advice to enter only those vocations appropriate to the entire plan of the life of the Buddhist.

The last three portions of the Eight-fold Noble Way attempt to deal as pragmatically with the concentration practices of the Buddhist as do the first two with the rational and the affective and the next three with the ethical. Through proper efforts, reflection, and meditation the Buddhist is expected to progress to the state of *nirvana*. Despite the Buddha's dying admonition to work out one's own salvation, it would not be correct to assume that *nirvana* is accomplished merely by following the recipe. The Eight-fold Noble Way leads to *nirvana*, but it does not guarantee it. *Nirvana* is realized—and realization stands somewhere between production and discovery. The details have been disputed ever since the departure of the Buddha.

The Buddhist therapy may be described as psychological rather than philosophical. According to tradition the Buddha refused to engage in discussions about the eternity or noneternity of the cosmos, the finitude or infinitude of the world, the identity or nonidentity of the human self and the human body, and the survival or nonsurvival beyond death of the enlightened person. His refusal was based on the grounds that such metaphysical questions sidetrack man from the real problem of doing something practical about the miserable condition of human existence. The Buddha was determined not to fall into the error of Upanishadic seers: the error of offering philosophical speculations to people seeking a remedy for existential anxiety.

The Buddha, like Mahavira, organized a group of dedicated celibates; unlike Mahavira, he was reluctant to allow an order of nuns, but eventually he did. The lay followers of the Buddha were not as well organized as were the Jaina laymen. During his lifetime the Buddha began the practice of meeting with the monks during the rainy season to teach and to plan strategy. The practice has been continued in Buddhism, although not at regular intervals. Two such congregations within the century after his passing settled the problem of the basic scriptures, the *Tripitaka*, but they also provoked serious differences of opinion which ultimately divided the Buddhist community into the conservatives and the liberals, i.e., the Theravadas and the Mahayanas. When King Ashoka embraced Buddhism in the third century B.C., he did not establish Buddhism as a state religion in any Western sense. The difference was that for the first time an Indian monarch assumed that he had obligations and responsibilities for his people. His concern as a Buddhist for the lives of animals was not welcomed by the sacrificial priests, but it was by the peasants whose flocks and herds had been plundered by monarchs seeking benefactions through the ancient blood and fire sacrifices. Ashoka sent Buddhist missionaries to Ceylon and probably to Mesopotamia and the Mediterranean area. The strength of Buddhism and Jainism in India at this time is indicated in the fact that of more than fifteen hundred inscriptions belonging to the period 200 B.C. to A.D. 300 fewer than fifty are non-Buddhist or non-Jaina. It was in the fifth century A.D. that the famous University of Nalanda was founded, a Buddhist institution to which students came from many countries. But by the seventh century Buddhism had begun to decay in India. The introduction of Tantric practices, often of debased sexual forms, was one of the factors in its growing unpopularity. Another was that by taking a receptive attitude toward other religions, Buddhism became assimilated into Hinduism; e.g., the Vaishnavites made the Buddha an *avatara* of Vishnu. A third factor in the decline and fall of Buddhism in India was the invading Muslims. They destroyed many monasteries and murdered the monks. Today Buddhism flourishes in eastern Asia, but in India it is largely a memory.

Charvaka, Jainism, and Buddhism were the chief challenges which the *brahmins* faced from the east from the sixth century B.C. onward. The challenges were not entirely negative, for we read of *brahmins* who, after completing their studies in the west, went down the Ganges to learn from eastern intellectuals their interpretations of the sacrifices and the *Upanishads*. They must have found the interpretations too radical for their tastes. Although the Jains and the orthodox interpreters of the Vedic tradition shared similar views of the self and of the importance of *tapas,* both Jains and Buddhists disagreed with the orthodox on such matters as *shruti,* Brahman, the ceremonies, and the rising class distinctions. The possibility of finding a meeting of minds with the Charvaka philosophers must have been fruitless. The *brahmin* monopoly had been broken in the east.

CHAPTER 8

Bhagavata

The eastern end of the Ganges valley was not the only area from which early challenges to the religion of the *Upanishads* originated. In the west the Upanishadic authors in rebelling against the elaborate and mechanical systems of sacrifice and ceremony had established a pattern of change within their own ranks. Moreover, since intermarriage between Aryan males and non-Aryan females was common, many Vedic Hindus were exposed to foreign gods and strange religious rituals in their own households. Worshipers of *yakshas* (vegetation spirits) and *nagas* (snake gods) remained in the forests and valleys. Tribal gods were still worshiped along the Ganges and the Jumna, but in general Brahminism and Upanishadic learning were well established in the west. The challenge was to come from those who found meaning in the worship of personal gods and who could not identify with an impersonal Absolute to be realized through a very special form of knowing. The sacrifices also were challenged in the west, although the grounds were their inefficacy rather than the sanctity and equality of all forms of life. The western challenge, like the eastern, came from the *Kshatriyas*. Jainism was developed by the Jñatrika tribes, Buddhism by the Shakya tribes, and Bhagavata by the Satvata tribes.

The Western Challenge

The western challenge was less radical than the eastern, but its impact on Hinduism was in the long run greater because, unlike

Charvaka, Jainism, and Buddhism, it became completely assimilated within Hinduism as one of the principal cultic forms. Jainism and Buddhism offered a way of liberation from *samsara* by effort: Jainism required self-restraint and *tapas,* and Buddhism demanded careful attention to one's thoughts, words, feelings, and actions. But the path offered in the west was the easy path of *bhakti.* Single-minded devotion to God would be followed by the gift of grace (*prasada*) from the deity, as was promised so beautifully in the *Gita*:

> Give me your whole heart
> Love and adore me,
> Worship me always,
> Bow to me only,
> And you will find me:
> This is my promise
> Who love you dearly.

> Lay down all duties
> In me, your refuge.
> Fear no longer,
> For I will save you
> From sin and bondage.[1]

The way of *bhakti* was not a post-Vedic creation in the western end of the Ganges, for the germ of the idea can be traced in many of the Vedic hymns. All of the Vedic deities, with the possible exception of Rudra, were beneficent. On the principle of *dehi me dadami te* (I give to you that you may give to me) the *devas* were believed to confer upon man that which made life good. Varuna, above all the *devas,* was responsive to man's devotion:

> If we have sinned against the man who loves us,
>   have ever wronged a brother, friend, or comrade,
> The neighbor ever with us, or a stranger, O Varuna,
>   remove from us the trespass.

> If we, as gamesters cheat at play, have cheated, done
>   wrong unwittingly or sinned of purpose,
> Cast all these sins away like loosened fetters, and,
>   Varuna, let us be thine own beloved.[2]

The term *"bhakti"* appears first in Hindu literature at the close of the *Shvetashvatara Upanishad* when the *rishi* says that the condition for receiving liberating knowledge is that one have "the highest devotion (*bhakti*) for God," [3] but, as we shall note in the next chapter, this late *Upanishad* is unique in its teaching of the existence of a personal god. For the most part, the way of *bhakti* is not Upanishadic teaching.

The religion which arose to challenge the religion of the *Upanishads* in the west was a monotheistic religion of devotional love for god. The name of the religion is "Bhagavata," which seems to mean merely that which relates to god. The specific geographical area was the city of Mathura and the surrounding region, and the people were a number of cow-herding tribes. The god was called Krishna or Vasudeva or Vasudeva-Krishna. There is so much uncertainty and conjecture about Krishna as compared with the core of reliable historical data for Gautama and Vardhamana that the place to begin in trying to follow the development of Bhagavata is to look for evidence that there actually was a Krishna-worshiping people. Fortunately, we do have reliable evidence. An inscription discovered at Besnagar records the erecting of a column in honor of Vasudeva, "the god of gods." In the inscription the man who erected the column is named—Heliodora—and he is identified as a Bhagavata. Also in the inscription the name "Amtalikita" is found, which is probably the Antialkidas of Bactro-Greek coins, and, if so, this would date the erection of the column in the second century B.C. A second external evidence comes from the records of Megasthenes. He wrote about the worship of "Herakles" by a tribe he called "Sourasenoi" which he located at "Methora" near the "Jobares" river. The *Kshatriya* tribe called Shurasenas was located at this time at Mathura on the Jumna. A reference to a "Krishna" in *Chandogya Upanishad* 3. 17. 6, who is identified as the son of Devaki and the pupil of a *rishi* named Ghora Angirasa, ought not to be taken seriously as a reference to the Krishna of Mathura since the word "Krishna" meaning black was a name commonly given a dark child in a family. Indologists have speculated that Krishna was a solar deity associated with Surya, that he was a vegetation deity, and that he was a hero or king elevated to divine status in the stories built around him. The matter which concerns us, however, is that there was a Krishna-worshiping cult in the west which challenged the religions of sacrifice and knowledge at about the same time that a second challenge was being made in the east.

The Pañcharatra

The term "Pañcharatra" (five nights) is associated with the western challenge. Pañcharatra may denote a ceremony lasting five days and five nights, or it may be a corruption of *pañcharatha* (five vehicles, ways, or paths), which could indicate the syncretism of five monotheistic religions. The latter seems plausible since there were five religions, each directed to the worship of a single god in the vicinity of Mathura.

The first of these monotheistic religions was the worship of a very ancient *deva* who was probably of Indo-European origin, a *deva* named Bhaga. He is mentioned in the *Rig,* but his function is indistinct. We can assume from his name that he had something to do with the bestowing of wealth, and we are also informed that he presided over marriages. In *Rig* 2. 17 Agni is praised as a *bhaga,* i.e., as one who rules over wealth. Wealth and the sun are associated, and the worship known as Bhagavata around Mathura on the Jumna River appears to have developed from an ancient sun worship. The term "Bhagavat" came to mean one who graciously disposes wealth, and as such was applied to several gods, especially Vishnu. The composite religion resulting from the union of many religions in the Mathura area came in time to be called Bhagavata, the religion of graciousness.

Another of the "five ways" was the religion known as Ekantika (one presence), a term which also was used as an alternate title for the Bhagavata religion. Ekantika was an ancient, anti-Vedic monotheism. Its deity was a god of youth. The worshipers were known as Krishnas (blacks). According to the *Rig* the Krishnas were bitter foes of the Aryans, which probably means only that they fought well in defending their land against the invaders. The religion of the Krishnas was a conservative religion, and, although opposed to the

Vedic tradition, it was finally accepted within developing Hinduism as it presented no serious threat to the status quo.

The third monotheistic religion of the Pañcharatra was known as Narayaniya. The *rishi* assigned to the *Purusha* Hymn (*Rig Veda* 10. 90) was named Narayana, and therefore in time the term was used to denote *Purusha* as the Cosmic Soul, the Supreme Being in the universe. "*Purusha* is verily all this visible world, all that is, and all that is to be; he is also the lord of immortality," [4] sang the *rishi*. In *Mahabharata* 12. 346 the *rishi* Narada goes to see the Supreme God Narayana, and is surprised to discover Narayana engaged in religious rites. He wishes to know to whom the Supreme God pays religious devotion. Narayana replies that he is worshiping his original form, the source of all that is: "There is no one that is superior to me. Who is there whom I myself may worship or adore with rites? Who, again, is my sire in the universe? I myself am my grandfather. I am, indeed, the grandsire and the sire. I am the one cause of all the universe." The worshipers of Narayana were called Narayaniyas, and in the course of the development of Vaishnavism the name of the god became one of the most revered names for Vishnu.

A fourth monotheistic group which contributed to the Bhagavata religion was called the Vaikhanasas after the *rishi* Vaikhanas. Their chosen deity was Vishnu, and their special form of adoration was in living the life of a recluse. Both male and female anchorites dedicated themselves with purity of conduct to their god. Although many of the Vaikhanasas were assimilated into Bhagavata, some remained as members of an independent cult until the seventh century A.D. Their contributions to temple worship and iconography were outstanding.

The fifth group of the Pañcharatra was the Satvata, a non-Aryan and non-Vedic people who specialized in black magic and sorcery. They appear to have come from the aboriginal tribes and to have had disdain for *brahmins*. Among their primitive rites was a ceremonial branding.

These five religions had sufficient commonality for them in time to merge into one. All of them appear to have originated in connection with some form of sun worship. All of them inclined to monotheistic worship of a god who was benevolent and who was anxious to bestow gracious gifts upon his devotees. They all agreed in condemning both the Vedic fire and blood sacrifices with their accompanying austerities and penances and the Upanishadic approach to man's liberation from *samsara*. But one element was missing which could bring the five religions into unity: that was a common legend. This was supplied by the stories of Krishna which had been growing around the city of Mathura.

The Early Krishna Legends

Krishna was probably non-Aryan, and certainly non-Vedic and non-*Brahmin*. Thus his popularity was a serious challenge to *shruti*-minded Hindus. Perhaps only in Hinduism could a god so out of step with traditional views and values become the most beloved of the gods. The stories about Krishna have appealed so intensely to the imaginations of Hindus that they have been told and retold, altered and augmented for almost two thousand years. The earliest stories go back to the century of the Buddha, and additions were made as late as the sixteenth century A.D. under the stimulus of Chaitanya. We shall consider in this chapter only those circulating at the beginning of the fourth century A.D. The stories begin with a king of the solar line named Yayati, a king who ruled so wisely and so well that no one in his kingdom was ill, no one was evil, and no one died. When Yama, the lord of death, complained to Indra that none came to his palace from the kingdom of Yayati, Indra sent Kama, the god of love, to excite the passions of the king and thus to cause him to rule unwisely. Under the influence of Kama the king fell in love with Devayani, the daughter of a priest, and married her. From this marriage of a *Brahmin* woman and a *Kshatriya* man came Yadu, the ancestral king of a lunar line, who is referred to in the *Rig* as a slave. The *rishi* Durvasas placed a curse upon Yadu for an unfilial act, a curse which predicted that his posterity would not rule long in the land. Yadu married the five daughters of a serpent king named Dhumavarna (smoke-colored), and from this polygynous marriage sprang the tribe known as the Yadava, into which in due time Krishna was born. All Yadavas or Yadus, according to the Vedic *brahmins*, were *daityas* (aboriginals), but they were not uniformly condemned in the Vedas. This can probably be accounted for by the fact that warfare in northern India was one in which there was continual reshuffling of foes and comrades in arms.

According to the legends which grew up among the cow-tending tribes around Mathura, Ugrasena, the king of Mathura, affianced his daughter Devaki to Vasudeva, the son of Shurasena, the king of the Yadus. Devaki thus joined the harem of Vasudeva, which consisted of seven sisters. The youngest of the seven was Rohini. Shortly after the marriage Kamsa, the brother of Devaki, imprisoned their father, King Urgasena, and made himself king. But the tyrant's peace of mind was disturbed by a prophecy of the sage Narada that he would die by the hand of one of Devaki's sons. Kamsa, determined that this would not happen, killed each son of Devaki and Yasudeva at birth. Six male children were thus dispatched. Before the birth of the seventh son Yasudeva magically transferred the foetus from the womb of Devaki to that of Rohini. Thus was born the fair-complexioned Balarama. Kamsa, sensing that something was amiss, took extra precautions during the next pregnancy of his sister. When birth was imminent, he imprisoned and chained both Devaki and Vasudeva. But when the dark-skinned Krishna was born at midnight, the chains fell from Vasudeva, and the prison guards passed into an unnaturally deep sleep. Vasudeva took the child out of the city and across the Jumna—later legends say the river parted so the crossing was on dry land—and gave the child to a couple named Nanda and Yashoda in exchange for a girl that had just been born to them. He brought the girl back to the prison and placed her in the arms of his sleeping wife. When Kamsa realized he had been tricked, he ordered a massacre of all male children. Krishna escaped because by this time Nanda and Yashoda had moved with the cattle herders to the green pastures of Brindaban. There Krishna grew to manhood in the company of cowherds and milkmaids. The stories of the boyhood of Krishna are among the favorites of Hindus, even among those who do not worship Lord Krishna. The boyhood stories were added to the legend about the first century A.D. when a tribe called the Abhivas moved into the area. One of the early stories of Krishna's childhood was that the demoness Putana took the form of a nursing mother and offered her breast to the infant after she had covered it with deadly poison, but the infant Krishna was not affected by the poison. Instead, he held tightly to the breast and drained the demoness of both milk and blood. When another demon attempted to destroy Krishna, he kicked it with such force that the demon died. A five-headed serpent who dwelt in a pool in the Jumna was defeated by the boy in combat; the serpent was allowed to escape to the ocean on condition that it never return again. A story of a mortal combat between Krishna and Indra is demythologized as a replacement of food-gathering and plunder by agriculture and domesticity.

The Krishna legends which have had the most influence in the shaping of the cult were those about his boyhood pranks and his youthful dalliances with the milkmaids. As a boy he was given to mischievousness. He developed a great appetite for butter and frustrated every effort of his foster mother to restrain him, but when she brought herself to the point of punishing him, she always broke down in forgiving love. By the fourth century A.D. stories began to circulate about the love of the milkmaids (*gopis*) for Krishna, but it was not until the composition of the *Bhagavata Purana* in the ninth and tenth centuries that the erotic exploits of Krishna were delineated. Two forms of love were offered as the pattern of *bhakti* devotion: maternal love and sexual love.

The early legends report that when Krishna and his heroic brother, Balarama, left Brindaban, they went to Mathura, where, after fighting giants, demons, and beasts, Krishna slew his uncle Kamsa according to the prophecy and established a Yadu on the throne. Krishna lived for a time in Mathura before setting out to establish his own kingdom in Dvaraka. His exploits were those befitting a culture hero, except for the fact that some are of dubious morality. For example, in the great battle between the Pandavas and the Kauravas on one occasion when Drona, the military leader of the Kauravas, had almost vanquished the Pandavas, Krishna sent a false message to Drona that his beloved son had been killed. When Drona heard this, he lay down his arms and thus became an easy prey to the Pandavas. Again when Arjuna was nearly defeated in single combat with Karna, the chariot of Karna suffered an accident to the wheel. Karna dropped his weapons and asked Arjuna to stay his hand while he repaired the wheel, but, when Arjuna stopped fighting in accord with the customary rules of warfare, Krishna urged him on, and Arjuna decapitated the defenseless Karna while he was working on his chariot. Such blemishes in the character of Krishna are difficult to explain. At last Krishna's luck turned, and he was killed in a manner Greek rather than Indian: a hunter, mistaking him for a deer, shot an arrow at him and hit him in his one vulnerable spot—his foot.

The bodies of Krishna, his father Vasudeva, and his brother Balarama were cremated in the same funeral pyre. According to the legend, some of their wives threw themselves on the pyre in the rite of *suttee* (widow immolation), a rite which was unknown at the eastern end of the Ganges until the sixth century A.D. After the funeral the sea rose and engulfed Dvaraka, thus fulfilling the ancient prophecy of Durvasas that the rule of the Yadus would not last long.

The Krishna legend gave to Bhagavata a common god and a common story to which other stories could be attached. Thus it could offer a viable alternative to the Upanishadic speculations and the Vedic sacrifices. But more than this, it could offer a new soteriology. Jainism and Buddhism offered the way of effort. Bhagavata offered the way of *bhakti*.

Bhagavad Gita

One can argue either that the *Bhagavad Gita* is the most used and best loved scripture of Hinduism because it contains Krishna as its chief character or that Krishna is the best loved god because he is glorified in the *Gita*, the most popular book in Hinduism. At least the *Gita* is to be regarded as part of the historical upheaval which shook the ritualistic religion inherited from the *Samhitas* and the *Brahmanas* and the intellectualistic religion inherited from the *Aranyakas* and the *Upanishads*. Unlike Jainism and Buddhism it offered a way which could be assimilated easily within Hinduism. Some students of the *Gita* have said bluntly, "The *Gita* appeals to the masses." [5] This is true, but to state this without qualification is to misrepresent the *Gita*, because it is far more than a popularization of Hinduism designed to win the allegiance of the common people. There is something in the

Gita for everyone. The ways of action, thought, devotion, and *yoga* are presented and supported. It is a book for all the people, not solely for the lower classes. It is anthropocentrism at its best, since it accepts its hearers where they are and shows how they can within the broad limits of the path which is naturally theirs progress to the attainment of the highest good.

The date offered by scholars for the composition of the *Gita* ranges from the fifth to the second century B.C. It is an independent work which was later fitted into the *Mahabharata*. It has the honor of being the only *smriti* listed among the *prasthanatraya* (three great sources, literally three great supports) of the informed Hindu, the other two being the *Vedanta Sutras* of Badarayana and the ten or twelve principal *Upanishads*. The *Gita* has been widely praised, but for many different reasons. Shankara thought it was "an epitome of the essentials of the whole Vedic teaching," and in his commentary on 18. 66 expressed his opinion that the *Gita* teaches that "self-knowledge alone is the means to the highest bliss." Also in commenting on 2. 10 he wrote, "Thus it is clearly proved that in the *Gita* the cognition of Self-knowledge without any admixture of works is marked as the only path of liberation." Gandhi praised the *Gita* as a guide to works: "What effect the reading of the *Gita* had on my friends only they can say, but to me the *Gita* became an infallible guide to conduct. It became my dictionary of daily reference. Just as I turned to the English dictionary for the meaning of English words that I did not understand, I turned to this dictionary of conduct for a ready solution of all my troubles and trials." [6] Schweitzer, likewise, saw it as seeking recognition for the idea of self-devotion to God by action and as defending the "secular" life: ". . . an attempt to prove that the man who stays at home and follows his calling is able to attain the same holiness and redemption as the monk who goes forth to homelessness and devotes himself to inactivity." [7] D. D. Kosambi agrees that the teaching is on action, but he doubts the moral worth of the teaching: "The *Gita* with its brilliant Sanskrit and superb inconsistency is a book which allows the reader to justify almost any action while shrugging off the consequences." [8] And others contend that the *Gita* teaches the way of devotion to a loving god, e.g., "A greater and more ardent attempt is nowhere made to turn philosophy into practical religion and bring the individual and the universe into personal relation with a living god." [9] This is also the view of Edgerton: "And no means for attaining salvation is more emphasized in the *Gita* than *bhakti*, 'devotion to God, or fervent love of Him.' " [10] R. C. Zaehner agrees: "The revelation of the totality of God is very gradual, but for anyone who will but take the trouble to read the *Gita* from beginning to end—that is, in the order in which it was presumably written—the emergence of a loving God out of an impersonal Brahman in and out of the experience of liberation cannot fail to stand out." [11] R. D. Ranade once attempted to list the "labyrinth of modern interpretations" of the *Gita*. He concluded there are eight: (1) Interpolationism (Garbe, Holtzmann, Olden-berg, Schrader, Otto), (2) Devotionalism (Bhandarkar), (3) Chris-tianism (Lorinser, Weber, Lassen, Garbe, Farquhar, Edgerton), (4) Buddhism (Buddhiraja), (5) Activism (Tilak), (6) Numenism (Otto), (7) Detachment (Gandhi), (8) Divinization (Aurobindo).[12] E. W. Hopkins dismissed the *Gita* as "an ill-assorted cabinet of primitive philosophical opinions." [13] Brejendra Nath Seal observed, "Each commentator accepts those passages of the *Gita* which support his own preconceived dogma and distorts the meaning of the conflicting passages to harmonize them with his dogma." [14] Seal distinguished three interpretations of the *Gita*'s teachings on self-real-ization: (1) either knowledge or works or devotion as the sole way, or the way required by certain temperaments, (2) an eclecticism of the disciplines, and (3) a synthesis of the disciplines such that by stressing one the values inherent in the others may also be realized. The opinions on the *Gita* are obviously extremely diverse, but there is one about which there is no doubt as to its truth: Warren Hastings wrote in the preface to the first English translation (1875) that the *Gita* would "survive when the British dominion shall have long ceased to exist."

There is an aspect of the *Gita* to which insufficient attention has been called: this is the fact that the *Gita* is composed in the framework of an instruction about the means of attaining that which matters most. Krishna is the teacher (*guru*) and Arjuna is the pupil (*shishya*), and here, as in all *guru-shishya* relationships, the teaching is given in terms of *adhikara* (the pupil's competence) and *bhumika* (the pupil's stage of development). This means that the first teaching is the simplest rather than the most important, and that the last teaching is the most difficult—and possibly the most important and the one toward which earlier teachings point. This, in fact, is the way in which the *bhakti* message quoted at the opening of this chapter from the *Gita* is presented, for it is described both before and after the presentation as "the highest secret of all," "the wisdom which is the secret of secrets," "my supreme message," and "my supreme secret." In other words, the advice to love Krishna with one's whole heart is the *upanishad* of *upanishads*. This simple, but often omitted, observation about the composition of the *Gita* will help us understand the *Gita* both as a positive teaching and as a challenge to *karma-kanda* and *jñana-kanda*.

The *Gita* is not only the teaching of a divine guru, it is also a poem—The Blessed Lord's Song. It should therefore be read as a poem. To literalize it, e.g., to insist that it describes an actual battle, is to stress the inconsequential and, possibly, to miss the teaching. In the reading of poetry and myths Indians and Westerners suffer from different obstacles: the Indian is apt to be too gullible, too imaginative, too uncritical, and the Westerner is apt to be too historical-minded, too scientific-oriented. If the fault of Indians is to fail to see the relevance of demythologization, the fault of Western readers is to demythologize in such a manner as to fail to grasp the point of the myth.

In order to locate the dramatic situation of the *Bhagavad Gita* we must outline part of the story of the *Mahabharata*. The *Mahabharata* is the epic of India. Its position in Hindu culture is suggested in the fact that it is often called "the fifth Veda." It began as a simple epic narrative, but in time it became a veritable encyclopedia of popular Hinduism. The plot is almost lost in the moral teachings which are four times as long as the story. The *Mahabharata* is chaos both in plot and in teachings, yet it is the repository of much that is alive in Hinduism. The epic is the account of activities of the descendants of Bharata, the mythical hero for whom India is named. The Bharata tribe, whom some identify as the Dravidians, merged with other tribes, including the Kuru. The fifth in lineal descent from Bharata was Hastin, who established his capital, Hastinapura, on the Ganges in the modern district of Meerut. Many generations later Vyasa the king on the throne at Hastinapura impregnated two widows of his childless half-brother in accord with the ancient custom of *niyoga,* and thus were born the half-brothers Pandu and Dhritarashtra. Pandu as the elder assumed the throne upon the death of Vyasa, and upon his death Dhritarashtra became king at Hastinapura and took into his home the five sons of Pandu to rear with his own one hundred sons. The five, who are known in the *Mahabharata* as the Pandavas, and the one hundred, who are known as the Kauravas from the old tribe of Kurus, are to be understood in the epic as representing the ancient conflict between *devas* and *asuras*. The epic reminds us that according to Hinduism good and evil, gods and devils, come from the same source: Pandavas and Kauravas are grandsons of Vyasa and descendants of Bharata. More than this the five Pandavas are incarnations of Vedic deities: Yudhishthira of Dharma, Bhima of Vayu, Arjuna of Indra, and the twins Nakula and Sahadeva of the Ashvins. Among the Kauravas the eldest, Duryodhana, is Kali, the evil spirit of the Kali Yuga, the incarnation of *Adharma* (The Lie). The epic is not so much a contrast of good and evil as is sometimes supposed, but a conflict of greater evil and lesser evil. There are no white knights among the sons of Pandu and Dhritarashtra. There is one paradigm in the epic—Bhishma—and he is the head of the family representing the *asuras*. Bhishma embodies the *dharma* teachings of the *Gita* in that he acts out his role, fulfilling his duties unmindful of the results, which in his case is the ultimate victory of his opponents—a victory which he anticipated.

According to the epic the one hundred sons of Dhritarashtra became jealous of the Pandavas who were being reared in their midst. Duryodhana, the eldest of the sons of Dhritarashtra, made a palace of inflammable materials for the Pandavas and enticed them to move into it. Then he had the palace set on fire. But the Pandavas escaped and fled into the forest where they disguised themselves as priests in order to escape death at the hands of Duryodhana. After many years in disguise the Pandavas surfaced to engage in an archery contest in a neighboring kingdom in which the trophy was the daughter of the king. Arjuna won the contest and the princess Draupadi, but he was forced by the foolish words of his mother Kunti to share her with his brothers. Duryodhana, still bent upon the destruction of the Pandavas, challenged Yudhishthira to a gambling match. Yudhishthira, who had an uncontrollable urge to gamble, accepted the challenge, lost the kingdom, and finally was forced by reason of the loss of a wager to go into exile for twelve more years plus one year in which the Pandavas were to live unrecognized in the city. When at last the Pandavas had fulfilled all the stipulations of the wager, Duryodhana refused to give back their kingdom. Thus war broke out between the Pandavas and the Kauravas.

At this point Krishna enters the epic—or perhaps we should say that at this point the *Bhagavad Gita* has been inserted into the epic. Krishna is now clearly of divine status. According to the story, Arjuna, the military brain of the Pandavas, and Duryodhana went to Dvaraka to ask Krishna's aid in the forthcoming war, but Krishna had taken a vow not to enter actively into the war. However, he gave them the choice of either his army or himself. Duryodhana chose the army; Arjuna chose Krishna. The *Bhagavad Gita* begins at the eve of the first battle. Even though Krishna has vowed to serve in a noncombative role, he joins Arjuna in his war chariot. The lines of battle are drawn. Conch shells, drums, cymbals, and trumpets have sounded, and all is ready for the fight to begin. Suddenly Arjuna stays the chariot in order that he might look once again at the battle lines. He becomes aware that it is a family fight; blood relatives, teachers, and friends are on both sides. Arjuna drops his bow and announces to Krishna his charioteer that he will not give the signal to start the battle. Why should he lead men to their death so he can have an empire? Does power and happiness mean so much to him that he is willing to kill for it? The hedonic satisfactions of ruling a kingdom cannot outweigh the pain of the killing of kinsmen. It is better to be killed than to kill for such motives.

Krishna replies by reminding Arjuna that he is called "the scorcher of the foe." He adds that his words show some wisdom, but he is not wise in mourning for the dead or for the soon-to-be-dead. Bodies are killed, but the body is not the person. The inner reality, the true reality, the *Atman,* has never been born and will never die. Death comes to all bodies, but never to the *Atman.* But beyond this he reminds Arjuna that he is a warrior, and that to turn from battle is to reject his *dharma* (duty). Neither winning the kingdom nor not winning the kingdom is the issue. The only relevant question is whether one does the work which is his to do. Action should be done from a sense of duty without regard for the results of action. Man is so constituted that he must act. The important issue is the motivation of his action. Only the *dharma* act is right.

Thus Krishna the *guru* helped Arjuna discover his self-identity. Arjuna had been in such a state of mind that he had forgotten who he was. Ruling and warring both express and form the nature of a *Kshatriya*. The advice to kill, since killing merely destroys the body, was very inferior advice, but it was all that Arjuna was ready to receive in his highly emotional state at the opening of the battle.

Krishna then promised to instruct Arjuna in the discipline he had taught Manu the first man. This is the knowledge which enables a man to see Brahman in his action. Through this knowledge man learns that the Absolute can be realized in himself, in others, and in his chosen deity. Even the body can be trained so it becomes the instrument of realization of its identity with Brahman. Through yogic discipline and meditation it is possible to live in this world of delusion and illusion and still to know the Real.

Arjuna makes such progress that whereas he first asked, "How can I avoid playing my role as a *Kshatriya*?" he changes his question to "Show me beneath what forms and disguises I must learn to behold you. Number them all, your heavenly powers, your manifestations. Speak, for each word is immortal nectar. I never grow weary." Krishna begins, "I am the *Atman* that dwells in the heart of every mortal creature: I am the beginning, the life-span, and the end of all. . . . I am the divine seed of all lives. In the world, nothing animate or inanimate exists without me. There is no limit to my divine manifestations." But Krishna stops and asks, "Why do you need to know this? You need only to know that I am." However, Arjuna's readiness (*adhikara*) exceeded what Krishna offered, and he requested that he be granted a vision of the Absolute. At this point we have in the eleventh chapter of the *Gita* one of the rare attempts in literature to state the content of a theophany. Arjuna was privileged to behold "the entire universe, in all its multitudinous diversity, lodged as one being within the body of the God of gods."

This is clearly the high point of the *Gita* but it is not the denouement, for the *Gita* is a religious tract, not a philosophical one. Its purpose is to bring to ordinary men the values inherent in the liberating knowledge of the *Upanishads* which could be attained only by the seers. Therefore the *Gita* seeks to save men in their existential situation not from their existential situation, and so the remainder of the *Gita* brings Arjuna back from the heights of the vision to the world of his *dharma* accompanied by a god whom to love is to know. "United with me," Krishna assures Arjuna, "you shall overcome all difficulties by my grace. . . . The Lord lives in the heart of every creature. . . . Take refuge in him. By his grace you will find supreme peace and the state which is beyond all change." And Arjuna replies, "I will do your bidding."

The Gita as Bhagavata

The *Gita* was composed over several centuries. It is the work of many hands. Its inconsistencies, its contradictions, its undeveloped ideas, and its lack of logical development have often been pointed out. The *Gita* is not a systematic work; it is not even a scholarly work. Although it seems less confusing when considered as the teaching of a patient *guru* to an impetuous young military leader, we run into many difficulties in trying to trace a thread of argument throughout the work. It must be understood as Bhagavata religion in the making. Here for the first time in the Hindu tradition we find an exposition of a religion of loving devotion to a god who graciously bestows benefits upon his followers. This is popular religion, not the religion of sacrificial priests nor philosophical seers. This is a religion that appeals to the heart rather than to the hand or head. Bhagavata is *Ekantika Dharma,* a singular love and devotion to the Supreme Lord. There is no demand for fire and blood sacrifices, no austerities, no abstract thought—just devotion to the God of gods. The *Gita* does not solve the problems of human life, but it does attempt to put the problems in a different light. Work done with detachment and attempts to see Ultimate Reality in Its pure state are but propaedeutic to the path of union and loving communion with God. God enters the human condition. Arjuna does not need to step from his chariot to find Krishna. Man does not need to search for the divine. The Presence is with him and for him. This was totally new in Hinduism. The idea was too novel to be clearly expressed and too wonderful to be easily understood. It challenged the old ways of ritual and knowledge such that *brahmin* and *rishi* were never again to have the singular hold upon the religious life of India which they had enjoyed before Bhagavata. Bhagavata was the first of the *bhakti margas*—the first invitation to take refuge in the mercy of a forgiving god.

CHAPTER 9

Shvetashvatara

The Hindu religion may be divided into two large groups: orthodox or traditional Hinduism which claims to find its source in the *shruti* tradition—i.e., in the Vedic literature—and cultic or sectarian Hinduism which, while not neglecting *shruti*, contends that the great body of *smriti* literature must be added to the Vedic ideas and practices. The Bhagavata religion with its *Bhagavad Gita* is the foundation of the large collection of religions subsumed under the general heading of Vaishnavism with a common devotion to Vishnu. The second largest body of sectarian forms of Hinduism is Shaivism, the worship of Shiva or of gods associated with Shiva. Shaivism also takes its origin from the area of the western end of the Ganges watershed, and it also arose as challenge and reaction to *shrauta* sacerdotalism and intellectualism. In the absence of a name for this movement we shall use the term "Shvetashvatara" to designate the tendencies of thought, attitudes, and actions which culminated in the appearance of Shaivism. The term comes from the title of a late *Upanishad* which contains marked theistic tendencies. The importance of the *Shvetashvatara Upanishad* for Shaivism is suggested in the fact that it is sometimes referred to as a Shaivite *Bhagavad Gita*.

The Shvetashvatara Upanishad

The *Upanishad* known as the *Shvetashvatara* is unique among the Vedic writings. Max Müller described it as "the most difficult, and at

164

the same time one of the most interesting works of its kind." [1]
Shankara found its existence something of a problem, since its theism
did not square with his own monistic interpretation of the *Upanishads*. Consequently, Shankara felt the necessity of writing a long
introduction to the work in which he argued by leaning heavily on
smriti material that the *Shvetashvatara* is in truth monistic. Müller,
who was himself perhaps overly persuaded by Shankara, argued that
the *Upanishad* is not late and that it does not contain dualistic
elements. Recent scholars usually agree that it is late and that it does
contain dualistic and theistic elements. The *Shvetashvatara* gives
every appearance of being a work of arbitration. The author, in the
words of Radhakrishnan, was seeking "to reconcile the different
philosophical and religious views which prevailed at the time of its
conception." [2] He seems to have been reacting to the challenges
offered by the devotional monotheisms we examined in the previous
chapter. His problem was to find a *modus operandi* which would
preserve the Upanishadic insights in the face of demands for a
devotional religion.

The name of the *Upanishad* is the name of its author, the *rishi*
Shvetashvatara (white mule). The name probably means no more
than "the man who owns a white mule." Such animals were highly
prized in India from early times. There is no basis for reading color
prejudice nor indebtedness to white Syraic Christians into the term.
Although this work is classified as *shruti,* one may be able to
understand it better in a *smriti* context, because the tone is not
pontifical pronouncing but honest examining of inherited wisdom. It
opens with philosophical questions rather than with theological
affirmations: What sort of a cause is Brahman? What causes us to be
born into this world? What sustains our lives? Are there any beings
who rule over us and determine our destinies? What impact does
time, inherent nature, fate, and chance have upon us? Should the
physical elements, the womb, and the male contribution be considered as the only explanatory factors? The soul exists, continues the
rishi in dialogue with himself, but it is powerless with respect to
pleasures and pains. Man is not the determiner of his own destiny;
man is not an ultimate cause, even of his own life. There does seem
to be One that rules over events in the life of man, who from his own

self-power controls time rather than is controlled by time. At least this is the claim of those who have practiced yogic meditations.

The humility, the honest questioning, and the willingness to make a fresh start in seeking answers to fundamental questions about the human condition are features of the introduction to the *Shvetashvatara Upanishad* which make it a fascinating book to study. It gives the reader confidence that the author is going to be frank and fair, that he will not appeal to a *deus ex machina* to bail him out when he reaches a stalemate.

Man in his existential distress, continues the *rishi,* supposes he has three paths of liberation open to him: the path of wisdom (*jñana*), the path of religiousness (*dharma*), and the path of irreligiousness (*adharma*).[3] The first path is the path offered in the other *Upanishads:* the realization that our true nature is not *jiva* but *Atman,* and that *Atman* is Brahman. The third path—the path of irreligiousness —is the path of the *hoi polloi,* the unthinking masses, whose "philosophy" was systematized in the work of the Charvaka philosophers. This philosophy was also known as Lokayata, the view of the people of this world. It is a foolish way, adds the *rishi.* The second path—the path of religiousness—must refer to the paths of those, such as the followers of the Bhagavata, who worshiped a god from whom they expected gracious benefits. The impact of the *Shvetashvatara Upanishad* is to interpret the Brahman personally. As an *Upanishad* the *Shvetashvatara* supports knowledge as the means of salvation, but the object of knowledge is not Brahman-as-Absolute but Brahman-as-God. Six times in this short *Upanishad,* almost as a *mantra,* we read, "By knowing God one is released from all fetters." [4] The distinction between knowing and revering is not very sharply drawn, for the author also stresses devotion as a *marga:*

> The One who rules over every single source,
> In whom this whole world comes together and dissolves,
> The Lord, the blessing-giver, God adorable—
> By revering Him one goes for ever to this peace.[5]

The god of Shvetashvatara is a hidden god, but by the practice of meditation "one may see the God who is hidden, as it were." [6] The

personal names given to the god are Hara (The Bearer),[7] Agni
(Fire),[8] Aditya (The Sun),[9] Vayu (The Wind),[10] Chandra (The
Moon),[11] Bhagavat (The Supreme One),[12] Mahad Yashas (Great
Glory),[13] Rudra,[14] and Shiva.[15] The preferred name for the personal
Brahman in *Shvetashvatara* is Rudra (The Howler), or perhaps,
oxymoronically, Rudra-Shiva (The Kindly Destroyer). Rudra was
the Vedic *deva* of storms characterized by their unpredictability and
by dangerous aspects. Rudra was a god of appeasement. The *suktas*
addressed to him asked him to go away, rather than to come near. He
was a dread-inspiring god. Calling him Shiva (The Kindly One)
may have been a petition rather than the naming of an attribute. Yet
Rudra was both slayer and healer, destroyer and creator, and so he
remained when he became absorbed into Shiva, the god who danced
the dance of destruction-creation, the god who both ended a world
cycle and opened the next world cycle, the god of death whose
symbol is the *linga,* the organ of reproduction.

Brahman personalized is still One—the One without a second.
"The One . . . He is God!" [16] sang the *rishi* Shvetashvatara. This
oneness, however, shifts between the oneness of monism and the
oneness of monotheism, but the *rishi* seems to realize that he cannot
have it both ways, so the emphasis is on the immanence of god rather
than on the oneness of Absolute Totality. He is the god "who has
entered into the whole world." [17] He describes the immanence
poetically:

> Thou art woman. Thou art man.
> Thou art the youth and the maiden too.
> Thou as an old man totterest with a staff.
> Being born, thou becomest facing in every direction.
>
> Thou art the dark-blue bird and the green parrot with
>   red eyes.
> Thou hast the lightning as thy child. Thou art the
>   seasons and the seas.
> Having no beginning, thou dost abide with immanence,
> Wherefrom all beings are born.[18]

The statement that Rudra-Shiva faces in every direction is expressed in sculpture in portraying Shiva with five faces. The three eyes of Shiva—one for the past, one for the present, and one for the future—indicate his omniscience. The *Shvetashvatara* describes the god as "having an eye on every side and a face on every side, having an arm on every side and a foot on every side." [19] The adjective "supreme" (*parama*) is lavishly used: "the supreme Mighty Lord," "the supreme God of gods," "the supreme Ruler of rulers." [20]

Monotheistically, Rudra-Shiva is "the Creator of all," [21] "the maker of the creation and its parts," [22] and "the maker of both existence and non-existence." [23] It is he who created the Golden Germ (Hiranyagarbha) from which the world was born.[24] Monistically, Rudra-Shiva is that of which all things are made: "the source of all" [25] and "the origin of all beings." [26] From him all beings are born.[27] He is even "the source and origin of the gods." [28] At the close of the *Upanishad* in answer to the first question raised in the introduction, viz., "What is the cause?" the *rishi* affirms, "He [Rudra] is the Cause." [29] And again

> He who is the maker of all, the all-knower, self-sourced,
> Intelligent, the author of time, possessor of qualities,
>   omniscient,
> Is the ruler of Primary Matter and of the spirit,
>   the lord of qualities,
> The cause of reincarnation and of liberation, of
>   continuance and of bondage.[30]

This bifurcation of monism and monotheism runs throughout the *Upanishad*, and affords to the objective student valuable clues for understanding the problems faced by the seers who like Shvetashvatara tried to work out a position which would be true to the Upanishadic vision and still take seriously into account the devotional strains from the aboriginal peoples who were at this time making themselves more visible in the syncretic processes at work in northern India.

Rudra's functions do not end with creation, for he is also the support, ruler, protector, overseer, and guide of the world. "He is indeed the protector of the world in time, the overlord of all." [31] He is "the firm support, the Imperishable." [32] He "supports it all." [33] Emphasis is placed on Rudra as ruler: he rules over "both the perishable and the soul." [34] "The One spreader of the net, who rules with his ruling powers, who rules all the worlds with his ruling powers." [35] He is "the Protector," [36] "the embracer of the universe," [37] "the lord of biped and quadruped," [38] and "the overlord of the gods." [39]

Although Rudra creates the world, protects and guides the world on its course, is immanent in all the world, "surrounds the earth on all sides, and stands ten fingers' breadth beyond," [40] and merges with all beings at the end of time,[41] he does not make his presence overtly. He spreads "a net of illusion." [42] There is no likeness of him so that one can see him: "His form is not to be beheld. No one soever sees Him with the eye." [43] Rudra is the "illusion-maker" (*mayin*); Nature (*prakriti*) is illusion (*maya*)." [44] This is one of the few places in the *Upanishads* where the term *maya* is used in which the meaning is unquestionably that of the hiding of reality. Elsewhere where it appears, e.g., *Brihad-Aranyaka* 2. 5. 19, the notion is that of magical powers but not necessarily illusion. Although the individual in his normal powers cannot see Rudra, by practicing meditation (*dhyana*) he can see the hidden god.[45]

> By meditation upon Him, by union with Him, and by
>   entering into His being
> More and more, there is finally cessation from
>   every illusion (*maya-nivritti*).[46]

Meditation or devotional response to Rudra will destroy distresses, will satisfy the deepest desires of man, and above all will cause the cessation of birth and death.[47] Rudra is described as

> The One who rules over every single source,
> In whom this whole world comes together and dissolves,
> The Lord, the blessing-giver, God adorable—
> By revering Him one goes for ever to this peace.[48]

He is the god of grace (*prasada*).[49] He is bountiful and kindly.[50] Shiva is his name. And yet the prayers in the *Upanishad* reveal that the memories of Rudra the Vedic god who was sometimes malevolent have not been altogether eliminated:

> O dweller among the mountains, the arrow
> Which thou holdest in thy hand to throw
> Make kindly, O mountain-protector!
> Injure not man or beast! [51]

The devotee, remembering that Rudra has many faces, pleads,

> O Rudra, that face of thine which is propitious—
> With that do thou protect me ever!
> Injure us not in child or grandchild, nor in life!
> Injure us not in cattle! Injure us not in horses!
> Slay not our strong men in anger, O Rudra!
> With oblations ever we call upon thee. [52]

Max Müller, pointing out that the term *bhakti* appears only in the last stanza and that this portion is a later addition to the text, argued that the *Shvetashvatara Upanishad* does not present a *bhakti* approach to Rudra. This seems to be a strange argument in that it overlooks the fact that throughout the *Upanishad* the emphasis is on worshiping Rudra, meditating upon Rudra, and seeking Rudra's *prasada*. The next verse may be "a palpable addition," as Müller claimed, but the statement

> To one who has the highest devotion (*bhakti*) for God,
> And for his spiritual teacher even as for God,
> To him these matters which have been declared
> Become manifest if he be a great soul—
> Yea, become manifest if he be a great soul! [53]

is certainly in keeping with the teaching of the entire work. Knowing, worshiping, and being devoted to Rudra as the personal Brahman, the God of gods, is the thrust of this late *Upanishad*. Without devotion there will be no end of evil:

When men shall roll up space
As it were a piece of leather,
Then will there be an end of evil
Apart from knowing God.[54]

Rudra-Shiva

Why was Rudra, the god of the ruthlessness of nature, the power of the storm, and the destructiveness of lightning, chosen as the personalized Brahman? It was not because Rudra was one of the great gods of the *Vedas*. Although he is mentioned in many of the hymns of the *Rig*, he is invoked in only three hymns. While he is sometimes described as a god of good will, e.g.,

Let thy good will, O father of the Maruts,
Light on us: part us not from Surya's vision,[55]

he is more often suspected of displaying ill will toward men. A common petition was to leave man alone:

May Rudra's missile turn aside and pass us,
May the fierce Rudra's great ill will go by us.
Relax thy rigid bow to save our patrons;
Spare, O thou god of bounty, child and grandchild.[56]

He was the god who spread diseases among men and cattle, but he could also heal. His lightning destroyed, but it also purified. He was unpredictable, unfathomable, and unknowable. What *deva* could better symbolize the Brahman that is the negation of both *sat* and *asat* and also the negation of neither *sat* nor *asat*? A god who could not be established by rational categories was ideally suited to be correlated with the Absolute which could be best characterized by *neti, neti*.

Rudra gives every appearance of being a non-Aryan god. He was a *deva* who refused *soma* and who enjoyed blood. His name is said to come from a word meaning "to weep," but there is a high probability that it comes from *rudhira* (blood). He was the Bloody One. He was probably once appeased by nothing less than human sacrifices. The cults of Rudra-Shiva may go back to the Indus valley civilization; at least that was the claim of Sir John Marshall. He thought that the seal of "The Lord of the Animals" was an indication of a proto-Shiva worship in Mohenjo-daro. Today we are less convinced that this is the correct interpretation. The more common speculation is that Rudra was a Dravidian god who was adopted by the Hindus. He was a god of dark, wild, and awe-inspiring scenes: graveyards, dense forests, canyons, and caves. Sometimes he was the special god of thieves, cutthroats, and outlaws. Even after he was associated with Shiva, the dark side of his character remained, and to this day the Shaivite cults encourage a sentiment of fear and a feeling of the numinous toward their god, whereas the Vaishnavites look to their god with love and admiration.

There are a number of references to an early religion of Rudra worship. In the Narayaniya section of the *Mahabharata* a religious school called the Panchacratros is said to have been founded by Lakutin (or Lakulisha). Rudra is the supreme god in this religion. Panchacratros seems to have had the same relationship to the Rudra-Shiva cult that the Pancharatra had to the Vasudeva-Krishna cult. Patanjali, the author of the *Yoga Sutras* (second century B.C.), made the first reference we possess to a sect of Shaivites known as Shiva-Bhagavatas. In *Vayu Purana* 23 and in *Linga Purana* 24 there is recorded a legend that at the time of the birth of Krishna in Mathura the god Shiva entered a corpse in Kayavatara, the village of Karvan in Baroda. The appearance of Vishnu as a baby and Shiva as an animated corpse is suggestive of the difference of these two gods. This appearance of Shiva in a corpse is regarded by some as an *avatara* (incarnation) of Shiva, although *avataras* are usually associated only with Vishnu. One of the legends is that when his father, the Creator Brahmā, named him "Rudra," he also bestowed upon him seven other names: Bhava, Sarva, Ishana, Pashupati, Bhima, Urga, and Maha-deva. These seven are also said to be either the sons of Rudra or the manifestations (*avataras*) of Rudra. The claim for *avataras* for Shiva may indicate conflicts between these two early monothestic religions. When Rudra and Shiva became assimilated into Rudra-Shiva, Rudra acquired the 1008 names of Shiva. Moreover the iconography of the god became established: a five-faced figure with three eyes and four arms. In paintings he is shown with a blue neck. This is said to have been the result of the drinking of the poisonous scum which appeared when *devas* and *asuras* churned the ocean to rediscover the chalice of immortality and the other treasures which had been lost in the Deluge. His matted hair is gathered up like a horn, and contains within it the cresescent moon. The Ganges River is symbolically caught in his hair, reminding his worshipers of the legend of his having saved mankind on an occasion when the Ganges was released from heaven with the intention of destroying all mankind. His clothing is the skin of a tiger held in place by a serpent. He has an elephant skin cloak. All of these are trophies of ferocious fights with animals sent against him by jealous *rishis* whose wives had fallen in love with him. Thus Shiva became a god of tremendous vitality. He reached his apex in the tenth century in the conception of the Cosmic Dancer.

Although the worship of Rudra-Shiva began in northwest India and established itself at Banaras, it had spread throughout India by the time of the Christian era.

The Bhakti Element in Hinduism

The western challenge to *yajña* and *jñana* was to offer *bhakti* as an alternative to sacrifices and saving knowledge. It called attention to a devotional void in Hinduism. Intellectual vision was too sophisticated for the common people, and the Vedic rituals easily became a routine ceremonial program of cold bargaining. *Bhakti* changed Hinduism so that devotion in one form or another has been a distinguishing mark of living Hinduism since the third century A.D. Although *bhakti* is essentially the worship of a personal god, the "personal" characteristics have sometimes been regarded symbolically rather than literally. The success of Buddhism in India for many centuries is an indication that the Indian mind can indulge in moral discourses unassociated with a theistic faith, but the simultaneous outcropping of devotion in the west and the many outbursts of *bhakti* movements in India show that the Indians, like humans everywhere, cannot sustain themselves on barren intellectualism. Students of Indian philosophy who stress the remarkable profundity and perspicuity of the ancient Vedic *rishis* ought not to overlook the fact that during the centuries in which the *rishis* were seeking to penetrate behind the practice of rituals and the belief in gods to a metaphysical Absolute, others were approaching the mystery of life from a different perspective. These were the bards or poets (*sutas*) who lived in royal courts, and who sang of the heroic deeds of ancient warriors. They composed and kept alive the bardic poetry which was finally recorded in the great epics of India. They were generally outcasts from society who had been born of a *Brahmin* mother and a *Kshatriya* father. We can assume from the attitudes taken toward *sutas* that they were born out of wedlock, but as royal entertainers they often held favored positions in the courts. They must have been despised by some of the court followers, for the word "*suta*" came to mean "pimp," and one of the Sanskrit synonyms for prostitute was "wife of a *suta*." Since the *sutas* were jacks-of-all-trades including cooking, healing, and the training of elephants, it is not improbable that procuring may have been part of their services in the courts of kings. But their chief function was preserving and embellishing the folklore by presenting it to listeners in a form which was emotionally gratifying. Similar poets wandered from village to village singing songs of heroes and heroines.

The popular ballads which the *sutas* kept alive were the basis of the two great epics of India, the *Mahabharata* and the *Ramayana*. By the end of the third century A.D. both epics had been put into written form. The epics as collections of legends and semilegendary materials are called the *Itihasas* (this indeed it was). This term may indicate that the Hindus recognized the epics were folklore rather than records of historical events.

The *Mahabharata* was originally the story of Bharata, the legendary founder of all Indian families. It was chiefly on account of the war of annihilation between two familial lines which had descended from Bharata—the Kauravas and the Pandavas. In the alterations of the materials between 200 B.C. and A.D. 300 Krishna was made the chief deity in the epic. At least three-fourths of the *Mahabharata* is material which has been affixed to the original epic.

One of the additions was the *Bhagavad Gita*, which today appears as sections 13 to 42 of Book Six. In its present form the *Mahabharata* is a huge miscellany of both Aryan and non-Aryan materials. One scholar has suggested that we can understand the fate that has overtaken the *Mahabharata* if we can imagine "the *Iliad* survived to us only in Pope's translation, and our theologians had scattered through it, say, metrical renderings of Bunyan's *Pilgrim's Progress*, the Thirty-nine Articles of the Church of England, and the Westminster Confession of Faith, Fox's *Book of Martyrs*, and a few representative theological works of rival sects!" [57] But even this is not sufficient, for there is no standard text of the *Mahabharata*.

The other epic, the *Ramayana*, recounts events which are supposed to have happened two centuries before those of the *Mahabharata*. It is the story of Rama, a hero about whom there is much dispute. The chief events are his marriage to Sita, her abduction by the demon Ravana, the rescue of Sita, the reunion of Rama and Sita, and finally the death of Sita. The *Ramayana* has suffered seriously from rewritings by *Brahmins* desiring to glorify Aryan civilization and to demean foreign civilizations and the Buddhist religion. The characters of Rama and Sita are still held as models for men and women in India. Rama was later made an incarnation of Vishnu. Both the *Mahabharata* and the *Ramayana* have greatly enriched the *bhakti* tradition in India.

The term *"bhakti"* comes from *bhaj*, which means "to partake of," "to be attached to," or "to resort to." It first meant full participation in a ritual, but the meaning shifted to dedication to a god. The chief ingredient of the emotional linkage to one's chosen god is love, but in addition there are elements of dependence, fascination, awe, and fear. The Vedas do not ordinarily recommend this relation to the *devas*. Perhaps it would be more accurate to say that a relation of loving devotion was not considered a possible relation between men and gods in the *Rig*. The *devas* were the powers inherent in the nature of things, and the sacrifices were the means of manipulating the powers. Loving devotion to wind, sun, rain, and fire were not options. The notion that an individual human being might take an attitude of devotion to a god was largely a non-Aryan and non-Vedic innovation, and it seems to have as its place of origin the area now known as the Punjab, but its richest later developments were in South India and in Bengal.

Sanskrit has many terms for love. An eighteenth-century author named Narahari wrote a treatise entitled *Bhakti-ratnakara* in which he distinguished 350 kinds of love. However, the many loves can be classified into three general types: *prema, kama,* and *bhakti. Prema* is the gentle and pure love with no element of sexual desire in it. It is the romantic or troubadour love. In *prema* the lover is completely concerned in fostering the happiness of his beloved. *Kama* is craving erotic love in which the lover seeks his own satisfactions, usually sexual in nature. *Bhakti* is the devotional love of a human for his chosen god. There are five fundamental features of *bhakti.*

The first characteristic of *bhakti* is that it is monotheistic; it is the emotion appropriate to belief in one god. The belief, however, is not necessarily a belief in the reality of only one god; it may be the belief that there is only one god who is real for a particular worshiper. There is a latent henotheism in all forms of Hinduism: this is the belief in what is known as *ishta devata* (chosen god). *Ishta devata* has nothing to do with theology but much to do with worship. One's chosen god is the god one worships, not necessarily the only being which one believes to be a god. There is no assumption that the god that is right for one worshiper is necessarily right for another worshiper. Each person may select his own deity. The Hindu is repelled by the notion prevalent in Christianity and Islam that devotion to one god necessitates an obligation to oppose the worship of other gods and to propagandize the worship of one's own. In India more value is placed on the quality of worship than on the number of worshipers.

The second feature of *bhakti* is the belief that the god of one's worship is personal in the sense that god responds to the approach of the worshiper as a person. The attitude of god to man is that of love, mercy, and forgiveness. The term used by *bhaktas* is *prasada* (grace). The grace of god cannot be earned by a devotee. To petition for grace would miss the mark altogether. Grace is not something the god bestows or withholds. Grace is the very nature of god. A gracious god no more chooses to be gracious than a circle chooses to possess 360 degrees. Therefore, all the recipient can do is celebrate the *prasada* of god.

The third characteristic of *bhakti* is that man must love his god as a free response rather than as a calculated means to win god's favor. Vaishnavite love is a consuming love; Shaivite love tends to be more complex because of the admixture of awe and fear in the devotee's response to Shiva.

The fourth aspect of *bhakti* in the period we are considering was the attitude known as *prapatti* (surrender). The *bhakta* was a total believer who resigned himself in complete submission to his god. The self-surrender was sometimes likened to Yashoda's inability to punish the mischievous Krishna, and sometimes to the helplessness of the *gopis* when they heard the flute of Krishna. The *prapatti* in Shaivism had more of the flavor of surrender to the majesty and strength of the god of destruction-creation. Differences in the conception of the nature and necessity of *prapatti* created divisions later in the *bhakti* cults.

Finally, there is in *bhakti* the notion of *sharanagati*, i.e., the coming to one's god as a refuge. This was the final word of Krishna to Arjuna in the *Gita:* "Take your refuge in me, and have no fear, for I will save you." The linkage was called *para anurakti* (superior attachment).

The nature of *bhakti* has been considered from every conceivable viewpoint in the history of Hinduism. The *bhakti* relationship between man and god is usually described analogically in terms of human relationships. The main *bhavas* (attitudes between god and man) are (1) *dasya-bhava* (the attitude of a servant for his master), (2) *sakhya-bhava* (the attitude of friendship), (3) *vatsalya-bhava* (the love of a parent for the child), (4) *shanta-bhava* (the love of a child for a parent), (5) *kanta-bhava* (the love of a wife for her husband), and (6) *madhura-bhava* (the sexual love of man and woman). If it is possible to distinguish Hindu philosophy from Hindu religion, the difference is the absence of *bhakti* in the former and the presence of *bhakti* in the latter. To this day there remain covert tensions between those Hindus who look back to the Vedas as the fountainhead of all

Hindu beliefs and those who temper the Vedic tradition with *bhakti* elements. The tension becomes overt when orthodox *Brahmins* are confronted with extreme *bhakti* forms such as those of the left-hand Tantric cults.

10

The Smriti Tradition

The religions which had taken root directly from the Vedic literature were severely challenged by the movements at the two ends of the Ganges valley from the sixth century B.C. to the fourth century A.D., but the *shruti* literature—the *Samhitas,* the *Brahmanas,* the *Aranyakas,* and the *Upanishads*—had established itself firmly in Hinduism. This establishment Hinduism was to undergo many changes—the fire and blood sacrifices on open-air altars were to change to idol worship in dark rooms in temples; the way to liberation by means of knowledge was to make room for *bhakti* and *yoga* techniques; the *Brahmin* monopoly on learning was to adjust to concepts from post-Vedic and even anti-Vedic sources; and the aristocratic royal orientation was to be jeopardized by egalitarian devotion to gracious gods—yet it was never to break completely from the Vedas. This was the *shruti* tradition. It is also called the *Sanatana Dharma* (the ancient system of law). Those who look exclusively to the Vedic literature as the authority on all religious matters are known as *shrautas* (the followers of the *shruti*). Philosophically they are called the *astikas* (the yes-sayers). In opposition to the *shrautas* were those designated as *nastikas* (those opposed to Vedic scriptures and the main teachings of the scriptures, e.g., the Charvakas), as *avaidikas* (those opposed to the Vedic scriptures as authoritative but not necessarily to everything taught by the Vedas, e.g., the Buddhists), and as *shramanas* (those who rejected the concept of Brahman).

By the year A.D. 300 a term was needed to identify a fourth group whose opposition to *shruti* was not rejection but an effort to extend the teachings of the Vedic literature. The term was *"smartas"* (those who are followers of the *smritis*). The *smartas* did not deny the sacred quality of the *shrutis*; on the contrary, they acknowledged *shruti* literature as the recordings of directly inspired seers, but they believed that these writings of original revelation required extension, augmentation, and application. The enormous body of post-Vedic writings to which the terms *"smriti"* (remembered) and *"shastra"* (instruction) are applied is classified into eight groups: (1) *Vedangas,* the collection of materials on rituals, morals, astronomy, phonetics, etymology, and grammar, of which the best known are the *Dharma Shastras* (Law Codes), and of these the most important are Manu's and Yajñavalkya's; (2) *Darshanas,* the writings of the leaders of the six orthodox philosophical schools; (3) *Itihasas,* legendary works such as the *Ramayana* and the *Mahabharata;* (4) *Puranas,* eighteen collections of legends which in many cases have acquired a heavy load of aboriginal ideas and stories; (5) *Upavedas,* the materials which have been added as appendages to the principal Vedas, e.g., the *Ayurveda* which was added to the *Atharva;* (6) *Tantras,* the enormous collections of writings on occult topics often of an esoteric and erotic nature; (7) *Agamas,* the writings which are unique to the three great sectarian branches, i.e., Vaishnavism, Shaivism, and Shaktism; (8) *Upangas,* a broad term for writings related to the logical and ritualistic forms of thought. Much of the *smriti* material is written in the *sutra* form, i.e., in short pithy aphorisms designed to suggest an entire line of thought. The *sutra* form was particularly used in the philosophical systems, thus creating a need for commentaries to make the *sutras* intelligible. The distinction between *shruti* and *smriti* may seem to be quite simple: if it is not a *Samhita,* a *Brahmana,* an *Aranyaka,* or an *Upanishad,* then it is *smriti.* However, since Hinduism has no closed canon, new *shruti* material theoretically can be added at any time. The *smriti* body, of course, grows without limitation.

The term "the *smriti* tradition" refers not only to the body of writings called *smriti* but also to the entire way of living and thinking which had been fixed in India by the end of the third century A.D. Although the orthodox often claim their Hinduism stems straight from the *Vedas*, the truth is that much of Hindu *sadhana* is the outgrowth of *smriti* extensions of *shruti*. Our concern in this chapter is to spell out the fundamentals of the *smriti* tradition as it was before the period of development which we are calling "The Reformation." Much of what we call "the *smriti* tradition" is taken for granted by all Hindus today.

The Trimurti

The pattern of dividing the gods into groups of three has ancient standing in India. We have already noted that the Vedic *devas* were classified into the celestial, the atmospheric, and the terrestrial. Sometimes a single *deva* was selected as the ruler of each sphere, e.g., Savitri (sun), Indra (heavens), and Agni (fire), or Surya (sun), Vayu (wind), and Agni. The best known grouping of three is that of the Trimurti (three forms) which is first mentioned in the latest of the *Upanishads*, but which is not found in the *Bhagavad Gita*. The Trimurti consists of Brahmā (Creator), Vishnu (Preserver), and Shiva (Destroyer). The outstanding sculptural representation of the Trimurti is a magnificent three-faced bust nineteen feet in height in a Shaivite cave on the island in Bombay harbor named Elephanta (or Gharpuri), a work of art dating from the eighth century A.D. Although the Trimurti is often referred to in modern Hinduism, and although cogent arguments can be given for the wisdom of referring to the godhead as the principle of creation-preservation-destruction, the truth is that the three-fold godhead is not an object of worship, and the Trimurti must in all honesty be considered a post-Vedic experiment which failed.

When the word "Brahman" is introduced in the *Upanishads* it is neuter in gender, but occasionally it becomes personal and masculine, and as such it is "Brahmā." In the *Chandogya Upanishad* 8.15 we are informed that the teaching of the *Upanishad* was taught by Brahmā to Prajapati, by Prajapati to Manu, and by Manu to human beings. In *Kaushitaki Upanishad* 1. 5 Brahmā is described as sitting on the throne of Brahman. In *Mundaka Upanishad* 1. 1 Brahmā is said to be the first of the gods to appear, the maker and protector of the world, and the one who taught the knowledge of Brahman to Atharvan, his eldest son. The word "Brahmā" is used twice in *Shvetashvatara Upanishad*—5. 6 and 6. 8—but in this *Upanishad* the personal Brahman is usually called Rudra. In *Maitri Upanishad,* one of the last of the *Upanishads,* we find the only place where the Trimurti is listed: Brahmā, Rudra, and Vishnu.[1]

Brahmā is always listed first among the Trimurti, but this does not indicate priority in dignity or power; rather it may be merely a reminder that creation is first in chronological order. Brahmā has never been a popular deity in India. There are only two temples to him: one at Pushkar near Ajmere, and the other at Khedbrahmā. Neither is an active temple. Brahmā suffered the fate of creator gods in other cultures in becoming a forgotten god because his creative act was eons in the past. Moreover the worshipers of Vishnu and Shiva have made Brahmā subordinate to their chosen gods: the Vaishnavites claim that Brahmā sprang from a lotus which grew from Vishnu's navel, and the Shaivites prove the superiority of Shiva over Brahmā in their myth that Shiva in anger once destroyed the fifth head of Brahmā.

In art Brahmā is depicted as red in color with four heads and four arms. He is shown with a beard. In his hands he holds a drinking cup, a bow, a scepter, and a *Veda*. His vehicle is Hamsa, a bird which looks like a white swan or goose, but is in fact a mythical bird which had the ability of separating *soma* and milk from water. Brahmā's consort is Saraswati, a Vedic river goddess who has become the patron of music and scholarship. She rides upon a peacock, and is depicted holding a vina in her hand. She remains to this day one of the worshiped gods of Hinduism.

The two other gods in the Trimurti are the great gods of modern Hinduism. Whereas lip service is paid to Brahmā, worship is directed to Vishnu and Shiva. Vishnu, as we have noted, was a god of second rank in the Rig-Vedic pantheon; but he grew in importance, and by the time of the composition of the *Mahabharata* was of the first order of gods. According to the Vaishnavites he is the God of gods. It is in the *Puranas* that he is elevated in rank and given attributes of mercy and goodness. His name is said to be derived from *vish* (to pervade), and he is regarded as the all-pervading spirit associated with waters.

He is said to recline in the coils of the serpent Shesha which floats upon water. The Ganges springs from his feet. Vishnu's association with water is perhaps derived from the Indians' vital dependence upon water. The climate of much of India is such that the entire year's supply of water falls in a two-month period, and the difference between food and starvation is the timing and the quantity of the monsoon.

Vishnu is the most gracious of all the gods of Hinduism. This is indicated most of all in his *avataras* who are incarnated into the human scene to save mankind and to destroy evil. When Vishnu sleeps, he rests upon Shesha; but when he is active, his vehicle is the Garuda bird, a mythical half-giant and half-eagle creature. In art forms Vishnu is blue in color. He is dressed as an ancient monarch. In his four hands he holds a conch shell, a battle discus (*chakra*), a club, and a lotus. Other marks of his royalty are a jewel worn around his neck and a star-shaped sign of immortality shown on his breast from which a tuft of curly hairs grows. His consort is the lovely and loving Lakshmi, who has submerged her personality in dedication to her spouse.

"Shiva" prior to about 200 B.C. was not the name of a god but of an attribute (auspicious), and it was applied to Rudra with the hope that it might encourage him to be auspicious. Shiva's association with Rudra and his general character and appearance have been described in the previous chapter. His vehicle is the bull Nandi. Perhaps more important than Shiva are his Shaktis (female energies). The spouse of Shiva is said to be Parvati, who is portrayed as a beautiful young woman quietly sitting beside her husband or on his knee engaging in discourses on love and metaphysics. But Shakti as energy has the power to appear in different forms. Parvati has at least ten other forms besides that of the quiet and loving wife. The three most significant are Uma (a practitioner of the harshest of asceticisms), Durga (a ten-armed demon-slayer mounted upon a lion), and Kali (the black goddess who drinks blood and feeds upon corpses, and whose devotees have occasionally been restrained by civil authorities from practicing some of the extremes to which their worship has led them).

The inclusion of Shiva in the Trimurti reminds us that in

Hinduism destruction is not a malfunctioning of the universe which requires explanation and justification, but it is an inherent and necessary aspect of reality which is incorporated into the godhead. Destruction is a divine function, not a devilish perversion. Creation and destruction, birth and death, and good and evil are necessary aspects of the nature of things. The devil is inherent in the nature of god rather than antithetical to god.

Another feature growing out of the conception of the multiple godhead is that since Brahmā, Vishnu, and Shiva are equally divine, the god one worships is a matter of personal choice. There is no true god as contrasted to a false god, but there may be a right god for a worshiper. Another way to state this is that in Hinduism one's "god" is whatever one chooses to worship, and a new god can be added at any time. Margaret Sinclair Stevenson in her book, *Without the Pale,*[2] reports that once in a certain temple in Kathiawar a cow died within the temple yard, and the Dheds, the group whose responsibility it was to remove dead animals, refused to take the cow away because they had been offended by the temple authorities. So the old head priest announced that the cow was a god, had it buried in the courtyard, set up a marble image over the grave, and "to this day its worship is regularly carried on." The doctrine of *ishta devata* (chosen deity) is more than an expression of Hindu tolerance; it is also a fitting expression of the belief that all gods are symbolic of the cohesion of existence (*sat*), consciousness (*chit*), and value (*ananda*). (*"Ananda"* is usually translated "bliss," but it also means that which produces bliss, i.e., value.)

Time and Eternity

From earliest times the Hindus began to distinguish the time-bound and the timeless. Time (*kala*) was a measurement within that which is unmeasurable. The body was subject to the ravages of time, but the soul was the unborn portion. Birth and death, creation and destruction, and beginning and end were limitations of events within the context of the limitless.

Calendar time among the Hindus seems to have been based on a five-day week prior to the third century A.D. The seven-day week of the Chaldean system was introduced into northwest India by the Greeks and was made universal in northern India during the Gupta period (A.D. 320–480). The days of the week were named after the Indian equivalent for the presiding planets according to the Greek-Roman system: Ravivara (Sunday) from Ravi, the sun; Somavara (Monday) from Soma, the moon; Mangalavara (Tuesday) from Mangala, the planet Mars; Budhavara (Wednesday) from Budha or Mercury; Brihaspativara (Thursday) from Brihaspati or Jupiter; Shukravara (Friday) from Shukra or Venus; and Shanivara (Saturday) from Shani or Saturn. The signs of the zodiac were also brought to India by the Greeks, and the months were named after these signs translated from their Greek equivalents. The six months of the year during which the sun progresses northwards, i.e., from the winter to the summer solstice, came in India to be known as *uttarayana* (northward path), and it is the auspicious season of the year; the six months of the year during which the sun moves southward came to be known as *dakshinayana* (southward path), and it is the inauspicious season. Weddings, in particular, are scheduled during *uttarayana*. Even deaths should occur during the auspicious season. Bhishma assured Yudhishthira, "I will never pass out of the world as long as the sun is in the southern solstice. This is my resolve. I will proceed to my own ancient abode when the sun reaches the northern solstice." [3] *Uttarayana* is also called the day of the gods, and *dakshinayana* is called the night of the gods. Thus one human year equals a divine day and a divine night.

Cosmic time according to the *smriti* tradition is measured in great cycles (*kalpas*). A *kalpa* is 12,000 divine years, and a divine year is equal to 360 human years, so a *kalpa* is 4,320,000 human years. Each *kalpa* is divided into four *yugas* (ages); *Krita, Treta, Dvapara,* and *Kali.* These terms come from the four throws in the ancient Indian dice game: four, three, two, and one.

Krita Yuga is four times the length of *Kali Yuga*; i.e., it is 4800 divine years or 1,728,000 human years. It is the golden age. During this *yuga* men devote themselves completely to their duties and responsibilities as determined by their station in life. In the words of the *Manu Dharma Shastra*: "All men are free from disease, accomplish their aims, and live four hundred years." *Treta Yuga* is three times the length of *Kali Yuga,* i.e., 3600 divine years or 1,296,000 human years. The life span is three hundred years during this *yuga,* and the quality of human life begins to decay. *Dvapara Yuga* is twice as long as *Kali Yuga,* i.e., 2400 divine years or 864,000 human years, and life expectancy is diminished to two hundred years. Men and women are blinded by passion in this *yuga. Kali Yuga*—our present age—lasts for 1200 divine years or 432,000 human years. The life span is only one hundred years, and these years are spent in strife, quarreling, and war. Some have estimated that the present *Kali Yuga* began 3102 B.C.

One thousand *kalpas* constitute a Brahmā Day, a period of time which begins with the creation of a universe and ends with its dissolution. Each Brahmā Day is followed by a period of equal length known as a Brahmā Night. A Brahmā Day is a period of activity; a Brahmā Night is a period of dormancy. Cosmic creation (*srishti*) and cosmic quiescence (*pralaya*) follow one another without end. The Hindu thus computes time within the framework of endlessness. The psychological impact of such a view of the cosmos may seem strange and depressing to the Western mind, although the same motion of unlimitedness is required by the view of space held in modern physics and astronomy. The Westerner may be justifiably more disturbed by the cyclical theory of time—a view which some have called "the squirrel cage theory of time." But this may be an improper conception, since there is nothing in the *smriti* literature which would require that time be thought of as following a two-dimensional spiral; it may also be thought of as moving in the path of a three-dimensional helix. A coiled spring theory of time would allow for both repetitive cycles and progressive movements. Such a view is certainly more consistent with the Hindu view that qualitative changes can take place in the life of both individuals and societies.

Karma and Samsara

At the very time when the ancient Hindus believed in the reality of millions of gods they also believed in one cosmic order (*Rita*).

This order was operative not only in the realm of natural events but also in morality. Causality in the moral realm, known as *karma*, is frequently defined as "the law of the deed." According to this law any moral act, like any physical act, is both the result of causes and the cause of other acts. A billiard ball is caused to move by the impact of the cue, and will cause another ball to move when it hits the second ball. Causality in moral affairs is not quite that simple, but the same principle holds. Each act of the human being, whether it be intentional or unintentional, whether it be right or wrong, and whether it be directed to good or bad goals, is the result of causes set in operation by the actor in previous acts, and at the same time this act creates causes which will in the future yield other effects. *Rita* and *karma* are denials of chance in the universe. Nothing is accidental; everything is caused. *Karma* is not a form of fatalism (*niyati*), although it is so asserted by the *guru* Vaishampayana in the *Mahabharata*: "That which has happened was ordained to happen. Destiny . . . is incapable of being resisted." [4] But *karma* cannot be fate, for the individual himself is the determiner of *karma*, whereas the doctrine of fate is the doctrine that one's future has been set for him by forces not in his control.

The doctrine was well established by the time of the Buddha. Charvakas and Ajivikas attempted to defend the concept of fate against *karma*, but few Hindus since the sixth century B.C. have doubted the law of *karma* or offered alternatives to it. Correlative with the theory of *karma* is the belief in transmigration of the vital self. The reason for this is the impossibility of locating the cause of each act within the limitations of a single birth and death, and also the observation that some causes do not yield results within a single lifetime. *Karma* and *samsara* (passage, or the impermanence of things) require each other. This was noted by many *rishis* in the *Upanishads*: "Obtaining the end of this action, whatever he does in this world, he comes again from that world to this world of action." [5] "Those whose conduct has been good will quickly attain a good birth, the birth of a *Brahmin*, the birth of a *Kshatriya*, or the birth of a *Vaishya*. But those whose conduct here has been evil, will quickly attain an evil birth, the birth of a dog, the birth of a hog, or the birth of an untouchable." [6] "The individual soul roams about in reincarnation according to its deeds." [7] "The soul being overcome by the bright or dark fruits of action, enters a good or an evil womb." [8]

The incarnation need not be in human form; in fact, gross observation tells us that most lives are not human lives. Some Hindu sects have even attempted to list the number of bodies into which a migrating *jiva* may enter, and others have worked out schemes of how many thousands of births are required before a *jiva* has the opportunity and privilege of entering the human form. But such calculations do not seem central to Hinduism.

Karma is divided into *aravdha karma* (the results of actions which have begun to produce effects) and *anaravdha karma* (the results of action which have not yet begun to produce effects). The second form of *karma* is further divided into *praktana karma* (the results of action done in previous incarnations which have not yet begun to produce effects) and *kryamana karma* (the results of action done in this incarnation which have not yet begun to produce effects).

What prevents *karma* from being a form of fatalism is the belief that ways of acting differ in the degree to which they produce *karma* and that the individual person is an effective agent in choosing how he will act. The implication seems to be that *karma* determines the action but not the modes of the action. Jyoti's *karma* may cause him to perform a specific act, but Jyoti determines whether he acts greedily, cruelly, selfishly, charitably, kindly, lovingly, etc. Krishna advised Arjuna that acts done from a sense of duty use up *karma* without creating new *karma*. If one's goal is to terminate the series of incarnations, as Hinduism assumes it is, then the aim is to exhaust *karma*. The Hindu expression is "to eat up one's *karma*." When all *karma* is "eaten up," there are no causes of another incarnation.

Reincarnation is not punishment for sin. An incarnation according to the Hinduism of the *smriti* tradition is the natural consequent of acts. A divinity is not necessary to control and direct *karma*, although some sects have introduced a divinity for such purposes.

Arguments for believing in the doctrine of reincarnation may take the form of appeal to empirical experiences or recall of events which one could not have experienced in the present life span, or of the strange feeling that some people have at one time or another that they are repeating an act or revisiting a scene when that is not the case. Other arguments are of the rational type: the appeal to the irrationality of the one-life hypothesis of Christians, Jews, and Muslims, or to the waste of life spent in years of preparation for creativity which lasts only for a few years, or to the premature death of promising youths. While such arguments may have their place, they neither persuade nor aid Hindus in their belief. Reincarnation is for them a received assumption which does not depend upon empirical evidence or rational argument. It is a remarkable fact that none of the classical philosophers of India attempted to examine the validity of the doctrine of reincarnation. A learned Hindu once remarked in private conversation, "It is an irrational idea, but no more irrational than the Christian conception of immortality!" *Karma* and *samsara* have one great psychological advantage: they make it impossible for the Hindu to blame anyone other than himself for his good or bad fortune.

The most common Western misunderstanding about the concept of reincarnation is that it is chiefly concerned with the continuation of consciousness, i.e., that one will, therefore, be able to remember previous existences. But *samsara* is much more relevant to the conservation of values than to the preservation of memory. The good that has been attained will be effective beyond the life of the body, and the evil which has not yet been rooted out may still be eliminated. So interpreted, *karma* and *samsara* are removed from the realm of the occult and placed in the realm of the good, the beautiful, and the true.

Caste

According to *shruti* tradition the division of mankind into four classes dates from the beginning of things, since *Rig Veda* 10. 90 states that when cosmic man was sacrificed *Brahmins* were made from his mouth, *Kshatriyas* from his arms, *Vaishyas* from his thighs, and *Shudras* from his feet. But according to *smriti* tradition the fourfold division was formulated by Manu the Lawgiver. The law or code of Manu is known as *Manu Smriti*, or *Manu Dharma Shastra*, or *Manu Samhita*. From its references to Greeks, Scythians, and

Persians the dates A.D. 100 to 300 are required for its composition. This book is regarded by *Brahmin* scholars as the most important in Hinduism next to the Vedic literature, an evaluation based no doubt on the high position assigned to *Brahmins* in it, a position which *Brahmins* did not have without challenge in the Vedic period but which has been steadfastly maintained by them since A.D. 300. An indication of how some non-*Brahmins* regard the *Manu Dharma Shastra* is the fact that Dr. B. R. Ambedkar, the Untouchable leader and chairman of the committee which wrote the Indian constitution, once burned a copy of the *Manu Dharma Shastra* in a public ceremony.

The first structuring of Hindu society, like that of most early societies, was into the free (*arya*) and the slave (*dasa*), but by the beginning of the fourth century A.D. the fourfold division had become traditional. Although some scholars say the number of theories or origin of caste is at least as large as the number of persons who have studied caste, they are usually variations of six fundamental theories. The first is that the division is based on color pride and prejudice. The Sanskrit word for the traditional classification is "*varna*," and *varna* means color. But it also means species, kind, character, and nature. Those who support the color hypothesis maintain that the light-complexioned Indo-Aryans wished to avoid assimilation with the dark-complexioned aborigines whose lands they invaded. To this day fair skin is prized in India. Almost all matrimonial advertisements state that the wife must be fair complexioned. But this color evaluation has not always prevailed in Hinduism. White has not always meant good, nor has black meant evil. Both Rama and Krishna were said to be dark. In *Kaushitaki Upanishad* 3. 1 a man named Pratardana is said to have won Indra's favor and is invited to select a boon. Pratardana, feeling he is not qualified to select a boon, asks Indra to select the boon which would be most beneficial to mankind. Indra says that the boon most beneficial to mankind would be to understand Indra, and the reason is that this understanding is so powerful that no evil, not even the murder of parents, would cause the dark color to depart from the face of the person who has this blessing. The implication is that dark color is associated with goodness, and pale color with evil. Color has for centuries been associated with the four *varnas*: white with *Brahmins*, red with *Kshatriyas*, yellow with *Vaishyas*, and black with *Shudras*. But this is not to be regarded as any form of color prejudice; rather it is a way of identifying the moral virtue associated with each *varna*: white stands for wisdom, red for courage, yellow for desire for wealth, and black for physical activity.

A second type of theory of caste origin is that the division grew out of racial, tribal, and familial solidarities. Again another Sanskrit word has been used to support the theory: the word *"jati"* which is used for the subclasses comes from *jata* (race). Both the invading Aryans and the people whose lands they invaded were divided into tribes and clans. Such differentiations tend to become rigid when challenged. There were also tribes whose specialty was performing as priests and teachers, others as warriors, others as traders, and still others tended herds and tilled the land. However, we learn from the *Rig* that *rishis* came from all classes of the people.

The third theory of caste origin is based on trade guilds, professions, and vocations. The divisions may have been consciously made as an economic device to insure each community would be supplied with all necessary occupation groups, or they may have grown out of monopolistic desires to restrict and control certain vocations. The word *"jati"* is used in India today to denote subclasses based on occupational differences. The divisions of this nature are constantly growing, and are often based on what seems to an outsider to be ridiculous differentia. For example: in South India cocoanut harvesters are separated from cocoanut cultivators; in Bengal those oil pressers who ladle the oil from the presses are socially inferior to those who employ a spigot to drain off the oil; in Cuttack potters who turn their wheels while sitting have no intercourse with potters who stand while they work; and in certain parts of India fishermen who weave the meshes of their nets from right to left may not intermarry into fishing families who weave their nets from left to right. The number of *jatis* is said to be over 25,000.

A fourth theory of caste origin is based on religious beliefs, cult practices, social habits, and even eating habits. Dr. Ambedkar argued in his book, *The Untouchables,* that the distinction between caste Hindus and outcaste Hindus arose when tribes in settled communities gave up the eating of beef, while "Broken Men," i.e., families whose tribes had been broken by wars, lived outside the settled communities and did not change their food habits. Although this thesis seems much too contrived, it typifies many theories of this nature which call attention to the differences in life-styles which may have contributed to the caste divisions. In October 1956 Dr. Ambedkar as President of the Scheduled Castes Foundation on the occasion of the 2500th anniversary of the Buddha's birth led 300,000 Untouchables out of Hinduism into Buddhism. The Untouchables took the threefold vow of Buddhism in a ceremony conducted at Nagpur by the oldest Buddhist priest in India. The effort was a failure, for these "Buddhists" later became a *jati* within Hinduism.

A fifth theory of caste origin is that the social divisions grew out of the distinction between victors and vanquished in wars. Radhakrishnan has supported this theory: "Caste enabled the Vedic Indian to preserve integrity and independence of the conquering as well as the conquered races and promote mutual confidence and harmony." [9] Radhakrishnan does not miss the opportunity to remind his readers that India solved peaceably the problem which others solved by slavery and death: "When European races conquered others, they took care to efface their human dignity and annihilate their self-respect." [10] While he is correct in shaming Western peoples for killing war captives, for making slaves of them, for raping their women, and for putting them on reservations, the caste system ought not to escape its share of reproach. Ambedkar once wrote out of his own experience, "To the Untouchables, Hinduism is a veritable chamber of horrors." [11]

Caste divisions have been supported by appeal to myths and legends. Some subcastes claim solidarity because of ancestral relations with sacred rivers, hills, trees, and stones. A subcaste in Gujarat known as the Kumbi claims it has descended from the perspiration that appeared at the waist of the goddess Parvati. In rural India it is sometimes very difficult to distinguish a social subcaste and a religious cult. Alchemy, astrology, snake worship, transvestitism, scatalogy, sexual habits, etc., have sometimes divided Hinduism so radically that the result is a new grouping. Such were the Thugs who worshiped by murdering, the Nathas who claimed to be wizards who could transform themselves into any form at will, and the Siddhas who specialized in intoxicants and drugs.

Probably the reason why no theory of the origin of caste is adequate is because caste is too many things: marriage restrictions, dining restrictions, occupational restrictions, clothing restrictions, and even restrictions about touching, being near, or seeing another human being. The chief ingredient in the caste division is the notion of purity, but to say that the *Brahmins* are the most pure, the *Kshatriyas* less so, the *Vaishyas* still less so, the *Shudras* hardly pure at all, and the Untouchables not at all is to suggest a hierarchy easily misunderstood. The misunderstanding is in assuming that purity is a private or even a class possession. Caste purity is a community possession. Just as Plato contended that the wisdom of the state is the wisdom of the guardians and the courage of the state is the courage of the warriors, so according to Hinduism the purity of the community is lodged chiefly in the *Brahmins*. But it is the community's purity, not the *Brahmins*'. The *Brahmins* are only one of the custodians of purity. Purity is preserved by *Brahmins* who study and teach the Vedas and who avoid contact with that which defiles, and it is also preserved by the *Shudras* and the Untouchables who wash clothes, cut hair, carry away garbage, and remove dead animals. A Hindu might extend Donne's "Ask not for whom the bell tolls, for it tolls for thee," to the observation that just as each is diminished in another's death so each is augmented in the community's wisdom, goodness, beauty, truth, and purity. Caste is one of the ways—strange though it may seem—in which Hinduism symbolizes the solidarity of life.

The word "caste" is an anomaly which probably ought to be eliminated. It comes from the Portuguese word *"casta"* (pure race). *Varna* is the preferred term for the fourfold division: the *Brahmins*, who trace their lineage to preservers of learning; the *Kshatriyas*, who developed from ruling families; the *Vaishyas*, who are the merchants and traders; and the *Shudras*, who are the "blue-collar workers." Those not in the caste system would appear to be descendants of aboriginal tribes, war captives, criminals, or other groups not well received by the in-group. The subcontinent of Asia has been a melting pot of peoples for centuries, and a basic conservatism has

X

restrained the tempo of the melting. Megasthenes observed in the third century B.C., "It is not permitted to contract marriages with a person of another class, nor to change from one profession or trade to another, nor for the same person to undertake more than one, except he is of the class of philosophers, when permission is given on account of his dignity." The *varna* distinction was well established in the early centuries of the Christian era, and already the *varnas* were beginning to break into *jatis*. The *Manu Dharma Shastra* both expressed and reinforced the *varna* division, giving to each a psychological basis: the *Brahmin* is quiet and studious, the *Kshatriya* is energetic, and the *Vaishya* is impelled by desire. The *Shudras* and those outside the *varna* system are difficult to place psychologically because they are too inconsistent, too undeveloped, too much swayed by momentary impulses. In terms of the *atmansiddhi* ideal the first three are well on their way to realizing the highest good for man, whereas the last two are as yet only candidates for the higher values.

Westerners are repelled by the idea that by birth one is *Brahmin, Kshatriya, Vaishya, Shudra,* or outcaste. Hindus may remind the Westerners that a *Brahmin* is not a *Brahmin* because of his birth but rather that his birth into a *Brahmin* family was the result of his having attained that status by reason of his reincarnations. *Varna* is determined by *karma*. Birth into a *varna* is not an accident. It is the natural result of karmic causes. One is born where one belongs by reason of his acts over many incarnations. If reincarnation is taken seriously, the injustice of the *varna* system vanishes. But this is not to justify the entire *jati* system with its notion of the obligation to engage in the occupation of one's father, nor the practice of Untouchability with its denial of the essential humanity of millions of people. The *varna* system has degenerated and requires a thorough overhauling. Untouchability has been outlawed by the Constitution of India, and efforts are being made to assist the lower classes to enter fully into the life of the modern nation.

Already by the third century A.D. the fourfold *varna* system was deteriorating into castism by making it into a rigid system which was finally to choke life and hope out of Hindus caught in vocational, social, and economic binds. *Varna* appears as a qualitative distinction in *shruti* literature; e.g., *Chandogya Upanishad* 4. 4. 1–5 reports that a young man named Satyakama once came to *guru* Gautama saying, "I wish to become a student of Vedic knowledge. May I become your pupil?" When the *guru* asked about his birth and lineage, Satyakama replied that he did not know because he had been conceived out of wedlock of a servant girl who could not identify the father. The *guru* replied, "A non-*Brahmin* would not have explained this as you have. Bring the fuel. I will receive you as a pupil. You have not deviated from the truth." Brahminhood was, according to this story, indicated by moral character, not by birth. But in the *smriti* tradition *varna* as a moral distinction deteriorated into *jati* as a birth distinction.

Chaturvarga

By the time of the formation of the *Mahabharata* the good life for man had been spelled out in terms of four goals. They were called the *chaturvarga* (tetrad of goods). These were *kama* (the goal of hedonic satisfactions), *artha* (the goal of material possessions and physical comforts), *dharma* (the goal of the fulfillment of the duties and obligations pertaining to one's station in life), and *moksha* (the goal of release, liberation, and salvation). The four goals were also called the *purusharthas,* the means by which one becomes a full man. No one should be missed or slighted, but because of the supreme importance of *moksha,* it was called the *paramartha,* the highest wealth. In early times in India the first three, the *trivarga* (group of three), were known as the goals of the village (*grama*). They were secondary goals, i.e., means to the realization of *moksha,* the primary goal of life. They were also called the goals of time, and *moksha* was the goal of liberation from time. *Moksha* was also known as the forest (*vana*) goal, since elderly people often broke the ties with their joint families in order to live in remote spots in the forest where they could seek liberation unmolested.

The goal of *kama* denoted the whole range of sense gratifications: tastes, odors, sights, sounds, and a wide variety of touches (smooth, rough, wet, dry, cold, hot, soft, firm, itching, scratching, tickling, smarting, etc.). *Kama* above all referred to the pleasures of sex. The god of love, Kama, according to the Vedic *sukta* of creation (*Rig*

Veda 10. 129) was the primal force which stirred the formless and brought about the creation. Kama is portrayed in art as a boy with a bow of sugar cane, a bowstring of honeybees, and a quiver of arrows tipped with flowers. Although this goal of life was usually called *kama*, a more appropriate term might have been *bhukti* (enjoyment) since pleasures in the generic sense rather than solely in the sexual life were intended. *Kama* was not an innovation of the *smriti* tradition; the *Rig* is filled with expressions of hopeful expectations of benefactions from the gods.

The drinking of *soma* was part of the hedonic life, although it was not for profligates but for intelligent and pious men: "May I, the wise and devout, enjoy the delicious abundantly honored *soma* food, which all gods and mortals, pronouncing sweet, seek to obtain. . . . We drink the *soma*, may we become immortal. . . . O *soma*, drunk by us, be bliss to our hearts. . . . I praise thee now for exhilaration . . . thou art the bestower of heaven." [12] *Soma* is celebrated in one hundred and twenty hymns in the *Rig*. It was a drink enjoyed by both men and gods. The Vedic deities, unlike the Olympians, did not mind sharing divine pleasures with men.

One of the most remarkable literary sources for understanding the path of pleasure (*pushti marga*) is the *Kama Sutras* of Vatsyayana, a work of the fourth century A.D. Here the daily life of a gentleman of leisure and culture is described in detail. After the morning bath, he perfumes his body, rubs his lips with red juice, sweetens his breath by chewing betel, puts on clean clothing, and adds a flower to his coat. After his breakfast, he relaxes in a swing while being entertained by talking parrots, myna birds, and fighting cocks. During the morning he engages in amateur art activities such as drawing, painting, sculpting, playing music, and writing poetry. After his lunch, he enjoys a nap, followed by social calls. In the evening musicians and dancers entertain him until he returns to his private quarters where everything is in readiness for love play with his mistress. Excursions, picnics, drinking parties, games, and worship add variety to his life. The *Kama Sutras* contain full directions for sexual love with amazing lists: sixty-four arts auxiliary to the joys of love, six classes of signs for lovers, fifteen excellent go-betweens, eight signs which reveal the dawn of love, twelve noncoital forms of embrace, ten kinds of kisses, eight kinds of scratchings, eight types of bitings, twenty-six kinds of men who are successful with women, thirty-four types of women who are easy prey to men, seventeen signs a woman has lost interest in a man, and eighty-four coital positions! Many of the directions are intended more for the wooing of a young bride than for illicit love; e.g., there is the charming method of inducing a bride into the first kiss by playing a game in which a betel leaf is passed back and forth by using only the lips.

Two views of women came into being in this period, and have remained side by side in India. One is the view that Sita is the ideal woman: the pure and obedient wife of Rama. According to this view, a woman is never impure. She is essential for the man's proper performance of his religious duties, and sexual ecstasy is paradigmatic of the man-god relationship. The other view is manifested in Draupadi, the vigorous wife of the five Pandava brothers. According to this view, a wife stands in the way of her husband's liberation since she constantly tempts him to desert his religious duties. Marriage, according to this second view, is a conflict between feminine lust and male *dharma*. Therefore a woman as a constant threat to man's salvation must never be independent; she must always be controlled by father, husband, brothers, brothers-in-law, and sons. For example, in the *Mahabharata* the beautiful Tapati upon receiving a marriage proposal from a king replies, "O king, I am not the mistress of my own self! Know that I am a maiden under the control of my father. If you really entertain an affection for me, demand me of my father. . . . I am not the mistress of my body. Therefore, O best of kings, I do not approach you. Women are never independent. . . . If my father bestows me upon you, then, O king, I shall be thy obedient wife." [13] Some Hindu sects have maintained that liberation is impossible for a woman, and others hold that a woman has no god other than her husband: "The husband is the wife's god, and he is her refuge. Indeed, there is no other refuge for her." [14] The two views of women have never been reconciled. One of Gandhi's legacies was a puritanical view of sex, but other Hindus have held a vastly different view; e.g., Bhartrihari in praising the joys of embracing a lovely woman wrote, "The heaven sung by the scriptures is merely secondary." [15]

Kama was well established in the *smriti* tradition as one of the *purusharthas* of a full life, and for the most part it has remained as such in Hinduism, although it is kept within the context of the other three goals, being balanced especially with *dharma* and *moksha*.

Artha, the second goal, means literally a thing or an object. It denotes all the things a person can amass, possess, share, enjoy, lose, and destroy. It includes the materials for maintaining a home, rearing a family, engaging in a vocation, and performing religious duties. *Artha* is the means and the sign of worldly success. According to the *Artha Shastra* material gain is the most important of the three ends of human life because on material gain depends the realization of *kama* and *dharma;* but the *Yajñavalkya Smriti* places *artha* at the bottom of the hierarchy of values by which a person ought to be honored. These are in the rank from most honorable to least honorable: learning, piety, old age, family line, and wealth. To realize the *artha* ideal one must concern himself with *vartta* (the direct means of earning a living, e.g., agriculture, husbandry, industry, trade, moneylending, etc.) and also with *dandaniti* (the indirect means, e.g., politics and jurisprudence). He must be a man of *niti* (practical morality), combining friendship, knowledge, morality, and action in such a manner that they pay dividends in wealth and success.

The *Artha Shastra* of Kautilya is one of the books which remain from the post-Upanishadic treatises on worldly success. It is primarily a handbook for rulers, presenting itself as "the science which treats of the means of acquiring and ruling the earth." [16] According to this work statecraft is largely an efficient system of espionage. Officers must be rotated, lest they become entrenched in power. In all judicial matters the king is the final authority. Total destruction of enemies is advised. Enemy kingdoms are to be weakened by fomenting disturbances within them. Personal enemies are to be tortured, blinded, exposed to contagious diseases, and murdered. Similar advice is given to Yudhishthira when Bhishma, arguing that the primitive state of man is an intolerable anarchy, recommends that the best remedy is to embrace absolute monarchy: "If a powerful king approaches kingdoms weakened by anarchy, from desire of annexing them to his dominions, the people should go forward and receive the invader with respect." [17] Such a monarch rules by divine right: "The man that bends his head to a powerful person really bends his head to Indra. . . . A person who is desirous of prosperity should worship the king as he should worship Indra." [18] The man who "even thinks of doing an injury to the king, without doubt meets with grief here and goes to hell hereafter." [19]

Poverty is not glorified in the *smriti* tradition. The stereotype of the Indian as an ascetic peasant complacent in his destitution can be destroyed by reading a volume of folktales of India called the *Pañchatantra* (five books), which was put together in northwest India in the second century A.D., but which did not assume its present form until the sixth century. The *Pañchatantra* is a collection of stories told by an aged priest to the dull sons of a king as a means to instruct them in human psychology and practical politics. The characters are animals who study the *Vedas*, show up the hypocrisy of *Brahmins*, declare the faithlessness of women, and affirm the dishonesty of servants. The praise of *artha* is open and unabashed:

> A fangless snake; an elephant
> Without an ichor-store;
> A man who lacks a cash account—
> Are names and nothing more.[20]

> The wealthy, though of meanest birth,
> Are much respected on the earth;
> The poor whose lineage is prized
> Like clearest moonlight, are despised.[21]

The third *purushartha* is *dharma*, the principle of restraint. *Dharma* means the whole complex of law, justice, custom, ethics, and manners. The term comes from *"dhri"* (to sustain), and the implication is that preservation of the person and his highest values depends upon restraining wayward appetites and desires. *Dharma*, as another of the concepts developing from the ancient Vedic conception of *Rita*, is in its widest and fullest meaning the view that the sustenance of the physical world and the sustenance of society depend upon order. *Dharma*, as the factor of regulation operating on all the goals of life, is sometimes assigned first place among the *purusharthas*. *Dharma* has the connotation of an ordered social hierarchy; it is an order in which everyone plays roles with reference to others. The station of each person determines the duties he has to others, the duties linked with *varna, jati,* joint family, and the stage of individual development. Duties and responsibilities have first priority. Freedom is not the opportunity to do as one pleases but the psychological state of living harmoniously and happily within the framework of the *dharmas.*

Dharma has been forced in Hinduism to bear a wide interpretation as it includes duty, obligation, responsibility, virtue, justice, law, goodness, and truth. Economics, vocation, jurisprudence, politics, and religious ritual have all been brought into subservience to *dharma.* To do one's *dharma,* as Krishna says in the *Gita,* is to do the work that is required solely by reason that it is one's duty so to do. If one acts according to *dharma,* one ought not to be concerned about the results or the rewards. Yudhishthira, who is described in the *Mahabharata* as the incarnation of *dharma,* says, "I never act, solicitous of the fruits of my actions. I give away, because it is my duty to give; I sacrifice, because it is my duty to sacrifice. I accomplish to the best of my power whatever a person living in domesticity should do, regardless of the fact whether those acts have fruits or not. . . . The man who wishes to reap the fruits of virtue is a trader in virtue." [22]

There are many ways of classifying the *dharmas* which govern the life of the Hindu. One of the simplest and best is into the following five *dharmas:* (1) *varna dharma,* the duties pertaining to one's caste—e.g., in most *Brahmin varnas* the use of wine is forbidden; (2) *ashrama dharma,* the rules that belong to one while in a certain stage of life—e.g., a student is required to carry a staff but not an umbrella; (3) *varnashrama dharma,* the rules for a person of a particular *varna* while in a particular stage of life—e.g., a *Brahmin* student is expected to carry a staff cut from the branch of a palasa tree; (4) *naimittika dharma,* the acts forbidden to everyone—e.g., every Hindu is forbidden to act disrespectfully to his parents; (5) *sadharana dharma,* the obligations which are common to all by reason of the human status—e.g., the obligation to act non-violently.

Dharma as a duty ethic has occasionally been put to questionable uses in India since the ethic of acting for duty's sake does not always specify just what one's duty is. *Dharma* can become a blank check which is filled out by another. Also a conflict of duties is not an uncommon situation. Yet *dharma* has permeated all Hindu thought. Unlike the Westerner, who often regards his duty as something he must do but would rather not, the Hindu has been conditioned to do all that comes under the heading of *dharma* without anguish since the *dharma* act is simply the way to act. Not to do one's *dharma* is seldom entertained as a viable alternative.

Moksha, the fourth goal of life according to the Hindu analysis, was once described by Paul Deussen as "the most precious jewel of Indian faith." [23] Hindus refer to it as the *parampurushartha* (the highest wealth). The term *"moksha"* means freedom, but it may also symbolize liberation, release, escape, salvation, deliverance, fulfillment, and realization. The goal of *moksha* was slow to develop in Hinduism. The term appears only three times in the *Upanishads,* and these are in the latest *Upanishads: Shvetashvatara* 6. 16 and *Maitri* 6. 20, 30. Some orthodox schools refused to recognize the goal for many centuries; e.g., the Mimamsa defied the doctrine of *moksha* until the eighth century A.D. In the epics, although the emphasis was on *dharma,* there was also stress on the disquieting and nonsoteriological aspects of life. *Mahabharata* 11. 5 contains an interesting parable of "the wilderness of life." A *Brahmin* once lost his way in a great forest teeming with wild beasts. Lions, elephants, and snakes pursued him. He ran desperately seeking a place of safety. He came to the edge of the forest, thinking he might get out of the wilderness, but he found that the entire forest was surrounded by a net, and that a frightful female demon stood just outside the forest ready to pounce upon him the instant he got through the net. He turned back into the forest, and at last stumbled into a deep pit. He did not fall to the bottom of the pit because he became caught in creeping vines, and there he hung upside down unable to free himself. A large snake at the bottom of the pit waited for him to fall; a huge elephant stood at the top of the pit waiting for him to crawl out. Rats were gnawing on the creepers which held him. In this distressful situation a few drops of honey from a comb in the vine fell into his mouth. He relished the taste, never losing hope of prolonging his life. Such is the human condition. *Moksha* is the goal of escape from this samsaric world.

In the period 600 B.C. to A.D. 300 there was conflict between the *dharma* ideal and the *moksha* ideal, between doing one's duty and being relieved from the round of births and deaths. There is some truth in saying that it was a conflict between the short view of life within an incarnation and the long view which looked at the human situation from the standpoint of many rebirths and redeaths. The conception of *moksha* as the transcendence of the limits of mortal existence had not yet been worked out. *Moksha* as freedom was first conceived as freedom from the wheel of birth and death; the conception of *moksha* as freedom for the realization of the full potentialities of man was yet to be worked out. A quotation from the *Mundaka Upanishad* illustrates the situation: "Taking as the bow the great weapon of the *Upanishads*, one should place in it the arrow sharpened by meditation. Drawing it with a mind engaged in the contemplation of Brahman, know that Imperishable Brahman as the target." [24] The arrow is released from the bow in order to hit the target. *Moksha* is freedom from *samsara* in order to attain supreme goals. Freedom *from* and freedom *to* were at this time not well thought out, although this distinction had long been adumbrated in an ancient prayer:

> Lead me from unreality to reality.
> Lead me from darkness to light.
> Lead me from death to immortality. [25]

It was the responsibility and the privilege of the philosophical systems to spell out the opportunities of realization which were made possible because of the negative freedom of being released from the weary round of incarnations.

Ashramas

By the beginning of the fourth century A.D. the ideal human life was considered to be divided into four periods of equal length. Since for generations the ideal length of life had been one hundred years, each of the periods (*ashramas*) was thought to be twenty-five years. The *ashramas* are not mentioned by name in the *Rig*, although references are made to students, householders, and ascetics. But by the time of the Buddha the four *ashramas* were established, and one of the heresies of the Buddha was to encourage the skipping of the two middle *ashramas*. The term *"ashrama"* comes from *"shram,"* meaning to exert energy. Each of the stages of life is supposed to be a time for a unique effort toward the realization of *moksha*. The *varnas* stress human nature; the *ashramas* stress human nurture. The *ashrama dharmas* are the duties appropriate to the individual in each of the four stages on the path to the supreme goal.

The four *ashramas* are the *brahmacharya* (student), *grihasthya* (householder), *vanaprasthya* (hermit), and *sannyasa* (wandering mendicant). The division, it should be noted, are the divisions of those for whom *moksha* expectations in this incarnation are realistic, i.e., the twice-born. In the *brahmacharya* the student receives instruction in the *Vedas*, learns meditative disciplines, develops self-control, and prepares himself for life responsibilities. *Grihasthya* is the time of marriage, vocation, and family responsibilities. *Vanaprasthya* is the period for releasing attachments to worldly goods, for turning over the family vocation and possessions to sons, for guiding others on the basis of one's own experiences, and for paying more and more attention to the liberation of one's self from worldly attachments. In the *sannyasa* stage of life a break is made from all worldly ties, and full attention is given to the goal of *moksha*.

The *ashrama* program is a functional division. The four *ashramas* are in chronological order: preparation, production, service, and retirement. They constitute a rhythm of inner-direction and outer-direction. The student is inner-directed; his task is to prepare himself for the life ahead. The *grihastha* and the *vanaprastha* are both outer-directed: the former supports the entire society; the latter shares his experiences for the good of all. The *sannyasi* is inner-directed; having contributed to society at least as much as he received, he prepares himself for the final release.

It is a mistake to pair the four *ashramas* with the four *purusharthas*. But the *ashramas* do correspond roughly to the four parts of the Vedic literature; i.e., the Hindu as student memorizes the *suktas* of the *Rig*, as householder he performs the rites and ceremonies, and as *vanaprastha* and *sannyasi* he seeks the ultimate enlightenment depicted in the *Upanishads*. It is also interesting to note that stage one is preparation for stage two, and that stage three is preparation for stage four; but in another sense the first three are as a group preparatory for the fourth stage. Although Manu condemned anyone who sought *moksha* without going through the first three *ashramas,* there are many deviations from this norm. A *sadhu* (holy man) may skip the second, or the third, or both. In practice few other than *Brahmins* participate in the third and fourth *ashramas.* The fourfold ideal remains an ideal which few carry out in detail. Nevertheless even today the *ashrama* pattern influences the life of the Hindu. He does feel an obligation to apply the pattern in some fashion to his life. Hindus relate the *ashramas* to the *varnas* by observing that *Brahmins* ought to move through all four, *Kshatriyas* and *Vaishyas* ought to reach the third, and *Shudras* are not expected to go beyond the second.

According to Manu the formal education of a *Brahmin* boy began by the time he reached his eighth birthday. His first seven years were to be years of free exploration of the world of sound, color, form, taste, and odor. The boy was to go to his prospective *guru* with a small faggot, requesting permission to become a pupil (*shishya*). A *guru* was under no obligation to accept a boy as his pupil; in fact, he might be very unwilling, since a *guru* took on special obligations which could have serious karmic effects for himself. Also the *guru* received no fixed remuneration for his services. The *guru* was faced with the serious responsibility of determining whether the boy was ready to begin Vedic studies. The estimation of *adhikara* (fitness or eligibility) of the pupil was the task of the *guru.* When the boy was accepted, he was invested with a three-strand thread which was part of his costume for the rest of his life—subject to renewal each month in interest of hygiene. The boy was expected to live in the home of his *guru* five months of each year during the *brahmacharya* period in order that the *guru* might nurture his development.

The purpose of this form of education was to prepare the twice-born boy for participation in his cultural heritage. It was a disciplined education. He collected fuel for his *guru's* fire, tended his cattle, helped in the house, ate only simply food, wore but the minimum of clothing, and observed complete chastity. The formal training was Vedic study. If he was to become a priest, this would include much memorization of *suktas*. To make sure that the memorization was perfect, some *gurus* required their students to recite *suktas* both forwards and backwards. If the boy was in training to become a teacher rather than a priest, less stress was made on correct memorization and more on the ability to interpret the meaning of the *Vedas*.

When the young man left his *guru* at about age sixteen, he was expected to have considerable knowledge of the *Vedas* plus the habits of study which he would continue throughout his life. As part of the closing ceremonies of his education the student took a ceremonial bath, made a formal offering to his teacher, and returned home to be honored by gifts of clothing and an umbrella.

The education of *Kshatriyas* and *Vaishyas* began later, usually at about age twelve, and continued until age twenty-two or twenty-four. The early educating of *Brahmins* was based on the assumption that they had more to contribute to the community and therefore ought to become productive as soon as possible. Girls of all three twice-born *varnas* were educated in the home, where they learned the duties of wife, mother, homemaker, and participant in the home rituals.

The second *ashrama* is *grihasthya*, the life of a householder. According to the *Mahabharata*, "The life of domesticity is the most difficult of all the four modes of life." [26] Yet when Yudhishthira expressed a desire to renounce the householder state and become a *sannyasi*, Vyasa reminded him that the highest duty of man lies in living the full life of a householder. One of the reasons why Shankara was sometimes called a crypto-Buddhist was because he introduced the practice of celibacy into Hinduism. The *Mahabharata* also contends that the *grihasthya ashrama* is the most valuable: "The four different modes of life were at one time weighed in the balance. The wise have said that when domesticity was placed on one scale, it required the three others to be placed on the other scale for balancing it." [27] The reason for this high regard is that the householder is the supporter of everyone else: "The gods, *pitris*, guests, and servants all depend for their sustenance upon the person leading a life of domesticity." [28] Marriage was regarded in the *Mahabharata*—and is still regarded—as a social duty and a sacramental necessity. Marriage is woman's sacrament. According to the *Dharma Shastras,* marriage is primarily for the begetting of offspring, but it also is required for the performing of proper worship of the gods. Marriage is a contract between families. Therefore, the question of the happiness of the couple most immediately involved is secondary. The Westerner who compares the family in the West and the family in India discovers how different are the expectations about marriage in these two cultures. This was brought out in a study of the Hindu family by Aileen D. Ross. In this study of Hundu families in urban Bangalore the emotional attachment of the mother-son relationship was discovered to be almost eight times greater than that of the husband-wife relationship.[29]

The daily life of the householder from the time of awakening before rising from bed to the last moment before going to sleep has been prescribed in the many *Dharma Shastras.* It is unbelievable that many Hindus attempt to follow the codes of rules of domesticity in every detail; e.g., the householder is advised while dining to face the east for long life, the south for fame, the west for prosperity, and the north for truth. However, the five daily *dharmas* of the twice-born householder, the *pancha-maha-yajña* (five great sacrifices), which were laid down in the *Dharma Shastras* are still taken seriously in many Hindu homes. (1) *Deva yajña* (deity worship). This is the obligation to burn a simple offering to the gods, or to make an oblation of milk, curds, or butter, or to place a bit of wood sprinkled with *ghee* in the fire. (2) *Brahmā yajña* (Brahmā worship). Each day the householder expresses his debt to the ancient sages by studying, teaching, repeating, or meditating upon some portion from the Vedic scriptures. (3) *Pitri yajña* (ancestor worship). Libations of water or the setting aside of rice balls (*pindas*) constitute a daily remembrance of ancestors back to the seventh generation. (4) *Bhuta yajña* (spirit worship). This is interpreted either as a daily recognition of spirits both good and bad, or as a daily offering to animals, birds, or insects. (5) *Nara yajña* (man worship). This is the obligation each day to honor ties of fellowship with humans by a gesture of hospitality to guests, to friends, to a stranger, or even to a beggar.

Another reason for the importance of the householder stage of life was that this was the stage which perpetuated and supported the *samskaras*, the ceremonial rituals which were the extensions of the *Brahmanas* into the *Dharma Shastras*. These were the sacraments of Hinduism particularly related to the life of the home and designed to celebrate important steps in the life of the twice-born. Gautama in his *Dharma Shastra* listed forty *samskaras*, but in *Grihya Sutras*, i.e., the rules of the domestic life, there are but sixteen. They are the following:

1. *Garbhadhana*, a ritual to insure conception.

2. *Pumsavana*, a *samskara* to protect and nourish the child in the womb after it is obvious that the wife is pregnant.

3. *Simantonnayana*, a rite performed in the last month of pregnancy for the purpose of encouraging the mental formation of the child.

4. *Jatakarman*, the birth ceremony.

5. *Namakarana*, a ritual for the naming of the child.

6. *Nishkramana*, a ceremony for taking the child out of the house for the first time.

7. *Annaprashana*, the first feeding of solid food.

8. *Chudakarana*, the first cutting of the hair.

9. *Karnavedha*, the boring of the ear lobes for ornaments.

10. *Vidyarambha*, the beginning of study by the learning of the alphabet.

11. *Upanayana*, the ceremony for initiating study of the *Vedas* under the tutelage of a *guru*.

12. *Vedarambha*, the actual beginning of Vedic studies.

13. *Keshanta*, the first shaving of the beard.

14. *Samavartana*, the homecoming after the completion of Vedic studies.

15. *Vivaha*, the marriage ceremony.

16. *Antyeshti*, the funeral rites.

Only three of the *samskaras* are regularly observed today:

upanayana, vivaha, and *antyeshti. Upanayana* marks the progression of the boy from childhood into the life of a student. The investiture with the sacred thread reminds him that as a Hindu he will always live under *dharma.* A thread ceremony for girls has been added by the more progressive Hindus. The marriage ceremony is a long and complicated ritual. The actual completion of the ceremony is the taking of seven steps by bride and groom. The first three nights after marriage the couple are expected to be continent as a reminder that marriage is not license for sexual pleasures but a contract controlled by the community. The funeral rite in most cases uses fire to dispose of the corpse. The customs vary throughout India. For example, among the more primitive communities the mourners drop seven stones from their left hand as they return from the burning ghats in order to delay and confuse the evil spirits who seek to follow the mourners back to their homes. These spirits are believed to be unable to resist counting, but they are notoriously bad counters! The practice of *suttee* (widow immolation) was quite common in India until stopped by law in the middle of the nineteenth century.

Hindus have through the centuries added innumerable ritualistic and ceremonial customs to the life of the householder. Among these can be mentioned: ceremonial bathing; calculation of auspicious times by astrologers; taking of vows, often of an ascetic nature; veneration of trees, rivers, stones, snakes, etc.; fortune-telling; pilgrimages to sacred places; vigils before shrines; avoidance of mentioning names of one's self, one's *guru,* one's eldest son, and one's spouse; *guru* worship; celebration of holy days.

The holy days and religious festivals vary throughout India. The two most important and most universal are Dipavali and Holi. Dipavali (or Divali) is a five-day celebration in October-November, which in reality is five festivals rolled into one. The first day is dedicated to Lakshmi and Parvati, the second to Shiva and Parvati, the third commemorates the victory of Vishnu over the demon Bali, the fourth recalls the return of Rama to Ayodhya and his coronation, and the fifth remembers Yama's visit to the home of his sister. On the evening of the third day of Dipavali small bowls of oil are lighted and placed throughout the house and yard to express joy in the victory of good over evil. Holi is a three- or four-day celebration in February-

March which began as a fertility festival and which includes the lighting of bonfires, the erection of a pole and dancing around it, the making of loud noises, and the throwing of colored water, mud, and refuse at passersby. The rationale behind the celebrations has been lost. Some speculate that Holi is a time when all act like *Shudras* as an expression of common humanity.

An interesting feature of Hindu festivals, feasts, and fasts is that they are regenerative breaks in the regular pattern of the daily life of the householder. Many of them involve disorder, flux, transgression, and chaos. They afford a period of relief from the monotony of the programmed life of the Hindu, and make it possible for the householder to return with satisfaction to his *dharma*-dominated life. Rhythmical polarities are found throughout the Hindu pattern of life.

According to Manu, when grandchildren have arrived, gray hairs appear, and the wife has reached the age when she is incapable of conceiving, the married couple enter upon the *vanaprasthya ashrama*. This is a transitional period between the busy life of the householder and the retirement of the *sannyasi*. It is a time when the responsibilities of home management and family vocation are gradually turned over to the next generation. Since interest in the affairs of daily life still concern the *vanaprastha*, his counsel and advice are available even though he is not active in his profession or vocation. Semi-retirement is a good description of this *ashrama*. The relations of husband and wife are not broken, and they may still enter fully into the social life of the joint family and community. But their attitudes toward occupation, profession, and family affairs undergo change during this period. Home maintenance, professional reputation, vocational competency, and financial security become secondary matters. Toward the end of the period they retire more and more to themselves. This may take the form of pilgrimages to holy spots, or the spending of more time in temples, or increasing the amount of time spent in private rooms.

At last comes the *sannyasa ashrama*, the period in which full attention is given to the goal of *moksha*. While the word *"sannyasa"* means renunciation, it means the renunciation of *kama, artha,* and worldly *dharmas,* rather than the renunciation of life. It is the time of life when *moksha* is the sole pursuit. In ancient India the grandsire of the family separated himself from all ties. He left the home to wander in the forest, feeding upon roots and plants, begging food from householders, accepting and possessing no money, owning no property, and engaging in no activities resembling those of the householder. No frivolous word passed his lips. Some spoke only the name of God. *Sannyasa* was the second period of *brahmacharya;* the first was a preparation for life, the second a preparation for death. The emphasis was not on the retirement from worldly activities but on the preparation for complete release from the *samsara* condition.

The meaning of *sannyasa* has changed through the centuries. Many modifications must be made in modern India. It remains an ideal, though it is realized by few. Aurobindo has expressed the rationale of the *sannyasa ashrama* by saying that Hindu culture says to the individual, "When you have paid your debt to society, filled well and admirably your place in its life, helped its maintenance and continuity and taken from it your legitimate and desired satisfactions, there still remains the greatest thing of all. There is still your own self, the inner you, the soul which is a spiritual portion of the Infinite, one in its essence with the Eternal. This self, this soul in you you have to find, you are here for that, and it is from the place I have provided for you in life and by this training that you can begin to find it." [30]

The *smriti* tradition was shaped largely by the epics and the codes of law. It changed Hinduism from a religion of kings and courts, of priests and philosophers, and of sacred books and rigid ceremonies to a practical program of human conduct adapted to different stages of human development and to different conditions of life. *Smriti* brought Hinduism to the populace and gave it an appeal which it has never lost. Those who rejected the ancient sacrificial rites and who could not understand the *Upanishads* found meaning, consolation, and guidance in the ordering of life in terms of *varnas, purusharthas,* and *ashramas.* The *smriti* tradition is a reminder that Hinduism should not be considered exclusively from literary sources. The *dharma* of the common man is largely *dastur* (custom).[31]

CHAPTER **11**

The Early Astika Darshanas

The hiatus between popular belief and practice and intellectually elaborated speculation and technique is a wide one in India. The rise and development of the *smriti* tradition was a rude shock to the supporters of the *shruti* tradition. It served notice that Vedic scriptures had failed to capture the minds of the Hindus. If the *Upanishads* were to be efficacious in the lives of men and women, the message they propounded had to be presented in a different format. The day of pontifical pronouncements of supposedly revealed truths was over. "Where there is conflict between *Veda* and *smriti*, the *smriti* should be disregarded," states *Mimamsa Sutras* 1. 3. 3., but the intellectuals who wished to teach what is embedded in *shruti* realized that the time had come when they must develop systematic presentations of *astika* and *vaidika* concepts if they were to make the *Veda* meaningful and convincing. Therefore, from about A.D. 200 an effort was made to present Vedic insights in a new style. This was the literary form known as *sutras*. A *sutra* (thread) is an aphorism

211

which uses the minimum of words to convey the meaning of an ancient truth. *Sutras* adumbrate lines of thought so the reasoning can be reconstructed and examined for validity and truth. According to a famous definition, *sutras* show "the beginning, the end, the repetition, the novelty, the objective, the glorifications and the argument." [1] *Sutras* were intended as teaching devices for the instruction of pupils in Vedic learning, but they were also reformations of Vedic thought which attempted to show that the insights of the ancient *rishis* were true, not because they carried the stamp of direct revelation, but because they could be made acceptable to the rational mind. The authority of argument replaced the authority of insight. *Smriti* had broken tradition. *Sutras* were the beginning of the effort to re-establish traditional wisdom on new grounds. The *sutras* and the commentaries upon them were dedicated to the preservation of *shruti* truths on rational bases, but, as often happens, the defenders sometimes unconsciously altered the original teachings.

Mimamsa

One of the early attempts to reform the *shruti* tradition by placing it on a different epistemological foundation was that which came to be known as the Mimamsa (investigation). The Mimamsa and the other attempts to reform *shruti* are known as philosophical systems by Western scholars, but to call them systems of philosophy is to invite comparisons with Western systems. Among the many Sanskrit terms used to denote these philosophies, the one which best indicates the nature of Hindu philosophy is the word "*darshana*," meaning to see from a point of view deliberately chosen. *Darshana* connotes selectiveness rather than comprehensiveness. Therefore, a Hindu philosophical system must be thought of as an approach to a subject matter rather than as complete analysis and systematization. Mimamsa, in particular, will be found to be incomplete as a system, although it is intelligible as a viewpoint. The Mimamsa *darshana* is the attempt to solve problems arising from Vedic literature by conducting an investigation from the standpoint of rational and critical inquiry. The founder was Jaimini, who may have lived in the third century B.C., but the *Mimamsa Sutras* which is extant is from a version dated between A.D. 200 and 450.

The Mimamsa philosophers (whom we shall hereafter designate as Mimamsakas) were horrified that people were doubting the *Vedas* as infallible authorities and questioning the efficacy of the Vedic rituals. As the most orthodox of the orthodox, the Mimamsakas held that the *Vedas* are eternal and therefore always valid in the life of man. The *Vedas*, they held, have no authors. The *rishis* did not create them; they apprehended the eternal truths and transmitted them to us. However, the transmission was through words, and words need to be interpreted; hence, there is a need for investigation. The Mimamsakas as old-fashioned purists wanted to go back of the *Upanishads* to the original revelations. When they spoke of "the *Vedas*," they meant the *Samhitas* and the *Brahmanas*, i.e., the *karma-kanda* of the Vedic literature. *Shruti*, for them, was not the secret knowledge of the Upanishadic *rishis*; it was the formulated duty (*dharma*) to engage in the activity (*karma*) associated with the sacrificial rituals (*yajñas*). The whole *dharma* of man was to perform the rituals as prescribed in the *Brahmanas*. According to *Mimamsa Sutra* 1. 1. 2 "*Dharma* is that which is indicated by means of the *Vedas* as conducive to the highest good." Mimamsa may be said to be philosophical insofar as it supplied a justification for the beliefs on which the Vedic ritualism depended. Later philosophers called the Mimamsa *darshana* "Purva (earlier) Mimamsa," "Karma (action) Mimamsa," and "Dharma Mimamsa" to distinguish it from the "Uttara (later) Mimamsa," "Jñana Mimamsa," "Brahman Mimamsa," or Vedanta which explicated the *Upanishads*.

According to the Mimamsakas, knowledge alone is not sufficient for the realization of *moksha*, not even the esoteric knowledge of the *Upanishads*, for the human self must fulfill and realize itself through acts, specifically ceremonial religious acts. Without the *dharma* of the ceremonial act, Upanishadic knowledge is pointless, and true *ananda* (happiness) will be missed. According to the Mimamsa philosophy there are three kinds of acts considered from the point of view of the degree of necessity which accompanies them: (1) the obligatory (*nitya*), e.g., the morning and evening prayers; (2) the conditional (*naimittika*), e.g., the requirement of taking a bath during an eclipse, which is conditional upon there being an eclipse; (3) the optional (*kamya*), e.g., the horse sacrifice. The optional act depends upon wanting the specified reward, upon the capacity (*adhikara*) of the performer, and upon the possession of the means for the performance of the rite.

The ceremonial act will produce its fruit, but the fruit does not always appear immediately after the act. To account for this, Jaimini assumed the existence of an unseen force which he called *apurva* (unseen). *Apurva* was regarded as a transcendental potency which acted as a metaphysical link between an act and its result. *Apurva* is brought into existence by the sacrifice itself, and it continues to exist until it has brought about the result it is able to produce. *Apurva* controls the entire world; in other words, the world process is a ritual event. The concept of *apurva* appears to have been created by the Mimamsakas to explain how *karma* acts in the absence of a god. Religiously it is the after-state of the ceremony; philosophically it is the bondage between cause and effect. By the tenth century the Mimamsakas felt that *apurva* as an impersonal principle could not explain the functioning of cause and effect in the natural world, so they postulated a god as the custodian of *karma*. But the early Mimamsakas were atheistic.

The main intent of Jaimini and his followers was to establish the Veda as authoritatively true. The Mimamsakas, realizing that the claim that the *Veda* is *shruti* was no longer convincing, attempted to give rational arguments for what was basically a dogmatic position. They based their reasoning upon the doctrine of *svatah-pramanya*, the self-validity of knowledge. This cornerstone of their philosophy was the claim that knowledge is by nature direct and immediate. A cognition which is the result of direct apprehension carries with it such a weight of intrinsic validity that the knower must accept it as true. But what is "direct apprehension"? This, they said, is any form of awareness which meets these four criteria: (1) it is free from contradiction; (2) it does not arise from defective causes; (3) it is a novelty—i.e., it is not a memory; (4) it represents the object. Practically this means that any direct and immediate apprehension is a basis upon which it is safe for humans to act. Truth is normal; error is abnormal. Human existence is far superior when a person makes the assumption of the truth of that which comes to him directly and immediately than when a person takes an attitude of doubt and skepticism toward knowledge claims. The presumption of intrinsic validity of direct and immediate apprehension is pragmatically justified. If it seems to be unjustified, perhaps one has not taken sufficiently into account the long-range view of *apurva*.

Although the Mimamsakas held that all immediate cognitions are to be treated as true, they were not so foolish as to deny that there are errors in knowing. This they explained in two ways. One was to point out that the so-called "erroneous cognitions" are not cognitions at all. They are a mixing of a perception and a recollection. For example, if upon seeing a piece of shell on the beach one were to say, "This is silver," the "this" refers to the perception of the piece of shell and "silver" refers to the recollection of the appearance of silver. The sentence "This is silver" is a verbal hybrid of perception and recollection; it is not a unit of knowledge. The second way is to point out that "This is silver" is an identification due to the omission of distinctive features of shell and silver because of defects in the eye of the perceiver, or of conditions under which the image is seen, or of hasty and superficial examination.

The Mimamsakas denied that a knowledge claim is neutral, i.e., that a proposition is to be judged neither true nor false until tested. They were defending the practical rightfulness of acting on the assumption that a knowledge claim is true. Their "true until proved false" was the epistemological equivalent of the legal "innocent until proven guilty." Their reason for this claim was not because they were establishing a principle for all knowledge, but because they wanted to establish this principle for Vedic knowledge. They wanted to establish that the instructions for the Vedic sacrificial rites were to be taken as mandates unless or until experience proved that in some way the rituals ought to be modified, and even then one ought to proceed very cautiously because the *apurva* which the ritual brings into existence cannot be measured, and its results are seldom immediate. Furthermore, if the whole universe is a ritual, one ought to hesitate to give up the rituals which are in some unseen manner linked with the cosmic event itself.

The Mimamsakas were conservatives who were cautioning radicals from hastily giving up the ceremonies on the grounds that the benefits were not obvious and immediate. They claimed that the Vedic rites were efficacious, and they thrust the burden of disproof upon their opponents. The Mimamsakas as total believers did not need the verification and validation processes they expounded. Verification was the business of the nonbelievers. The Mimamsakas desired to make matters as difficult as possible for the critics of the *Brahmanas*. Their doctrine of *apurva* was in practice a device by which they could always declare disbelievers wrong. They could point out that the force of the Vedic rituals was "unseen," that it had not yet appeared, and that the results when they did appear might not be recognizable. By placing the cause-effect relationship of rituals in such remote and unperceivable relationships, the Mimamsakas may have thought they were protecting the rituals, but we today are inclined to regard their defense as the work of tenacious believers rather than rational defenders. They did serve as effective custodians of inherited religious practices and theories during periods of widespread disbelief, but it was surely a questionable service to the *shruti* tradition to say, "We have faith in the *Vedas,* and to those who wish to disprove us, we say that the confirming evidence of faith is unseen and unprovable." The impact of the Mimamsa *darshana* in Hinduism was to support those who wished to continue believing in the effectiveness of Vedic rituals and to drive further away those who were already inclined to put their faith in the gracious gods of the rising *bhakti* movements or to join the Buddhists or the Jains.

Samkhya

Concurrently with the development of the Mimamsa *darshana* there came into being in India another philosophy which, because of its systematic view of the world, merits a careful consideration. Samkhya was both a *darshana* (viewpoint) and an *anu-ikshiki* (survey of all things). As early as the seventh or sixth centuries B.C. some Indian intellectuals began to suspect that the *Upanishads* might be interpreted nonmonistically. Even in the earliest *Upanishads* there are passages which suggest a latent dualism. For example, in

Chandogya Upanishad 6. 2 the original Being created the world of things and then entered into them, and in *Brihad-Aranyaka Upanishad* 1. 4. 6 the entire world is said to be food and eater, i.e., matter and spirit. Again in *Brihad-Aranyaka* 3. 9. 10–17 a distinction is made between the *Atman* and that which the *Atman* pervades. Such passages do not constitute a sufficient basis for concluding that a dualistic conception of reality was being fashioned alongside the monistic, but they do indicate that the concept of dualism was not foreign to the thinking of the *rishis*. A. Berriedale Keith has said that "it is impossible to find in the *Upanishads* any real basis for the Samkhya system. The *Upanishads* are essentially devoted to the discovery of an absolute, and, diverse as are the forms which the absolute may take, they do not abandon the search, nor do they allow that no such absolute exists. There are, however, elements here and there which mark the growth of ideas which later were thrown into systematic form in the Samkhya, but it is impossible to see in these fragmentary hints any indication that the Samkhya philosophy was then in process of formation." [2] Keith adds that the Samkhya "goes radically and essentially beyond the teachings of the *Upanishads*." [3] The Samkhya philosophers in going "beyond" rather than "against" the *Upanishads* were able to escape the charge of being *nastika*. The Samkhya remains the most genuinely creative philosophical system and the most successful nonmonistic philosophy in the Hindu tradition. John Davies in his study of Samkhya declared that it "contains nearly all that India has produced in the department of pure philosophy." [4] To a large extent Samkhya became the catalyst of Hindu philosophy. N. V. Thadani once expressed the opinion that all other Hindu philosophies are but amplifications, commentaries, or criticisms of Samkhya ideas and conclusions.[5] Shankara, the great apologist for the monistic interpretation of the *Upanishads*, paid the Samkhya the high compliment of identifying it as his main opponent within Hinduism. In spite of its dualistic interpretation, Samkhya was regarded as a reforming orthodoxy rather than a revolting heresy. Its role has been that of the loyal opposition.

The first Samkhya philosophers may have been pre-Buddhistic, and Buddhism may have borrowed its emphasis on *duhkha* from an early form of Samkhya. The legendary founder of Samkhya is

Kapila, a half-mythic figure located in the seventh century B.C. He is reputed to have spent the latter part of his life at the mouth of the Ganges. The earliest surviving work of the *darshana* is the *Samkhya Karika* of Ishvarakrishna, a work of the third century A.D. The *Samkhya Karika* begins with the recognition of the misery of life: all human beings are subject to three sorts of suffering—that due to their own foolishness and errors, that originating from others, and that which can only be assigned to a divine or demonic origin. Three remedies are offered: (1) empirical methods will get rid of some; (2) religious practices may remove some, although in the slaying of sacrificial animals more suffering is caused; (3) *samkhya* (discriminative knowledge) is a third way. This is the best way: ". . . different from and superior thereto is that means derived from the discriminative knowledge of the evolved, the unevolved, and the knower." [6]

Samkhya discriminates two sorts of causes, one which evolves and one which does not, and two sorts of effects, one which is a cause of other effects and one which is not. The two primal causes are *prakriti* and *purusha*. The former is the principle of matter from which the entire physical universe evolves; the latter is the principle of consciousness from which nothing evolves. *Prakriti* and *purusha* constitute an ontological dualism which, although going counter to the Upanishadic monism of *Atman*-Brahman, was sufficiently implicit within the *Upanishads* that the Samkhya philosophers could not be charged as being *avaidika* (non-Vedic). Although their philosophy was godless (*nirishvara*), its dualistic metaphysics was soon made adaptative to and supportive of theism.

Prakriti is similar to Tat Ekam (That One Thing) in the *Rig*. The word is composed of *pra* (before) and *kriti* (creation). *Prakriti* is not a being but a force, not a thing but a principle, not an experienced reality but an abstraction created to explain experienced reality. The argument for *prakriti* is cosmological: effects presuppose a material first cause in which the effect is immanent; the physical world is an effect; so there must be a material first cause from which all that has come or will come into being in the physical universe emanates, evolves, or is manifested. Nothing new comes into being in this world, for all things exist potentially in *prakriti*. This theory, known as *satkaryavada* (pre-existent effect) is a distinguishing feature of the

Samkhya philosophy. *Prakriti* is the root-cause of the world of our experience. It is universal potency. Everything is latent in *prakriti*. The Latin for *prakriti*—*procreatix* (cosmic energy)—is a better translation than words like "nature," "matter," or "the objective," which are the usual English translations. *Prakriti*, the unevolved material principle, contains immanently all things. *Prakriti*, though one, is internally complex. It is constituted of three factors called *gunas*. These are strands or constituents, not qualities nor attributes. The *gunas* are sub-principles of the principle of materiality. They are mutually dependent. As a unity in trinity they can be separated only in thought for analytic purposes. They are *rajas* (the sub-principle of activity), *tamas* (the sub-principle of resistance), and *sattva* (the sub-principle of order). The psychologizing tendency to refer to the *gunas* as pain (*rajas*), pleasure (*sattva*), and delusion (*tamas*) is of questionable assistance in understanding them. The importance of the *guna* theory is that it indicates that the physical universe is the result of an evolving from an orderly whole composed of elements out of whose opposition a harmony results. Because of this harmonious opposition events take place in the world. A common analogy is that of a swimmer who moves through the water because the water offers resistance to his movements, because the water also allows passage, and because there is an orderly sequence of the swimmer's movements of legs and arms. The *gunas* are ever in a state of change with reference to each other. This perpetual change is movement balanced by countermovements, and the result is that *prakriti* remains in a state of interior balance or equilibrium. All is flux within *prakriti*, and in this state of equilibrial flux *prakriti* causes nothing, produces nothing, evolves nothing.

Purusha as the principle of subjective reality corresponds to *prakriti* as the principle of objective reality. But there is a striking difference. Whereas *prakriti* as cause of the physical world evolves into the physical and mental beings of the world, *purusha* does not evolve. Yet *prakriti* would not evolve were it not for *purusha*, for it is *purusha's* presence which disturbs the constant internal counterbalancing of the *gunas*, and by creating a disequilibrium among the *gunas* alters the functioning from a homogeneous mode of action to a heterogeneous one. Thus the cosmic evolutionary process takes place within *prakriti's* evolvents. But *purusha* does not act, is not aware, and does not function as a subject. The notion of unconscious consciousness, of that which makes things happen without acting, may seem a bit strange, although the analogy of a national symbol may help; e.g., Uncle Sam and John Bull do nothing but they inspire citizens to do things.

Perhaps it was the doctrine of *purusha* which prevented this philosophy from sharing the fate of Charvaka, i.e., of being rejected as a materialistic philosophy. *Purusha,* as a metaphysical principle, was no more established by empirical evidence than was *prakriti.* The argument for *purusha* was teleological: the world is a kingdom of ends, and *"purusha"* is the name given to the end or goal of the cosmic process. This argument rests on the assumption that things which exhibit design always have a transcendent reference to an extraneous end. Hence, *prakriti's* evolving must be for the sake of some end outside its own nature, and that end is the liberation of *purusha* from the bondage of identifying itself with the evolvents of *prakriti.*

Purusha, unlike *prakriti,* is many. Samkhya dualism is unusual in that one of the two realities is a unity-in-trinity, and the other is a plurality of units which are referred to jointly as *"purusha."* There was for the early Samkhya philosophers no great *Purusha,* no cosmic *Purusha,* no God. The *purushas* were numberless, and they were egalitarian—at least the *Samkhya Karika* does not attempt a hierarchical classification of *purushas.* Therefore, bondage and liberation pertain to individual *purushas. Moksha* happens only to atomic units generically identified as *purushas.* Their bondage consists in forgetting who they are as they identify themselves with the evolvents of *prakriti.* Each *purusha* is simple, static, and passive; it is a witness (*sakshin*). But in the condition of bondage it considers itself to be actor or agent. It becomes ignorant of its true selfhood and becomes involved in the evolutionary processes of *prakriti.* However, according to the amazing dualism of Samkhya, the very process of evolving by which *purushas* become bound is also the process of liberating by which *purushas* become free. The activity of the *gunas* in which *purushas* are somehow involved is part of the total *sadhana.* According to *Samkhya Karika* 20, from the joining of *purusha* and *prakriti*, the insensitive and unconscious principles which have evolved from *prakriti* appear as though they were sensitive and conscious; and similarly, the *purusha* which is a witness, appears as though it were fully involved in the activities of *prakriti*. In the next *sutra* the author states that the evolution proceeds for dual purposes: in order that *purusha* become aware of *prakriti* as other than itself, and secondly, in order that, having made this discrimination, *purusha* withdraw and isolate itself from *prakriti*. For the liberation of *purusha* the two unite like a blind man carrying a crippled man on his back. *Prakriti* is the blind but active man; *purusha* is the seeing but inactive man. Here, however, as throughout the speculations of the Samkhya philosophers, problems bristle. A blind man and a crippled man would join forces consciously for their mutual benefit, but *prakriti* and *purusha* are not aware of each other. *Purusha* is inactive, and liberation is not an advantage to *prakriti*. Keith writes as follows about this "union": "This conception is the fundamental point of the whole Samkhya system, and its difficulties are obvious. There is no possibility of mediation between the spirit which is removed from all action, and the active but unconscious nature. . . . Spirit cannot act, and on the other hand, nature, being unconscious, is not capable of receiving directions from the conscious spirit. . . . Unconscious nature cannot experience misery: spirit in itself does not experience misery, and the union of the two, which results in the apparent experience of misery by spirit, which wrongly thinks that the misery which it brings to light in nature is misery which it itself endures, thus creates the very misery which it is the object of the union to abolish." [7]

According to Samkhya philosophers nothing emerges from *prakriti* until *purusha* disturbs the balance of the *gunas* by its presence, although, as we have noted, just how insentient *prakriti* and a *purusha* which can have no objects of awareness can establish a relationship is a mystery. The first to emerge from *prakriti* is *mahat* (the cosmic principle of knowing) and *buddhi* (its psychological counterpart in the life of the individual). By "emergence" or "evolution" these philosophers meant the appearing in the order of reality of that which was latent in *prakriti* and its evolvents. The terms "causes" and "effects" do not seem appropriate for the relation of *prakriti* and that which emerges from the imbalance of the *gunas*, yet there are no better terms; therefore, translators of Samkhya tend to place the words "cause" and "effect" in quotation marks. Again the evolution appears as if it were for the sake of *prakriti*. (Lavish use is made of the Sanskrit word *iva* in the *Samkhya Karika* since unconscious *prakriti* is thought to act *as if* conscious and *as if* it were acting for its own sake.) One of the analogies is that *prakriti* acts for the liberation of each *purusha* in the manner in which milk appears in the cow for the nourishment of the calf.[8] From *mahat* evolves the principle of individuation known as *aham-kara*. This is the functioning of ego identification, i.e., the discriminating between the ego of you and me, between thine and mine. *Mahat* and *aham-kara* are thought to emerge due to the preponderance of *rajas* among the *gunas*. At this point in the evolution a distinction is made between the further evolution which is the result of the preponderance of *sattva* and the further evolution which is the result of the preponderance of *tamas*. The former results in the appearance of *manas* (the principle of arranging perceptions into percepts and concepts), the five sensory organs (sight, sound, touch, taste, and odor), and the five motor organs (speaking, handling, walking, excreting, and reproducing). The latter results in the five *tanmatras* (subtle elements) which are the physical counterparts of the objects of the sensory organs, and from the *tanmatras* evolve the five *bhutas* (gross elements), i.e., (1) space from elemental sound; (2) air from elemental sound and touch; (3) fire from elemental sound, touch, and color; (4) water from elemental sound, touch, color, and taste; (5) earth from elemental sound, touch, color, taste, and odor.

All of this evolution is known as primary evolution. It is the appearance of principles or categories (*tattvas*) by which the world exists, by which it is talked about, and by which it is known. In addition to the primary evolution, there is a secondary evolution by which the common things of the world come to be, e.g., trees, mountains, physical bodies, etc. Primary evolution yields *tattvas*; secondary yields things. Secondary evolution is the rearranging of the gross elements. Secondary evolution can be reversed, but primary evolution cannot; i.e., a tree can be reduced into its gross elements, but fire cannot be reduced into its subtle elements. Secondary evolution takes place in time, but primary evolution does not.

In another analogy the author of the *Samkhya Karika* 59 says, "As a dancer desists from dancing, having exhibited herself to the audience, so does *prakriti* desist, having exhibited herself to *purusha*." This important *sutra* is open to many misinterpretations; e.g., it does not mean that *prakriti* ceases to exist after liberating a *purusha*, for after all *prakriti* is one and *purushas* are many. *Prakriti* does not "desist" at the liberation of each *purusha*. It cannot mean that *prakriti* ceases to act in time, for *prakriti's* evolution is not a temporal process. What it must mean is that *prakriti* and *prakriti's* evolution vanish from the point of view of each *purusha* upon its liberation. The "dance" of *prakriti* is solely for the liberation of the *purushas*. When a *purusha*, because of the functioning of *prakriti*, discriminates its true nature as *purusha* (pure consciousness) from the *antah-karana* (internal organ)—i.e., the collection of *buddhi, aham-kara,* and *manas*—and also from the *linga-sharira* (subtle body)—i.e., the entity which migrates consisting of internal organs, sensory organs, motor organs, and subtle elements—then the bondage of ignorance is broken and for liberated *purusha, prakriti* ceases to "dance." Both bondage and liberation from the point of view of *purushas* are phenomenal: "Of a certainty, therefore, not any *purusha* is bound or liberated, nor does any migrate; it is *prakriti*, abiding in manifold forms, that is bound, is liberated, and migrates." [9] The "change" which appears in *purusha* is unreal and fictitious; and the change which takes place in *prakriti* is the cause of both "bondage" and "liberation" of *purushas*. In the state of liberation resulting from *prakriti's* evolution *purushas* recognize themselves as pure subject. What that can mean is very difficult to grasp. Radhakrishnan says they are "mirrors with nothing to reflect." [10] *Moksha* is described as follows in the *Samkhya Karika*: "When the separation from the body has at length been attained, and by reason of the purpose having been fulfilled, *prakriti* ceases to act, then he attains eternal and absolute isolation." [11] According to *Pravacaya Sutra* 6. 59 the liberated *purushas* have knowledge of the whole universe—but there is nothing to know when *prakriti* vanishes! The general tone of liberation in the

Upanishads is one of joy, but the Samkhya denies that there is any bliss in the liberated state. All that can be said about it is that it is an end of suffering. How can unconscious *prakriti* suffer, or how can inactive *purushas* experience suffering? If they cannot experience suffering, how can they experience liberation as the cessation of suffering? Samkhya holds that there is no real union between a *purusha* and *prakriti*, and that which was never united cannot be released from the bondage of union. Thus the Samkhya separation of *purushas'* bondage to *prakriti* turns out to be an illusory separation from an illusory bondage.

What was it that the Samkhya philosophers were trying to do? The answer is that they were not satisfied with the absolute monistic interpretation of the world as it was understood by the Vedic interpreters of their day. So they tried to offer a dualistic ontology as an alternative to the monistic interpretation, and, in order not to have the charge of heterodoxy brought against them as had been brought against the Jains, Ajivikas, Buddhists, and Charvakas, they attempted to show that their views were at least not inconsistent with some of the views expressed in the *Upanishads*. This was not too difficult as the *Upanishads* had always been a miscellany of *rishi* speculations with no editor to establish consistency and system. They were a potpourri of metaphysical suggestions collected over a period of about five hundred years. The Samkhya philosophers made blunder after blunder in their efforts to work out a rational alternative to the monism of *shruti*. In order to have an alternative to the monism of the Absolute, they postulated the complete duality of *purusha* and *prakriti*, and then in order to account for the evolution of *prakriti* by which *purushas* are liberated from *prakriti*, they postulated the functional union of *purushas* and *prakriti*. They wanted *prakriti* to be an object without a subject and *purusha* to be a subject without an object. They affirmed that *purushas* as pure consciousness cannot be conscious of *prakriti* and *prakriti* as unconscious matter cannot be aware of *purushas*, yet it is the presence of *purusha* which is the catalyst that triggers the evolutionary processes of *prakriti* so the latent causes will have their fruition. Somehow the whole process works for the *kaivalya* (independence) of the *purushas* who are always independent save for the fiction of bondage which they cannot entertain since they are not conscious beings.

The Samkhya philosophy was an amazing labyrinth of confusions and contradictions, yet it became the foundation of Indian psychology, of much of the asceticism which pervades Hinduism, and of *yoga* theory and techniques. In addition, by offering a thoroughly new and creative dualistic metaphysical system as an alternative to the unquestioned acceptance of the monistic view propounded in the *Upanishads,* the Samkhya philosophers had presented, however inadequately, a position which no future Hindu philosopher could ignore. Thus the Samkhya philosophers extended and reformed the *shruti* tradition.

Yoga

In approximately the second century B.C. a man named Patañjali, who was familiar with the Samkhya philosophy and who accepted its general position, decided that discriminating knowledge was not sufficient as a means by which individual selves could detach themselves from the existential conviction they were identical with the transmigrating agent. In order to determine what more was needed, he studied the *shruti* literature available to him and found references to the use of physical and sensual means to assist the individual in his attainment of independence (*kaivalya*) from *prakriti.* For example, the *Brihad-Aranyaka Upanishad* describes the essential mystical experience in terms of colors and sounds: "The form of this person is like a saffron-colored robe, like white wool . . . like a flame of fire, like a white lotus, like a sudden flash of lightning." [12] "It is the sound thereof that one hears by covering the ears thus. When one is about to depart this life one does not hear this sound." [13] Elsewhere light and form are used to indicate the nature of the experience: "Therefore, verily, on crossing that bridge, if one is blind he becomes no longer blind." [14] "When there is no darkness, then there is neither day nor night, neither being nor non-being, only the auspicious one alone. That is the imperishable, the adorable light of

Savitri the ancient wisdom proceeded from that." [15] "Fog, smoke, sun, wind, fire, fireflies, lightning, a crystal, a moon—these are the preliminary forms which produce the manifestation of Brahman in *yoga.*" [16]

The word "*yoga*" is almost unknown in the early *Upanishads,* but it does appear in the two latest, the *Shvetashvatara* and the *Maitri.* In *Maitri* 6. 10 the term "*yogi*" first appears, where it is treated as almost identical with *sannyasi,* but in *Shvetashvatara* 2. 8–15 is found a remarkably systematic description of the practices and results of *yoga.* One should select a pleasant, clean, level spot, free from gravel and ashes, near the sound of running water. It should be secluded and protected from the wind. The body must be held steady with the head, chest, and neck erect. The breathing is to be diminished, and all movements are to be arrested. Concentration begins by selecting some natural object upon which to fix one's senses and mind, e.g., fog, smoke, fire, wind, fireflies, lightning, a crystal, the moon, etc. The results are said to arise from man's intimate relationship with the five cosmic elements: earth, water, fire, air, and space. The first signs of progress are purely physical: a feeling of lightness, health, clearness of countenance, pleasantness of voice, sweetness of body odor, etc., but if the practitioner continues, his being will reflect "the God who is in fire, who is in water, who has entered into the whole world" like a mirror reflects objects after it has been cleansed of dust.

The term "*yoga*" comes from the root *yug* (unite, join, yoke). It appears to have been used originally for the breaking and training of horses. Although in time it shifted, at least in popular usage, to denote the uniting of man and god, or man and his world, or man and his true Self, the original connotation of control or discipline has remained and ought to be stressed. The yoke placed on the neck of oxen does in truth unite the two animals, but the more significant fact is that it unites them for the purpose of getting work done. *Yoga* should be related to such British expressions as "to buckle down to a job" or "to harness oneself to the task." To do yoga is to "buck up," i.e., to regain control of one's emotions and desires. *Yoga* connotes rigorous control of one's being; the opposite of "doing *yoga*" is drifting, showing no enthusiasm, and playing it cool. Exertion, diligence, and zeal are marks of the yogic man. He is the most alive of men, acting like others, yet with a different flare, for he lives consciously and intensely.

Yoga as a conscious effort to realize the meaning of the human condition may be pre-Aryan. One of the seals from the Indus valley civilization is a figure in a yogic posture. *Yoga* may have developed out of forms of primitive magical ritualism, for to this day yogic disciplines are so cluttered with occultism and sorcery that authentic yogis are constantly warding off gullible people who want them to do magical wonders. Swami Sivananda, who devoted much of his life trying to teach *yoga* to Westerners who visited his forest university at Rishikesh, was finally compelled to write, almost in anger, "There is no such thing as miracle or *siddhi*. Ordinary man is quite ignorant of higher spiritual things. He is sunk in oblivion. He is shut up from higher transcendental knowledge. So he calls some extraordinary event a miracle. But for a Yogi who understands things in the light of *Yoga*, there is no such thing as a miracle." [17]

The *yoga* which Patañjali described in the *Yoga Sutras* is not his. He was not an originator of *yoga*. His work was that of an editor. The book that we have called the *Yoga Sutras* is probably an emendation of Patañjali's original work. The first three chapters are thought to be from the second century A.D. and the fourth is from the fifth century A.D. The first chapter is on the theory of *yoga*, the second is on technique, the third is on the *siddhis* which may result from the physical and spiritual exercises, and the final is on *kaivalya*, the desired result.

Yoga, according to the *Yoga Sutras*, is the voluntary restraint of mental states so the ego may separate itself from the nonego, and thus may discover its true identity. Not all types of minds (*chittas*) are able to make this discovery. The *yoga* philosophers distinguished five kinds of minds, and pointed out that only two of these can hope to progress in *yoga*. The *kshipta chitta* (wandering mind) is far too much a slave to passions to profit from *yoga*. This is the mind in which *rajas* is dominant. The second type of mind, the *mudha chitta* (forgetful mind), is the mind which easily becomes absorbed in an emotional state and forgets its true good. Such a mind is said to be moved by *tamas*. The third mind is the *vikshipta chitta*, the distracted but occasionally steady mind. Because of its spasmodic control by *sattva guna,* it may tend to good, but it is likely to slip back into evil. The fourth type of mind is called the *ekagra chitta.* This is the one-pointed mind, the mind which easily concentrates on a chosen object. It is the teachable mind. Such a mind can, and should, practice *yoga.* But the mind which is the mind prized by yogis is the *niruddha chitta* (restrained mind). This mind is subject to the will of the individual; it can enter *samadhi* (contemplation).

The *Yoga Sutras* as a handbook for guidance into spiritual exercises warns the neophyte that there are obstacles or hindrances (*kleshas*) which must be faced. *Klesha* is a highly technical term in *yoga.* *Kleshas* are the roots of the body, birth, life, and suffering. They cause existential pains, and they are also the root of all pleasures: "They have pleasure or pain as the fruit, by reason of virtue or vice." [18] In other words, the *kleshas* are the fundamental motivators of human action which can be channeled for good or for ill, for liberation or for bondage. Thus the *kleshas,* as is true for so many elements in *yoga,* are capable of reversal such that the motivator for evil can become the motivator for good. The yogi is not one who steps outside the normal life of the average individual, rather he is the one who is able to turn the human drives so the same dynamic can be structured toward the realization of a diametrically different goal. The *kleshas,* according to *Yoga Sutras* 2. 5–9, are *avidya* (ignorance), *asmita* (egoism), *raga* (emotional attachment to pleasure), *dvesha* (aversion to pain), and *adhinivesha* (attachment to life). The first two and the second two are pairs: *avidya* and *asmita* are wrong notions about things objective and things subjective; *raga* and *dvesha* are wrong notions about things pleasant and painful. The meaning is that there is nothing wrong in having these emotionally toned notions; what is wrong is that error has been made in identifying the object toward which the drives are directed—e.g., the fifth *klesha* is a reflection of the drive to self-preservation, and this is an important and valuable drive, but the error is in wrongly identifying what makes for self-preservation. Clinging to physical life as though it were an intrinsic value is utilizing the life-drive wrongly, for the physical life is only an instrumental value. So, in the case of each of the *kleshas,* the error is in failure to comprehend the true nature of facts and values. "All is pain to the discriminating," advises *Yoga*

Sutras 2. 15. That is, the one who sees man's passage correctly sees *duhkha* (impermanence, change, temporality, frustration, anxiety). Whereas the typical Westerner tends to account life good despite occasional miseries, the *yoga* philosopher discerns life to be evil despite occasional joys. But the pain-of-living is not without remedy.

The heart of the *Yoga Sutras* is 2. 28 to 3. 54 which contains the techniques of self-awareness, the means by which a *purusha* can detach itself from the ignorance which binds it to *prakriti* and thus learn to discriminate its *purusha* nature and attain *kaivalya*. The *angas* (limbs or parts) are the practical and necessary steps leading to the goal. At no point in the discipline should the yogi confuse an *anga* with *kaivalya* to which the *angas* point. According to the *yoga darshana* all life is *yoga*, but one must not confuse the means with the goal. The *Yoga Sutras* offer a list of *angas* in an effort to spell out the aspects of the total *yoga* that each may see more clearly how he ought to proceed on the human pilgrimage. There are eight *angas*.

The first *anga* is *yama*, the moral restraints: ". . . abstinence from injury to others, abstinence from lies, abstinence from theft, abstinence from sexuality, and abstinence from avarice." [19] These are almost the same as lists for similar purposes in Buddhism.

The second *anga* is *niyama*, the positive moral requirements which balance the negativity of the *yama* list: cleanliness of body and mind, contentment, practice of asceticism and silence, study of philosophy, the reading of sacred books, and meditation upon Ishvara.[20]

The third *anga* (*asana*) denotes the bodily postures and positions, Patañjali selected no specific *asana* for approval; his only suggestion was that the posture be steady and easy. Later yogis devised scores of different *asanas*, and sometimes engaged in quarrels over the relative merits of the postures. They listed as many as eighty-four ways of sitting on the ground.

The fourth *anga* has to do with the regulation of the breath. The term "*pranayama*" literally means the pause after an exhalation. Regular slow breathing is the aim. Again yogis after Patañjali worked out elaborate schemes for proper breathing with various ratios of inhalation, exhalation, and pause, and with various patterns of breathing in one nostril and out the other.

The last four *angas* involve the intellectual and spiritual aspects of the technique. The fifth *anga* is *pratyahara*. This is identified in the *Yoga Sutras* as "that by which the senses do not come into contact with their objects and follow as it were the nature of the mind." [21] The fifth is the stage in which the individual has mastered control of his senses. His senses are obedient to his will. To describe *pratyahara* as "withdrawal of the senses" is not quite correct since what is meant is that one can will to hear and not to see, to see and not to hear, etc. All *yoga* means discipline, and *pratyahara* is discipline related to sense experiences.

Anga number six applies the same discipline to the mind. *Dharana* or steadfastness of mind is the development of the ability to hold the mind to one idea, to give full attention to a chosen topic. *Dharana* and the last two *angas* are called *samyama* (inner discipline) by Patañjali.[22] They are both mental disciplines and the fruits of the physical disciplines. They are "more intimate" [23] than the preceding five. *Dharana* is not regarded by Patañjali as a special condition to be sought on rare occasions. Instead it means that the yogi should develop the habit of looking at every fact and every thought squarely and fairly. He is to become so developed in concentration that he enters into each experience as a fully awakened person. He is to be completely aware of the reality and value of what he is doing, whether it be eating, reading, walking, talking, making love, etc.

The seventh *anga* is *dhyana* (meditation). By *dhyana* the *sutras* mean the continuous and complete flow of thought with reference to the object of concentration. The difference between *dharana* and *dhyana* is that whereas the former is concentration on the object of concentration, the latter is expansion on the object of concentration. *Dharana* holds the object in mind; *dhyana* creatively utilizes the object of thought as a springboard for other thoughts. Patañjali's words are: "By potency comes its undisturbed flow." [24]

Finally, the last *anga* is named: *samadhi*. "The trance-modification of the mind is the destruction and rise of all-pointedness and one-pointedness, respectively." [25] *Samadhi* denotes a unity of contemplator and contemplated which might be called intuitive. The grave danger is that the yogi may mistake *samadhi* for the goal; but it is only an *anga*, i.e., part of the means for the realization of the goal. Although the yogi is tempted to stop with *samadhi*, to enjoy it, and even to display it before his disciples as an attainment, he must resist this temptation. *Samadhi* has been often regarded as one of the *siddhis* (miracles) of *yoga,* and India for generations has had more than its quota of charlatans who display their "trances" in order to astonish the crowds. Competition in yogic tricks has little if anything in common with *yoga* as a discipline for self-realization. The yogi must go beyond *samadhi,* as he must go beyond all the *angas,* to that to which they lead: *kaivalya* (absolute independence, absolute freedom, absolute isolation). The yogi is to desire desirelessness—and then to cease even the desire for desirelessness! "The seed of bondage having been destroyed by desirelessness even for that, comes absolute independence." [26]

According to the last *sutra* of the *Yoga Sutras,* "Absolute freedom comes when the qualities, becoming devoid of the object of the *purusha,* become latent; or the power of consciousness becomes established in its own nature." [27] *Kaivalya* is the state of the *purusha* freed from *prakriti.* The efforts to describe *kaivalya* always fail. Perhaps one of the better efforts is found in *Yoga Sutras* 4. 7 where the author says the *karma* of the yogi who attains *kaivalya* is "neither white nor black." The meaning of this *sutra* has been debated by the commentators, but the surface meaning is not difficult to grasp. White means good, black means evil. There are four types of *karma*: (1) black, the *karma* of *asuras*; (2) white, the *karma* of the completely righteous (*devas?*); (3) both white and black, the *karma* of most people; and (4) neither white nor black, the *karma* of the perfected yogi. The yogi's actions are beyond good and evil. He is not subject to the moral evaluations placed upon the actions of ordinary men. This does not mean that he flaunts common morality; rather he marches to a different tune.

The impact of the *angas* is to place the person fully in control of his own existence. The sanctions that control behavior are now internal rather than external. He does not require the law court, social pressure, or a god to control his behavior. He has taken upon himself his own moral sanctions. He is so in tune with Reality that he does what is natural for him to do, and what he does is right. His acts are morally right, but no longer because he consciously seeks the good and avoids the evil. He transcends the usual moral sanctions.

The Yoga *darshana* never tried to stand alone as an independent system of philosophy. It assumes the Samkhya metaphysical system, except at one point it attempted to improve upon Samkhya: it introduced Ishvara as a supreme *Purusha,* a *Purusha* which is not subject to the bondage of other *purushas,* a *Purusha* which guides the evolution of *prakriti* and accounts for the relationship between the *purushas* and *prakriti.* The joint system of Samkhya-Yoga is sometimes called "Theistic Samkhya."

The development of *yoga* after Patañjali is a long, long story. On the one hand, it was adopted by each of the philosophical systems as part of the solution to the problems of man's estrangement from his true identity. Each *astika* system combined discipline (*yoga*) and inquiry (*vicara*). Disciplined curiosity might be said to be the methodology of all the *darshanas,* and it can be said to Hinduism's credit that the philosophical systems have been remarkably successful in combining psychological discipline and intellectual inquiry. On the other hand, *yoga* techniques were subjected to many variations on the common theme: ascetic, sensual, atheistic, theistic, absorptionistic, devotional, Tantric, puritanical, naturalistic, supernaturalistic, magical, medicinal, physical, spiritual, etc. It has been subjected to so many abuses through the centuries that it is surprising that it still has any respectable standing. Yet *yoga* as a psychological discipline and Samkhya-Yoga as a philosophy remain important contributors both to the development of Hinduism and to living Hinduism.

Nyaya-Vaisheshika

Philosophy, both in the East and in the West, may be divided into the synthetic and the analytic. The former attempts "to see life steadily and see it whole"; the latter seeks to examine the elements which make up the whole. The synthetic philosopher regards the analytic as a nit picker; the analytic philosopher regards the synthetic as a hasty generalizer. The synthetic can't see the trees for the forest; the analytic can't see the forest for the trees. In approximately the third century B.C. two analytic *darshanas* appeared in India; both presumably were reacting against the synthetic methods of Samkhya speculation. These two, like the Samkhya and the Yoga, later joined forces to become a single *darshana*. The Nyaya (literally "going into" a subject) analyzed the process of thought and the nature of knowledge; the Vaisheshika (meaning the particularity of things) analyzed the nature and meaning of the units of reality. Both were thoroughly *vaidika* (*Veda*-supporting), agreeing that the fundamental goal of their analysis was to assist in the attainment of liberation and accepting knowledge as the principal technique of liberation. Both were set against the skepticism and nihilism which had infiltrated from Jainism, Buddhism, and Charvaka. Gotama, the founder of Nyaya, began the *Nyaya Sutras* with the observation that the reason for studying logic is to attain "supreme happiness," and in his second aphorism promised that the study of logic would annihilate "pain, birth, activity, faults, and wrong notions" and lead to *moksha*. Likewise Kanada, the founder of Vaisheshika, opened the *Vaisheshika Sutras* noting that *dharma* is the subject matter and that through a detailed study of the authoritative *Vedas* the supreme good would be attained. Scholars who delight in drawing East-West parallels call Gotama the Aristotle of Hindu philosophy because he was the founder of Indian logic and Kanada the Democritus of Indian philosophy because he advanced an atomic theory. The Nyaya philosophers, choosing as their subject matter how man knows, attempted to show the origin and nature of human knowledge. The Vaisheshika philosophers, picking up the theme of plural entities from the Samkhya doctrines of manifold *purushas*, attempted to show how monadic spiritualism implied materialistic atomism.

"Nyaya" in a narrow sense means syllogistic reasoning and in a broad sense the science of correct knowing. As a philosophy of language the Nyaya *darshana* was concerned not only with the methods of knowing but also with the meanings of words and sentences, the modes of persuasion, the forms of debate, and even the significance of accents. It was a rebuke to the Samkhya philosophers who had used new patterns of thought without examining them. According to the Naiyayikas there are four methods of knowing: perception, inference, analogy, and authority.

Perception (*pratyaksha*) is the most important means of acquiring knowledge because it is certain; i.e., one always knows when he is having a sensation. It is inexpressible in words, since one can never express verbally exactly what one senses. And it is without error in the sense that one senses exactly what one senses, although he may be in error when he tries to express the sensation. Perceptions may be either indeterminate or determinate. The indeterminate perception is immediate, uncritical, unanalyzed sense experience; the determinate perception is the same sensation identified and named. The indeterminate may be of red color, large size, warmth, animal odor, etc.; the determinate would be its identification as a cow. According to the Naiyayikas, indeterminate perception "arises from the contact of a sense with an object." [28] This contact is actual, not metaphorical. This is obvious in the cases of taste and touch, but the Nyaya philosophers contended that physical contact is also a fact in the cases of seeing, hearing, and smelling. Knowledge derived from perception is the result of the conglomeration and movement of physical causes. Perception was also divided by the Naiyayikas into the ordinary and the extraordinary. The ordinary consisted of both external and internal perceptions. The external perceptions are due to the senses of smell, taste, sight, touch, and sound which the Naiyayikas associated respectively with the elements earth, water, light or fire, air, and ether. This parallelism is based on the theory of like-perceiving-like—i.e., the nose is composed chiefly of earth, and therefore the nose perceives the earthy in objects; the tongue of water; the eye of fire; the skin of air; and the ear of ether. Internal perceptions are the result of the activity of the mind (manas) which is in contact with psychical states and processes such as desire, aversion, striving, pleasure, pain, and cognition. The objects of internal perception are themselves activities of the mind rather than activities and aspects of the external organs. Manas as the organ of internal perception functions as a central coordinator of all man's knowledge. Extraordinary perceptions are of three kinds: perception of classes, perception of "complication," and yogic perception. A class like mankind, triangle, or hardness is a perceived reality, not an abstraction. Perhaps what they had in mind is that Devadatta can be perceived as Devadatta or as man. Perception of "complication" refers to the process by which sensations of different senses become so closely associated that they become integral parts of a single perception; e.g., one may say "The orange looks sweet" or "The grass looks soft" when of course sweetness and softness are not directly perceived by the sense of sight. Yogic perception is the extraordinary intuitive powers said to be possessed by some yogis, e.g., the ability to "see" events taking place hundreds of miles away.

Inference (*anumana*), the second means of knowing, is "knowledge which is preceded by perception." [29] Perception is the primary mode of knowing; inference is the secondary mode. The Nyaya logicians were remarkably original in their analysis of the syllogism. For them the syllogism was chiefly a pedagogical or persuasive device to remove doubt in another's mind. For this reason, they often presented the syllogism with the conclusion first; e.g., "There is fire on the mountain, because there is smoke on the mountain, and wherever there is smoke there is fire" rather than "Wherever there is smoke there is fire, and there is smoke on the mountain, so there is fire on the mountain." This order is strictly in accord with the established custom in Indian thought of identifying an event as an effect, and then seeking the cause—an order expressed in the Sanskrit word for causal relationships, the word "*karya-kartva*" which means literally "effect-cause relationship" in contrast to the usual Western expression "cause-effect relationship."

The Nyaya logicians worked out a five-part syllogism which differs strikingly from the Aristotelian in being inductive-deductive rather than solely deductive. The five parts are:

1. Statement.   The thesis is to be established. The statement is offered as a conviction of the speaker or author and as that which he intends to establish in the mind of the hearer, e.g., "That mountain is on fire."

2. Reason.   The naming of the middle term (i.e., the term which does not appear in the conclusion), e.g., "Because the mountain has smoke."

3. Example.   The statement of the major premise plus an example, e.g., "Whatever has smoke has fire, as in the case of an oven."

4. Application.   An assertion of the presence or absence of the ground suggested in the minor term, e.g., "That mountain has smoke such as is invariably accompanied by fire."

5. Conclusion. A restatement of the thesis to be established, except that this time it is stated as confirmed, e.g., "So it follows that that mountain is on fire."

The differences between the Greek and the Indian syllogisms can be indicated by placing an example of the two side by side, using in this illustration the old one on the mortality of Socrates:

Greek	Indian
All men are mortal.	Socrates is mortal.
Socrates is a man.	Because he is a man.
Therefore Socrates is mortal.	Whoever is a man, is mortal, e.g., Pythagoras.
	Socrates is a man, a being invariably mortal.
	Therefore Socrates is mortal.

The third way of knowing, according to the Naiyayikas, is "the knowledge of a thing through its similarity to another thing previously well known." [30] The author was well aware that analogy or comparison (*upamana*) is not fully reliable, because he admits that some reject analogy as a means of right knowledge,[31] but he adds that it can still be accepted, "for comparison is established through similarity in a high degree." [32] The problem is the determination of what constitutes "a high degree" of similarity.

The fourth source of knowledge is authority (*shabda*), and for the Naiyayikas this meant Vedic authority: "The *Veda* is reliable . . . because of the reliability of their authors." [33] They did not elaborate what constitutes the criteria of reliability.

Another interesting aspect of the Nyaya philosophers was their analysis of the concept of truth. The test of truth for them was its capacity to lead to successful action (*samvadi-pravritti*). All knowledge is an incitement to action, and the test of truth is the application of the act indicated. "This is a horse" is inferred if, after hearing the statement, one were to walk closer to the object until all signs indicate that the object indeed is a horse. But workability is the test of truth, not the meaning of truth. That is, although truth is known by means of workability, it means a correspondence between statement and object. Truth is, whether it has or has not been tested. For example, "This wine is sweet" is a truth about the wine before sipping to test its sweetness. "We hold right knowledge to be an independent impression which corresponds to the reality," declared the author of a tenth-century Nyaya work.[34]

The Vaisheshika philosophers were also realists, but they analyzed the realistic syndrome from the point of view of the object rather than from the point of view of the knowledge of the object. Their realistic metaphysics was the counterpart to the Nyaya realistic epistemology. All knowing is discursive; i.e., the subject and the object are separate. The object of thought remains external to the thought. "The universal experience of the objects of the sense is the mark of the existence of an object different from the senses and their objects."[35] These external objects of thought were called *padarthas* (categories) by the Vaisheshika philosophers. This word is composed of *pada* (word) and *artha* (meaning). A *padartha* is an object which can be thought and named, a reality which can be known. *Padarthas* are categories of reality; but, since reality is always knowable, they are also categories of knowledge. A *padartha*, therefore, is both a metaphysical and an epistemological concept. The world is a plurality of these realities which are characterized by uniqueness and difference. The Vaisheshika philosophers, seizing upon the realistic passages in the *Upanishads* and ignoring the idealistic passages, offered a pluralism diametrically opposed to the monism expressed in the *tat tvam asi* doctrine. The bulk of their philosophizing consisted in classifying the *padarthas*. Their classification was a mere listing of the realities, and thus the result was a far less systematic metaphysic than that offered by the Samkhya philosophers.

According to the Vaisheshika philosophers the existence of things is a characteristic of things. To exist does not mean to make an impression upon a knower. Existence is a feature of things in, of, and for themselves. The existence of things in no way depends upon being perceived or thought. The state of being the object of awareness is incidental to the being of things.

The *padarthas* are seven: substance, quality, action, universality, particularity, relation, and nonexistence. Substance (*dravya*) is the most important category, for it is in substance that actions and qualities inhere. Substance is the self-subsistent, absolute, and independent nature of things. It is the unity which persists through change. The *dravyas* are the self (*atman*), mind (*manas*), time (*kala*), space (*dik*), and the physical elements (*bhutas*)—i.e., earth, water, fire, air, and ether.

The most distinctive feature of the Vaisheshika metaphysics was its atomic theory. The term for atom was "*anu*," a point in space. Each atom possessed size, mass, weight, shape, fluidity or hardness, viscosity or its opposite, potential velocity, potential color, potential taste, potential odor, and potential touch. Each atom was distinct from every other atom. This feature was regarded as so important that the notion of the particularity (*vaishesha*) of the atoms gave the name to the school. Atoms are passive. Their movement is due to external impact only. A prime mover was believed to be needed to account for motion, and this was supplied in the form of so-called "ultimate atoms" which move by reason of their special *dharma*. These special atoms were called "unseen agencies" (*adrishtakaritam*), and these mystical agents appear to have been reified into a Lord of *Karma*, a controller and guide of the moral law. By the action of this unseen power atoms were made to vibrate and to form dyads, i.e., compounds of two atoms. Dyads in turn were caused by the unseen power to form into triads, and so on until the combination reached a diameter of one-millionth of an inch, at which stage the substance could be identified as earth, or air, or fire, or water. All coming-into-being and passing-away the Vaisheshika philosophers accounted for in terms of atomic combining and atomic dissolving.

Universality (*samanya*) and particularity (*vaishesha*) were important *padarthas* in Vaisheshika metaphysics. A universal, for them, was not merely a name; it was a property residing in objects. This property is what is denoted when one classifies an object. Particularity was believed to be equally objective in things. It is what one denotes when one distinguishes one thing from another. This means that Devadatta-as-man and Devadatta-as-Devadatta are both objective realities. The philosophers of this school were unfortunately not very helpful in explaining how all universals can be objective; e.g., how does the manness of Devadatta-as-man and the manness of Basu-as-man come together to form a universal man? By making both universality and particularity objective the Vaisheshika meta-physicians seem to have attempted to encompass both absolute monism and absolute pluralism.

The seventh *padartha*—nonexistence *(abhava)*—was added after the time of Kanada to denote negative facts which in the context of the epistemological realism of the Nyaya-Vaisheshika school meant the realities which are represented by the statements designating nonexistence, and whose reality confirms or disconfirms the truth of the statement. For example, the statement "There is no cow in the yard" is true because of the reality of there not being a cow in the yard. Four kinds of *abhavas* were distinguished: (1) antecedent nonexistence, the nonexistence of a thing before its production; (2) subsequent nonexistence, the nonexistence of a thing after its destruction; (3) mutual nonexistence, the nonexistence of a thing as another which is different from it—e.g., a clay pot is not a wooden spoon; (4) absolute nonexistence (i.e., a complete impossibility), e.g., the son of a barren woman. The significance of the *padartha* of *abhava* was that it was required to bring out clearly the difference between the Samkhya-Yoga and the Nyaya-Vaisheshika conceptions of causality. According to the Samkhya-Yoga the effect resides in the cause prior to its appearance so that coming-into-being is but the fruition of the cause; e.g., the evolvents of *prakriti* are inherent in *prakriti* as a pre-existent effect *(satkaryavada)*. But according to the Nyaya-Vaisheshika the effect does not reside in the cause prior to its appearance so that coming-into-being is the appearance of a novelty; e.g., the wetness of water is not in the atoms which come to be water.

Bondage, according to the Vaisheshika philosophers, was due to the ignorance of the *padarthas,* and particularly to the tendency of confusing the *atman* with the *manas* and the physical body. Liberation was regarded as the separation of the self from all karmic powers. In the condition of liberation there is no life, no consciousness, no pain, and no bliss. It is a state of the individual *atman* devoid of all qualities and all activities. *Moksha* becomes the qualityless, indeterminate, pure nature of the individual *atman* as an inactive substance. It knows nothing, feels nothing, does nothing. No wonder a Vaishnava saint is reported to have said it would be better to be a jackal in the forest of Brindaban than to be liberated according to the Vaisheshika formula!

The early *astika darshanas* did not offer completely satisfactory reasoned alternatives to the authoritative view of the Vedic scriptures, but they marked the beginning of the reforms of *shruti*. Each left its lasting mark on Hinduism. Mimamsa reinstated the importance of ritual and ceremony; Samkhya provided the essential harmonious tension of spirit and matter; Yoga offered the means by which the physical and mental could be disciplined to attain goals which transcended both; Nyaya provided the logical structure without which valid reasoning cannot arrive at truth; and Vaisheshika offered a classification for distinguishing the realities which are discovered rather than created. These five movements constituted the foundation upon which Hinduism as religious philosophy and philosophical religion interpreted and reformed its Vedic tradition.

CHAPTER 12

Vedanta

Yudhishthira on one occasion in the *Mahabharata* observes, "Argument leads to no certain conclusion, the *shrutis* are different from one another; there is not even one *rishi* whose opinion can be accepted by all; the truth about religion and duty is hid in caves." [1] This is an accurate assessment of the intellectual condition of Hinduism in the first seven centuries of the Christian era. But, during the very centuries of the composition of the *Mahabharata,* efforts were being made to develop a consistent *shruti* doctrine. The most successful of these was that of Badarayana, who in his *Vedanta Sutras* (or *Brahma Sutras*), which is dated as early as 250 B.C. and as late as A.D. 450, summarized the teachings of the *Upanishads* into 555 pithy aphorisms so brief and concise that they make no sense without a commentary. It was his *sutras* which prompted the observation that a *sutra* writer rejoiced more in the saving of a word than in the birth of a son. A *sutra* is only a note. It allows a limited amount of freedom in its interpretation. A *sutra* may be compared to a *raga* in Indian music which sets the structure for the musician yet allows considerable freedom for variation within the structure. A *sutra* is two steps removed from the original spiritual experience: first the experience, then the *Upanishad,* and then the *sutra*. Since a spiritual experience is essentially unshareable, the proper response ought to be silence; but some who have religious experiences set for themselves the impossible task of verbalizing the truths revealed in the experiences. Such were the Vedic *rishis*. Poems, analogies, metaphors, and stories were the media of their efforts. The *rishis* in their desire to express the inexpressible truths paid little heed to matters of internal consistency. Badarayana, however, sought to summarize the essential teachings of the Upanishadic *rishis* with a view to philosophical consistency and completeness. The orderly mind of Badarayana is evidenced in the titles of the four chapters of his work: "The Theory of Brahman," "Objections to the Theory of Brahman," "Ways to Attain Knowledge of Brahman," and "The Fruits of the Knowledge of Brahman." The philosophy of the *Upanishads* was known hereafter as "Vedanta," i.e., the last and culminating doctrine of the Vedic literature. The basic works of this philosophy, the *prasthanatraya* (Triple Support), were the *Upanishads,* the *Vedanta Sutras,* and the *Bhagavad Gita.* The three outstanding commentaries on the *Vedanta Sutras* are those of Shankara (ninth century), Ramanuja (eleventh century), and Madhva (thirteenth century), and their forms of Vedanta are known respectively as Advaita (non-dualism), and Vishishtadvaita (nondualism qualified by difference), and Dvaita (dualism). Each regarded his as the correct interpretation of the *Vedanta Sutras,* and therefore of the *Upanishads.* Shankara's interpretation, because his commentary is one of the earliest and perhaps the most thorough, is usually assumed to be *the* Vedanta. The authors of the other commentaries kept an eye on Shankara's as they wrote. The Vedantins agreed that the world is the manifestation of Brahman, that knowledge of Brahman is the *marga* which leads to liberation, and that Brahman can be known only through the *shruti* teachings of the *Upanishads.* They differed regarding the nature of Brahman, how Brahman causes the world to be, the nature of the world, the relation of the individual self to Brahman, and the condition of the self in the liberated state.

Shankara is probably the greatest intellectual India has produced, yet we know very little about his life. This is consistent with the Indian claim that it is the work of a person, not the person, that is important. He was a Malabar Brahmin, and he lived in the ninth century. He broke Hindu tradition by moving from *brahmacharya* to *sannyasa* and introduced within Hinduism the pattern of the celibate monk, a pattern of life which he undoubtedly borrowed from the Buddhists. He established four monasteries (*mutts* or *maths*) at widely separated parts of India, and he wrote commentaries on nine

Upanishads, on Badarayana's *Vedanta Sutras,* and on the *Bhagavad Gita.* Although a staunch defender of *jñana* as the only way of liberation, he composed poems, prayers, and songs to the gods, principally Shiva. Perhaps his loveliest prayer is this one:

> Forgive me, O Shiva, my three great sins. I came on a pilgrimage to Kashi forgetting that you are omnipresent; in thinking about you I forget that you are beyond thought; in praying to you I forget that you are beyond words.

Although not a ritualist, he broke his *sannyasi* vow in order to perform his mother's funeral rites. He was very conservative with respect to caste, holding that *Shudras* had no right to study the *Vedas* nor to perform Vedic rituals. Perhaps the best clue to the character of the man is to be found in the four prerequisites he stipulated for anyone who wished to study at his *mutts:*

1. The prospective student must have a knowledge of the distinction between the eternal and the noneternal.

2. He must have subjugated all desire for the fruits of action either in the present life or in any future life.

3. He must possess the attitudes of tranquility, self-restraint, renunciation, peace of mind, patience, and faith.

4. He must desire release from this world.

One other item about Shankara needs to be mentioned before we examine his systematization of Upanishadic thought. Shankara is often described as the greatest philosopher of India—and so he was—but Western students must be reminded that he was a religious philosopher. It is a serious mistake to identify his interests with those of philosophers who seek knowledge from a sense of wonder. Shankara did not seek philosophical wisdom in order to know; he sought it in order to be saved. He wrote in the introduction to his commentary on the *Vedanta Sutras,* "With a view to freeing one's self from that wrong notion which is the cause of evil and attaining thereby the knowledge of the absolute unity of the Self, the study of the Vedanta texts is begun." The comprehension of Brahman, he wrote in his comment on *Vedanta Sutras* 1. 1. 1, is the highest end of man because it destroys the root of evil and the seed of the entire *samsara*. Again in his commentary on 1. 4. 14 he observed that "a conflict of statements in the Vedanta passages regarding the world would not even matter greatly, since the creation of the world and similar topics are not at all what scripture wishes to teach." In other words, scripture according to Shankara wishes to teach that a man can be set free rather than how the world came into being or what is the nature of the world. Conflicts on metaphysical issues are of little consequence as long as there is no error on how the individual can be liberated. Shankara, of course, is not unique among Indian philosophers in his soterial interest, but his fundamental religious motivation is sometimes forgotten by students who are carried away by the profundity of his metaphysical speculations and arguments. As philosopher he inherited, used, and extended the methods, concepts, and arguments of Buddhism, Nyaya, Vaisheshika, Mimansa, Samkhya, and Yoga, and as an *astika* Hindu his intention was to make his philosophy an accurate interpretation of the authoritative Vedic scriptures. Although he shared with the Buddha disenchantment with the material world and its allurements and the hope of a quiescent liberation, he disagreed completely with the Buddha at one point: he did not share the Buddha's skeptical and agnostic distrust of inherited learning. Shankara was unwilling to break with the past, yet he was open to the needs of his own times. Therefore he set himself to an interpretation of the *Upanishads* which would make them acceptable to the intellectuals of his day and preserve them as authoritative for future generations.

Shankara's Method of Interpreting the Upanishads

Shankara, realizing that the *Upanishads* do not teach one metaphysical and theological view, sought a schema of interpretation which would enable him to formulate a systematic Vedanta. He found what he needed in the distinction made in *Mundaka Upanishad* 1. 1. 4 between *para* (higher) and *apara* (lower) kinds of knowledge. The *apara* kind of knowledge is that which utilizes the *upadhis*, i.e., the limiting conditions of the intellect which include the use of the discursive mind (*manas*), the five senses, and the five organs of action of the body. In the language of Samkhya, all forms of knowing which involve the evolvents of *prakriti* are of the *apara* kind of knowing. *Upadhi* from the point of view of the object means all forms of knowing which refer to space, time, change, or any genuine cause and effect relationship. The *para* kind of knowledge is free from the *upadhis*. It knows by direct insight. According to Shankara, *shruti* is not intended to replace perception and inference; it presents only that knowledge which cannot be attained in any other way. The *para-apara* distinction gave Shankara a powerful apparatus to eliminate from serious consideration all empirical data and all reasoned conclusions which did not start with *shruti*. Furthermore, the *para-apara* distinction made it possible for Shankara to treat all passages in the *Upanishads* which described Brahman as One as a *para* presentation of Reality, i.e., Reality as it is, and all passages which described Brahman dualistically as an *apara* presentation of Reality, i.e., Reality as it seems to be to the sensing mind and the discursive intellect. Shankara wrote in commenting on *Vedanta Sutras* 3. 2. 21, "The preferable theory therefore, is to distinguish with us two classes of texts, according as Brahman is represented as possessing form or as devoid of it."

The *para-apara* distinction cannot be regarded literally as two points of view. *Apara* is the phenomenal view of things, i.e., things viewed by the senses, and thought about discursively. But *para* knowledge is things experienced from no point of view. "Higher" and "lower," or "primary" and "secondary," forms of knowing are inferior translations of *para* and *apara*. A better translation would be to interpret *apara* as "knowledge" and *para* as "insight confirming *shruti*," for Shankara was a scholastic who had committed himself to the *Upanishads* as the final, complete, and infallible authority on the ultimate truths about man and the universe. He based his authoritarianism on the view that the ancients had better insights than the wise of his day, since they had direct concourse with the gods. His first allegiance was always to Vedic authority. For example, in commenting on *Vedanta Sutras* 1. 1. 2 he said that "the comprehension of Brahman is effected by the ascertainment, consequent on discussion, of the sense of the Vedanta-texts, not either by inference or by the other means of right knowledge." Later in this paragraph, as if to reassure his readers that he did have a place for reasoning, he added, "Scripture itself, moreover, allows argumentation; for certain passages . . . declare that human understanding assists scripture." Again in 2. 1. 6 he wrote that Brahman "is to be known solely on the ground of holy tradition." To those who interpret 2. 1. 6 "But it is seen . . ." to mean that reasoning also is to be allowed its place, Shankara replied that "the passage must not deceitfully be taken as enjoining bare independent ratiocination, but must be understood to represent reasoning as a subordinate auxiliary of intuitional knowledge."

Shankara used two secondary devices in his interpretation of the *Upanishads*. One was the principle of earlier and later: a conflict between two passages was sometimes settled by pointing out that the later view was a correction of the earlier. The other device was to regard a passage as metaphorical when it conflicted with Shankara's own view, e.g., 2. 4. 2, and as literal when it confirmed Shankara's view, e.g., 1. 1. 6. Thus Shankara had an arsenal for pointing the Upanishadic nose of wax in the direction he chose, and the *Upanishads,* like all proper authoritative religious texts, proved to be sufficiently enigmatic to permit such latitudes of interpretation.

Shankara began his commentary on the *Vedanta Sutras* by arguing that it is by *avatah-pramanya* (intrinsic validation), a concept he borrowed from the Mimamsa philosophers, that we know that the whole sphere of the ego and the whole sphere of the nonego cannot be identified. Yet man seems intent upon coupling these spheres. He has a natural propensity to superimpose the nature and attributes of the one upon the other. This superimposition (*adhyasa*) is particularly pernicious when objective qualities are superimposed upon the interior self. He ignorantly turns the "I" into "me." He separates the self into an existent "I" and an existent "me," and thus suffers the anguish of self-ignorance. The proof of the self's reality is the act of immediate awareness. Shankara believed it is possible to become free from the wrong views of the self, and thus to be free from the causes of existential evil in human life. Shankara's philosophy was an effort to overcome the error of superimposition and to see reality as an integrated whole. Shankara was convinced that the deplorable condition of man is due to a gross misunderstanding of value and reality, and that through correct understanding man can find the highest values.

Shankara's Philosophical Method

The goal of philosophy according to Shankara is to discover that which when known will make everything known. But knowing is far more than intellectual awareness. Shankara, in accord with an ancient tradition in India, held that to know is to attain and to possess. The Hindus, even when they were most sacerdotal, held that knowing was a critical part of the ritual, or, to state this negatively, that not understanding the meaning of the ritual would vitiate it. For example, in *Atharva Veda* 8. 10 almost every line ends with the phrase "who knows this," which is a reminder that knowledge of the meaning of the sacrifice was a necessary condition of the proper performance, and that ignorant carrying out of rituals was ineffectual. The knowledge which philosophy seeks and which religion requires, according to Shankara, is a knowledge which is coherent throughout. Such knowledge is found in the *Upanishads* if one will apply to the teachings of the *rishis* the formula of *para-apara*. Shankara did not hesitate to treat the *Upanishads* as authoritative when he deemed it necessary, e.g., "the fact of everything having its self in Brahman cannot be grasped without the aid of the scriptural passage: That thou art." [2] Reason, he believed, can assist *shruti* when it goes beyond "knowledge" rooted in experience. Empirical knowledge is satisfactory for purposes of successful activity in the world of the senses, the world of *apara* knowledge, but it is dangerously deceiving in the world of *para* knowledge. Perceptual relations have no validity in the world which only insight confirming *shruti* can grasp. As far as the real world is concerned, perception yields ignorance. All our sense knowledge is nonknowledge (*avidya*). Shankara did not condemn human beings for trusting in *avidya* which leads to the superimposition (*adhyasa*) of the objective upon the subjective, for this is the very condition of the finite human existence. What he asked is that humans understand that the human condition is itself the assessment of our real nature from the *apara* form of knowing. Reasoning (*tarka*), he said, is not an independent source of knowledge. It is chiefly a means for the strengthening of faith in the *Upanishads* and for the refutation of error by means of the examining of assumptions and the testing of the validity of arguments. Shankara did not think of himself in the role of a teacher of truth; rather his self-image was that of an unmasker of ignorance. He believed that when error is exposed, truth shines forth by its own light. Shankara said truths are revealed to man in four sorts of revelation: (1) a general revelation open to all mankind in the human experience of living in a world of name and form; (2) the Vedic revelation which is given in all the Vedic literature, but primarily in the *Upanishads;* (3) the revelation given through incarnations of the gods; (4) *anubhuti* revelation, which is direct experience of truth arising from meditation on Upanishadic texts.

In support of his view of revelation Shankara called attention to passages in the *Upanishads* which point out four states of consciousness, e.g., *Brihad-Aranyaka* 5. 14. 3–7; *Maitri* 6. 19 and 7. 11. 7; *Mandukya* 1–12. The first is the waking state, a state said to have "nineteen mouths," i.e., the five organs of sense, the five motor organs, the five vital breaths or winds of the inner body (associated with the heart, rectum, navel, throat, and genitals), the organizing intellect (*manas*), the wisdom intellect (*buddhi*), the egoizing intellect (*aham-kara*), and the universalizing intellect (*chitta*). In the waking state the individual never doubts but that his "mouths" are the avenues to reality, and that the world he is aware of by means of the "mouths" is the real world. The second is the dreaming state of consciousness in which cognitions are inward rather than outward. It is the state in which the objects of awareness are created by the dreamer himself. When he awakens from dreaming, the objects cease to exist. The third state of consciousness is the dreamless or deep sleep state. In this condition there are no objects whatsoever, but there is consciousness; e.g., one may say upon awakening, "I slept well. I was conscious of nothing." That is, one recalls that one had a sound sleep, yet it was an awareness without any objects. In deep sleep it is the mind that goes to sleep, not the self. *Turiya*, the fourth state, can perhaps only be described as being beyond the third state. *Mandukya* 12 says it is "the cessation of development, tranquil, benign, without a second." In *turiya* there is nothing to distract. It is the ideal condition for *ekagrata* (one-point mindedness). It is a witnessing, transcending state which defies description. By appealing to *turiya* Shankara was calling attention to a life deep within the self of each of us where we find a nondual reality. While on the surface of things we experience a dual world, we arrive at a kind of "knowledge" about it which is really nonknowledge, and we superimpose upon ourselves the objective features of the experienced world, but there is also a nondual world of which we have occasional intimations. This is Reality. In *turiya* the *avidya* which rose so naturally in our waking states of consciousness can be seen for what it is, and we can by an integral intuitive experience discover what Reality is and at the same time who we are, for they turn out to be identical. In pointing out that the *turiya* state transcends both the dreaming and the dreamless state Shankara was avoiding the solipsistic view that each of us is the author of experience. Shankara was, in the language of Western philosophy, an idealist but not a subjective idealist. Shankara's choice of the word *"jñana"* for the means of becoming aware of the Reality within was an unfortunate one, since knowledge necessarily implies the *triputi*, i.e., a knowing subject, a process of knowing, and a known object. All knowledge prevents us from knowing Brahman! The term *"anubhava"* (intuitional consciousness) might have been better. Shankara's problem was the problem of mystics who betray the subject-object transcending experience when they try to talk about it. All language objectifies. Terms like "perfect knowledge," "direct awareness," "pure consciousness," and "absolute intuition" can only hint at the ineffable. "Taste and see for yourself" is the least misrepresenting statement a mystic can make about his mystical experience.

Shankara has suffered through the years from the adulation of his followers. He has even been declared to be an *avatara* of Shiva. Unfortunately, his followers have sometimes failed to recognize the necessity of endless revisions of even Shankara's interpretations if the Absolute is to be expressed in the shifting categories of temporally limited human concepts. Shankara interpreted *shruti*, but his interpretation is not *shruti*.

Atman

When Shankara applied his interpretation of the *Upanishads* and his philosophical method, he produced a reformation which was the fruition of the philosophy of his predecessors and the starting point for his successors. The simplicity of his reformation has often been lost by those who do not distinguish the essentials from the peripherals. The essentials of his reformation consisted of two parts: (1) he turned inward rather than outward, and (2) what he sought first and foremost was value rather than reality. The most striking aspect of his reformation was that what he found within he affirmed to be identical to the external: *Atman* is Brahman. He called his philosophy "Advaita" (nonduality) in order to stress the identity of inner reality and outer reality and perhaps to call attention that, although he used much Samkhya language, he was not a Samkhya philosopher. In his nondualism he also argued for the untenability of other dualities: cause and effect, Brahman and god, Brahman and the world, and Brahman and the individual self.

Shankara believed that man's greatest need was to discover the Self. His philosophical predecessors had arrived at conceptions of the self, but in Shankara's opinion their selves were pseudo-selves. The self in Nyaya-Vaisheshika was a substance, a thing among things. Consciousness for these philosophers was an accidental property of the embodied self and not even an accident of the liberated self. The self in Samkhya-Yoga was said by the defenders of this *darshana* to be conscious, but they would not allow it to be conscious of any thing. Moreover, the Samkhya-Yoga self was a pluralistic concept, and every self was limited by other selves. Both Samkhya-Yoga and Nyaya-Vaisheshika thinkers erred, said Shankara, in failing to grasp the unity and subjectivity of the true Self.

According to Shankara when the Upanishadic *rishis* promised to teach the knowledge which when known would make all things known, they did not have in mind any object of knowledge. Instead they were attempting to nudge their pupils to the discovery of the knower. The self as knower was to be discovered by an immediate intuitive experience, not by discursive reasoning. But alas—the pupil who happily announced that he understood because he knew the self as the subject of knowledge was still far from the Advaita view of the Self, for the Self according to Shankara is neither a subject nor an object, neither an "I" nor a "me," but the basis of the subject-object distinction-distortion.

When one looks within, the first entity one finds is the atomic self, the agent of acting, the knower of the known. This is the *samsarin,* the transmigrating entity, the *jiva.* This individual self is that which distinguishes one person from another. It is the self identified with different minds and bodies. It is finite, separate, and temporal. It is the phenomenal self of the individual living being. All living beings—gods, demons, humans, lower animals, plants, and even so-called inanimate objects—at least for some Hindus and for all Jains, are *jivas.* The *jiva* is always limited both by other *jivas* and by what is not *jiva* at all, the non-*jiva.* I-thou and I-it are relations common to all *jivas.* The *jiva* as the principle of identity through change is often confused with the body and the mind in such statements as "I am here," "I am fat," "I weigh more now than I weighed last year," "I am in pain," "I remember," "I think," etc. The *jiva* is the self seen from a point of view, the self objectified, the self with *upadhis* (limiting adjuncts). Shankara did not deny the experience of the *jiva,* but he called attention to *jiva*-consciousness as part of the *apara* view of the world. It is integral to the way of appearance. The *jiva* is as real as the convergent rails one sees when looking down the parallel rails of a railroad track. Convergence is an *upadhi* we superimpose on the rails. The *jiva* is the self conceived as an object associated with psycho-physical attributes and functions. The *jiva* is the appearance of the Self in various forms of dignity and power. It is the revelation in a graduated series of psychic beings of that which is eternally unchanging and uniform. In commenting on *Vedanta Sutra* 1. 3. 19 Shankara argued that the Upanishadic formula *tat tvam asi* (that thou art) refers to the difference between "the real nature of the individual self" (the *tat*) and the "second nature, i.e., that aspect of it which depends on fictitious limiting conditions" (the *tvam*). This difference, however, is often overlooked. We tend to take the "second nature" as the real. We are like a person who in twilight mistakes a post for a man. We do not rise to the knowledge of the Self. We remain at the level of the individual self. "But when, discarding the aggregate of body, sense-organs and mind, it [the individual self] arrives, by means of *shruti*, at the knowledge that it is not itself the aggregate, that it does not form part of transmigratory existence, but is the True, the Real, the Self, whose nature is pure intelligence; then knowing itself to be the nature of unchangeable, eternal cognition, it lifts itself above the vain conceit of being one with the body, and itself becomes the Self, whose nature is unchanging, eternal cognition."

The Self is the *Atman*. The *Atman* is the *jiva* with *upadhis* removed; or, to state this conversely, the *jiva* is the *Atman* hidden by *avidya* (false knowledge, nonknowledge, or ignorance). *Atman* and *jiva* are not two selves. Railroad companies do not lay down two sets of rails, one that is parallel and one that is convergent! The *Atman* is the self vis-à-vis *para vidya*; the *jiva* is the self vis-à-vis *apara vidya*. To translate *"Atman"* as "self" is always a risk, as it reminds the hearer of terms like "mind," "mental states," "soul," and "spirit." Also it tends to introduce the connotation of an existent substance. But the *Atman* according to Shankara is the Reality which substantiates mental and spiritual states such as thinking, remembering, imagining, willing, feeling, valuing, etc. It is the *Atman* by reason of which these states are experienced as the functioning of a substantial ego rather than the flux of psychical processes (*skandhas*) as they are conceived in Buddhism. Shankara expressed his rejection and revulsion of Buddhism by calling it "the full destroyer of the world." Shankara appealed again and again to the experience of his readers in two analogies. One illustrated the illusive nature of the *jiva* by comparing the *Atman* to a real juggler who stands on the ground performing the rope trick, and the *jiva* to the illusive juggler who climbs up the rope. The other illustrated the limited nature of the *jiva* by comparing it to the space within a pot as related to the space outside the pot. The *jiva* is the embodied self which acts, enjoys, builds up *karma,* knows, and is affected by pleasure and pain. The *Atman* is the self which has no relationships with anything.

The reality of the *Atman* is self-validating. Its reality is intuited. It is the ground of the being of the self of everyone. "For everyone is conscious of the existence of his self, and never thinks 'I am not.' If the existence of the self were not known, everyone would think 'I am not.' " [3] A twentieth-century Advaita Vedantin has said, "The truth is that there is no need to look for the self. We simply cannot deny it. It is the denier of the denial. What is needed is not to prove the reality of the self. For while we can never prove this reality, there is also no need to prove it. The self is the presupposition of every proof. Any proof is a proof of the self. It is the self that approves or ascertains. Self-certainty is thus the only absolute certainty. It is the ground of all certainties. We conclude that it is wrong to look for the self as some kind of enduring mental entity which is to be known through introspection, or to deny it because we can find no such entity. . . . How then is the self known? We contend that it is not strictly known. The knowing self is never known. But are we ignorant of it? Shall we treat the self as something that is real, but which is forever unknowable? This conclusion too is unwarranted. We have no ignorance of the self. We have, in an important sense, perfect knowledge. . . . There is no knowledge appropriate to the self except to be the self. And no one can assert that he is at anytime not his self. . . . What we understand by self-knowledge here is that between the self and the so-called knowledge of the self no distinction can be made. The self is the knowledge. . . . Instead of ourselves mentally approaching the self in order to be what it is, we must let the self approach us, declare itself to us." [4]

The uniqueness of man is that he among the *jivas* is *jiva*-aware, and thus he transcends his *jiva*-ness. He knows himself as *Atman.* He can understand that the qualities and acts which he identifies as his are in fact a way of looking at the universal substratum which makes the psychic appearances possible. This true Self is the "One without a second." It is independently real. But to say this is not to affirm that the *Atman* exists. The *Atman* is the transcendental ground of experience which under the conditions of causality, time, and space—which Advaitins often denote as *nama-rupa*—appears as existent *jivas*. Shankara sometimes referred to *Atman* as "self-exis-tent." His intention must have been to call attention to the independent character of *Atman,* but since "existence" is a relational term requiring reference points with other entities, we are likely to misunderstand Shankara if we use terms like "existent" or "self-exis-tent" with respect to *Atman.* "Existence-ness" might be appropriate, although not very informative. *Atman* does not belong to the order of objectively real things, and, consequently, it cannot be said to be the highest real being among beings, yet it is that whose reality makes all conscious existents exist. Students of Shankara do not agree as to the contribution, if any, the *jivas* make to the *Atman.* Since the *Atman* is both immanent in and transcendent to conscious states and processes, a new category is sometimes used to signify the *Atman* as an abiding reality present in the life of *jivas:* identity-in-and-above-difference. The doctrine of *maya* is the watershed which divides the interpreters of Shankara. Those who regard the world of name and form as a meaningless and unfortunate diversion from the true life of the spirit stress the independence and transcendence of the *Atman.* Those who regard the world as a meaningful and necessary manifestation of the *Atman* stress the immanence of the *Atman* in the *jivas,* and may indicate that the activity of *jivas* is essential to the fullness of *Atman's* reality, although this comes close to reading *Atman* as a potentiality rather than a reality.

A serious problem lingers in all discussions of the self: how can one treat the self so due consideration is given both to the demands of the empirical facts of the activity of the self and also to the demands of the transcendental unity of the self? David Hume after writing his *A Treatise on Human Nature* added an appendix in which he stated misgivings about his own analysis: "In short, there are two principles which I cannot render consistent, nor is it in my power to renounce either of them, *viz.* that all our distinct perceptions are distinct existences, and that the mind never perceives any real connection among distinct existences. Did our perceptions either inhere in something simple and individual, or did the mind perceive some real connection among them, there would be no difficulty in the case." It was the genius of Shankara and of the Upanishadic *rishis* to have been aware of this problem and to have proposed as their answer "something simple and individual" in which perceptions inhere: the *Atman* as the presupposition and basis of all the experiences of all *jivas*. Hume saw the problem, but he could not find a solution. He wrote, "For my part, I must plead the privilege of a sceptic, and confess that this difficulty is too hard for my understanding. I pretend not, however, to pronounce it absolutely insuperable. Others, perhaps, or myself, upon more mature reflections, may discover some hypothesis that will reconcile these contradictions." But Hume in his more mature reflections did not arrive at a reconciling hypothesis, and, unfortunately, he was not aware that Shankara had discovered such a hypothesis in the *Upanishads*.

One might be tempted in the context of Samkhya-Yoga metaphysics to identify the Vedanta of Shankara as a spiritual monism of a universal *Purusha* as opposed to the *purusha-prakriti* dualism. The argument in support of this is that according to Shankara the only clue we have for understanding the *Atman* is an individual's awareness of being a *jiva*. But to argue from the spirituality of the *jiva* to the spirituality of the *Atman* is to forget that the *jiva* is an object in the world of objects and the *Atman* is not an object; and to argue from the spirituality of the self, i.e., the subject-knowing-*jiva*-as-object, is to forget that *Atman* is not a subject. *Atman* transcends completely the subject-object category. *Atman* is not a Samkhya Purusha of *purushas*. Nevertheless, it is correct to identify the *Atman* as Reality comprehended subjectively, the highest Self, the *Paramatman*. *Atman* is Reality as transcendental pure consciousness, i.e., as consciousness which is not the limited consciousness of objects, but which when manifested in the *nama-rupa* world as a *jiva* is a being whose essence is the functioning of conscious awareness.

Atman as pure consciousness is not conscious. A *jiva* is conscious, and, as a being whose essence is the functioning of consciousness, it requires an object of awareness in order to exist as a conscious being. When Shankara advised human beings to turn from the world of sense objects and thought objects to the *Atman,* he was not asking *jivas* to substitute knowledge of *Atman* for knowledge of non-*Atman;* rather he was asking them to recognize the *upadhis* under which conscious beings are aware of objects and to allow self-luminous Reality to shine forth.

Brahman

Reality comprehended subjectively is *Atman,* and Reality comprehended objectively is Brahman, but Reality is One—the *Atman-Brahman.* Man's chief goal, says Shankara, is "the complete comprehension" of Brahman, since it destroys the root of all evil, the *avidya* which is the seed of the entire *samsara.* There is a sense in which Brahman is known before the knowing, because Brahman is the Self, the knower. So the "thatness" of Brahman is established, but the "whatness" of Brahman is not established—and on that there is "a conflict of opinions." Shankara as a lover of debate thrived on intellectual conflict. Hence much of his commentary on the *Vedanta Sutras* is reasoned refutations of those whom he believed held erroneous views both Vedic and non-Vedic. We noted in Chapter Six that there are three views of the Cosmic One in the *Upanishads*: (1) personal, (2) impersonal and not abstract, and (3) impersonal and abstract. Shankara supported the third as the *para* view, the first two as the *apara* views. Although he conceded the validity of all three views, he condensed them into two: "Brahman is apprehended under two forms; in the first place as qualified by limiting conditions owing to the multiformity of the evolutions of name and form (i.e., the multiformity of the created world); in the second place as being the opposite of this, i.e., free from all limiting conditions whatsoever." [5] The former, Shankara claimed, is Brahman as the object of knowledge; the latter is Brahman as the object of ignorance. This is not a very clear way to distinguish the two forms. The former is the Para Brahman, the Brahman which has no attributes or qualities, the Nirguna Brahman; the latter is the Apara Brahman, the Brahman which has attributes or qualities, the Saguna Brahman. The unqualified or unconditioned Brahman is the Brahman devoid of all *upadhis.* Such a Brahman, of course, cannot be known since objects are known through their attributes. Every attribute which is applied to Nirguna must be eliminated by the Upanishadic *"neti, neti"* (inadequate, inadequate). This is the Brahman of negations: "It is not coarse, not fine, not short, not long, not glowing like fire, not adhesive like water, without shadow and without darkness, without air and without space, without stickiness, colorless, tasteless, without eye, without ear, without voice, without wind, without energy, without breath, without mouth, without measure, without inside, and without outside." [6] Later redactions of these passages included in addition that Brahman is "intangible, without personal or family name, unaging, undying, without fear, immortal, stainless, not uncovered, nor covered." The list of negatives could be extended *ad infinitum*. Saguna Brahman is described as "He who consists of mind, whose body is life, whose form is light, whose conception is truth, whose soul is space, containing all works, containing all desires, containing all odors, containing all tastes, encompassing this whole world." [7] Nirguna is usually designated as "It" and Saguna as "He."

The Nirguna-Saguna distinction is an effort to differentiate Reality and appearance, the numinous and the phenomenal; but there is something more profound in the two forms than a distinction between how things are and how things appear to be. Shankara had in mind two definitions of Brahman or two different roles of Brahman, and he was not willing to give up either. He defined Brahman as the cause of the world and also as the substratum of functions associated with the self such as knowing and valuing. Unlike the Samkhya, he contended that there was an Absolute One which was both efficient and material cause of the world. He did not hold to an evolutionary theory of the world out of Brahman. Nothing actually evolved from Brahman. But he held that Brahman was the substratum of the world such that unless there were Brahman there would be no world. Shankara had inherited from his philosophical predecessors of the reformation period two distinct views of causality: (1) the non-pre-existent effect theory (*asatkaryavada*) and (2) the pre-existent effect theory (*satkaryavada*). The former, which was held by the Nyaya-Vaisheshika philosophers, is the theory that the effect does not exist in the cause as a potential or undeveloped effect. Cause and effect are two different substances. The cause in the process of production ceases to exist. Coming-into-being is a process in which a novelty appears. This theory is therefore sometimes called the *arambhavada* (the doctrine of new creation). An example is the wetness of water which is not found in the elements hydrogen and oxygen. The example given by the Indian philosophers was that of clay which due to the skill of the potter becomes an urn. The latter theory, which was held by the Samkhya-Yoga philosophers, is the theory that the effect does exist in the cause prior to its appearance as an effect. The effect is the cause transformed. Hence the theory is sometimes called the *parinamanvada* (the doctrine of modification). According to this theory nothing really new comes into being since the effect pre-existed in the cause. The effect is the cause transformed. Those who supported this view contended that a pottery urn was somehow in the clay all the time, for unless this were the case the clay would never become an urn.

Shankara rejected both theories on the ground that they established a duality of cause and effect, and also on the ground that both were concessions to the Buddhistic view of a dynamic changing world. Shankara offered his *satkaranavada* theory (the existent cause theory) as contrary to the theories held by the Nyaya-Vaisheshika and the Samkhya-Yoga philosophers and as contradictory to the *asatkaranavada* (the nonexistent cause theory) held by the Buddhists. According to Shankara's theory the effect is only an apparent manifestation of the cause. The cause alone is real; the effect is illusory. It is also called the *vivartavada* (the doctrine of appearance). The "cause" (which is not actually a cause since it never produces an effect) remains ever the same. The "effect" is a superimposition (*adhyasa*) upon the "cause." The substance called "cause," though unchanged, does have an appearance from a point of view of having undergone modification or transformation. Shankara's theory is a transformation theory like the Samkhya theory, only, whereas the Samkhya transformation is real, Shankara's transformation is false. Hence Shankara spoke of the nondifference of cause and effect: "In reality, however, that distinction does not exist because there is understood to be non-difference (identity) of cause and effect. The effect is this manifold world . . . the cause is the highest Brahman. Of the effect, it is understood that in reality it is non-different from the cause, i.e., has no existence apart from the cause." [8] We can see why Shankara was so concerned to reject the two doctrines: he held that the world had no existence apart from Brahman, and he regarded both doctrines of causality as contending that the effect was an independent existent. This was a curious *non sequitur* on Shankara's part, for "cause" and "effect" are relational terms like "husband" and "wife" and do not denote independent entities. Shankara interpreted the two theories to mean that both Brahman as cause and the world as effect had independent status, and this, when applied to the entire world of gods, physical universe, and *jivas,* Shankara would not allow: "The entire body of effects has no existence apart from Brahman." The world is Brahman with *upadhis,* i.e., Brahman falsely transformed.

We have said that Shankara defined Brahman as both the "cause" of the world and as the substratum of knowing and valuing. The former definition is sometimes known as *tatastha-loksana* (definition by appeal to an accidental feature of the thing defined) because, according to Shankara, the entire world is accidental to the nature of Brahman. Brahman would be Brahman with or without the world. The second definition is known as *svarupa-loksana* (definition by appeal to an essential part of the thing defined). An example of the two types of definition is found in *Taittiriya Upanishad* 3. 1–6. A son asked his father to define Brahman for him. The father answered in five definitions, ranging in customary *guru* fashion from the first, the easiest and most misleading definition, progressively through the better definitions to the final and best definition. The first definition offered is "That whence beings here are born, that by which when born they live, that into which on deceasing they enter . . . That is Brahman." This is definition *per accidens.* It is a fact that things have no existence other than insofar as they depend upon Brahman, but the existence of things is accidental to the nature of Brahman. In the next three definitions Brahman is defined as life, as the mind, and as knowledge. Each successive definition moves further away from that which is accidental to Brahman and closer to that which is essential to Brahman. The fifth definition is: "Brahman is *ananda.* For truly beings here are born from *ananda,* when born they live by *ananda,* on deceasing they enter into *ananda.*" "Ananda" is customarily translated as "bliss," "joy," and "delight." But these translations do not bring out the full meaning. "The highest values" would be a better translation. Brahman is the ground of beings, the foundation of existence; but this does not indicate the essential nature of Brahman, for Brahman undergoes false transformation not for the sake of existence but for the sake of values. Brahman is the ground of all values. Insofar as values require a physical substratum, the physical world is, but the real goal of existence is value. Shankara offered as his reformation of the *Upanishads* an axiology, a theory of value, rather than an ontology, a theory of reality. Hence the multiple term *satchitananda* (being-consciousness-value) which Shankara used to denote the Brahman meant that Brahman was *sat* (the foundation of being) in order that consciousness be, and that Brahman was *satchit* (the foundation of being and consciousness) in order that values might be. Therefore, Brahman is to be known as *satchitananda* (the foundation of being and consciousness as telic to the essential nature of Brahman, i.e., the foundation of all values). Thus it becomes clearer why Shankara regarded the understanding of Brahman as the highest end of man.

Maya

Shankara as Hindu scholiast started with the authoritative *Upanishads*, but Shankara as Hindu defender of the faith often started with the contingent physical world as an effect, particularly when refuting the Samkhya philosophers whom he called "the semi-destroyers of the world." Whereas the Samkhya separated the material cause and the operative cause of the world, Shankara rejected such separation on the grounds that this would be inconsistent with his fundamental *advaita* position. Yet his rejection seems dangerously close to Samkhya: "If we admitted some antecedent state of the world as the independent cause of the actual world, we should implicitly admit the doctrine that all is derived from an eternal fundamental substance. What we admit is, however, only a previous state dependent on the Highest Lord, not an independent state. A previous state of the world such as the one assured by us must necessarily be admitted, since it is according to sense and reason." [9] Nirguna Brahman creates nothing; but Saguna Brahman, who is known by the religious term "Ishvara" (Highest Lord), does create the world by acting upon the "undeveloped principle" which Shankara says can be denoted by terms like *akasha* (ether), *akshara* (the imperishable), and *maya*: "For *maya* is properly called undeveloped or non-manifested since it cannot be defined either as that which is or that which is not." [10]

Shankara as a Vedic fundamentalist was usually uncreative in his approach to the *Upanishads*, but in his doctrine of *maya* he was creative—and he left for his followers a concept over which they have wrangled ever since the master's death. The word *"maya"* is sparingly used in the Vedic literature. In the *Rig* it means magical power, and in the *Upanishads* it is the power of the gods to create an illusion. *Maya* as the ontological negative principle is coupled with *avidya* as the principle of ignorance. Another term was used more often by Shankara for the foundation of his doctrine of *maya*: this is the term *iva* (as it were). For example, in *Brihad-Aranyaka* 4. 3. 13 a *rishi* describes a dreamer who is "now, as it were *(iva)*, enjoying pleasure with women; now, as it were *(iva)*, laughing and even beholding fearful sights," and again in the same *Upanishad rishis* refer to duality itself as an example of *iva*.[11] Shankara also made good use of *iva* in his commentary; e.g., *Vedanta Sutras* 2. 3. 43 reads, "The self is a part of the Lord," and Shankara comments, "By 'part' we mean 'a part as it were *(iva)*,' since a being not composed of parts cannot have parts in the literal sense." Shankara brought together the Upanishadic concepts of *avidya*, *iva*, and *maya* to form his doctrine of the ontological status of everything in the *apara* world.

Maya denotes both the "activity" and the "effects" of Nirguna Brahman because there are neither acts nor effects. But what can this mean? Some Advaitins have taken Shankara literally and have claimed that Shankara taught an illusionism; e.g., K. C. Bhattacharyya, "The acosmism of Shankara goes beyond realism and idealism by reducing the world to absolute illusion," [12] and P. D. Shastri, "It is true beyond doubt that Shankara means by *Maya* nothing but illusion." [13] Other equally qualified interpreters of Shankara disagree; e.g., S. Radhakrishnan writes that for Shankara "unreal the world is, illusory it is not," [14] and W. S. Urquhart says, "It [*maya*] was only a symbolic expression of that consciousness which lies in the depths of religious devotion, and which is content to see the world pass away and the glory thereof, if only it may abide in the Eternal." [15] We cannot settle this quarrel among scholars in this brief space, but

Shankara's own words seem to support Radhakrishnan and Urquhart. For example, in his commentary on *Vedanta Sutra* 3. 2. 21 Shankara puts in the mouth of "our opponent" the observation that the *Veda* prescribes the annihilation of the world as a condition of final release. Shankara in reply asks what sort of annihilation does his opponent have in mind, and he suggests two possibilities. The opponent may mean that the prescribed annihilation of the world is analogous to the annihilation of hardness in butter which is effected by bringing it into contact with fire. But if this is what he means, says Shankara, then "the Vedic injunctions bid us do something impossible, for no man can actually annihilate this whole existing world with all its animated bodies and all its elementary substances such as earth and so on." But the opponent may mean that the world of name and form which is superimposed upon Brahman by nescience (*avidya*) is to be dissolved by knowledge, just as the phenomenon of a double moon which is due to a curable disease of the eyes is removed by application of medicine. If this is what the opponent means, then "the only thing needed is that the knowledge of Brahman should be conveyed by Vedic passages sublating the apparent plurality superimposed upon Brahman by nescience." This text from Shankara would seem to indicate that Shankara did not regard the empirical world as unreal and worthless but that humans should strive toward their liberation by attempting to see the opaque Unity which is manifested through the obvious pluralities.

Much of the confusion about the doctrine of *maya* arises from the fact that its relational nature is either ignored or unknown. Shankara does not say the world is *maya*, as though this were a factual statement, for from the *apara* point of view the world is very real, and only a fool would attempt to deny it. There is a story in India about a man who refused to move out of the path of an elephant because he learned from the village teacher that the elephant was *maya*. The elephant threw him off the road and into the ditch. When he went to the teacher for an explanation, he was told that the next time he met a *maya* elephant he better get his *maya* body out of the way! A question like "Is the world an illusion?" cannot be answered by yes or no because it has not been fully put. The question must indicate by whom the world is regarded as an illusion. "The world of *maya*" is not merely a descriptive ontological statement; it is also a prescriptive axiological statement. The world is—and ought to be—*maya* for the enlightened man when considering the world from the point of view of *para vidya*. The man in pursuit of enlightenment is advised to place his mind and affections on matters other than immediate and pressing material needs and satisfactions. The world is very much with the unenlightened man; but the enlightened man takes toward the world, its joys and its sorrows, an attitude of sufficient detachment and good humor so that neither its pains nor its pleasures can deter him from the pursuit of the perfect realization of the Self.

The term "*maya*" appears in but one *sutra* of the *Vedanta Sutras*: "But the dream world is mere appearance (*maya*) on account of its nature not being manifest with the totality of attributes of the waking state."[16] Shankara makes no significant comment on this *sutra*. According to Shankara the clue to the presence of *maya* is the use of "I" or "me" or "mine" in their individualistic senses; i.e., any experience constituted by or following from the distinction between subject and object, or between self and nonself, is a *maya* experience. *Maya* is that ontic-noetic state in which limitations (*upadhis*) are imposed upon Reality. We are in a state of *maya* whenever we fail to recognize the oneness of Reality. *Maya* is beginningless, because time is a distinction within *maya*. *Maya* is unthinkable because thought is subject to *maya*. *Maya* is indescribable because language is a result of *maya*. To understand *maya* one must transcend the understanding made possible by *maya*. The Advaitins thus found themselves in a double bind: to "know" Brahman they had to fashion a false dichotomy between knower and known, and to "know" *maya* they had to escape the dichotomy without which there is no *maya*. If the Advaitins were challenged because their doctrine of *maya* and their *vivartavada* theory of causation did not explain the world in terms of the world, they replied that this was exactly the point—the world as an appearance can only be explained in terms of that of which it is an appearance. Post-Shankara Advaita Vedantists split on *maya* and *avidya*: some held the terms are the same; others contended that *maya* is positive and *avidya* is negative, by which they meant there is a difference between Ishvara and *jivas* in that the former is to be described as *maya,* the latter as *avidya.* But for Shankara *avidya* or *maya* is the cosmic principle by which manifested things are neither real nor unreal. Shankara held rigid notions of *sat* (reality) and *asat* (unreality). Only Brahman is *sat* in the sense of Absolute Being which is permanent, eternal, and infinite. *Asat* or absolute nonbeing is for Shankara complete impossibility, e.g., the son of a barren mother. *Maya* partakes of *sat* and *asat,* yet it is neither *sat* nor *asat.* It is contrary to and other than both Absolute Reality and absolute nonreality. The physical world and its effects, the gods, and the *jivas* are the entities within the "world" of *maya.* They are said to be *satasatvilaksana* (other than real or unreal) and *anirvacaniya* (indescribable in terms of being and nonbeing). A *maya* object is one in which both the name and the "what" are conventional.

Shankara had two sorts of *maya* in mind: the *maya* of substance and the *maya* of attribute. An example of the first is the mistaking of a rope for a snake. The false reality of "snake" is superimposed on the rope. This is the *maya* of experiencing the physical world as though it were Reality. The person in this state of *avidya* does not know that the world is but the appearance of Brahman. The second sort of *maya* consists in applying a false quality to an object; e.g., a person looking at a white stone through amber glass sees the stone as yellow. This is the *maya* of regarding a self as an atomic *jiva* rather than as *Atman.* This distinction is important for Shankara, for if the *jiva* were *maya* as the "snake" is *maya* there would be nothing to be liberated.

One of the puzzling questions arising from Shankara's reformulation of the Upanishadic insights has to do with the rationale for the world of *maya.* Why the world? Shankara quotes *Taittiriya Upanishad* 2. 6, "Would that I were many! Let me procreate myself!" This, says Shankara, "is declared to have originated the entire creation." [17] Shankara does not indicate why the Brahman would desire to multiply. One of the complications is that Brahman here must mean for Shankara Saguna Brahman, and Saguna is Himself a *maya* product, so Shankara is not actually dealing with the question of why there is *maya* but why the *maya* Brahman would create a *maya* world and *maya* selves. In his commentary on *Vedanta Sutras* 2. 1. 14 he says, "He [Ishvara] stands in the realm of the phenomenal in the relation of a ruler to the so-called *jivas.*" Ishvara is the phenomenal Lord of the phenomenal world and the phenomenal ruler of phenomenal souls. In 2. 1. 33 he speculates that the creative activity by which the *maya* world comes into being is mere sport (*lila*), i.e., free whimsical activity with no end in view. *Lila* is related to the Latin *ludere* (to play) from which the English term "illusion" comes. *Vedanta Sutras* 2. 1. 32 states, "Brahman is not the creator of the world, on account of beings engaged in any action having a motive." The world is the product of Ishvara's joyful spontaneous expression of power. No telic factor is involved. Such views cast doubts on the value of the world, and give credence to those who maintain that India's principal philosophy is world illusion and world denial. Attempts to refute this view may take the form of arguing that the world is Brahman's art by which attention is called to the rich values inherent in Reality, or that pluralization is integral to Totality, and without this mode of explication Totality would be less than totality, e.g., "In a certain sense *Maya* represents the possibility for Being of not being. The All-Possibility must by definition and on pain of contradiction include its own impossibility. It is in order not to be, that Being incarnates in the multitude of souls; it is in order not to be, that the ocean squanders itself in myriads of flecks of foam. . . . Nothing is external to absolute Reality; the world is therefore a kind of internal dimension of Brahman. But Brahman is without relativity; thus the world is a necessary aspect of the absolute necessity of Brahman. Put in this way, relativity is an aspect of the Absolute. Relativity, *Maya,* is the *Shakti* of the Absolute, Brahman." [18] In connection with Schuon's suggestion, it is interesting to note that Shankara himself said that "Brahman is, in a secondary sense of the word, called non-being." [19]

Much of the conflict and confusion arising from Shankara's doctrine of *maya* might have been avoided if his critics had kept in mind that he was not arguing that the world is of no value, for the world of *maya* is always the *maya* of Brahman. Shankara did not ask his followers to treat the world and other selves as though they did not exist, rather he was asking them to keep in mind the conditions under which the world and other selves are perceived, and to recognize that the characteristics that the world and other selves have are the characteristics Reality must have in order for it to be experienced by sense organs and minds. We from the West must temper our criticisms of the inadequacies of Shankara's conceptions of Brahman and *maya* by keeping in mind we are heirs of the Greeks in our passion for clarity and precision, whereas the Hindus, and particularly the Vedantists, are inclined to the view that the human mind is an intruder on Reality and has no authority for dictating the conditions of existence. Reality does not wait breathlessly for the human verbalization of its nature. Moreover, the aim of Hindu *sadhana* is not to yield true statements but to bring freedom and peace to the human spirit.

Bondage and Liberation

Vedanta is primarily a religion. It is a philosophy only insofar as a philosophy is needed as a foundation for Vedantic religion. Shankara did not seek knowledge to satisfy intellectual curiosity. He was engaged in no mere speculative adventure to delight the mind. He created a metaphysic to set men free. He sought knowledge in order to attain and to promote the highest state of spiritual evolution. He opened his commentary on the *Vedanta Sutras* with these words: "With a view to freeing one's self from that wrong notion which is the cause of evil and attaining thereby the knowledge of the absolute unity of the self . . ." Again in commenting on *sutra* 1. 4. 14 he notes that "a conflict of statements regarding the world would not even matter greatly, since the creation of the world and similar topics are not at all what Scripture wishes to teach." In other words, the Vedic literature is to be approached as religious tracts, not as works on cosmogony and cosmology. It teaches how to go to heaven, not how the heavens go.

Shankara inherited from the *shruti* tradition the view that man's existential situation was one of bondage. According to Samkhya some *purushas* had fallen into *prakriti's* condition as victims of a primeval ignorance (*avidya*). Shankara was also aware of the fourfold roots of medical science which had been appropriated by the Buddha: the identification of the illness, the identification of its cause, the determination of the possibility of cure, and the prescription of the means of cure. Shankara's analysis of human bondage was at a crucial point remarkably different from theirs. Bondage is not man's *real* situation. Bondage is *maya;* bondage is part of the *apara* view of things. Man as *jiva* is in bondage, but man is *Atman* upon which *jiva* characteristics have been superimposed. Therefore, man is in bondage *iva* and man is liberated *iva.* Does this mean that bondage and liberation are not to be taken seriously? Not at all, Shankara would reply, but it does mean that bondage and liberation are empirical, phenomenal, *maya.* Man's state of lostness is a self-creation, not the curse of gods or the result of destiny. Shankara assumed *karma,* but he did not stress it; he emphasized more how right choices can avoid building *karma* than how present status is determined by past *karma.*

Since bondage is a self-creation, then liberation is also a self-creation. The doctrine of divine grace was therefore rejected. A god cannot do for a person what he must do for himself. *Bhakti marga* is to be rejected as an ingredient in liberation. There is no divine *prasada.* But Shankara did allow for the *bhakti* emotion as part of the full life for man, and, as we have already noted, he wrote many beautiful devotional poems and songs. When he visited his dying mother, he first spoke to her of his philosophical tenets, but when he realized these gave her no consolation, he sang her the *bhakti* songs of Shaivite worship. He says in his *Vivekachudamani,* "Of all things which help the attainment of liberation, *bhakti* is the greatest." But *bhakti* is only a "help." In his commentary on *Bhagavad Gita* 3. 16 he distinguishes four kinds of *bhakti*—the devotional feelings of those in distress, of those who desire knowledge, of those whose object is to attain some particular end, and of those based on *jñana*—and affirms that the fourth is the highest, and in commenting on *Bhagavad Gita* 18. 54–55 he makes the highest form of *bhakti* identical with *jñana.* Shankara as a practical man did not quibble over the means for the realization of a desired end. Although he spoke disdainfully of those who put complete trust in *yoga,* he recognized *yoga* as helpful in developing the habit of concentration and of purifying the individual for the consummating enlightenment. Shankara was always afraid that the *bhakta* or the yogi might become so infatuated with his god that he would never get to the Reality behind the gods.

He was more charitable toward *karma marga* than to *bhakti* or *yoga*. Works may be co-operative with knowledge, he says in commenting on *Vedanta Sutras* 3. 4. 33. Works, he says, can be the means for the origination of knowledge. Works can help to purify the mind, to strengthen control of the passions, and to induce calmness. But they remain means. Works of intense concentration are also recognized as fruits of knowledge. One great problem in works is that they tend to give the illusion that liberation is attained, but liberation is no attainment. Liberation is only the awakening to the fact that the innermost self is identical with Brahman. Nothing happens which makes one liberated; nothing comes into being that was not already. One only realizes what has always been. This is why Shankara consistently denied that liberation is accomplished through works, through moral improvement, or through a divine gift. No reality changes. All that takes place is the forsaking of an accidental self caused by ignorance. *Avidya* is given up for *atmavidya*.

Shankara recognized that the theoretical understanding of the oneness of Reality is not sufficient to eliminate the pervading feeling of individuality and limitation. There must be an illuminating awareness of identity, an experience which is not the result of discursive knowing but one which can even be described as mystical. An individual is unlikely to be argued out of his *upadhis*. The transforming awareness must come about through a deep understanding of the *maya*-ness of empirical experiences in this *nama-rupa* world. Shankara's *marga* moves through a growing awareness of the *maya* nature of the physical world, the gods, and the *jivas* into an identity consciousness by which the person becomes fully aware of the Absolute manifested in the relative.

Moksha is whenever the individual is ready for it. Shankara was the only one of the Vedantists who taught the doctrine of *jivanmukti*, i.e., liberation while in the flesh. When his doctrine of *moksha* is characterized as absorptionism and regret is expressed that individuality is lost, it must be pointed out that one cannot lose what one never had.

Shankara's reformation of the *shruti* tradition has often been misunderstood because he tried to express the Absolute in language which is necessarily relative, but he has to a large extent become within orthodox Hinduism the sage "whose opinion can be accepted by all." In fact, in this respect he may have succeeded far too well, since for centuries the Advaitin followers of Shankara have been inclined to accept his teachings as final rather than make a fresh examination of *shruti* and *smriti*. But there were and are objectors to Shankara, and one of the greatest of these was Ramanuja.

CHAPTER 13

Vaishnavism

From the fifth to the eighth centuries there was a conflict of many Hindu cults in a struggle to win the allegiance of the common people. Two cults survived: Vaishnavism and Shaivism. Their conflict included the telling of rival legends which enhanced their own deity. For example, according to the Shaivites Shiva had bitten off a head of Brahmā, given a kick to Yama, and knocked the teeth out of the sun; in other words, he had made himself victor among the gods. The Vaishnavites countered with a tale in the *Padma Purana* about the sage Bhrigu who once visited the Trimurti for answer to an important question. Brahmā was too busy in a metaphysical discussion to listen to Bhrigu's question, Shiva was dallying with his wife and would not leave her, and Vishnu was asleep. Bhrigu in disgust gave Vishnu a kick. Vishnu awoke and began to stroke the feet of the holy man, expressing appreciation of the new mode of honoring deity. The Shaivites reminded the Vaishnavites that Shiva never sleeps whereas Vishnu alternates between activity and rest.

Royal Patronage

In the conflict among the religions and sects a new factor entered during this period: appeal to kings for support. Buddhism had benefited tremendously from the support of the Mauryan emperor Ashoka in the third century B.C., but it was not until the Gupta period, i.e., the fourth and fifth centuries A.D., that Hinduism enjoyed royal subsidies. Chandragupta I and his successors used with some justification the title "King of Kings." The Gupta reign began modestly with the triumph of one petty dynasty over its neighbors. According to an inscription placed as an addendum to an Asoka pillar at Allahabad, Chandragupta I began his rule over the ancient kingdom of Magadha with his capital at the ancient city of Pataliputra on February 26, A.D. 320. The Guptas were desirous of restoring the traditional religion. Samadragupta, the son of Chandragupta I, was given the title "Restorer of the Horse-Sacrifice" for having celebrated that long-neglected rite. The Guptas were favorably disposed to Vaishnavism, and as they expanded their empire until it covered all of northern India and the Deccan plateau, they built temples and encouraged the arts associated with Hinduism. The Gupta support of Vaishnavism was one of the causes for the popularity of the rule throughout India. The coins of Chandragupta II represented the king as receiving a gift from Vishnu.

Even though Buddhism and Jainism had begun within short distances of Pataliputra, both had by this time lost the fervor of their early years. The Buddhist holy places had begun to suffer from neglect. However, Buddhism's day in India was not yet over. King Harsha (606–648), who emerged after the devastations of the Hun invasions, was a zealous Buddhist who was finally assassinated by *Brahmins*. The last royal patronage the Buddhists enjoyed was that of the Pala kings. Gopala, the founder of the line, ruled from 750 to 770. The Pala kingdom, which covered roughly the area of modern Bihar and Bengal, lasted for four centuries. Gopala's most significant contribution to Buddhism was the establishment of the University of Nalanda, the greatest Buddhist seat of learning in India. He also subsidized the building of many temples and the establishment of monasteries. Although the Palas were Buddhists, they maintained good relations with the Hindus, employing Hindus as some of their chief ministers. Buddhism enjoyed royal patronage, but it was beginning to lose vitality by reason of the growth of Tantric ideas and practices within its ranks. Some were using Tantrism as an excuse for licentiousness, sexual depravity, worship of demons, magical spells, and exorcisms.

In South India fearful struggles took place between Vaishnavites and Shaivites as each sought to win the favor of ruling monarchs. Between the eighth and eleventh conturies the Shaivites were successful in winning the support of the Salambhas with their capital at Haruppeshvara, the Kalachuris of Tripuri, the Mushanas of Chamba, the Chalukyas of Vengi, the Somavamsis of Kosala, the later Pallava kings, and the Chola kings of the great sixth century Tamil dynasty. Support often included persecution of the vanquished; e.g., the Vaishnavite Mahapurna, a teacher of Ramanuja, had his eyes gouged out by the Shaivite Chola king Rajendrachola, and Ramanuja took sanctuary in Mysore for twelve years in order to escape royal persecution.

Jainism lacked royal support in northern India, but it was popular among the trading classes, and it had some support from southern kings. In the eighth, ninth, and tenth centuries about one-third of the people of the Deccan were Jaina. The Ganga rulers in the Deccan and the Chapa rulers of Vardhamanapura were patrons of Jainism. During these three centuries the Jains built many temples and erected huge statues of their *tirthankaras*. Conflicts within Jainism, especially between the Digambaras and the Shvetambaras, weakened the religion. Also the Jains appear to have lost ground through having adopted so many Hindu ideas and practices that Jainism appeared to be but another Hindu sect.

Avataras

During the Gupta age the worship of *avataras* (descents or incarnations) became an important aspect of the Vaishnavite religion. The origin of the *avatara* concept is unknown. Central Asia has usually been suggested as its source. It is the belief that the divine nature becomes incarnate in animal or human form in order to conquer an evil being, to arrest the growth of unrighteousness, or to induce men to reform their lives. The concept is not clearly found in the *Vedas*, although *Rig* 6. 49. 13 refers to Vishnu's three steps as having been taken for "man in distress." In the *Mahabharata* Shiva on one occasion appears in the form of a man of the Kirata tribe in order to test the sincerity of Arjuna. In the *Shatapatha Brahmana* the figures of a dwarf, a fish, and a tortoise are associated with Vishnu. The aboriginal peoples of India had tales of gods appearing *incognito* among men. During the Gupta age the *avatara* concept became firmly established in Vaishnavism. Vishnu was growing as a redeemer god, and what was more natural than that he should on occasion visit man in a redemptive function? A cycle of legends of his incarnations grew, absorbing many indigenous savior-myths and primitive fairy tales of animals displaying helpfulness to needy human beings. The number of *avataras* of Vishnu varied, but by the eighth century the number had been stabilized as ten. Some originally had little to do with Vishnu. The first five *avataras* are clearly mythological; the next three are heroic; the ninth is an effort to assimilate Buddhism into Vaishnavism; and the tenth is eschatological.

1. *Matsya.* Vishnu appeared as a fish to rescue Manu Vaivasvata (the Hindu Noah) from the Flood, to recover the *Vedas* which had been stolen by a demon, and to instruct Manu in the *Vedas*.

2. *Kurma.* After the Flood, when things were in a chaotic state, the gods discovered that the nectar of immortality had been lost and was at the bottom of the ocean. They decided to churn the ocean in order to bring up the chalice which contained the nectar. Vishnu volunteered to become a tortoise in order that the back of the tortoise might serve as a pivot for the enormous churning stick.

3. *Varaha.* When the demon king Hiranyaksha once dragged the earth to the bottom of the ocean, Vishnu assumed the form of a boar, slew the demon, and raised the earth from the ocean's depths.

4. *Narasimha.* Upon the death of Hiranyaksha, his twin Hiranyak-sasipu assumed the throne of the demons. His tyranny became a threat to gods, men, and animals. Since he had received a boon that he could not be killed by either man or beast, Vishnu assumed the form of a man-lion and slew him.

5. *Vamana.* The origin of this incarnation myth is Vedic inasmuch as the three strides of Vishnu are referred to in the *Rig*. According to this myth, the demon Bali had acquired domination over the three worlds. To win back the worlds, Vishnu took on the form of a dwarf and begged that he be allowed as much land as he could

cover in three steps. Bali agreed. Vishnu then assumed giant proportions, and took two strides to cover earth and heaven. But he did not take the third step, leaving the underworld to Bali.

6. *Parashurama.* "Rama of the Axe" is Vishnu incarnated to deliver the *Brahmins* from the tyranny of the *Kshatriyas.*

7. *Rama.* Vishnu as Rama, the hero of the *Ramayana,* the slayer of the powerful king Ravana.

8. *Krishna.* The incarnation of Vishnu as Krishna of the *Bhagavata Gita* and of the *Bhagavata Purana* is the most popular of the *avataras.* However, in some Vaishnavite subsects Krishna is exalted into full divinity and his brother Balarama is given his place among the *avataras* of Vishnu.

9. *Buddha.* The adoption of the Buddha as an *avatara* of Vishnu is explained in two ways: one is that in so doing Buddhism could be assimilated into Vaishnavism; the other is that this was a method to encourage the wicked to despise the *Vedas,* reject caste, and bring about their own destruction. The second explanation, we might add, does not seem consistent with the benevolence usually associated with Vaishnavism.

10. *Kalki.* Kalki is the name of the incarnation yet to come in this Kali Yuga. Vishnu is to come again to renovate the earth and to restore its lost purity. *Kalki* (white horse) signifies the steed upon which he will ride.

It was the concepts of *avataras* which transformed Bhagavata into Vaishnavism. Without such a transformation Vasudeva Krishna might have remained only a culture hero. But in making Krishna an *avatara* the foundation was laid for the development of Hinduism's most popular sect. The common man, who could not understand the *Upanishads* and who found Shankara's interpretation far too intellectual, received the comfort and consolation he needed from the gracious god who demonstrated his love in taking on human and animal forms in order to redeem mankind. Epigraphic records and archeological remains from the fourth to the eighth centuries attest to the popularity of *avatara* worship.

Bhagavata Purana

Between the sixth and the sixteenth centuries A.D. a great body of *smriti* literature was written in the Sanskrit language which is known as the *Puranas*. The word "*Purana*" means "ancient." A *Purana* was supposed to give a legendary account of ancient times dealing with five subjects: the creation of the world, the genealogy of gods and *rishis*, the royal dynasties, cosmic cycles, and the destruction of the world. The *Puranas* are called "the Veda of the common people" since they present much Vedic material in the form of legends and stories. They always stress *bhakti*. Their uncritical presentation of miracles and superstitions gives them a fairy tale appearance. There are eighteen major *Puranas* (*Maha-puranas*) and an indefinite number of secondary ones (*Upa-puranas*). Of the eighteen, six are addressed to Vishnu, six to Shiva, and six to Brahmā with emphases respectively on *sattva*, *tamas*, and *rajas*. But this stylistic division is weakened by the fact that Vishnu is prominent in most of the *Puranas;* it is therefore proper to consider them in the context of Vaishnavism. Indeed the most celebrated is the *Bhagavata Purana* (also known as *Shrimad Bhagavatam*), a huge work of 18,000 stanzas which was written in the ninth or tenth century A.D. The dramatic structure is a dialogue between a dying king and a holy man. The former has unwittingly killed a *brahmin*, and is doomed to die in one week. The *Bhagavata Purana* is recited to him during the week.

The importance of the *Bhagavata Purana* for Vaishnavism is largely centered in the tenth book wherein is recounted the birth of Krishna, his mischievous boyhood, his amorous delights with the *gopis*, his destruction of the tyrant Kamsa, his marriages, his miracles, and his heroic exploits up to the time when he left Mathura and Brindaban. Attention is often called to the fact that it was this book with its emphasis on the amorous exploits of Krishna which changed the Bhagavata sect from Vaishnava *dharma* to Vaishnava *bhakti*, but a more accurate assessment might be to state that due to Book 10 of the *Bhagavata Purana* Vaishnavism moved beyond *bhakti* to *prema* and *kama*. Here one finds the accounts of the *gopis* slipping away from their husbands at night in order to dance in moonlight on the banks of the Jumna River with Krishna and to enjoy the fullness of sexual embraces. The tenth book also records his marriage to eight first wives and to 16,100 secondary wives, each of whom gave birth to ten sons and one daughter. Hindus make widely different evaluations of these passages. Radhakamal Mukerjee thinks the stories of Krishna and the *gopis* represent "man's profoundest communion with God." [1] Chintaman V. Vaidya rejects them completely: "We entirely disbelieve the truth of these stories; no more mischievous though well-intentioned misrepresentations have ever sullied the fair name of a great man." [2] S. Radhakrishnan relieves the Aryan conscience by expressing his opinion that they "clearly indicate the non-Aryan origin of Krishna." [3] Without trying to evaluate the matter, we can recognize that the author of the *Bhagavata Purana* was presenting the most intense human emotion as an approximation of spiritual devotion, and also as the most trustworthy road to liberation.

No reference is made in the *Bhagavata Purana* to Radha as Krishna's favorite *gopi,* but she was so established a few generations after the composition of this book. The Radha-Krishna love is sexual love consummated outside of marriage on the grounds that such passion is more intense than the expression of love within marriage. This was to open the floodgates to extreme forms of eroticism. The gain for literature was tremendous. One of the first literary products was the *Gita-govinda* of Jayadeva (twelfth century), a series of monologues on the theme of the love of Radha and Krishna strikingly similar to "The Song of Songs" of the *Old Testament.*

Alvars

In the seventh and eighth centuries there appeared in South India twelve wandering troubadors who proved to be the most formidable opponents of Buddhism and Jainism, the authors of a fascinating chapter in the development of Hinduism. They did what Shankara was unable to do: they drove Buddhism out of India, and Jainism out of South India—and they did it with music. They composed and sang songs of devotion to Vishnu in the Tamil language. Some of these minstrels were of low birth, one was an outcaste, and one was a woman. In the tenth century their songs were collected and compiled in a single volume, the *Nalayira Prabandham* (Book of Four Thousand Songs). This is today the chief prayerbook and hymnbook of Tamil Vaishnavism. This collection is so highly regarded that it is sometimes called "The Tamil Veda."

The word "*alvar*" means one deep in wisdom, but the *Alvars* were not philosophers, and they added no new dimension of thought to Hinduism. They believed in the existence of a personal God and of the ability of man to establish relations with God. The love and compassion of Vishnu as manifested in his *avataras* was their constant theme. Caste had no significance whatsoever for them. They believed that worldly enjoyments were unprofitable, holding that the only durable satisfaction was in loving surrender to the will of Vishnu. Knowledge and works, they held, would not take man to God. They sang their songs in temples, villages, markets, anywhere. The place did not matter, since for them Lord Vishnu was wherever he was worshiped.

The greatest of the *Alvars* was Nammalvar, a *Shudra* by birth. His preparation for his singing to Vishnu was said to have been sixteen years of silent meditation under a tamarind tree. He is the author of 1296 hymns in the *Nalayira Prabandham*. This hymn gives the flavor of his work:

> When shall I join my lord, who poison is
> For evil deeds, and nectar for the good?
> Husband of her who haunts the lotus-bloom,
> Cowherd who thought no scorn to graze the cows:
> Who overpaced the world in his two strides.[4]

In another hymn from Nammalvar the author chides his emotions for going so far ahead of his works; *bhakti* and *karma* ought to move in lock step:

> Alas! my heart, wouldst thou now start ahead
> Of me to reach His feet and praise His grace
> So fired by zeal, so goaded by thy love?
> But tarry now, I prithee, let us work

> Together up to Him of hue of puvai flower
> And weave into wreathes of honied song
> Which welleth forth from tongue, unhelped by mind.[5]

For the most part the *Alvars* did not attempt to refute false views. They were too God-intoxicated to waste time in intellectual arguments. The *Alvar* Tirumalishai in one of his hymns did indicate disapproval of other religions: "Jains are ignorant; Buddhists have fallen into a snare; Shaivites are without enlightenment; and those who will not worship Vishnu are low indeed." The typical *Alvar* attitude toward knowledge as a way of liberation is expressed in this hymn from Tondaradipodi:

> Truth have I forsworn! Caught in the snares
> Of wily dames of flowing locks, come I
> An erring soul. Refuge for all the sins
> That teem the world, O gracious Lord Ranga!
> 'Tis but my certain hope Thy grace will save
> Which makes me bold to come to Thee and wait.[6]

Acharyas

Coincident with and immediately following the *Alvars* there appeared in South India a group of Vaishnavite teachers known as the *Acharyas* (teachers). An *Acharya* was one who observed the rules of his order, a spiritual guide and interpreter. In the hierarchy of religious leaders an *Acharya* was said to be worth ten *upadhyayas*, i.e., teachers who taught only by rote. The first of the Tamil *Acharyas* was Nathamuni, who collected the *Alvar* hymns and compiled them into the *Nalayira Prabandham*. He opposed the Advaita emphasis on knowledge and the Mimamsa stress on ritual. He even disapproved of the doctrine of *karma* on the grounds that it encouraged a manipulative attitude toward life. Salvation is a gift from God. The liberated individual is not absorbed into the being of God but enjoys eternal fellowship with him.

Ramanuja was the greatest of the *Acharyas*. In his long life—he is said to have lived from 1017 to 1137—he bridged the gap between Vedism and Vaishnavism and worked out a view which attempted to satisfy both the religious longings of the common people and the desire of philosophers for intellectual respectability. The followers of Shankara in the two centuries after his death had increasingly interpreted Vedanta as a *mayavada,* i.e., the view that the entire world is an emptiness, a void without meaning. *Moksha* was called *vivartavada,* the theory of illusory self-modification, and the gods were but figments of the imagination which an intelligent person did not take seriously. Ramanuja, who had from earliest childhood been taught that devotion to Vishnu was the way of liberation, set for himself the task of stemming this interpretation of the *Upanishads* and of restoring *bhakti* as a *marga* within the context of the Vedic tradition. He referred to Shankara and his followers as his opponents. Madhva, who extended Ramanuja's thought to a complete dualism, regarded Shankara as the incarnation of a demon. Ramanuja wrote with great dedication and some rancor; e.g., he began his commentary on the *Vedanta Sutras* with this statement of the Advaita view of the Brahman: "Eternal, absolutely non-changing consciousness, whose nature is pure non-differenced intelligence, free from all distinction whatever, owing to error illusorily manifests itself . . . as knowing subjects, objects of knowledge, acts of knowledge," and then he gave as his own evaluation of Shankara's view: "This entire theory rests on a fictitious foundation of altogether hollow and vicious arguments, incapable of being stated in definite logical alternatives. . . . The theory must needs be rejected by all those who, through texts, perception and other means of knowledge—assisted by sound reasoning—have an insight into the true nature of things." Ramanuja's vituperative manner set a tone of conflict between the defenders of Shankara and the defenders of Ramanuja which has persisted to this day. Rudolf Otto records a conversation with a Ramanuja follower who told him, "I would sooner become a Christian than acknowledge the teachings of Shankara." [7] George Thibaut in the introduction to his translation of Shankara's commentary on the *Vedanta Sutras* stated after much argument and evidence that "in some important points" Ramanuja's commentary more accurately

interprets the *Vedanta Sutras* than does Shankara's.[8] Thibaut reports
that for having made this statement he was charged by Advaita
Vedantists with "philosophical incompetency" and with being
"hopelessly theistic due to early training." [9]

Ramanuja was born at Shriperambattur in Tamilnad about
twenty-six miles west of Madras. When he began Vedic studies, his
guru realized that he was a prodigy. At age sixteen he married to
satisfy his mother's wish. Shortly after the marriage, his father died
and he was in charge of the joint family. One of the first things he
did was to move the family to Kanchipuram in order that he might
study with Yadava Prakasha, a famous teacher of the Advaita
philosophy. The relationship between pupil and teacher was soon
strained, since Ramanuja did not agree with the nondual interpretation of the *Upanishads,* and did not hesitate to challenge his *guru.*
There is a tradition that Yadava Prakasha tried to bring about the
death of Ramanuja—a tradition kept alive by the Ramanuja followers
in South India. Alavandar, the chief priest at Shrirangam, learned of
Ramanuja, and followed his growth with interest. When Alavandar
felt that his end was near, he sent for Ramanuja, but before Ramanuja
could reach Shrirangam, the priest died. When Ramanuja arrived,
the corpse had three fingers of the right hand closed. Ramanuja
learned that there were three unfinished tasks in the life of Alavandar. One of these was to write a commentary on the *Vedanta
Sutras* which would modify the nondualistic views expressed in
Shankara's commentary. Ramanuja vowed he would fulfill Alavandar's desires. This explains not only the emotional quality of
Ramanuja's commentary, but also the name of the movement—Vishishtadvaita (modified nondualism) Vedanta. Shortly after this experience Ramanuja sent his wife home to her family, became a *sannyasi,*
established a *mutt* (school) near the temple at Shrirangam, and spent
the rest of his life as a scholar and teacher.

All of Ramanuja's work was an expression of his own *bhakti.* He
had from childhood been deeply impressed by the *Alvars,* and his
lifework was an effort to harmonize the *Upanishads* and the attitude
of devotion to a personal god. He sought to give a rational defense for
the claims of the heart. His Vedanta differs from Shankara's in that
whereas Shankara sought to reconcile Upanishadic speculation and

religion in general, Ramanuja sought to reconcile Upanishadic speculation and a particular religion, Vaishnavism. Shankara was a Shaivite, but he was primarily a student of the *Upanishads;* Ramanuja was first and foremost a Vaishnavite. He was more concerned about human liberation than the validity and truth of philosophical arguments. Among the many legends preserved by Vaishnavites is that Ramanuja learned Vaishnavism from a *guru* who pledged him to the customary vow of secrecy, but Ramanuja broke his pledge because he believed that the teaching was a message of salvation for all. Perhaps the best way to formulate the Vaishnavite evaluation of Ramanuja is to say that he is regarded as the one who completed the Hindu *bhakti* that was begun in the *Bhagavad Gita.*

Ramanuja agreed with Shankara that Reality is one, not two, as the Samkhya philosophers maintained; but the One according to Ramanuja is internally complex (*vishishta*), not absolutely simple as Shankara maintained. Brahman consists of three reals: (1) the unconscious universe of matter (*prakriti*), (2) the conscious community of finite selves (*atmans*), and (3) the transcendent lord (Ishvara). The individual soul and its body is a perfect analogy of the macro-cosmic world of the Lord and his world. *Prakriti* is the gross body of the Lord, transmigrating souls are the subtle body of the Lord, and liberated souls are the blissful body of the Lord. Ishvara is the transcendent Soul of the universe. Ishvara is a person capable of entering into personal relations with souls both bound and free.

The Upanishadic proposition *tat tvam asi* (That thou art) is interpreted by Shankara to affirm the absolute identity of Brahman and the individual self. For Advaitins there is no difference between the "that" (Brahman) and the "thou" (individual self). The individual self is Brahman in association with a particular psychical apparatus and a particular physical body. "That" is Pure Consciousness; "thou" is Pure Consciousness associated with a psycho-physical organism. The "thou" is the "that" temporarily limited. But for Ramanuja *tat tvam asi* affirms a relationship. It is a relationship of identity—a peculiar kind of relationship. Every relationship must have at least two relata, two things that partake of the relationship. If there are not two relata, there cannot be a relation. So the "that" and the "thou" can only be identical in a sense; their nonduality (*advaita*) must be modified (*vishishta*). There must be a difference between two entities even in an identical relationship. *Tat tvam asi* means for Shankara that the two are really one, no matter how different they may appear; *tat tvam asi* means for Ramanuja that the two are sufficiently different to be identified as "that" and "thou." Shankara's apparent difference is a real difference for Ramanuja. Ramanuja will not accept Shankara's *para vidya* and *apara vidya* distinction. In Ramanuja's own words: "In texts, again, such as 'Thou art that,' the co-ordination of the constituent parts is not meant to convey the idea of the absolute unity of a non-differenced substance; on the contrary, the words 'that' and 'thou' denote a Brahman distinguished by difference. The word 'that' refers to Brahman omniscient . . . the word 'thou,' which stands in coordination to 'that,' conveys the idea of Brahman insofar as having for its body the individual selves connected with non-intelligent matter. This is in accordance with the general principle that co-ordination is meant to express one thing subsisting in a twofold form." [10]

Both Shankara and Ramanuja made a distinction within the concept of Brahman. For Shankara it was a distinction between Nirguna Brahman, the Brahman without attributes, and Saguna Brahman, the Brahman with attributes; but it was a distinction between reality and appearance. For Ramanuja it was a distinction between Karana Brahman, the Brahman in the causal state, and Karya Brahman, the Brahman in the effect state, and it was a distinction within reality. Brahman in the causal state includes pure matter and bodiless souls in an unmanifest form. This is the *"tat"* of *"tat tvam asi."* Brahman as *Tat* is at once the material and the operative cause. In other words, Ramanuja agreed with the Samkhya that both matter and spirit are real, but rather than separating them in a dualistic schema, he put both of them in Brahman. His order of causal evolution is the same as the Samkhya, except for him everything evolves from the One rather than from *prakriti* under the stimulation of *purusha*. The causal Brahman rather than being without qualities (*nirguna*), has an infinity of good qualities: omniscience, omnipotence, benevolence, etc. He is the Highest Person (*Purushottama*). Brahman in the effect state is Brahman manifested as world and individual selves. This is the *"tvam"* of *"tat tvam asi."* The potentialities of Karana Brahman are now actualities. *Natura naturans* becomes *natura naturata.* The creation of the world is not *ex nihilo,* because it is a transformation within Brahman. Ishvara (Brahman as Creative Lord) manifests himself in *chit* (sentient nature) and in *achit* (insentient nature): "The entire aggregate of things, intelligent and non-intelligent, has its Self in Brahman insofar as it constitutes Brahman's body." [11] Ishvara's creation is a *lila* (sport) but not a *maya* (illusion). In other words, the Upanishadic accounts of creation were taken literally by Ramanuja, whereas Shankara insisted on using *"iva"* (as it were) with respect to creation. Ramanuja was not entirely consistent in his descriptions of the relation of Ishvara and the created world; sometimes he said the relation of God and the world is like that of the soul and the body, and at other times he said it is like that of a king and his subjects. He wanted the world to be both a mode of God and also a part of God. He had problems in making God the sole cause of the world and also in affirming the unchanging nature of God. This he attempted to resolve by distinguishing the "soul of God" and the "body of God." Just as a human being is the same from infancy to old age but his body changes radically, so God as the indwelling soul remains unaffected in the modifications of the creation and dissolution of the world. Ramanuja's theism seems to embody an interesting trinity: God as material cause which is affected by the transformation which brings about the physical world, God as spirit which is affected by the moral imperfections of the world, and God as Ishvara which is unaffected and immutable under all conditions.

The world is real for Ramanuja. He wrote, "Next as to the assertion that all difference presented in our cognition—as of jars, pieces of cloth and the like—is unreal because such difference does not persist. This view, we maintain, is altogether erroneous, springs, in fact, from the neglect of distinguishing between persistence and nonpersistence, on the one hand, and the relation between what sublates and what is sublated, on the other hand." [12] This attack on Shankara was not altogether fair, since Shankara in denying that the world is real (i.e., permanent) did not mean that it is therefore unreal but rather that it is neither real nor unreal. The passages in the *Upanishads* which Shankara took to imply that the world is *maya,*

Ramanuja understood to deny an independent existence of the world, but not its dependence on the being of God. Ramanuja wrote in his attack on Shankara and his followers, "According to the view of our opponent, this entire world, with all its endless distinctions of ruler, creatures ruled, and so on, is, owing to a certain defect, fictitiously super-imposed upon the non-differenced, self-luminous Reality, gives rise to manifold illusions, and cannot be defined either as being or non-being." [13] An unprejudiced reader of Ramanuja has the impression that Ramanuja was so anxious to disprove Shankara that he occasionally made errors and exaggerations.

Sometimes it is illuminating to read Shankara's and Ramanuja's commentaries side by side. For example, in commenting on *Vedanta Sutras* 3. 2. 3 where the word *"maya"* appears Shankara wrote that "it is mere illusion," but Ramanuja, as though he had Shankara's commentary before him, wrote that "the term *'maya'* denotes wonderful things" [rather than illusory things]. Shankara used *maya* and *avidya* interchangeably, but Ramanuja regarded *maya* as a metaphysical principle ultimately grounded in *avidya* as an epistemological principle. Therefore, Ramanuja attacked *avidya* in order to get at Shankara's conception of *maya* by pointing out that the *avidya* of Shankara cannot originate in the individual self, for the self is itself a product of ignorance, and it cannot originate in Brahman, for Brahman is self-luminous intelligence which is contradictory to ignorance. So *"avidya"* is a word without an existential referent.

The individual self—the knowing self—cannot be proved to exist since it is the basis of all proof, says Ramanuja. But while it cannot be proved, it is known by direct experience. The *atman* or *jiva* is both a spiritual monad and a spiritual mode, i.e., both a substance and an attribute: "The individual self is a part of the highest Self. . . . Hence there is no contradiction between the individual and the highest Self—the former of which is a distinguishing attribute of the latter—standing to each other in the relation of part and whole, and their being at the same time of essentially different nature." [14] This difficult view Ramanuja clarified by pointing out analogously that light is both a substance and an attribute of a lamp. Consciousness is an attribute of the self, said Ramanuja, and "the essential character of consciousness or knowledge is that by its very existence it renders things capable of becoming objects, to its own substrate, of thought and speech. This consciousness . . . is a particular attribute belonging to a conscious self." [15] But, whereas Shankara held that "the highest Self is not in real contact with anything," [16] i.e., that the Self can be conscious but not conscious of anything, Ramanuja held that the essential nature of consciousness is to be related to objects: "as the attribute of an agent and as related to an object." [17] A "consciousness" that does not make things into epistemological objects is no consciousness at all. Consciousness is an attribute, not the essence, of the self. Moreover, it is an attribute which appears and disappears: "We clearly see that this agent (the subject of consciousness) is permanent (constant) while its attribute, i.e., consciousness, not differing herein from joy, grief, and the like rises, persists for some time, and then comes to an end." [18] The self to be a self must have the attribute of potency of knowing an object, and the object is needed in order for the self to be a self. So the self can be in a state of knowing, or in a state of not-knowing, and it may be in a state of bondage, or in a state of not-bondage. Hence the self which the *rishis* of the *Upanishads* desired to set free must, in order to be a self, be a conscious agent, which in turn requires an object to be known, and therefore liberation cannot be absorption into a homogeneous being, a one in which there is "consciousness" but no agent of consciousness and no object of consciousness.

At this point in his argument, Ramanuja makes an appeal to the populace which is typical of the humanness of the man: "To maintain that the consciousness of the 'I' does not persist in the state of final release is altogether inappropriate. It, in fact, amounts to the doctrine—only expressed in somewhat different words—that final release is the annihilation of the self. The 'I' is not a mere attribute of the self so that even after its destruction the essential nature of the self might persist—as it persists on the cessation of ignorance; but it constitutes the very nature of the self. Such judgments as 'I know,' 'Knowledge has arisen in me,' show, on the other hand, that we are conscious of knowledge as a mere attribute of the self. . . . No sensible person exerts himself under the influence of the idea that after he himself has perished there will remain some entity termed 'pure light.' " [19]

Karma, for Ramanuja, is the way in which God expresses approval or disapproval of acts. Therefore, one cannot achieve *moksha* merely by the elimination of *karma*. Bondage is not an intellectual error to be eliminated by proper understanding of the nature of things. Neither *karma marga* nor *jñana marga* can bring *moksha*. "The cessation of bondage is to be obtained only through the grace of the highest Self pleased by the devout meditation of the worshiper." [20] Self-surrender (*prapatti*) to the Highest Lord with full reliance on His mercy (*prasada*) is the only way to liberation. However, Ramanuja did grant that knowledge and action can be forerunners of *bhakti*. For example, he wrote in his commentary on *Bhagavad Gita* 12. 12, "Hence, to him who is inept for *Bhakti-Yoga* (the Path of God-Love), soul-devotion is recommended as next best; but to him who cannot bring a mind peaceful enough to try this, let him devote himself to doing fruit-forsaken works, based on soul-faith. This would gradually lead to soul-contemplation and soul-vision in order." Again in the proem to his commentary on Book 13 of the *Gita* he wrote, "In the First Division comprising the First Six Lectures, it was shown that there were two Paths, viz., *Karma-Yoga* and *Jñana-Yoga* by which an aspirant can achieve actual soul-realization. It was also shown that such soul-realization or soul-cognition is ancillary to God-Love known as *Bhakti*, or the means by which to reach the Supreme Goal, viz., the Blessed Lord Vasudeva, Who is Para Brahman." Unlike Shankara, he rejected the concept of liberation in the bodily state (*jivanmukti*). Liberation means only *videhamukti* (freedom after physical death). The liberated self retains its individuality in the state of *videhamukti* because the cause of bondage is not individuality but self-centeredness and self-reliance. The liberated remain in the relationship of *bhakti* to the Lord. The goal is not to be lost in the identity of the Absolute but to be in a state of eternal blissful communion with God. The oneness in Vaishnavism—or Shrivaishnavism, as the Vaishnavism of the Tamilnad followers of Ramanuja preferred to call their religion—is the psychological oneness the lover feels toward his beloved. The experience is of oneness, but the identity of the two remains. The ontological nonduality of Shankara became psychological nonduality in Ramanuja.

CHAPTER **14**

Shaivism and Shaktism

According to Aurobindo there is "a tendency of the Indian mind which is common in all its activities, the impulse to follow each motive, each specialization of motive even, spiritual, intellectual, ethical, vital, to its extreme point and to sound its utmost possibility. . . . In life the ideal of opulent living and the ideal of poverty were carried to the extreme of regal splendour and the extreme of satisfied nudity." [1] Aurobindo praises this tendency, and adds, "In every extreme the Indian spirit seeks for a law in that extreme and a rule, measure and structure in its application. . . . the Indian mind returns always towards some fusion of the knowledge it has gained and to a resulting harmony and balance in action and institution." [2] One example of this movement is the Buddha, who as a youth before arriving at the Middle Path lived in a different palace each season of the year and as an ascetic reduced his diet to a few grains of rice a day. Another is Shaivism. Throughout the history of Shaivism there has been a tendency to excess. The earliest sect reveals this tendency. In the *Mahabharata* it is called the Pashupati, i.e., worshipers of the Lord (*pati*) of cattle (*pashu*). The devotees, referring to themselves as cattle, worshiped Shiva as the Lord. Later they explained the name as the Lord (*pati*) who assists his creatures (*pashu*) to free themselves from the bondage (*pasha*) of this world. The sect was also called the Lakulisha, i.e., worshipers of the one who carries a club (*lakula*). According to a legend Shiva once entered the corpse of an unknown person, picked up a club lying nearby, and went forth club in hand to teach the doctrines of the sect to four disciples: Kushika, Gargya,

Kaurusha, and Maitreya, each of whom established a subsect of the Pashupati. Non-Shaivites say that Lakulisha was the name of the man who, claiming to be the incarnation of Shiva, successfully started this form of Shiva worship. The teaching of the Pashupati was that in order to throw off the shackles of matter and to end the misery of human existence the individual must engage in ritual actions often of the most violent and repulsive nature, e.g., besmearing of one's body with ashes from cremation grounds; eating of excrement, carrion, and human flesh; using human skulls as drinking bowls; simulating the act of coition; engaging in loud laughter; and dancing to the accompaniment of bull-like roars. The sect was totally condemned by Shankara and by the Mimamsa philosopher Kumarila. By the eleventh century the most prominent branch was known as the Kalamukha (black-faced) because the members of the sect wore a black mark on the forehead. By this time they were widely known as perverts, drug addicts, drunkards, and murderers.

There has always been a psychological difference between Vaishnavism and Shaivism. Vaishnavism is more sophisticated, urbane, and moderate in its approach to the Hindu motif. Shaivism is more primitive, rural, and extreme. Vaishnavite priests tend to be suave *Brahmins* who bring to their priestly functions the dignity of a noble tradition. Shaivite priests, who are seldom *Brahmins*, bring to their office the zeal and enthusiasm of personal experience and dedication. The ascetic Hindu *sadhus* one sees in India today are almost without exception Shaivites. The two great branches of Hinduism reflect the nature of their gods. Vishnu was an orderly god who could establish himself in each of the three realms. He became the god experienced through love similar to human love. Rudra-Shiva was a taboo god to whom prayer was made that he accept the oblation and spare the lives of his worshipers. Whereas love was the principal emotion of the worshipers of Vishnu, the worshipers of Shiva stood in awe, fear, and dread of their god. He became the god of cremation grounds. This is not to deny that *bhakti* entered Shiva worship, but to remind us that Shaivite worship always includes an element of wariness in its approach to its chosen deity. The worship of Shiva, as we have already noted, may have originated in non-Vedic India, or even outside of India. An indication of this is that whereas Shiva worship often has a sexual pattern, the Aryans spoke contemptuously of the phallus-worshipers (*shishna-devatas*).

Another difference which ought to be noted in regard to Shaivism is that it tends to be more cultish than does Vaishnavism. It stresses the importance of outward and visible signs that one is a Shaivite, whereas the Vaishnavite emphasizes the importance of the emotional response of the individual to his god. Shaivism, because of its propensity to manifest itself in overt fashion through ascetic practices, pilgrimages, and temple worship, has sometimes been described by Westerners as the highest form of Hinduism, e.g., "Shaivism is by far the best that India possesses; judged by its intrinsic merits Shaivism represents the high water mark of India's deeply religious intuition and life." [3] G. U. Pope described Shaiva Siddhanta as "the most elaborate, influential and undoubtedly the most valuable of all the religions of India." [4] Shaivite cults, because of the tendency of the religion to adapt itself to the lives of its devotees, take on many local variations.

Adiyars

The developments in Shaivism between the time of the formation of the *Mahabharata* and the Muslim occupations were in South India. Shankara advanced the cause of Shaivism by selecting Shiva as his chosen deity, but the *maya* status which he conferred upon all gods and the arid intellectualism of his thought did not popularize the worship of Shiva. Shaivism had no Ramanuja to systematize its thought, but it did have its singers who, like the *Alvars* of Vaishnavism, made the religion emotionally meaningful to the common people. These singers known as *Adiyars, Nayanmars,* or *Nayanars* were both *"Alvars"* and *"Acharyas"*; i.e., they developed both the devotional and the intellectual sides of Shaivism, although their theology is implicit in their poetry rather than systematically developed. There were sixty-three of these saints or teachers. They composed in their native Tamil language rather than in Sanskrit, and their work was exclusively in hymns. Their lives are encompassed in the seventh to the tenth centuries. The four greatest *Adiyars* were

Sambandar, Apparswami, Sundaramurti, and Manikkavasahar. The hymns of the first three *Adiyars* were put in a collection of 787 stanzas about A.D. 1000. This collection known as the *Devaram* together with the *Tiruvachakam* (Sacred Utterances) of Manikkavasahar, a volume of 3000 stanzas, constitutes the bulk of the essential scriptures of the Shaivites. The remarkable growth of Shaivism in South India in these centuries was due not only to the work of the *Adiyars* but also to the fact that it was favored by the Pallava kings from the fifth to the ninth centuries and by the Chola kings in the tenth century.

These were centuries of conflict with Buddhism and Jainism. Enemies of Buddhism in the North burned the Bodhi-tree at Gaya, the tree under which according to legend Gautama received his enlightenment. Even the hymns of the *Adiyars* contain expressions of hatred of both Jains and Buddhists:

> False Jains have lit for me a fire:
> O, let it to the Pandyan ruler go,
> That he the torture of a slow flame may know.
>
> Those Buddhists and mad Jains may slander speak.
> Such speech befits the wanderers from the way.[5]

When Jainism and Buddhism began to wane, the vigorous Shaivites turned upon the Vaishnavites. According to a Shaivite myth the gods Brahmā and Vishnu once saw a pillar of fire which seemed to stretch from the depths of the earth to the highest heavens. They wanted to measure it, and agreed that Brahmā would become a swan to seek out the top of the pillar, and Vishnu would become a boar to investigate its roots. But neither could find an extremity of the pillar. Brahmā and Vishnu then acknowledged their limitations and prayed to the pillar, whereupon Shiva disclosed himself, for he was, indeed, the unmeasurable pillar of fire. This myth appears frequently in the hymns; e.g., Apparswami writes in one of his hymns,

> Vishnu, spouse of Lakshmi, and four-ways-facing Brahm,
> Searched the heights and depths, but Thy feet could never see.
> Yet, O only Lord, who in Athihai dost dwell,
> Formless, in Thy grace, grant the sight of them to me.

And in another hymn Apparswami says,

> Brahm sought in vain on high.
> Vishnu delved vainly underground.
> Him in my soul found I.

Sundaramurti also refers to the myth in one of his hymns:

> Delay not to do good
> But praise Keteram's king,
> Whom Vishnu and great Brahm
> Vainly sought sorrowing.

Some of the hymns call attention to the superiority of Shiva to other gods; e.g., Manikkavasahar has written,

> Indra or Vishnu or Brahm,
> Their divine bliss crave not I;
> I seek the love of Thy Saints,
> Though my house perish thereby.
> To the worst hell I will go,
> So but Thy grace be with me.
> Best of all, how could my heart
> Think of a god beside Thee?

Although the gulf between Vaishnavism and Shaivism widened during these centuries, there were some attempts to bring the two branches together; e.g., a small group worshiped a deity known as Hari-Hara (Vishnu-Shiva), and represented their god in images with Shiva characteristics for the right side of the body, i.e., trident in his hand, snakes on his arms, tiger skin tunic, crescent moon and Ganges River in the matted hair, and even three abbreviated horizontal marks on the forehead, and with Vishnu characteristics for the left side of the body, i.e., *chakra* and conch shell in his hands, necklace of flowers, crown on head, and even half of the traditional V mark of Vishnu on the forehead.

Theology

Shaivism is strongly monotheistic. Shiva is portrayed in images and described in poetry with three eyes to denote his insight into past, present, and future, with a crescent moon in his hair to denote that he is the measurer of time, with serpents around his neck and arms to denote that he controls the *kalpas*, with a necklace of skulls to symbolize the dissolution and regeneration of mankind, with the Ganges caught in his hair to symbolize his protection of the earth from being crushed by the fall of the Ganges, and with a blue throat resulting from his drinking of the deadly poison which a demon prepared to destroy mankind. Despite this plethora of imagery, Shaivism eschews images as the focus of worship. The object of worship is usually a phallus, the symbol of creativity, or a *tiruvasi*, a semi-circular arch with a veil in front to symbolize the invisible presence of deity. Images of Nandi, Shiva's bull, rather than an image of Shiva, are likely to be found in temples. Even in the holiest of all Shaivite temples, the temple of Nataraja (Lord of the Dance) at Chidambaram, the famous statue of the dancing Shiva is obscured by the *tiruvasi*. Shiva, in other words, is a god of mystery; one does not easily understand this god, nor readily lay hold of his power.

The active side of Shiva is represented in his Shakti. Since Shiva's activities are manifold, his consorts are many—or, more accurately, his power is represented in a single consort who appears in diverse forms. The more important of the forms are Kali (destruction), Yoni (reproduction), Uma (beauty), Jaganmatri (mother of the universe), Yogini (asceticism), Durga (delighter in blood), and Parvati (mountaineer). Similarly Shiva is described as a destroyer who annihilates the world at the end of each *kalpa*, as a reproducer who regenerates the world after each annihilation, as an ideal ascetic who attains the highest perfection in austerity and meditation, as a contemplative who revealed grammar to Panini, and as a wild and jovial mountaineer who always acts effortlessly in hunting, drinking, and dancing, making the whole universe bright with his smile and alive with his joyous movements. It is not surprising that the best-loved image of Shiva is the Nataraja, with his right foot on the demon of evil, his left in the air poised for additional destruction if necessary, one hand raised in blessing, another pointing to the free foot to symbolize his power to liberate man, a third hand shaking a drum to symbolize sound as creation, and the fourth holding a bowl of fire to symbolize destruction. An elephant-hide cloak, a tiger-skin tunic, a snake neckpiece from evil beasts he has destroyed, and the skulls of his necklace represent the successive Brahmās he has slain.

The legends of Shiva are in no manner as rich as those which have been built around Vishnu. Although twenty-eight incarnations have been given to Shiva, the concept of *avataras* remains Vaishnavite. Shaivites love to dwell on the theme that Shiva comes to man uninvited and unannounced. Sambandar coined the appropriate expression, "He is the thief who stole my heart away." Shiva, according to Manikkavasahar, "Came down in grace and made even me to be His very own." One legend is that Apparswami received the stigmata of Nandi branded on his body. Thus Shiva is a god who comes to man on his own initiative, not when appealed to by man.

Sin and Grace

Shaivism as reformed by the Tamil saints begins with a feeling of deep-seated sin that borders on the fanatical. Calling one's self a dog was one of the favorite forms of penitence.

> The meanest cur am I; I know not how to do the right;
> 'Twere but what I deserve, should'st Thou my wickedness requite
> With the dread fate of those who never saw Thy flowery feet.

. . . .

> In right I have no power to live,
> Day after day I'm stained with sin;
> I read, but do not understand;
> I hold Thee not my heart within.

. . . .

Daily I'm sunk in worldly sin;
Naught know I as I ought to know;
Absorbed in vice as 'twere my kin,
I see no path in which to go.

. . . .

Evil, all evil, my race, evil my qualities all,
Great am I only in sin, evil is even my good.
Evil my innermost self, foolish, avoiding the pure,
Beast am I not, yet the ways of the beast I can never forsake.
I can exhort with strong words, telling men that they should hate,
Yet can I never give gifts, only to beg them I know.
Ah! wretched man that I am, whereunto came I to birth?

When the *Adiyars* attempted to spell out the sins of man rather
than lament upon the general tendency to waywardness, three sins
stand out: the sin of rejection of Shiva, the sin of fickleness, and the
sin of carnality:

I roamed, a cur, for many days
Without a single thought of Thee.
Roamed and grew weary, then such grace
As none could win Thou gavest me.

. . . .

My fickle heart one love forsakes,
And forthwith to some other clings;
Swiftly to some one thing it sways,
And even as swiftly backward swings.

. . . .

> The bond of lust I cannot break;
> Desire's fierce torture will not die;
> My soul I cannot stab awake
> To scan my flesh with seeing eye.

. . . .

According to the Shaivism of the *Adiyars*, when a person discovers the deplorable condition of his life, he learns of the grace of Shiva—and then finds he is unable to seize that grace:

> My spoon no hand hath when I
> Thy honey's grace to drink am fain.

But the anguish is falsely founded, for man does not come to Shiva—Shiva comes to man:

> Thou didst come into my vile fleshly body,
> E'en as 'twere into some great golden shrine;
> Soft'ning and melting it all, Thou hast saved me,
> Lord condescending, Thou gem all divine!

. . . .

> Fool's friend was I, none such may know
> The way of freedom; yet to me
> He shew'd the path of love, that so
> Fruit of past deeds might ended be.
> Cleansing my mind so foul, He made me like a god.
> Ah who could win that which the father hath bestowed?

The result is that man is cleansed, set free, and given a life of joy:

> Joy, day by day, unchanged
> Is ours, for we are His.

. . . .

Thou to me art parents, Lord,
Thou all kinsmen that I need,
Thou to me art loved ones fair,
Thou art treasure rich indeed.
Family, friends, home art Thou,
Life and joy I draw from Thee,
False world's good by Thee I leave,
Gold, pearl, wealth art Thou to me.

The one problem that remains is what can the devotee give in return to Lord Shiva?

Thou gavest Thyself, Thou gainest me;
Which did the better bargain drive?
Bliss found I in infinity;
But what didst Thou from me derive?
O Shiva, Perundurai's God,
My mind Thou tookest for Thy shrine:
My very body's Thine abode:
What can I give Thee, Lord, of mine?

Worship and Moksha

Worship in Shaivism is primarily an effort to express gratitude to Lord Shiva for grace freely given. The worshiper may take food to the temple which he gives to the priest, who in turn presents it before the symbolic representation of Shiva. The worshiper entering the holiest central part of the temple moves round the shrine clockwise while chanting appropriate sacred *mantras*. When he leaves, the priest returns a portion of the now-consecrated food to be dispensed to the poor or to be taken home for members of the family. *Linga* shrines, often very simple stones around the city or village, are honored with flowers and ghee. A rosary of *rudraksha* berries may be used in the recital of prayers.

Even though Shankara chose Shiva as his deity, Shaivism as a *bhakti* form of religion could not adopt his *maya* interpretation of gods nor his view that *moksha* is absorption into Absolute Reality.

God and man remain sufficiently separate that a relationship of devotion is always possible. Apparswami, looking forward to his condition beyond the death of the body, sang,

> How proud shall I be there,
> One of His heavenly host,
> At His fair feet who holds the deer,
> How proud will be my boast!

Likewise Manikkavasahar sang, "And ever more and more I'll bathe in bliss, with dance and song."

The path to liberation according to Shaiva Siddhanta, the largest group of Shaivites, is a fourfold path, a path upon which each of the four chief *Adiyars* are said to be an exemplar. The path of the servant (*dasa marga*) is the path of Apparswami. One cleans temples and gathers flowers for the deity as an expression of this path. The path of the good son (*kriya marga*) is the path of Sambandar. Acts of dedication to Lord Shiva express this path. The path of friendship (*yoga marga*) is the path of Sundaramurti, and it is marked by works of kindness to one's fellow beings. The path of wisdom (*jñana marga*) is the path of Manikkavasahar. It is the culminating path, the path of which the others are preliminaries, and it is marked by an understanding of Shiva's grace.

Shaivite Sects

Shaivism is the dominant form of Hinduism in South India. It has lost its hold in North India, even in Banaras, a city sacred to Shiva. The largest of the sects, the Shaiva Siddhanta, was dominant by the seventh century. The collective name for its scriptures is *Agamas,* a term derived from a word meaning "come down." The closeness in meaning to *shruti* (revealed) is obvious. The Shaiva Siddhantists recognize the *Agamas* as non-Vedic (*avaidika*), yet hold them to be equal in value to the Vedic literature. Since the term *"Agamas"* is also used by the Shaktas, the terms *"Shaivagamas"* and *"Shaktagamas"* are commonly used. But it is the hymns of the *Adiyars* which are chiefly treasured in Shaiva Siddhanta, and it is the teaching of this sect which we have thus far treated.

Four sects or offshoots from the main stem of Shaivism may be mentioned. One of these is Lingayat or Virashaiva, which was founded in the twelfth century by a *Brahmin* of South India named Basava. He broke from traditional Hinduism by refusing to undergo the sacred thread ceremony. His followers believe he was an incarnation of Nandi. The Lingayats are distinguished by a small stone *linga* enclosed in a metal box which they wear on a chain or string around the neck. They theoretically abandon all caste distinctions and grant women equal status with men. They are strict vegetarians, and they are opposed to all forms of magic and sorcery. They are encouraged to be zealous in vindicating any adverse remark about their religion and in working for the uplift and development of fellow cultists. The *linga* is not necessarily a phallic symbol for the Lingayats; rather it is regarded as a concentration of fire and light which purifies the body and mind of the individual. Fire is regarded as so pure that it is not to be used for cremation purposes, consequently the Lingayats bury rather than burn their dead.

In the ninth century a monistic form of Shaivism developed in Kashmir. Its founder was Vasugupta. He was much influenced by Advaita, and hence taught that Shiva was the Absolute Reality from which all else has emanated. Salvation for him was the intellectual recognition that the Absolute and individual selves are one. This cult is known as Kashmir Shaivism, or Shaivism of the Northern School. Also, since the founder treated the Absolute under the three principles of God, Soul, and Matter, the sect is known as Trikashastra or simply Trika. Kashmir Shaivism is a mediating, harmonizing *sadhana* which attempts to give matter more status than did Advaita and less than did Samkhya, and which stresses the importance of knowledge as a means of liberation yet finds scope for *bhakti*. It rejects the yogic view that one can by effort gain liberation, holding that only the grace of Shiva suffices.

A third cult of Shaivism is known as the Ganapatya since its deity is the elephant-headed god Ganesha, the son of Shiva and Parvati. There are varying legends to explain how their son happened to have an elephant head. One is that Shiva was once so angry at his son that he cut off his head. To console Parvati he agreed to replace the head with the head of the first being he met. The first being happened to be an elephant, so he placed an elephant head on Ganesha. The image of the pink, pot-bellied, one-tusked, elephant-headed god riding on a rat is a favorite in South India far beyond the limits of the small sect which worships Ganesha. The exclusive worship of Ganesha as the mover of obstacles dates from the middle of the seventh century. It is a cult with no caste distinctions, and hence is popular among *Shudras* and outcastes. A novel feature of the cult is the branding of the image of an elephant head on both arms of the devotees. The cult has split into many sub-cults, some adding the worship of many semidivine spirits, and some introducing wine drinking and promiscuous sexual activities.

The fourth offshoot from Shaivism cannot be called a sect; rather it is the development of a tendency latent within Shaivism: the *shakti* power. According to an ancient legend Shiva and Parvati once engaged in such violent sexual intercourse that they merged into one androgynous being. This is portrayed in sculptures known as Ardhanarishvara (Hermaphrodite Lord), the most famous of which may be seen in the cave at Elephanta near Bombay. This sculptured relief over sixteen feet high shows the male characteristics of Shiva on the right side and the female of Parvati on the left. The conception of Shiva as the perfect one embodying both sexes was well established by the Adiyars: "Our great one who is lord and lady too." (Sambandar) "Thou art half woman Thyself." (Sundaramurti) "The fawn-eyed maid is part of Thee!" (Manikkavasahar) Others carried this tendency further and developed a form of Hinduism which can be indicated by the generic term Shaktism.

Shaktism

Indian spiritual lore has not been exclusively philosophical, as some Western scholars like to believe. Concurrently with the composition of abstract speculation, manifested most spectacularly in the *Upanishads,* appeared techniques for the practical realization of physical and material goals. The *Atharva Veda* is an example of this tendency.

Another is the collection of short sayings known as *dharanis* from the fourth to the eighth centuries A.D. which were often written on the bark of trees and used as amulets to protect the wearer from evil spirits, kings' punishments, snakes, wild animals, fire, disease, theft, untimely death, etc. The Indian sought to make things happen, to avoid unhappy experiences, and to attain desired results of a very concrete nature as well as to seek liberation from the round of incarnations. Such a vigorous approach to nature can be regarded as the authentic inheritance of the *Rig rishis*. The Tantrics believed that all forms of production required an operation of something upon something else. The dual Shiva-Shakti was the formula for accomplishment. Shaktism is the result of emphasis on the feminine element in the formula. *"Shakta"* and *"tantra"* are interchangeable terms. The term *"tantra"* comes from *tan* (to spread) and perhaps from *tantri* (to know), and may have been used originally to mean to spread knowledge through mystic diagrams (*yantras*) with esoteric meanings (*mantras*). Shaktism or Tantrism is a vast collection of ideas and practices usually of occultic and sexual nature for the realization of practical ends. It is a delicate subject for Hindus to talk about, and a Westerner who writes or talks about it is open to severe criticism. Vivekananda, Gandhi, and Radhakrishnan avoided discussing Tantrism. Chandradhar Sharma in his fine study, *Indian Philosophy: A Critical Study,* devotes only two paragraphs to the subject.[6] Agehananda Bharati writes, "I have yet to meet an Indian-born scholar who stands squarely by the tantric tradition." [7] No translation of any Tantric text was published in India before 1900, and none in the West before 1913. Today over one thousand untranslated Tantric manuscripts are housed in the Asiatic Society of Bengal in Calcutta. Consequently, as yet our information about Tantrism is piecemeal.

We do not know the original home of Tantra. Bengal, Tibet, Nepal, and China have been suggested. Tantra is based on the belief that the union of lovers is the best analogy of the nature of the cosmos. Hence, "the yoga of sex" is a good characterization of Tantrism. The earliest Tantric writings come from the fifth century A.D. The importance of these writings is indicated in the fact that those who identify themselves as Tantrics refer to the Tantric writings as "the Fifth Veda"—an appellation shared with the

Puranas, the *Mahabharata,* the science of music, and the Tamil Shaivite literature!

The key concept for the understanding of Tantra is the inseparability of Shiva and Shakti, of the divine and the human, of the male and the female, of theory and practice, of the absolute and the relative, and of the macrocosmos and the microcosmos. Reality is fundamentally dual, but it is a duality of harmonious opposition. All discrepancies of speculation are lost in the doctrine of the identity of static and dynamic, negative and positive, empty and full. The nature of the cosmic polarity becomes best known to us when we experience the harmony of the male-female polarity. According to the literature of Tantrism the Hindu deities are in male-female pairs, e.g., Shiva-Shakti, Surya-Chandra, Agni-Soma, Ravi-Shashin (sun-moon), Purusha-Prakriti, etc. In the body the male-female pairs appear as right side of the body and left side of the body, right nostril and left nostril, soul and body, active state of the mind and passive state of the mind, semen and menstrual blood, etc. Beyond this is a vast collection of miscellaneous male-female pairs, e.g., blowing-sipping, consonant-vowel, cause-effect, lust-beauty, thunderbolt-lotus, etc. The Tantrics in other cultures created similar pairs, e.g., the Chinese *yang-yin* and the Tibetan *yab-yum.*

Tantrism accepted the fundamental Hindu view of *karma* and *samsara* and the ideal of *moksha* as liberation from incarnations for higher purposes. It did not claim that the Tantric *sadhana* is the best but that it was the only reliable means to liberation in the Kali Age. The Kali Age is the time when everything exteriorizes, but Tantra offers a reversal and interiorization—and, through interiorization, a liberation. The form by which intimations of *moksha* come to the Tantric is known as *chakrapuja* (circle worship). It is a form of worship in which male and female worshipers come together for the purpose of sharing in their efforts to attain *moksha.* Five *makaras* (things made of M's) are offered to the worshipers to be observed according to the extent of the development of the devotee. The five M's are *madya* (wine), *mamsa* (meat), *matsya* (fish), *mudra* (parched rice), and *maithuna* (copulation). The five symbolize in the order listed: the intoxicating knowledge of god, the consignment of all things to one's self, the identification of the pain and pleasure of the universe, the release from contact with evil, and the union of Shiva and Shakti. The so-called "Left-hand Tantrics" observe the M's literally; the "Right-hand Tantrics" use substitutes—e.g., the offering of flowers in proper gestures symbolizes union of Shiva and Shakti. The five M's are not engaged in for hedonic purposes but as an effort to participate in the delight of becoming (*lila*). Tantrism may also be regarded as an effort to transcend the illusion which denies reality to the physical world by insisting that it is only through the physical world that ascent can be made to the spiritual.

Tantrics in addition worked out an elaborate yogic technique for the interiorization of the macro-cosmos, a ritualization of the world. According to Tantrism vast stores of untapped energy lie within the human body. This is known as the *kundalini,* and is said in the occult physiology of the Tantrics to lie dormant at the base of the spine. This energy is to be aroused by yogic practices and raised through the *nadis* (occult tubes in the spinal cord) and the *chakras* (wheels of energy), and thus brought into creative action.

The problem in understanding Tantrism from the outside is that one is never sure which is literal and which is symbolic or occult. Its borrowing from the Purusha-Prakriti dualism of Samkhya-Yoga seems obvious, but the use it makes of the entities appears to be non-Indian. Its stress on man as the point from which an understanding of the world is possible is a refreshing change from those who first seek to know the world and then ask what is man in the vast reaches of time and space. Tantra seeks the recovery of a lost identity. Energy must be redirected from the external to the internal and from dissipation of the inner life to strengthening of the inner life. Tantrism attempts to open the awareness of man to his total environment that his life might be enlarged, his mind expanded, his emotions enriched. Woman is regarded as the greatest of all mysteries and the avenue to the fullest understanding of reality and the highest attainments of the human being. The sexual embrace is symbolic of and propaedeutic to the union of man and god. When we understand Tantrism better, we may have a far richer understanding of the breadth of the Hindu quest for reality and value.

CHAPTER 15

Islam, Christianity, and the West

Abu Raihan al-Biruni, an eleventh-century Muslim visitor to India, made the following observation of the Hindu character: ". . . the Hindus believe that there is no country like theirs, no nation like theirs, no kings like theirs, no religion like theirs, no science like theirs. They are haughty, foolishly vain, self-conceited, and stolid. They are by nature niggardly in communicating that which they know, and they take the greatest possible care to withhold it from men of another caste among their own people, still much more, of course, from any foreigner." [1] One does not need wide acquaintance with contemporary Hindus to find this attitude, but it would be grossly untrue and unfair to generalize this as the attitude of all Hindus. While there are some who believe that Hinduism is autochthonous [2] and a few who argue that the Indian is a European who has lost his identity,[3] the truth surely is that the Indian and Hinduism are the result of many ethnic and cultural strains. Hinduism has been modified by religions brought to the subcontinent, and it in turn has modified the immigrating religions. In this chapter we are concerned with the challenge to Hinduism offered by the Muslims, the Christians, and the European traders, merchants, and industrialists. The period from 600 B.C. to A.D. 300 was a period of internal challenge; the period from A.D. 1200 to the present day has been a period of external challenge. From the time of the coming of the Muslims to the time of entrance into the United Nations Indians have been adjusting and adapting to foreign ways. Of course the relationships have been symmetrical, although it is still possible to find in India protagonists of the view that Hinduism has borrowed nothing of value from *mlechchhas* (foreigners). This affirmation of a sociological miracle need not be taken seriously. Islam, above all religions, has modified Hinduism. In the words of an objective scholar, "So considerable has been the influence of Islam, that there is not an aspect of Hindu life, including its religion and domestic routine that has not been touched by it." [4]

Muslim Rule in India

Arabs and Indians had engaged in trade long before Muhammad founded the religion of Islam. We have already noted the commerce between Western Asia and the ancient peoples of the Indus valley. The first Muslims to appear on Indian soil were women and children captured by Hindu pirates early in the eighth century A.D. The captives were brought to the Sind. When Dahar, the ruler of the Sind, refused to give them up, an expedition of soldiers was sent from Arabia, and by 713 the Sind and part of the Punjab were in Muslim hands. The military leader, Muhammad ibn Qasim, remained as ruler of the territory, establishing a liberal and tolerant government. By the tenth century this early Arab rule had come to an end, but the evidence of Arabic rule can still be detected, e.g., the Arabic script of the Sindhi language. The Arabs were much impressed with Indian medicine and mathematics. They adopted the number system of the Indians, which they called "Indian numerals" (*al-ruqum-al-Hindiyyah*), and brought it to the West, where it became "Arabic numerals." Meanwhile other Muslim Arabs had established small colonies at each of the ports of the coastline of India, the largest settlements being in Malabar.

The next Muslim incursion into India came in 1001 when Mahmud of Ghazni conquered the area of the upper Indus. By 1020 Mahmud had established his empire as far east as Lahore. Mahmud, unlike Qasim, raided Hindu temples and carried off the wealth stored therein. The Hindu attitudes toward the Muslims are clearly indicated in al-Biruni's description of the raids: "Mahmud utterly ruined the prosperity of the country, and performed wonderful exploits by which the Hindus became like atoms of dust scattered in all directions, and like a tale of old in the mouth of the people. Their scattered remains cherish, of course, the most inveterate aversion towards all Muslims." [5] After Mahmud, the Ghaznavid empire broke up into small kingdoms or provinces, e.g., Delhi, Kanauj, Bundhelk-hand, Gujarat, Malwa, Bengal, and Lahore. The city of Lahore had become a rich cultural center. Poets in Lahore, such as Razi, Salman, and Ali Hujwiri, were influential in making the Persian language of Afghanistan and Central Asia the court language and the means of cultural expression throughout Muslim rule in India.

In 1175 a third Muslim invasion began. This one also originated in Ghazni, and the objective this time was not plunder but political power. The leader (sultan) of the invading forces was Muhammad Ghuri. By the time of his death in 1206 nearly all of northern India was under Muslim rule. His successor, Qutb-ud-din Aibak, who founded the Delhi Sultanate, can be properly described as the first Muslim ruler of Northern India. Aibak determined to consolidate the empire rather than extend it, but he is best known for the large mosque he built in Delhi. Consolidation was the work of his successors, especially of his son-in-law, Shams-ud-din Iltutmish. Iltutmish's task was made more difficult by the invasions of barbaric nomads from Central Asia who are known only as "Mongols," a term applied at that time to any Asian who was neither Hindu nor Muslim. Iltutmish, despite his preoccupation at the northwest border, found time for the Muslim fascination with architecture: he built the Qutb Minar, a magnificent tower which remains one of the showpieces of Delhi. The major task of the Delhi sultans throughout the thirteenth century was holding back the Mongol hordes. By 1335 under Muhammad Tughluq the empire had been expanded to include almost all the subcontinent. For the first time South and North were under one ruler, but even during the sultanate of Muhammad Tughluq disintegration began. In 1398 Timur of Samarqand sacked Delhi, with the result that independent kingdoms, some Muslim and some Hindu, displaced the united kingdom. When the last Tughluq king died in 1413 a series of weak kings known as the Sayyids took over the remnant of the empire. They were succeeded by the Lodi kings (1451–1526), who tried unsuccessfully to restore the empire to the dimensions of the Tughluqs.

The fourth, the last, and the greatest of the Muslim rulers in India was that of the Mughals. Some historians begin the modern history of India with the Mughal empire, an empire which lasted from 1526 to 1858. The dynasty began when Babur, a ruler of a kingdom whose capital was Kabul, invaded India in 1526. He was believed to have descended from Timur, and that was the only justification for applying the name "Mughal" to the dynasty. These sultans were in fact Turkish in origin. When Babur died in 1529, his kingdom reached to Patna at the eastern end of the Ganges. His son, Humayun, who ruled from 1529 to 1556, is remembered for two achievements: he brought more Persian-Turkish culture to India, especially the pageantry and pomp associated with royalty, and he was the father of Akbar. Akbar set a pattern of tolerance between Muslim and Hindu which has for the most part characterized the common life of Muslims and Hindus up to the time of the partition of the country into modern India and Pakistan. Akbar married Rajput princesses without asking them to give up their Hinduism, appointed Hindus to prominent administrative posts, abolished the pilgrim tax and the *jizya* (tax paid by non-Muslims in a Muslim country), gave land to the Sikhs on which they built their Golden Temple, and encouraged the classical Indian arts. One of the most interesting of his contributions to religion was the building of a House of Worship at the capital city of Fatehpur Sikri to which scholars of all religious faiths were invited to come to discuss religious matters on Friday after prayers. The hypothesis that Akbar attempted to form a syncretic religion called Din-i-Ilahi has very limited supporting evidence. Unfortunately, his efforts to harmonize Hinduism and Islam coincided with the efforts of Khwaja Baqi Billah and Shaikh Ahmad to strengthen the role of orthodox Islam in the affairs of state and with the effort of Chaitanya to revitalize Vaishnavism. Shaikh Ahmad fanatically demanded that orthodox Muslims not associate with non-Muslims or nonconforming Muslims. After the death of Akbar in 1605 the Mughals' increasing zeal for Islam peaked in the reign of Aurangzeb (1658–1707).

Aurangzeb was a Muslim zealot who claimed he acted always "for the sake of the true faith and the peace of the realm." He was determined to make India a genuine Muslim state. He attempted to stop drinking, gambling, and prostitution, forbade the sale and use of narcotics, issued edicts against *suttee,* reimposed the *jizya,* eliminated all taxes not authorized by Islamic law, stopped all music and festivities in the royal court, and abandoned the ceremony of public appearances of the emperor to the people. In one year (1679) Aurangzeb destroyed sixty-six Hindu temples in Amber, sixty-three in Chitor, one hundred and three in Udaipur, and razed to the ground an ancient Hindu shrine in Banaras and built a Muslim mosque on the site. He imposed a customs duty of five per cent on the goods of Hindus and two per cent on the goods of Muslims. His puritanical nature was such that he even criticized the extravagance of his mother's tomb, the famous Taj Mahal. But despite all his efforts against the Hindus, the Sikhs, the East India Company, and the unorthodox Muslims, neither the purity of life nor the strength of the empire was maintained during Aurangzeb's reign.

After Aurangzeb the Mughal empire slowly disintegrated into independent kingdoms which for a time paid annual tributes to the Delhi court, but the more powerful of these such as Hyderabad, Bengal, and Punjab passed from Mughal control. The British assumed overlordship of Delhi in 1803, and for fifty years preserved the fiction of Muslim sovereignty, but in 1858 following the Sepoy Mutiny the British deposed the last sultan, Bahadur Shah, and the Mughal empire came to an end. Muslims and Hindus, now brought together by their "common enemy," joined in a century of struggle for independence. But old tensions remained and in 1947 Pakistan went the way of the Muslim state to which Aurangzeb had aspired and India chose the secular state anticipated in the reforms of Akbar the Great.[6]

Islam

Islam is the religion of total submission to the one God. The essential doctrines call for absolute faith in Allah; in his prophets—especially Muhammad; in his book—the *Koran*; in his final judgment; and in his predestination. Whereas the way for man to go in Hinduism is a broad way with many *margas* from which the devotee may select his own, the way in Islam is a straight and narrow way, and the individual has no choice; e.g., the times of prayer, the words of prayer, and even the position of the body during prayer are prescribed. Fortunately, the Islam which came to India and made its imprint on Hinduism was not the Islam of the Arabs but that of the Turks and Afghans. The latter had recently become Muslims, and for them the relationship between their adopted religion and their traditional culture was still fluid. Thus in India Islam experienced many surprising changes. For example, Islam has traditionally held to the equality of man, yet in India Muslim castes are a familiar phenomenon. Again idol worship is forbidden in Islam, yet idols are worshiped by some Indian Muslims. The following news item appeared in *The Statesman* (Delhi) on March 11, 1959: "A Hindu temple near Suratgarh in Rajasthan has Muslim priests who perform worship of the idol and receive offerings from devotees. This has been going on for generations."

The impact of the Muslims on the Hindus is very hard to measure, and the student must take care in his reading to note whether the author is Hindu or Muslim. Yet it is correct to note that the Muslims brought about changes in architecture, painting, political organization, warfare, ceremonies, social behavior, etc. Tailored clothes, the turban, new forms of address and salutation, new foods and culinary delights, and new forms of details of domestic life were introduced and adopted. In the eighteenth century the puritanical Wahhabi movement triggered counter-puritanical movements in Hinduism.

Vedic authoritarianism was substantiated and strengthened by the authoritative attitude toward the *Koran.* Northern India, in particular, was altered by the Muslims. Benjamin Walker writes that "northern India may be said to have been permanently Moghulized, and the rest of India indelibly stamped with the impress received from Islam." [7]

The greatest impact of Islam on Hinduism was made by the movement known as Sufism. Islam grew out of the founder's experience of the presence of God, and from the earliest day of Islam the assumption was that this experience was unique to Muhammad. He was the greatest and the last of the prophets through whom God had spoken. God had recited to and through Muhammad his authoritative and culminating word to man, the *Koran.* The followers were to receive and obey that word; they were not to repeat the experience of Muhammad, an experience which Muhammad had not sought, did not prepare for, and did not want. But about A.D. 800 certain Muslims, desiring to achieve for themselves the experience of God's presence, began to practice methods to induce the experience, including the wearing of simple woolen garments. It was from the latter—*suf* (wool)—that they were called Sufis. Their predecessor had been Hasan al-Basri of Iraq (died 728), who engaged in asceticism as a protest against the worldliness of the Muslims of his time.

Sufism was at first a protest against the theological and juridical forms of Islam, but the movement could not long avoid developing its own rational defenses. While the orthodox stressed the separation of God and man by pointing out God was Creator and man was the created—"Allah created you from dust" [8]—the Sufis argued for the identity of man and God by quoting, "We are nearer to man than the vein of his neck" [9] and "Wherever you turn there is the face of God." [10] When the Persian mystic, al-Hallaj (858–922) identified himself with Allah by declaring, "I am the Truth" (*ana'l-Haqq*), the orthodox reacted with violence—al-Hallaj was crucified for his heresy. But they could not stop the movement, and soon the mystical insights were systematized into the doctrine that all being is essentially one, that all beings emanate from the divine, that before emanation they are ideas in the mind of Allah, and that man is the microcosm who is capable of reflecting the macrocosm. The essentials of Sufism were capsuled in the poem by al-Hallaj

> I am He whom I love, and He whom I love is I.
> We are two souls in one body.
> When thou seest me, thou seest Him,
> And when thou seest Him, thou seest us both.

The goal of Sufism was to promote the experience of union with the divine. A program of stages was formulated for the realization of that goal. The first stage was asceticism, including penitence for the past mode of living, renunciation of worldly affairs and concerns, and mortification of the flesh and appetites. The Sufis relinquished their personal property, abstained from even lawful pleasures, and engaged in silent meditation. The second stage was an effort to discover the esoteric knowledge which accompanies the direct personal mystical experience. Up to three years would be spent with a teacher (*shaikh*). During the early centuries of Sufism the studies were usually individual, but by the twelfth century Sufi orders and congregations had come into being, chiefly in Baghdad. Brotherhoods were formed in which the inmates worked, ate, studied, and worshiped together. The worship was usually the repetition of sacred formula, or the reciting of the excellent names of Allah counted on a rosary. Movements of the body were sometimes synchronized with the recitations. The third stage was the illumination which was expected to come. Sufi illumination, as is the case in mysticism almost universally, was described in terms of light:

> Allah is the light of the heavens and the earth.
> His light is like a niche wherein is a lamp.[11]

The Platonism of Plotinus was adopted and adapted for Sufi purposes. The third stage was the love of man and God. While the *Koran* does not explicitly state that Allah loves man, it does state that Allah knows all—"Whether ye hide that which is in your breasts or reveal it, Allah knoweth it" [12]—and this was interpreted as Allah's love for man. Human love was a reflection of divine love. This stage led to the God-intoxication of the Sufis which was manifested in trance and ecstasy. For this the Sufis were persecuted as heretics and some were forced to move eastward, where they found a sympathetic home in India. The *bhakti* elements of Hinduism and Islam found such common ground that they even came together to form a new syncretic religion, Sikhism.

Christianity in India

A Syraic work of the second or third century called *The Acts of Judas Thomas* reports that after the ascension of the Christ the apostles met in Jerusalem to cast lots to determine where each would go to preach the Gospel. When Thomas drew India, he protested that he would go anywhere except to India. Later he was sold into slavery, purchased by an Indian merchant, and taken to India. After many adventures he arrived at the port of Muziris near Cochin in the year 52. He is said to have established churches across South India and finally to have been martyred at Mylapore, now a suburb of Madras. Demetrius, Bishop of Alexandria, sent a visitor to a Christian congregation in India in the year 189. One of the delegates to the Council of Nicaea (325) was Bishop John, Metropolitan of India. Also there is the story of a group of Christian refugees from Persia who took asylum with Christians in Malabar in 345. Thus there is persuasive evidence that Christianity came to India soon after it was founded in the Levant.

The early Indian Christians lived isolated from the mainstream of Christianity until 1506 when the Jesuit Francis Xavier arrived in Calicut to establish the Roman Catholic Church in India. The relations between the Syrian and the Roman branches of Christianity, although cordial at first, became strained, and in 1599 the Syrians were forced to merge with the Roman Church. But in 1653 the Syrians broke from Rome and linked themselves with the Jacobite Christian Church of Antioch. In the nineteenth and twentieth centuries the Indian Christians were not immune from the denominational splits which divided Western Christianity. In India today there are in addition to those who are members of the Roman

Catholic Church and the various Protestant denominations Romo-Syrians who owe allegiance to the Pope, Jacobite Orthodox Syrians who are under the Jacobite Patriarch of Antioch, independent Mar Thoma Syrians, and Chaldean Syrians allied with the Nestorian Catholics of the East.

India was a prime target for Christian foreign missionary work for almost five centuries. Franciscans, Dominicans, Augustinians, and Carmelites arrived after the Jesuits. The first Protestant missionaries were German Lutherans who worked at Tranquebar near Tiruchirapalli. William Carey, the shoemaker-turned-linguist, was the first missionary to be sent by a Western missionary society. The missionaries were slow in coming to North India because until 1812 the East India Company refused to allow any missionaries in the area of its operation. When the policy was changed, the Church of England was established in India in 1814. Throughout the nineteenth century missionaries poured into India to found churches, hospitals, orphanages, tuberculosis sanatoria, homes for lepers, schools for the blind, printing presses, agricultural institutes, insane asylums, elementary and secondary schools, colleges, and other institutions for the improvement of the life of the people. By the middle of the twentieth century Protestants operated 46 colleges, 448 high schools, 553 middle schools, and 103 teacher-training institutions, and the Roman Catholics had 42 colleges, 474 high schools, and 4,362 primary schools.[13]

The impact of Christianity upon Hinduism is as difficult to measure as is the impact of Islam. Hinduism was stimulated by Christian example to do more than had previously been done for the poor and needy; e.g., there were no homes for lepers before Christianity came to India. Claims made by Christians that Christianity is reflected in the *Kural* and the *Bhagavad Gita* are difficult to support or refute. The claim that Krishnaism was an Indian plagiarism of Christianity based on the similarity of the words "Krishna" and "Christ" and on the parallelism of birth and childhood stories of Krishna and Jesus was popular among Indologists at the end of the last century but finds few supporters today. Much more defensible is the hypothesis that the *bhakti* developments with their emphasis on the sinfulness of man and the grace of God may reflect the impact of Christianity, and there is no doubt that Christianity was partly responsible for the appearance of the great modern Hindu reformers such as Rammohan Roy, Swami Dayananda, Keshub Chunder Sen, Ramakrishna, Vivekananda, and Gandhi, for each of these acknowledged his debt to Christianity. According to figures released by the Indian Government in 1964 only 2.4 per cent of the people of India are Christian. This is a very low percentage when one remembers that Christianity was in India before it was in Rome.

The West in India

Traders from Greece, Rome, Venice, and Genoa came to India seeking calicoes, silks, cloves, and pepper, but their relationships with the Indians were merely economic. The Portuguese were the first from the West who came to stay. Henry the Navigator in the middle of the fifteenth century expressed well the rationale of the West when he set as the goals of travel, exploration, and settlement of the East: to bring Christianity to the tribes lying "under the wrath of God," to overthrow Islam, and to increase national wealth and power. On May 17, 1498, four ships under Vasco de Gama landed near Calicut, and within a year regular trade had been established between Cochin and Portugal. In 1503 a fort was built at Cochin and a governor with 1500 soldiers were affixed. The Portuguese under the leadership of Albuquerque joined forces with the Hindus in opposition to the Muslims, and in 1510 drove the Muslims out of the excellent port city of Goa and established themselves and the Hindus there. Later they also made settlements at Diu and Daman. Since the Turks were more anxious to dominate the Mediterranean than to drive the Portuguese out of the Indian Ocean, the hold of Portugal on seaports in India remained largely unchallenged during the sixteenth century. The Portuguese were amazingly successful in propagandizing Christianity. Some of their means for promoting Christianity were ingenious; e.g., when a non-Christian died without sons, his property went to the nearest Christian relative. Most of the Portuguese settlers were males, with the result that nearly all the wives of the Portuguese were natives. Thus the Portuguese became

Indianized, and the Goans became Christianized. From 1609 to 1661 the Portuguese were harassed by the Dutch, who proved to be better shipbuilders and navigators than the Portuguese. The Dutch East India Company was interested in lands beyond India, and wanted only trading factories in India, leaving India open to other European powers.

The British East India Company was incorporated on December 31, 1600, with the intention of establishing trade with the archipelago, Indo-China, and the Malay peninsula, but after a few bouts with the Dutch it decided to limit its trade to India, where it was faced with a less formidable competitor. An Anglo-Portuguese treaty of 1642 prepared the way for full attention to India, where the British had first attempted to establish themselves in 1608. The British East India Company also discovered that trade in cloth was a good substitute for trade in spices. Its first trading post was opened in 1612 at Surat on the west coast of India. Factories for the production of cloth were established at Masulipatam in 1611, at Surat in 1618, at Madraspatam in 1639, and at Hooghly in 1651, and so thereafter at Patna and Kasimbazar. As the East India Company prospered, it watched the conflicts between Muslims and Hindus, particularly under the foolish policies of Aurangzeb. Sir Josia Child, director of the Company during the later Stuarts, noted its long-range purpose was "to establish such a politie and civill and military power, and to create and secure such a large revenue to secure both, . . . as may be the foundation of a large, well-grounded, sure English dominion in India for all time to come." The annual average return to stockholders of the Company from 1662 to 1691 was twenty-two per cent. The company's monopoly was virtually unchallenged until 1793. Difficulties were mounting, but so were profits. It was not the intention of the English to rule India except insofar as political power and authority might be necessary to insure a steady flow of financial profit. But slowly, step by step, the company found itself acting as ruler. The East India Company became a government within a government. It was impossible to determine which of its functions were trade and which were government. A more ideal arrangement for corruption would be hard to imagine, yet life under the "foreign devils" was far better than most Indians experienced in their villages and towns. Taxes were lighter and life more enjoyable under the British than under Muslim sultans or Hindu princes. The English-dominated cities of Bombay, Madras, and Calcutta grew rapidly. In the words of *The Cambridge Shorter History of India*: "The rapid growth of wealth and population of the three chief towns shows plainly that Indians found the rule of foreign traders milder, juster, safer, and more profitable than the government of neighbouring Indian princes, and, as conditions throughout the country became more disturbed, they sent their wealth and their families into the English settlements for safety, or came themselves to live and trade there." [14] In each company town the chief administrator was simultaneously the head of the civil administration, the administrator of justice, the commander-in-chief of the military forces, and the one who, because of his financial connections and power of nomination, was most sought out as a friend and most avoided as an enemy. The wonder is that under such conditions the British East India Company administrators were not more corrupt than they were.

The expectation of "English dominion in India for all time to come" was challenged in 1857. The Bengal army was at that time dispensing with the old smooth-bore musket and re-arming with the Enfield rifle. The new rifle required a much closer fit of cartridge and ball in the barrel, and the new cartridge needed to be heavily greased in order for it to be rammed down the barrel. These cartridges had to have the ends bitten off when they were put into the breech. Word spread among the sepoys of the Bengal army, who were selected largely from the *Brahmins* and *Kshatriyas*, that the cartridges had been greased with the fat of cows—and when the rumor got to the Muslim sepoys, it was the fat of pigs! Thus the cartridges were taboo for both Hindus and Muslims. This touched off a series of mutinies in the Bengal army throughout northern India. The mutiny was originally a religious rebellion. A rumor spread that the fundamental intent of the East India Company was to destroy both Hinduism and Islam and to Christianize and Westernize all India. The missionaries were reported to be working hand and glove with the effort. Many interferences with Hindu customs were recounted: the permission for the remarriage of widows, the laws against *suttee*, the ceasing of interest once shown in religious festivals, the new forms of education, the railroads which made it difficult to avoid pollution by contact with outcastes, the increasing encouragement and, in some instances, requirement of sea voyages for Hindus, the outlawing of Thugism, the introduction of Western forms of law, etc. The mutiny began at Dum-Dum on the outskirts of Calcutta and appeared more violently at Meerut near Delhi. Sepoys disobeyed and turned on their officers. Throughout 1857 violence broke out in scores of cities in the Ganges valley. Delhi was held for several months by the mutineers. There was no planned organization of the revolt, and no one was directing the activities. When the Muslims raised the standard symbolizing a holy war at the Jama Masjid in Delhi, the Hindus pulled it down. Thirteen bakers were killed in Delhi on the grounds they had sold bread to the English. The aged sultan, Bahadur Shah, who was only a figurehead, was carried in triumph through the city, while others attempted to raid his palace. Wealthier citizens went into hiding to avoid plunder and torture.

When the mutiny was finally put down in the spring of 1858, the British government assumed direct control over India, ending the pretense of the Mughal court at Delhi, and canceling the powers of the East India Company, a commercial organization which had never been qualified for ruling a country, above all an ancient country like India. The years 1600 to 1857 may be called "The Years of the Company" and the years 1858 to 1947 "The Years of the Crown," but both Company and Crown evidenced the truth of the adage that Great Britain is a nation of shopkeepers. Doing good for India was secondary to doing well for the United Kingdom. The India which had attracted the traders from the West was the India of riches and beauty; the India which was granted her independence was an India of overpopulation, disease, and poverty. But the legacy of the West to India has not been altogether negative. The railways and roads, the telephone and telegraph systems, the law courts and the Civil Service, a sense of the importance of obedience to law, Western medicine, modern technology, the English language, and systems of public education must be included as contributions of the British and the West to India. The West drained away much of the wealth of

India, but it also planted and nourished the hopes of a united and independent Indian nation.

The contributions of the West to Hinduism are very difficult to ascertain. Because of contact with Western peoples the Hindus began to ask questions about their own identity and destiny. A new sense of the importance of living entered Hinduism. Hindus began to examine their own history, art, science, medicine, literature, drama, music, dance, languages, social organizations, politics, law, ethics, and religion. Rational inquiry and critical evaluation began to replace the acceptance of tradition and convention. Contact with the West was the catalyst of the Hindu renaissance.

CHAPTER 16

Developments in Bhakti

The developments within Hinduism during the last seven centuries may be regarded as in part a reaction to the external challenges of the two great monotheistic religions, Islam and Christianity, and to Western peoples who came to India in quest of trade and commerce. We shall consider these developments under three headings. The first is the various forms of *bhakti* which came into being during these centuries; the second is the appearance of new forms of Hinduism, a revitalization which is often called "The Hindu Renaissance"; and the third is the rise of national aspirations culminating in the establishment of the independent nation of India. Innovations in *bhakti* appeared throughout India during these centuries, but in all cases they shared four characteristics: (1) the vernacular was used for preaching and writing; (2) the traditional *varna* distinctions were ignored; (3) there was little interest in the Vedic scriptures; (4) the *shruti* rituals and ceremonies were rejected. The *bhakti* developments in the north were more radical than those in the south; e.g., *varna* distinctions and the worship of images were far more rigorously attacked in the north. This difference was possibly due to the greater impact of Islam in the north.

Sikh Gurus and Saints

Sikhism, a religion with about five million followers, began as an effort to harmonize Islam and Hinduism. Nanak the founder

(1469–1538) was born into a *Kshatriya* family in rural Punjab. He came to the conclusion that neither Islam nor Hinduism should stand alone. "There is no Hindu and no Muslim," he declared. He wore a turban on his head and a Hindu sectarian mark on his forehead. He induced a Muslim to travel with him as he spread his message throughout India and Ceylon. He is reported to have made a pilgrimage to Mecca. He took his conception of God from Islam: a single existent conscious good Being both transcendent and immanent who created man and the world by his own unfathomable will. This sovereign God has no incarnations. If a name is to be given to God, let it be Sat Nam (True Name)—or, if one wishes, it may be Rama, or Shiva, or Allah, or any name one selects, for the name is unimportant. The *Japji* (remembrance) which the Sikh is expected to recite each morning begins: "There is but one God whose name is True, the Creator, devoid of fear and enmity, immortal, unborn, self-existent; by the favor of Guru repeat his name, The True One was in the beginning; the True One was in the primal age. The True One is, was and shall be." The mystery of God's being and his purpose in creation cannot be reasoned by the mind of man nor expressed in words: "By thinking I cannot obtain a conception of him, even though I think hundreds of thousands of times." But the divine mystery is revealed to man when he destroys his I-am-ness and recognizes his full dependence upon God. The chief moral attribute of God is kindness to human beings. All the lower creatures have been destined for the service of man, and man's destiny is found in the praise (*nam*) and service (*seva*) of God.

Nanak held to the Hindu doctrines of *karma* and *samsara*, but he rejected the *varna* system and the Vedic scriptures. He taught that man's reponse to God should be devotional adoration (*bhakti*) rather than the submissive attitude of Muslims. The *bhakti* he recommended was like the devotion of the Vaishnavite to the gracious Lord Krishna, but the object of his adoration was found not in a transcendent realm nor in a symbolic representation but within the heart. Nanak is believed to have learned the *bhakti* approach to deity from Kabir. The syncretism of Kabir the poet and Nanak the organizer must have been confusing to their followers. One legend is that when Kabir died Muslims and Hindus quarreled as to which had the honor of conducting the funeral rites. But when they removed the robe which had been thrown over the corpse, they found only a bouquet of flowers.

Nanak was not a philosopher, and he made no effort to formulate a theology. His disciples—the word *"sikh"* means disciple—called him and the nine leaders who followed in succession the *Gurus*. The tenth *Guru*, Govind Singh (1675–1708), changed the complexion of Sikhism from its original pacifism to a militant theocracy. He introduced a sword-baptismal ceremony and affixed the word "Singh" (lion) to all family names. He also terminated the Hindu tendency to *guru*-worship in no uncertain terms: "Those who call me God shall go to hell." The decision was reached that the term *"Guru"* did not refer to the person but to the words of the person. Thus the scriptures of Sikhism, the *Guru Granth*, displaced the historical *gurus* and is often referred to as "the eternal *Guru*." The history of Sikhism is full of violence and bloodshed—they have not been called "The Lions of the Punjab" without cause—but we are concerned here only with the Sikh contribution to *bhakti*.

The *bhakti* element in Sikhism is clearly seen in the nature of the *Granth*: it contains 3384 hymns, and in bulk is three times the size of the *Rig Veda*. Every line of the book is set to music. The assumption of Sikhism is that through poetry and music the devotee will lose himself in a rapture in which the truths of God will be revealed to him. The *Granth* is composed chiefly of the writings of the first five *gurus* and of sixteen saints (*bhagats*). We shall consider two of the saints: Ramananda (1400–1470) and Kabir (1440–1518). They, more than any others, provided a *bhakti* bridge between Islam and Hinduism.

Ramananda was at first a member of Ramanuja's Vaishnavite sect. He rose to become the leader of the sect, the fifth in succession after Ramanuja. In the course of his duties as leader he traveled through India visiting the various temples of the order, but when he returned to the monastery, the monks, concluding that he was polluted after his travels, refused to eat with him. Ramananda was so hurt by the insult that he left the sect, journeyed to Banaras, and began a new order which he called "Ramanandi." God, he declared, should be adored with fervent devotion under the name of Rama. He did not condemn idolatry, but he completely rejected the Hindu class distinctions. All men are equal in God's sight, he taught. "Whoever adores God is God's own." Most of his teaching was oral. Only one poem has been preserved—and it is in the *Granth*:

> Where shall I go? The music and the festivity are in my own house, my heart does not wish to move, my mind has folded its wings and is still. One day, my heart was filled to overflowing, and I had an inclination to go with sandal and other perfumes to offer my worship to Brahman. But the *guru* revealed that Brahman was in my own heart. Wherever I go, I see only water and stones worshipped; but it is Thou who has filled them all with Thy presence. They all seek Thee in vain among the Vedas. If Thou art not to be found here, we must go and seek Thee there. My own true *guru*, Thou hast put an end to all my failures and illusions. Blessed art Thou! [1]

To propagate his new religion he selected twelve disciples of whom one was a woman, one a Muslim, and several low in the caste hierarchy. The Muslim entered the discipleship by subterfuge. One dark night he lay in the path over which Ramananda walked. When Ramananda stumbled over the body, he spontaneously exclaimed, "Ram! Ram!" The person in the path declared that Ramananda's exclamation constituted an initiation. That person was Kabir.

Kabir was the son of a Muslim weaver of Banaras. His great hope was to unify the Sufism of Islam and traditional Hinduism, but his courage, cantankerous spirit, and sharp tongue were not suitable for the role of harmonizer and peacemaker. He married, had two children, and supported himself and his family by weaving. Asceticism he rejected: "If salvation is achieved by living on roots and fruits alone, the lives of birds and animals would be ideal lives." In one of his poems he wrote:

> If union with God be obtained by going about naked
> All the beasts of the forest shall be saved!
> What mattereth it whether man goeth naked or weareth a deerskin,
> If he recognize not God in his heart?
> If perfection be obtained by shaving the head,
> Why should not sheep obtain salvation?

> If, O brethren, the continent man be saved,
> Why should not a eunuch obtain the supreme reward? [2]

He ridiculed the philosophers, rejected all caste distinctions, scoffed at the *ashrama* division of life, and made no distinction between Hindu and Muslim. When a *Brahmin* challenged him to a debate he replied:

> Thou art a *Brahmin*, I am a weaver of Banaras;
>   How can I be a match for thee?
> By repeating the name of God I have been saved,
>   but thou, O pandit, shall be lost by trusting in the Vedas.

When a Muslim priest advised him to make a pilgrimage to Mecca, he turned upon the priest:

> Make thy mind thy Kaaba, thy body its enclosing temple,
> Conscience its prime teacher;
> Then, O priest, call men to pray to that mosque
> Which hath ten gates.
> Sacrifice, wrath, doubt, and malice;
> Make patience thine utterance of the five prayers.
> The Hindus and the Muslims have the same Lord;
> What can the Mulla, what can the Shaikh do for man?

When another Muslim condemned him for having a pig tied outside his door, Kabir said, "I have an unclean animal outside my house; but you have unclean friends inside your heart: greed, envy, pride, anger and avarice."

Kabir finally created so many enemies that they were successful in having the sultan Sikandar Lodi banish him from Banaras. He is said to have traveled throughout the Middle East, and, as an object lesson, returned to die in Maghar in northern India, since awful things were said to happen to anyone who died in this place.

> "One who dies in Maghar becomes an ass!" A fine thing, you have lost
>   your confidence in Rama!
> What is Banaras, what the waste land of Maghar, if Rama dwells in my
>   heart.

After Kabir's death his admirers collected his poetry. Many of them have been incorporated into the *Granth* of the Sikhs; others are in a volume known as the *Bijak* (treasury) which forms the sacred scriptures of the Kabir Panth (Kabir Brotherhood). Kabir's works are in an idiomatic form of Hindi. He is sometimes called "The Father of Hindi Literature"—a strange title for a man who could neither read nor write. Much of what passes today as Kabir poetry is in fact translations of inaccurate Bengali and Sufi reworkings of Kabir, but even these reflect the spirit of the weaver of Banaras.

The doctrine of Kabir is very difficult to determine, since he was a practical religious teacher rather than a philosopher. He was certainly a monotheist with pantheistic overtones: "He is one; there is no second." "Rama, Khuda, Shakti, Shiva are one: tell me pray how you distinguish them?" "In heaven, the realms below, in earth and waters, one alone, Rama, watches over all." In some passages he seems almost Advaitin: "How can I explain His form or outline? there is no second who has seen Him . . . He must be seen without qualities." Idolatry of all forms, he rejected:

> If God dwell only in the mosque, to whom belongeth the rest of the country?
> They who are called Hindus say that God dwelleth in an idol; I see not the truth in either sect."

Pilgrimages, ceremonial purifications, fasts, sacred threads, circumcision, and rosaries he denounced:

> Devotion, sacrifice and rosary, piety, pilgrimage, fasting and alms.
> Nine bhaktis, Vedas, the Book, all these are cloaks for falsehood.

. . . .

> You wear tilaks on your forehead, carry rosaries in your hands, and put on sectarian dresses.
> People think that God is a plaything.

. . . .

Some shave men's locks and hang the black cord on their necks.
And pride themselves on the practice of Yoga.
What credit is there in causing your seat to fly?
Crow and kite also circle in the air.

He denounced caste, holding that nurture is more important than
nature:

If birth from a Brahmin mother makes you a Brahmin,
Why did you not come by another way?
If birth from a Turk makes you a Turk,
Why were you not circumcized in the womb?
If you milk black and yellow cows together,
Will you be able to distinguish their milk?

"In the beginning," said Kabir, "there was no Turk nor Hindu—no
race, no caste."

Kabir believed that the great hindrance to man's experience of
God was sin. Only the pure in heart can see God. Pride in self, in
learning, in ceremony, and in ascetic practices were the great
obstacles.

My possessions are lust, wrath, covetousness, pride and envy.
Mercy, honesty, and service to the guru have not come to me even in
my dreams.

.   .   .   .   .   .

Unless you remove evil from your hearts, how shall you find God by
dwelling in the forest?

.   .   .   .   .   .

What availeth devotion, what penance, what fasting and worship,
To him in whose heart there is worldly love?
O man, apply thy heart to God;
Thou shall not obtain Him by artifice.

There is only one way to God—the way of loving faith in and devotion to the personal God: "By devotion I have obtained the Lord." The goal is re-absorption into God:

> When the godly die, to what abode shall the pious man's soul go?
> It shall unite with Him who is beyond expression and indestructible.

. . . .

> I no longer suspect that I shall suffer transmigration;
> Even in life I am absorbed in the infinite.

After the death of Kabir his followers asked his son for permission to found a sect, but the son replied, "My father strove throughout his life against all forms of sectarianism; how can I destroy his ideal and thereby commit his spiritual murder?" Nevertheless, the followers did establish a sect which they called the Kabir Panth, but they soon departed from the simple unadorned devotion of Kabir, and have since split into twelve schools based on differences in matters of form and ceremony. Today there is maintained in Banaras a shrine where a pair of sandals representing the feet of Kabir are washed daily. The wash water is given by the spoonful to worshipers at the shrine. Similarly the Sikhs have all but deified Nanak, who following Kabir denied that God has incarnations. Also they worship the *Granth* idolatrously even though Nanak was bitterly opposed to both idol worship and *guru* adoration. But Kabir's teaching of unencumbered *bhakti* was not lost altogether. The Sikhs have incorporated many of his poems in their scriptures; Christians find Nestorian piety in his works; Sufis have translated his Hindu poems into Persian; and his warm and simple *bhakti* poetry is used by liberal Hindus in the worship of their chosen gods.

Bhakti in Shri-Vaishnavism

The form of Vaishnavism which developed in South India after the *Alvars* and *Acharyas* split into two sects in the fourteenth century. Perhaps Ramanuja set a divisive mood in his writing, for he did write vituperatively against the Shankarites in his commentary on the *Vedanta Sutras*. We have already noted the abdication of Ramananda from leadership of Shri-Vaishnavism. Another dividing factor was the fact that some of the sacred scriptures were in Sanskrit and some in Tamil—and the Tamil-speaking people have deep affection for their beautiful language. But still more fundamentally, differences arose as to the interpretation of *bhakti*. While all agreed that the *bhakta* must surrender himself to the Lord, there were differences of opinion as to the worth and/or necessity of self-effort. Is anything expected of the worshiper? Does he make any contribution to his salvation? Or is salvation entirely the work of God? Two sets of answers were offered. The Vadagalais, who also stressed the Sanskrit scriptures, held that the individual must exert himself toward his own liberation. Without self-effort he can never come to the complete realization of his dependence upon the grace of God. He cannot save himself, but he will not resort to *prapatti* until he has tried self-liberation. Man turns to God only after he has turned away from himself, and he will not turn away from self until he has experienced the failure of his own struggles to purify his life, to attain the good, and to realize *moksha*. Not so, claimed the Tengalais, who favored Tamil over Sanskrit; the grace of Vishnu is spontaneous and self-sufficient. There is nothing at all that man can do about his own salvation, except turn to the Lord. To suggest the necessity of self-effort—even when it is admitted that self-effort will not suffice—is to imply that man makes a contribution to his own salvation. The two interpretations of the operation of *bhakti* came to be known as *markata-nyaya* (analogy of the monkey), since a young monkey contributes to its transportation by clinging to the back of its mother, and *marjara-nyaya* (analogy of the cat), since a kitten makes no contribution to its transportation.

The split widened as the implications of the two doctrines of grace were examined. The Vadagalais were charged with holding that God condones sin; sin is necessary in order for his grace to be operative. This leads to tolerance, or even to justification, of evil in the world. Moreover it means that God can be manipulated in the application of his grace. The Tengalais were charged with antinomianism. Morality for them, said their opponents, is of no worth in the working of *bhakti*, and hence of no consequence. Righteousness or unrighteousness make no difference in the sight of God. Man is at the mercy of the unpredictable dispensation of divine grace.

Differences arose as to the necessity of pilgrimages, caste observances, dietary obligations, and ceremonial purity. Finally, when the argument deteriorated to details such as the shape of the sect mark, the division was so great that subsects were formed which remain to this day.

Among the many who might be selected in Shri-Vaishanivism who contributed to *bhakti*, Vallabha (1473–1531) deserves consideration. He held that one begins by loving the Lord, and that service to the Lord and to man is an outgrowth of that love; works must never be regarded as means for generating the love of God. He especially objected to those who stressed, as did the Shaivites, the awe-inspiring aspects of deity. God should inspire love, not fear. The best example of the proper love of man for God is the love of the *gopis* for Krishna; therefore the name for God which Vallabha preferred was Gopijana-vallabha (the beloved of the *gopis*). All who seek salvation should emulate the feminine principle and have Krishna as their spiritual husband. Vallabha also contended that in this Kali Yuga the duties of the four *varnas* and *ashramas* cannot be properly fulfilled, and therefore such duties are secondary to the expression of love for Krishna. Whatever may have been Vallabha's intent, the cult members used his authority to justify immoral practices on the grounds that they did not matter anyway.

The Maharashtra Saints

A literary revival and religious awakening took place in Maratha country, i.e., west central India, from the thirteenth to the seventeenth centuries which is sometimes called "the Maratha renaissance." This *bhakti* movement was the product of about fifty poets who wrote short lyrical poems called *abhangs* expressing religious longings. Most of them were Vaishnavites, and many were devotees of Vitthoba of Pandharpur. "Vitthoba" is believed to be a corruption of "Vishnu." The shrine is quite primitive, but through the years it has become distinctive for the deep religious emotion of the pilgrims who flock there to listen to speakers and to join in song-services (*kirtans*) using the *abhangs* of the Maharashtra saints. These poet-saints were a remarkable cross section of Hindu society: *Brahmins, Shudras,* outcastes, tailors, gardeners, potters, repentant prostitutes, etc.

Jñaneshvar was the earliest of the poets. He, although a *Brahmin,* suffered persecution all his life because his father had deserted his *sannyasi* vow and returned to the householder *ashrama.* His chief production is the *Jñaneshvari,* a long paraphrase of the *Bhagavad Gita.* His devotion was directed to a god of transcendence and immanence, as can be seen in this section from his *Jñaneshvari* in which Krishna is speaking to Arjuna:

> To heaven they seldom go, but earth they fill
> Brim full of heaven, chanting my name until
> The world is cleansed from ill.
>
> Far not in heaven I dwell; nor in the sky
> In the sun's orb; than yogi's visions high
> Far higher still am I.
>
> Not in such places, Pandav (i.e., Arjuna), I abide,
> But those who sing my praises far and wide,
> Within their hearts I hide.[3]

The whimsical charm of some of the *abhangs* is illustrated in this one from Miktabai, the sister of Jñaneshvar, which describes a "topsy-turvy land" where all is one:

> An ant has leapt up to the sky
> And swallowed up the sun on high!
> A marvel this that I declare,—
> That barren wife a son should bear.
> A scorpion plumbs the nether Pit,
> And Vishnu's snake bows down to it.

A fly an eagle brings to birth.
Mukta, beholding, laughs with mirth.

Namdev (fourteenth century) was a tailor's son who became a robber and a murderer. His prayer-poem to Vitthoba contains the bittersweetness characteristic of so many of the *abhangs*:

When will the end of these things be?
Ah, tell me, Lord of Pandhari.
When wilt thou save unhappy me?

O tell me, tell me true, for I
Cry to thee with a bitter cry.

Why speakest thou not? Ah, Vitthal, why
Thus silent? Whither shall I fly?

Who else will bear my sore distress?
Smite me not in my helplessness.

As to the child is wholly sweet
His mother,—so to me thy feet.

Thou gracious Lord of Rakhumai,
Friend of the poor, hear Nama's cry.

Tukaram (1598–1649) was the greatest of the Maratha *bhaktas*. Almost five thousand of his poems have survived. He is called the Robert Burns of India. At one time the reading of his poems was required of all missionaries being sent from a British missionary society in order that none make the error of stating that Hinduism had no conception of sin and grace. He was a farmer who lost his parents, one of his two wives, and a son in a great famine. He suffered many persecutions at the hands of *Brahmins* who resented a *Shudra* as a religious teacher. Many legends have been built around Tukaram. One of the most charming is that of a *Brahmin* who insisted that Tukaram ought to hear a book expounding Advaita Vedantism. Tukaram agreed on condition that a blanket be placed over his head as he sat listening to the reading. When Tukaram made no movement under the blanket during a long reading, the *Brahmin*, suspecting that Tukaram was asleep, quickly jerked the blanket away and discovered Tukaram sitting with his fingers in his ears! "I cannot

listen to the doctrine that God and His worshiper are one," explained
Tukaram. "Between Himself and His worshiper God has drawn a
line; that line we must recognize. A man may have perfect insight
into God's nature, but he does not acquire God's power to create,
preserve, and destroy; these powers belong to God alone. So long as
God in His three forms exercises these powers Himself let us mortals
be humble and claim no identity with Him." This story illustrates
the two outstanding features of the religion of Tukaram: a deep sense
of sin, and opposition to Absolutism. His sense of sin appears in this
poem:

> No deeds I've done nor thoughts I've thought;
> Save as thy servant, I am nought.

> Guard me, O God, and O, control
> The tumult of my restless soul.

> Ah, do not, do not cast on me
> The guilt of mine iniquity.

> My countless sins, I, Tuka, say,
> Upon thy loving heart I lay.

He often compared his own sinfulness with the purity of his God:

> I am a mass of Sin;
>   Thou art all purity;
> Yet thou must take me as I am
>   And bear my load for me.
> Me Death has all consumed;
>   In thee all power abides.
> All else forsaking, at thy feet
>   Thy servant Tuka hides.

His dislike for Advaita Vedanta appears in this *abhang*:

> Advaita contents me not, but dear to me
>   The service of thy feet.
> O grant me this reward! To sing of thee
>   To me how sweet!

> Setting us twain, lover and Lord, apart,

This joy to me display.
Grant it to Tuka—Lord of all thou art—
Some day, some day.

Tukaram's *bhakti* was quite simple: we cannot understand God, but if we love God and completely surrender ourselves to him, God will grant to us his gracious care and take us unto himself. The claim that his message of divine redemption was the result of contact with Christianity is a possibility, but evidence is not sufficient. The moral overtones of his mysticism is strikingly similar to that in Judaic-Christianity.

The greatness of God cannot be comprehended, says Tukaram:

Thy greatness none can comprehend
　　All dumb the Vedas are.
Forspent the powers of mortal mind;
　　They cannot climb so far.
How can I compass him whose light
　　Illumines both sun and star?

Yet we can surrender ourselves to God:

Now Panddurang I've chosen for my part,
　　None, none but his to be.
In all my thoughts he dwells, dwells in my heart,
　　Sleeping and waking be.

God knows our needs and will care for us even as he cares for the birds and the creeping things of the earth:

Unwearied he bears up the universe;
　　How light a burden I!
Does not his care the frog within the stone
　　With food supply?

The bird, the creeping thing, lays up no store;
　　This great One knows their need.
And if I, Tuka, cast on him my load,
　　Will not his mercy heed?

The gracious God is ours—

> God is ours, yea, ours is he,
> Soul of all the souls that be.
>
> God is nigh without a doubt,
> Nigh to all, within, without.
>
> God is gracious, gracious still;
> Every longing he'll fulfil.
>
> God protects, protects his own;
> Strife and death he casteth down.
>
> Kind is God, ah, kind indeed;
> Tuka he will guard and lead.

But the grace of God is dependent upon man's surrender to God and his petition for that grace. Therefore, warns Tukaram, hurry to God for the world passes away:

> Who dares call aught his own
>   As swiftly speed the days?
> Time keeps the fatal score,
>   And not a moment strays.
>
> Hair, ears, and eyes grow old,
>   As, dullard, grow they must;
> The best is nigh thee, yet
>   Thou fill'st thy mouth with dust.
>
> Dying and yet thou buildest
>   As for eternity!
> Nay, haste to Pandurang!
>   'Tis Tuka says it: flee!

The Chaitanya Movement

The most significant development in *bhakti* during the period we are considering took place in Bengal in the sixteenth century. At this time Hinduism, particularly in the villages, was the worship of aboriginal gods like Mangala-Candi (a goddess of wealth) and Manasa (a goddess of snakes). Islam was being shaped by the Sufis. Chaitanya (1485–1533), a member of a *Brahmin* family at Navadvipa, had by age twenty-two earned a reputation as a scholar. He made a trip to Gaya to perform rites in honor of his departed father, and while there was converted to Vaishnavism. Upon his return to Navadvipa he deserted his school and his books in order to sing the praises of Krishna and to chant the holy names. Instead of teaching Vedic wisdom he organized *sankirtanas,* i.e., singing groups accompanied by simple musical instruments. Two years after his return from Gaya he took the vow of a *sannyasi,* and for the next six years journeyed throughout India winning converts to Lord Krishna. He lived the remaining eighteen years of his life at Puri, where he spent his days worshiping in the great temple. His acts of devotion became increasingly emotional. His singing, shouting, weeping, and dancing often ended in fits of ecstasy in which his legs and arms became rigid, his eyes rolled upward, and foam appeared at his mouth. On several occasions he attempted suicide. Guards were posted constantly lest he harm himself. His actions were often those of a madman. Chaitanya himself admitted he was a victim of epilepsy. His death was by drowning when he had a frenzied delirium while bathing in the surf near Puri.

Chaitanya wrote almost nothing after he turned from the life of a *Brahmin* scholar to that of a devotee of Krishna. He repudiated the *Vedas* as being antagonistic to the grace of God, and he vehemently opposed the Advaita Vedanta doctrine that the self loses its individuality in the state of *moksha.* He accepted anyone into his movement on the grounds that all *varnas* are equally pure. He approved of idolatry, and sometimes used a black stone in his adoration.

Chaitanya revived the Radha-Krishna theme of Vaishnavism. He identified himself with Radha and stressed the intensity of Radha's love for Krishna as the love of man for God. During his lifetime he was able to control the symbolic nature of the love of Radha and Krishna, but after Chaitanya, perhaps because of the Tantric elements in Bengal, there came into existence such cults as the

Sahajiya, which required that each male follower secure a woman other than his wife in order that they might imitate the coitus of Radha and Krishna, and the Sakhibhava, which required men to dress as women, to act as women, and even to pretend a monthly menstrual period, on the grounds that the devotee is always female and the god male.

Chaitanya was so involved in the hypnotic emotionalism of his own devotions that he did little to organize the cult. It was under his inspiration that Brindaban, the scene of Krishna's early life, was reclaimed from ruin, and after his life his followers erected a temple there. Those who descended from Chaitanya's original disciples were called *Gosvamis* (cow-lords). They became a hereditary priesthood and took unto themselves the prejudices of caste distinctions which Chaitanya had forbidden. Most of our information about early Chaitanya Vaishnavism comes from a huge book written in 1615 by one of the earliest *Gosvamis,* Krishnadasa Kaviraja. The book, *Chaitanya Charitamrita,* is a vast storehouse of biographical, philosophical, and anecdotal materials written as a labor of love by the aged *Gosvami.* The book indicates that even at this early date Chaitanya was beginning to be worshipped as a god. The biographical parts of the book make the early life of Chaitanya look very similar to those of Krishna as portrayed in the *Bhagavata Purana,* an effort no doubt to strengthen the view that Chaitanya was himself the incarnation of Krishna. "What the *Upanishads* call Brahman without a second is the halo of the body of Lord Chaitanya," declared Kaviraja.

The Chaitanyaism of the *Chaitanya Charitamrita* is a monotheism. The God is Krishna. Krishna's creative act was to bring into being three lesser gods: Brahmā, Vishnu, and Shiva. They were entrusted by Krishna with the creation of the world, although Krishna remains Lord of them and of their creation. Indeed, there are many Brahmās, Vishnus, and Shivas, but there is only one Krishna, the highest principle. The divine energy of Krishna is Radha or Hladini (delight). Radha is the highest manifestation of Krishna, i.e., the power of bringing delight. Radha and Krishna are fundamentally the same, but for the purpose of divine sport (*lila*) they are separated into two bodies. Krishna in his sport has manifested himself in many forms: *gurus,* devotees, *avataras, shaktis,* etc. But his supreme manifestation was the historic Chaitanya-Krishna. The unique feature of this manifestation was that Chaitanya was the unified Radha-Krishna. The body of Sachi, his mother, was radiant with light during her pregnancy. The child was born in the thirteenth month, and at birth had thirty-two auspicious marks. Many miracles were performed during his mischievous childhood. Even non-Hindus recognized that Chaitanya was divine; e.g., when the chief clerk of a king asked, "What does your heart tell you about Lord Chaitanya?" the king replied, "My heart tells me, Oh friend, that he is the God Himself." People are said to have sung, "Glory unto the Lord Krishna-Chaitanya; glory unto thee, Oh Holy Lord of Vraja: for you are incarnate to save the world."

A scholar has great difficulty in reading the *Chaitanya Charitamrita,* for the author turns from sections in which Chaitanya is God to other sections in which Chaitanya is only a God-intoxicated man: "And during the last twelve years of his life Lord Chaitanya felt incessantly the frenzy of separation from his beloved Krishna. As Radha went mad from seeing Uddhava, so did the Lord behave. He knew no rest, neither in the day, nor at night, for he felt incessantly the frenzy of separation. He raved like the mad and acted as such. His teeth began to shake and blood came out in drops on his skin. Now his body swelled and then at the next moment, it became awfully thin once more. And the Lord then had not a wink of sleep within the Gambhira room; he rubbed his face against the ground. And so his body was all covered with wounds." [4]

Perhaps the outstanding contribution to the development of *bhakti* made by the Chaitanya movement was its emphasis on the *sadhana* of *bhakti.* "No one can attain the object of desire without toil," Chaitanya is quoted as having said in the *Chaitanya Charitamrita.* Thus he settled in his mind the dispute between monkey-grace and cat-grace. For Chaitanya *bhakti* was more than a means to *moksha* or as a prelude to divine grace—*bhakti* was *moksha.* Steps were worked out leading to spiritual practice: faith in God, keeping company of holy men, purifying the mind, purging sins and evil desires from the mind, developing steadiness in religious practices, learning to enjoy religious practices, and attaching oneself to religious practices.

Devotees were classified according to the intensity of their love: the love of servants for masters, of friends for friends, of children for parents, and of *gopis* for Krishna. Chaitanya Vaishnavism became a *yoga* of love. One did not love the Lord, and then wait for the evidence of grace; one actively sought out and created the love. The weakness of the Chaitanya movement was inherent in its strength: in stressing the importance of the individual emotions it neglected the social implications. It had little regard for the moral life, individual or social. Personal emotional exaltation with no outlet becomes only sentimentality. But despite its lack of social concern, Chaitanya Vaishnavism ought not to be faulted altogether, for it made, and still makes, a tremendous contribution to Indian art. The Radha-Krishna theme is a favorite for artists and poets. The polarizing of Radha's love for Krishna and of his playful taunting of that love is a charming motif as can be seen in this English translation of a seventeenth-century Bengali poem:

> You do not choose right hours and times to play on your flute, my love. Out of season you play, and my heart goes forth to you without any control. When I sit in the company of my elders your flute calls me by my name. Can you not imagine, my love, to what shame I am put? From the other bank of the river you sound your flute and I hear its sound across the stream from this bank. Do you not know, my love, that it is my luckless fate that I know not how to swim across the river? [5]

CHAPTER 17

The Nineteenth-Century
Renaissance in Hinduism

When Job Charnock of the East India Company pitched his tents at the village of Sutanuti on the east bank of the Hooghly River on August 24, 1690, he did not realize he was founding the first British capital in India. The city which grew on this bog took the name of another village swallowed in the process, Kalikata, from Kali the spouse of Shiva. The name was later Anglicized to Calcutta. It was among the Bengalis of this sprawling city that the British approximated the admonition of Lord Macaulay: "We must do our best to form a class who may be interpreters between us and the millions whom we govern; a class of persons Indian in blood and colour, but English in tastes, in opinion, in morals and in intellect." The nineteenth-century renaissance in India radiated from Bengal. Bengalis are the Athenians of India. In the words of Jadunath Sarkar, "If Periclean Athens was the school of Hellas, the eye of Greece, mother of arts and eloquence, that was Bengal to the rest of India under British rule, but with a borrowed light which it had made its own with marvelous cunning. In this new Bengal originated every good and great thing of the modern world that passed on to the other provinces of India. From Bengal went forth the English-educated teachers and the English-inspired thought that helped to modernise Bihar and Orissa, Hindustan and Deccan. New literary types, reform of the language, social reconstruction, political aspirations, religious movements and even changes in manners that originated in Bengal

337

passed like ripples from a central eddy, across provincial barriers, to
the furthest corners of India." [1] We shall confine ourselves to the
renaissance in religion, i.e., to the Hindu reaction to the challenge of
the West. The term "renaissance" for these movements in nineteenth-century India must not be interpreted to mean that all Indians
experienced a rebirth or revival. The changes were made only among
a few city dwellers. They experienced in the nineteenth century
certain reorientations of life and thought which approximated what
Europeans experienced in the fourteenth, fifteenth, and sixteenth
centuries. Without demeaning the Indian renaissance, we must note
that while these changes were taking place in urban India, other
changes were taking place in the West, with the result that India by
the end of the nineteenth century was still at least a century behind
the West, especially in technology.

Brahmo Samaj

Rammohan Roy, the founder of the Brahmo Samaj, is often called
"the Father of Modern India." He was born in the Burdwan district
of West Bengal, not far from Calcutta, in 1772 (or 1774 according to
some records) of a wealthy orthodox *Brahmin* family. He was sent to
school in Patna, where he studied Arabic and Persian, and where he
was deeply impressed by Muslim culture, especially by Sufi ideas and
practices. For the rest of his life he wore Muslim dress and ate
Muslim food; but this never meant that he ceased being a Hindu, for
he continued to wear the sacred thread. Probably as a result of his
reading of the *Koran*, he became bitterly opposed to idolatry, and
wrote at age sixteen a paper condemning the use of images of the
gods in Hindu worship. The arguments with his father on the subject
were so acrimonious that he was forced to leave home. He led a
wandering life for the next three or four years, during which he may
have visited Tibet. Following this he spent a few years in Banaras,
where he learned Sanskrit and studied Vedic literature. In his
Upanishadic studies he was impressed by the *saguna* aspects of
Brahman, and concluded that the *Upanishads* present a monotheism
rather than the abstract monism of Shankara. In 1804 after the death

of his father he published a pamphlet in Persian in which he protested against the superstitions of religious creeds and attempted in his words "to lay a common foundation of Universal Religion in the doctrine of the Unity of the Godhead." In 1809 he was appointed as revenue official at Rangpur in the service of the East India Company, a position which he resigned within five years in order to give full attention to social and religious work.

The turning point of the life of Rammohan Roy occurred in 1811 when he witnessed the *suttee* of his sister-in-law. She had been persuaded by her relatives to immolate herself, but when the flames touched her body, she attempted to escape. However, her relatives held her down with long bamboo poles and drowned her screams with the beating of drums. The burning of widows at this time was common in northeast India. In Calcutta alone there were 253 immolations in 1815, 298 in 1816, 442 in 1817, and 544 in 1818. Rammohan pressured the British to interfere with Hindu practices to make *suttee* illegal, and as a result of his agitation it was so declared by Lord Bentinck on December 4, 1829.

During his five years with the East India Company Rammohan studied Tantrism and Jainism. He also organized an informal club which met regularly in his rooms to discuss religious topics. He insisted that the club should include members of all available religious groups. It was at this time also that he began the study of English and the reading of books on European politics.

Upon leaving the service of the East India Company he went at once to Calcutta, where in 1815 he founded the Atmiya Sabha (Association of Friends), which met once a week to study the monotheistic doctrines of the Hindu scriptures. He began publishing studies of the *Upanishads* in Sanskrit, Bengali, and English. Public debates were held frequently in which Rammohan defended Hindu theism and argued against the use of images in worship. His efforts to reform Hinduism were so unpopular with the Indians that, as he wrote in his autobiography, "I was at last deserted by every person except two or three Scotch friends, to whom, and the nation to which they belong, I always feel grateful." His relations with Christians had been cordial, although he was disturbed by the conflicts among the Christian denominations on matters of theology. He believed that the moral teachings of Jesus ought not be confused with the doctrinal positions of Christian theologians. He did not relish getting involved in theological arguments with the Christian missionaries, but he did want to make a point about Christianity, so in 1820 he published a book entitled *The Precepts of Jesus, the Guide to Peace and Happiness.* This book was an abstract of the four Gospels containing the moral precepts only; everything which suggested the divinity of Jesus was omitted. "I regret only that the followers of Jesus, in general, should have paid much greater attention to inquiries after his nature than to the observances of his commandments," he wrote in a letter dated September 5, 1830. Trinitarian Christians attacked him, charging him with the heresy of unitarianism because he had presented Jesus as a man and not as God. Rammohan soon found himself, against his will, involved in theological controversies with Christians, and in his characteristically thorough manner learned Hebrew, Greek, and Latin in order that he might understand the Old and New Testaments and their commentaries. Three volumes of defenses of his *Precepts of Jesus* were published in the next thirteen years. In the description of the second volume he wrote, "The contents of the following treatise are included under these two propositions: first, that the *Precepts of Jesus,* which teach that love to God is manifested in beneficence toward our fellow creatures, are a sufficient guide to peace and happiness; and secondly, that that omnipresent God, who is the only proper object of religious veneration, is one and undivided in person." He began to worship with a Unitarian congregation in Calcutta. His arguments both oral and written were so convincing that they converted the Reverend William Adam, a Baptist missionary from England. Adam's fellow missionaries at Serampore called him "the second fallen Adam." Rammohan's admiration for the Christian religion was well stated in a letter to the Reverend Henry Ware, an American clergyman: "I presume to think that Christianity, if properly inculcated, has a greater tendency to improve the moral, and political state of mankind, than any other known religious system." When one of his Christian antagonists affirmed that Jesus Christ was being degraded by Asiatics, Rammohan replied that Jesus was an Asiatic.

Rammohan was in no sense anti-European. He was nominated in

July 1824 by the Asiatic Society of Paris as its first Hindu honorary member. He regarded British rule as the benign act of Providence, and contrasted British rule with the despotism under the Mughals. In 1823 he was shocked when the government decided to found a new college of Sanskrit studies in Calcutta, and he wrote to Lord Amherst saying, "The Sanscrit language, so difficult that almost a lifetime is necessary for its acquisition, is well known to have been for ages a lamentable check to the diffusion of knowledge, and the learning concealed under this almost impervious veil is far from sufficient to reward the labor of acquiring it." The study of Sanskrit, he said, "can only be expected to load the minds of youth with grammatical niceties and metaphysical distinctions of little or no practical use to the possessors or to society." The funds should be "laid out in employing European gentlemen of talent and education to instruct the natives of India in mathematics, natural philosophy, chemistry, anatomy, and other useful sciences, which the natives of Europe have carried to a degree of perfection that has raised them above the inhabitants of other parts of the world." He did not miss the opportunity to make an attack on Advaita Vedanta: "Nor will youths be fitted to be better members of society by the Vedantic doctrines which teach them to believe that all visible things have no real existence, that as father, brother, etc. have no real entity, they consequently deserve no real affection, and therefore the sooner we escape from them and leave the world the better." Finally, he wrote in his letter to Lord Amherst that, if the calculated policy of the British were to keep India in darkness, there would be no better means than by promoting the study of Sanskrit; but, "as the improvement of the native population is the object of the government, it will consequently promote a more liberal and enlightened system of instruction."

Another social cause to which Rammohan devoted his energies was the improvement of the lot of the Hindu woman. He worked for educational opportunities for girls, for the elimination of child marriage and polygamy, for removal of the stigma on widowhood, and for legal equality for women and men. He opposed the debaucheries which had crept into Vaishnavism, the sexuality of Tantrism, and the animal sacrifices in Kali worship. He spoke often in defense of the freedom of the press and advised improvements in the judicial system of India.

On August 20, 1828, Rammohan Roy and a group of comrades formed the Brahmo Samaj (One God Society) for the sole purpose of worship. It was known among the English as "The Theistic Church of India." It was intended as a place where believers of the One God might join in worship whether their backgrounds were Hindu, Christian, or Muslim, but as matters turned out most of the worshipers were liberal Hindu theists. The society met each Saturday evening between seven and nine for a congregation worship service consisting of chanting of portions of the *Vedas*, a sermon, and the singing of hymns accompanied by instrumental music. In 1829 sufficient funds had been raised to purchase a house for the meeting place of the Samaj. The orthodox Hindus of Calcutta were furious with the establishment of the Brahmo Samaj, and organized a rival association, the Dharma Sabha. The entire Hindu community of Calcutta was involved in the controversy. On January 23, 1830, the new home of the Brahmo Samaj was dedicated as a building for "the worship of the one Eternal, Unsearchable and Immutable Being, who is the Author and Preserver of the Universe, but not under or by any other name, designation or title." There was also the stipulation that no image or picture would be allowed in worship. The intent, said Rammohan, was to revive monotheism in India on the basis of the Vedanta.

In November of that year he sailed for England at the request of the Mughal ruler, Akbar II, who had conferred on him the title of Raja. He was well received as he spoke on Indian affairs before a committee of the House of Commons on the need to assist the agricultural workers of India. Jeremy Bentham referred to him as an "intensely admired and dearly beloved collaborator in the service of mankind." Rammohan became ill in England and died at Bristol in 1833. His body was buried there by Unitarian friends.

After the death of Rammohan Roy the Brahmo Samaj weekly worship services were continued by Ramchandra Vidyabagish. Dwarakanath Tagore, a wealthy Calcutta merchant, paid the bills. But the enthusiasm which had characterized the Samaj was gone, and the congregation was small. In 1839 Devendranath Tagore, the eldest son of Dwarakanath, formed a society which he called the Tattvabodhini Sabha (Truth-teaching Society), and in 1843 he merged his society with the Brahmo Samaj in a ceremony in which he was made the spiritual successor to Rammohan. Under his leadership the Brahmo Samaj took on more of the trappings of a religious fraternity. Devendranath saw clearly that the Samaj had to steer a difficult middle course between the old and the new. He insisted that the Brahmos were "in and of the great Hindu community," that they were Hindus and were to remain Hindus, although they would purify the customs, usages, rites, and ceremonies of Hindu heritage and adapt themselves to the new situations of the mid-nineteenth century. One of his methods for calming the fears of the orthodox was to teach that according to Brahmoism the *Vedas* were infallible. By 1847 the Brahmo Samaj was on the verge of a split between those who with Devendranath accepted Vedic infallibility and those who with Akshoy Kumar Dutta were developing a rationalism which rejected the assumption of Vedic infallibility. Devendranath and four *Brahmin* scholars went to Banaras for an extended period to discover what was the opinion of the pandits of that holy city. By 1850 the doctrine of Vedic infallibility was given up. Devendranath was then instrumental in the forming of a "creed" that was used for a time as the definitive doctrinal position of the Samaj: "In the beginning there was only one Supreme Spirit; there was nothing else; He created all this that is. He is infinite in wisdom and goodness. He is everlasting, all-knowing, all-pervading, all-sustaining, formless, changeless, one only without a second, almighty, self-dependent and perfect; there is none like unto Him. Our welfare here and hereafter consists only in worshipping Him. To love Him and to do His bidding is to worship Him."

The rejection of the *Vedas* as infallible encouraged the Brahmos to return to the social reforms of Rammohan, and after much prodding the Samaj forced the marriage laws to be changed so that the bride had to be at least fourteen years of age and the groom at least sixteen. Devendranath, who was more of a mystic and a dreamer than a doer, retired to the Himalayas from 1856 to 1858. When he returned to Calcutta, he was delighted to find that a talented twenty-year-old youth had joined the Samaj, a youth destined to bring new life into the association. That youth was Keshub Chunder Sen. The Sen family was one of the most Westernized in Calcutta. Keshub spoke English far better than Bengali. Very soon Keshub became a close friend of Devendranath and one of the hardest workers of the Samaj. In 1861 he resigned his employment with the Bank of Bengal to become a fulltime missionary of the Samaj, and in 1862 he was made its *Acharya* or chief minister, but in 1866 when he started appearing at worship without wearing the sacred thread, he was rebuked by Devendranath. The relations between the two men cooled quickly. Keshub soon led a group of young men out of the Brahmo Samaj in order to form another society which he called the Brahmo Samaj of India.

Keshub was psychologically a revolutionist. He analyzed himself correctly when he once wrote, "I am partial to the doctrine of enthusiasm. To me a state of being on fire is the state of salvation. . . . Coldness and hell have always been the same to my mind. Around my own life, around the society in which I lived, I always kept burning the flame of enthusiasm."

When the Brahmo Samaj of India was established on November 11, 1866, Keshub offered a statement of faith which he called a "motto." It was accepted by the group at that time as a summary of their beliefs:

> The wide universe is the temple of God.
> Wisdom is the pure land of pilgrimage.
> Truth is the everlasting scripture.
> Faith is the root of all religion.
> Love is the true spiritual culture.
> The destruction of selfishness is the true asceticism.

Keshub, at last free from the restraining hand of Devendranath, introduced innovations. One was the confession of sin. Long and earnest pleadings with God for the pardon of sins became a part of the worship services. As an expression of joy that God forgives sins, Keshub introduced Vaishnavite hymns accompanied by drums, cymbals, and the *ektara* (a one-stringed lute). Street processions and open-air singing were also added, much to the disgust of the members of the Brahmo Samaj. Keshub's enthusiastic emotionalisms sometimes exceeded the bounds of common sense; e.g., in 1867 the slate of officers of the Brahmo Samaj of India were listed as:

> President—God
> Secretary—Keshub Chunder Sen
> Asst. Sec.—Pratapchandra Mazumdar.[2]

There was criticism of Keshub when he did not dissuade his followers from calling him "Lord," "Master," and even "Savior."

Meanwhile Devendranath Tagore held the Brahmo Samaj together, changing its name to the Adi (Original) Brahmo Samaj, and emphasizing that Brahmoism was Hinduism. Keshub in reply said that Brahmoism was broader than Hinduism. He called it "Human Catholicism." In a series of small pamphlets called *Tracts for the Times* Keshub wrote, "Brahmoism is anti-sectarian; catholicity is its distinguishing characteristic; love is its very life. It is not the religion of a particular community, epoch or country; it is universal religion; it is Human Catholic Religion."

Keshub was such an innovator, acting so quickly in the implementation of new ideas, that his followers must have been frustrated in efforts to keep up with their leader. From 1872 to 1877 he attempted to manage a commune seven miles north of Calcutta as a perfect example of the brotherhood of men. The members were organized according to the *marga* each preferred to follow: *yoga, bhakti, jñana,* or *karma.* One of the great achievements of Brahmoism was the Native Marriage Act of 1872 which abolished early marriages, made polygamy penal, sanctioned widow marriages, and allowed intercaste marriages. Six years later Keshub violated the Native Marriage Act by allowing his daughter to marry when neither the bride nor the groom had attained the minimum marriageable age. Moreover, the ceremony used was the orthodox Hindu ritual rather than the Brahmo ceremony. After a painful controversy the Brahmo Samaj of India split in 1878 into the Sadharan (common) Brahmo Samaj and the Nava Bidhana Samaj (The Church of the New Dispensation). The latter group was faithful to Sen, accepting his explanation that he had received a special revelation from God that he could marry his daughter in violation of the law he had himself promulgated!

The Church of the New Dispensation was an amazing religious organization. Keshub argued that it was to the religion of the New Testament as the New Testament was to the Old Testament. He called attention to a statement from Jesus: "I have yet many things to say unto you, but you cannot bear them now. Howbeit when he, the spirit of truth is come, he will guide you into all truth." Keshub claimed that he was "the spirit of truth," and that the Nava Bidhana Samaj was the place where the many things yet to be said were to be heard. "What do we see before us in India today but the fruit of that tree, whose seed Jesus planted, and Paul watered, centuries ago." He referred to the work of the Nava Bidhana Samaj as "the Acts of his Hindu Apostles." In 1881 he introduced baptism and a communion service into the worship services of his church. The congregation did not last long after Keshub's death in 1883. Only the Sadharan Brahmo Samaj survives in India today, and it cannot be regarded as an active force, but in the development of Hinduism Brahmoism made a contribution of rationalism, freedom of thought, the growth of nationalism, and the liberation of Hindus from many time-honored customs.

Arya Samaj

Christianity and the West elicited two types of reaction in India, one positive and one negative. Brahmoism was a positive reaction. In a speech in Calcutta shortly after Queen Victoria had assumed the title of Empress of India, Keshub Chunder Sen said, "Who can deny that Victoria is an instrument in the hands of Providence to elevate this degraded country in the scale of nations, and that in her hands the solemn trust has lately been most solemnly reposed? Glory then to Empress Victoria!" The Arya Samaj was opposed to the Westernization and the Christianization of India.

The Arya Samaj (Society of Nobles) was founded by Dayananda Saraswati (1824–1883), a man who was, if possible, more dynamic than Keshub Chunder Sen. Dayananda was born into an orthodox *Brahmin* family in a small town in Gujarat. His first serious thoughts about Hinduism occurred when at the age of fourteen he spent the night with his father in vigil before an image of Shiva. He was disturbed that his father and the priest fell asleep during the vigil and that mice ate the food set out before the image. "What sort of a god was it who could not prevent mice from eating his food?" he asked. Five years later when his parents planned a marriage for him, he ran away from home, adopted the life of an ascetic, and wandered throughout India for fifteen years. He was thrust into public view when he engaged in debates on religion with Hindu scholars at Banaras, and he soon began to have a following of those who were sympathetic to his views. He organized the Arya Samaj in Bombay in 1875, but it did not catch fire until it was transferred to Lahore in 1877. It remains to this day primarily a Punjabi movement. During the years of agitation for Indian Independence, the three branches of Brahmoism suffered from the joint stigmas of being pro-British and pro-Western, but the Arya Samaj grew because of its militant Hinduism and nationalism.

The outstanding feature of the Arya Samaj is its work of *shuddhi,* i.e., the reconversion of Hindus who have been converted to Islam or Christianity. Whereas orthodox Hindus usually refused to welcome back into the Hindu community those who had been converted to other religions, the Arya Samaj sought to bring them back. Dayananda taught that only through *shuddhi* could India realize religious, social, and political unity. The Arya became a strong missionary movement. It not only sought to win back those who had deserted Hinduism but also it invested hundreds of thousands of Untouchables with the sacred thread—an act regarded with the utmost horror by the orthodox. The members of the Arya Samaj are often called "the aggressive Hindus." The organization of the Samaj is on strictly democratic principles: each adult member male and female has one vote. Converts have equal standing with those born into the cult. The *varna* distinctions are regarded as divisions based on character rather than birth; hence in the affairs of the Samaj there is no *"Brahmin"* nor "outcaste"—there are only differences in intelligence and character. The Arya Samaj has been exceptionally active in establishing schools, colleges, hospitals, community centers, homes for widows and orphans, and in engaging in welfare work at times of flood and famine. There is today in Delhi an International

Aryan League which is the center of the propaganda activities of the Arya Samaj. The members of the Samaj have suffered criticism and even persecution because of the vigor of their activities, and there have been a few martyrs for the faith.

Dayananda organized the Arya Samaj as a "Back to the *Vedas*" movement. He rejected all post-Vedic developments in Hinduism, and would not shake hands with Brahmo leaders because they did not recognize the divine origin and infallibility of the *Vedas*. In place of *puja* before idols he attempted to restore the ancient sacrificial rites of fire and oblation. He held that the *Samhita* sections of the Vedic literature, and primarily the *Rig*, contain all the truths there are and all that will be. The *Vedas*, he said, are "the primitive scripture of humanity." In them are to be found all sciences, all technologies, and the solution to all social and political problems. He offered most incredible interpretations; e.g., *Rig Veda* 1. 2. 7, "I invoke Mitra and Varuna for the success of my poem" was interpreted to mean that water is the combination of hydrogen and oxygen!

The movement opposes monotheism as this is understood in Christianity and Islam, and it is equally opposed to polytheism. God is an objective presider over the processes of transmigration and *karma*. In 1877 a list of "Ten Principles" was formed by Dayananda which became the statement of faith all new members of the Samaj were expected to sign. It is still so used.

1. The first efficient cause of all knowledge and all that is known through knowledge is Paramashvara (Supreme Lord).

2. Ishvara is existent, intelligent, and blissful. He is formless, omnipotent, just, merciful, unborn, endless, unchangeable, beginningless, unequalled, the support of all, the master of all, omnipresent, immanent, unaging, immortal, fearless, eternal and holy, and the maker of all.

3. *Vedas* are the scripture of true knowledge. It is the first duty of the Aryas to read them, teach them, recite them, and hear them read.

4. One should always be ready to accept truth and give up untruth.

5. Everything should be done according to the dictates of *dharma*, i.e., after due reflection over right and wrong.

6. The primary object of this Society is to do good in the whole world, that is, to look to its physical, social, and spiritual welfare.

7. One's dealings with all should be regulated by love and justice, in accordance with the dictates of *dharma*.

8. One should promote *vidya* (knowledge of subject and object) and dispel *avidya* (illusion).

9. One should not be content with one's own welfare alone, but should look for one's own welfare in the welfare of all.

10. One should consider oneself under restriction to follow altruistic rulings of society, while in following rules of individual welfare one should be free.

The fact that the Ten Principles say nothing about the infallibility of the *Vedas*, the incarnation of souls, and vegetarianism has been the occasion of controversy, and even splits, within the Samaj. The Arya Samaj has never been a large group within Hinduism, but it has been a catharsis both of Hinduism and Indian nationalism.

Theosophy

Theosophy is not actually a form of Hinduism but it has been closely associated with India and Hinduism. The Theosophical Society was founded in New York City in 1875 under the leadership of Madame H. P. Blavatsky and Colonel H. S. Olcott and brought to India in 1882. The object was to form a universal society for the exploration of esoteric teachings, especially of the Gnostic variety, found in Hinduism, Greek religion, Egyptian religion, and early Christianity. The belief was that through such studies the divine powers latent within man could be released and utilized for the good of all mankind. The term "theosophy" came from the Greek words for god (*theos*) and wisdom (*sophia*). It is an ancient term, first used by the Greek philosopher Iamblichus in the third century A.D. for the inner knowledge of divine things.

The Theosophical Society from the beginning indicated that it was in quest of a lost knowledge called "The Wisdom." Man once had The Wisdom, as is indicated by cultural myths such as the Atlantis myth found in Plato's *Republic*. No single culture will be able to regain it; but by working together and by taking advantage of each other's insights, it may be recovered. There are certain "Mahatmas" or "Masters" who can help us in our efforts, if we can get in touch with them. Madame Blavatsky associated the Mahatmas with Tibet. The Theosophical Society lost credibility in 1885 when the British Society for Psychical Research exposed Madame Blavatsky's claims to occult powers as completely fraudulent.

The fortunes of the Society began to improve in 1893 when Mrs. Annie Besant came from England to the international headquarters of the Society at Adyar, Madras. She became President of the Society, and she more than anyone tied it closer to Hinduism with its doctrines of reincarnation, *karma*, and *nirvana*. She embarrassed some Hindus by her enthusiastic embracing of everything "Hindu" including idol worship. She also endeared herself to Indians by helping found Banaras Hindu University, by encouraging Indian resistance to the British government, and by becoming in 1917 the President of the Indian National Congress.

The tenets of the Theosophical Society were once stated by Mrs. Besant as these four:

1. There is one transcendent, self-existent Life, eternal, all pervading, all-sustaining, whence all worlds derive their several lives, whereby and wherein all things which exist live and move and have their being.

2. For our world, this Life is immanent, and is manifested as the Logos, the Word, worshiped under different names, in different religions, but ever recognized as the One Creator, Preserver, and Regenerator.

3. Under Him, our world is ruled and guided by a hierarchy of His elder children, variously called *rishis*, sages, or saints, among them are the world-teachers, who for each age re-proclaim the essential truths of religion and morality in a form suited to the age; this hierarchy is aided in its work by the host of beings—again variously named *devas* (shining ones or angels)—discharging functions recognized in all religions.

4. Human beings form one order of the creatures evolving on this
   earth, and each human being evolves by successive life-periods,
   gathering experiences and building them into character, reaping
   always as he sows, until he has learned the lessons taught in the
   three worlds—the earth, the intermediate stage, and the heavens—
   in which a complete life-period is passed, and until he has reached
   human perfection, when he enters the company of "just men made
   perfect" that rules and guides the evolving lives in all stages of their
   growth.

The goal of theosophy is to help individuals become "Masters of
the Wisdom" in order that they may help mankind individually and
collectively recover the goodness, beauty, and truth which have been
lost. The Masters as perfected individuals (*jivanmuktas*) may in fact
be regarded as *avataras* in that they are the Divine Consciousness
appearing with all the characteristics of humanity. These perfected
individuals together with the *devas* control the physical universe, are
custodians of the great religious truths, and supervise the cultural
developments of science, art, philosophy, commerce, etc. All is
according to a Great Plan of the Divine Consciousness. Each
individual finds meaning in life insofar as he becomes a conscious
co-operator in the Great Plan. This possibility is open to all, and each
religion makes its unique contribution. The Masters cannot as
individuals liberate mankind from its burden of suffering, ignorance,
poverty, and degradation, but through organizations such as the
Theosophical Society they can bring about the good of which all men
dream.

Ramakrishna Mission

The fourth movement which we are examining as representative
of many nineteenth-century revivals of living Hinduism is another
Bengali movement. It is the most successful and widespread of all
Hindu innovations of the nineteenth century. The prophet of this
movement was born in 1836 to a poor *Brahmin* family in a village in
the District of Hooghly. His name was Gadadhar Chattopadhyaya,

but he is usually known by his religious name, Ramakrishna. He is said to have had his first religious trance experience at age six or seven. He had very little formal education, and never was able to do more than the most rudimentary reading or writing. However, he developed a passionate love for music and poetry, and was instructed in the rudiments of the priestly functions of his *varna dharma*. At the age of nineteen he and his brother became priests at a new Kali temple in Dakshineshvar, about four miles north of Calcutta. When his brother died the next year, Ramakrishna was made the chief priest at the temple.

He became possessed with the idea that the Kali image in the main building of the temple grounds was not merely an image but the actual incarnation of the goddess. Day after day he pleaded before the image that he be granted a vision of Kali in all her glory. But there was no vision, and each day he wept in despair. "One day," reported Ramakrishna, "I was torn with intolerable anguish. My heart seemed to be wrung like a wet towel. I was racked with pain. A terrible frenzy seized me at the thought that I might never be granted the blessing of this divine vision. I thought, if that were so, then enough of this life. A sword was hanging in the sanctuary of Kali. My eyes fell upon it, and an idea flashed through my brain: The sword! It will help me to end it. I rushed up to it, and seized it like a mad man. . . . And lo! the whole scene—doors, windows, the temple itself—vanished. It seemed as if nothing existed any more. Instead, I saw an ocean of Spirit, boundless, dazzling. In whatever direction I turned, great luminous waves were rising. They bore down upon me with a loud roar, as if to swallow me up. In an instant they were upon me. They broke over me, they engulfed me. I was suffocated. I lost consciousness and I fell. How I passed that day and the next I know not. Round me rolled an ocean of ineffable joy. And in the depths of my being, I was conscious of the presence of the divine Mother." [3] The experience confirmed Ramakrishna's intuition that the image was more than an image, and throughout the rest of his life, which was spent entirely at Dakshineshvar, he was visited again and again by the goddess.

He became in every sense a "God-intoxicated man." He did not for a moment believe that Kali exhausted the full manifestation of

God, and he sought to see God in other forms. Visions of God as Rama and as Sita next came to him. Following this he was guided through the Tantric, the Vaishnava, and the Advaita *sadhanas,* and in every case experienced God. Later he lived as a Muslim and as a Christian, and, again, he had mystical experiences in keeping with these religions.

The high priest of Dakshineshvar became well known throughout Bengal with people coming to him, and he on occasion visited towns and villages. His tender heart ached with the misery he found, and, while he was pleased to find some efforts being made to assist the poor, the hungry, and the sick, he was not at all pleased with the motive of the charity. Humanitarianism was not enough. "They talk of mercy to the creatures! How audacious it is to think of showering mercy on the Jiva, who is none other than Shiva. One has to regard the creature as God Himself and proceed to serve it with a devout heart, instead of taking up the pose of doling out mercy." An act of kindness is not just an act of kindness. If an image is divine, then certainly a human being is divine. Ramakrishna did not mean that one should worship God through serving mankind; he meant that serving mankind was worshiping God. The realization of the divinity of man was the heart of his teachings.

A radiant joy permeated all of Ramakrishna's life. While he found God through Christianity, he believed that Christianity placed far too much emphasis on sin. He made the same criticism of the Brahmo Samaj. In a letter to Keshub Chunder Sen he said, "In your Brahmo Samaj the main topic is also [as in Christianity] sin. The fool who repeats day and night: 'I am a sinner, I am a sinner,' becomes a sinner indeed."

Ramakrishna told thousands of little stories, parables, and moral injunctions to the people who flocked to the temple. Often they were retellings of stories of folk wisdom, but the quality of the life of the teller gave them new meaning. Three will give a flavor of the charming wisdom and earthy quality of his teachings:

A man woke up at midnight and desired to smoke. He wanted a light, so he went to a neighbour's house and knocked at the door. Someone opened the door and asked what he wanted. The man said, "I wish to smoke. Can you give me a light?" The neighbour replied, "Bah! What is the matter with you? You have taken so much trouble to come and awaken us at this hour, when in your hand you have a lighted lantern!" What a man wants is already within him; but he still wanders here and there in search of it.

A man after fourteen years of hard asceticism in a lonely forest obtained at last the power of walking over the waters. Overjoyed at this acquisition, he went to his *guru,* and told him of his great feat. At this the master replied, "My poor boy, what you have accomplished after fourteen years' arduous labor, ordinary men do the same by paying a penny to the boatman."

Man is always restless, always moving from place to place. Why? Because he is never satisfied, because nothing brings him permanent satisfaction; and this fact that he is dissatisfied with his finite nature shows that it is not his natural condition. The fact that he has infinite ambition, that he has insatiable hunger for more and more, proves that he is infinite by nature, and that is why he is always dissatisfied with whatever is finite. . . . The contented man is no man; he is no more than a brute.

Among the young men who came to see and listen to Ramakrishna was a handsome young university graduate from Calcutta named Narendranath Datta. His was a wealthy, free-thinking family given to ostentation and extravagance. He was a superb athlete, a former member of the University of Calcutta wrestling team, a trained musician, and an obvious leader of men. The relationship between the semi-literate priest and the young gentleman was a curious one. Ramakrishna finally laid upon Narendranath, who was soon to become Vivekananda, the mission of looking after his disciples. Therefore, upon the death of the Master, Vivekananda rented an old house and organized the Ramakrishna Order of Monks. When some of the monks wanted to engage solely in spiritual exercises and studies, Vivekananda reminded them of Ramakrishna's belief that service to man was worship of God.

In order to think through what ought to be done with the Order, Vivekananda made a pilgrimage throughout India and in a memorable experience while standing on a rock off the southern tip of India he visualized the whole of the humanity of India before him with all its agony. He saw at once what was to be the direction of his life. But on his return to Calcutta he learned of the Parliament of Religions to be held at the Chicago World's Fair (1893), and, despite many odds, he reached Chicago, where he was the first Hindu to speak before American audiences. On September 19, 1893, he said in a speech, "Come up, O lions, and shake off the delusion that you are sheep; you are souls immortal, spirits free, blest and eternal; ye are not matter, ye are not bodies; matter is your servant, not you the servant of matter." In his last address at the Parliament he said, "The Christian is not to become a Hindu or a Buddhist, nor a Hindu or a Buddhist to become a Christian. But each must assimilate the spirit of the others and yet preserve his individuality and grow according to his own law of growth." After the Parliament Vivekananda spoke in many American cities, founded the Vedanta Society in New York in 1894, and taught in a two-month conference at Thousand Island Park on the St. Lawrence River in the summer of 1895.

Upon his return to India he formed the Ramakrishna Mission on May 1, 1897, a corporate body of monks and lay disciples, and two years later with funds from American and British admirers purchased land across the Hooghly River from Dakshineshvar at Belur and built a monastery as the headquarters of the Ramakrishna Order of Monks. Ever since its founding the Ramakrishna Mission has been engaged in a wide variety of charitable, missionary, and educational activities through its hospitals, dispensaries, orphanages, elementary and high schools, colleges, and cultural training centers for the masses. It remains to this day one of the most active agencies of social service in India.

Vivekananda died on July 4, 1902, at the age of thirty-nine. Four years before while traveling with American friends in Kashmir, Vivekananda surprised them on the anniversary of the American Declaration of Independence with a poem entitled "To the Fourth of July," the last six lines of which are

> Move on, O Lord, in thy restless path!
> Till thy high noon o'erspreads the world,

Till every land reflects thy light,
Till men and women, with uplifted head,
Behold their shackles broken, and
Know, in springing joy, their life renewed! [4]

CHAPTER **18**

Hinduism and Indian Nationalism

"Foreign dominion was nothing to peoples with no consciousness of nationality," [1] wrote the authors of *The Cambridge Shorter History of India* in explanation of why there had been so few rebellions against foreign rule in India prior to the nineteenth century. When the British assumed direct governmental control of India in 1858, the land was divided into more than six hundred princely states. R. C. Majumdar in a chapter entitled "The Indian People at the Beginning of the Nineteenth Century" writes, "It is hardly necessary to point out that there was no consciousness of unity among the peoples of India as a whole. The memory and tradition of the eighteenth century, when every man's hand was against his neighbour, persisted still in creating a wide gulf between the different regions of India." [2] He continues, "The Bengalis and the Rajputs remembered the horrors of the raid by the Marathas and cherished intense hatred of them. Similar feelings existed, for similar reasons, amongst other groups of Indian people. But even apart from such reasons, hardly any Indian ever regarded himself as a citizen of India owing allegiance to her, as against an alien power. This is best evidenced by the fact that an Indian soldier was ready to fight against any Indian power, including his own province or State, on behalf of any other power, which was willing to pay him for his service. This enabled the British to conquer India with the help of the Indians themselves. . . . The whole country was divided into a very large number of self-contained units, almost mutually exclusive in character, and the conception of India as a common motherland was still in the realm of fancy. There was no India as it is understood today. There were Bengalis, Hindustanis, Marathas, Sikhs, etc., but no Indians, at the beginning of the nineteenth century. There was, however, a complete revolution of ideas at the end of that century. One who speaks of an Indian nation at the beginning of the nineteenth century does as much violence to historical facts as those who refuse to recognize it at the end of that century." [3] Majumdar, no doubt, knew that he had to make this point because there are Indians who cherish the illusion of a long history of national unity; e.g., K. S. Ramaswami Sastri has written, "India has always felt herself to be a nation, though the obstacles to her realisation of her nationhood have been many and tremendous and though internal dissentions and external invasions have been ever and anon hindering such self-realisation." [4] An exaggerated statement such as Sastri's was probably a reaction to similar exaggerations made by the British, e.g., ". . . there is not and never was an India, no Indian nation, no 'people of India' " [5] and India "is a mere geographical expression like Europe or Africa." [6] Such conceptions are not limited to the British, nor to the nineteenth century. News analyst Robert S. Elegant of the *Los Angeles Times* in an article dated May 9, 1972, writes, "India is really not even a geographical expression, much less a nation, but rather a muddled state of mind." Kewal Motwani, an Indian sociologist in a book published in the very year of India's independence, says, "During the last thirty years or so, there has been a general belief that there is a renaissance in India and that India is a nation. Many books have been published on this subject, but it is the author's painful duty to join issues with these illustrious authors and thinkers, and he feels constrained to affirm that the core of Indian culture is in the course of disintegration and that India has all the characteristics of an amorphous, anonymous, unruly mob." [7]

We shall consider three outstanding Hindus of the twentieth century who have held differing opinions of the relation of Hinduism and nationalism: Rabindranath Tagore, Aurobindo Ghose, and Mahatma Gandhi.

Tagore

Rabindranath Tagore (1861–1941), the illustrious son of Devendranath Tagore and the winner of the Nobel Prize for literature in 1913, had serious doubts about the value of nationalistic emotions, which he called "the naked passion of self-love of Nations." He claimed that the very idea of a nation was foreign to Indians: "We have no word for 'Nation' in our language. When we borrow this word from other people, it never fits us." [8] Tagore's distrust of nationalism stemmed from his basic humanism: he feared that nationalism meant the leveling of people, the deadening of creativity, and the crushing of the spirit of man, since it placed the nation above the person. Tagore believed that Hinduism was a form of self-realization which rested upon the freedom of the individual to express himself in accord with the leanings of his own nature, and he feared that nationalism is destructive of the self. The nation, he believed, is a slave-producing institution which will in time drag human individuals to destruction. Therefore, he saw Hinduism and nationalism as diametrically opposed; the former stresses the moral greatness of man, and the latter turns men into means for the glorification of the state. Tagore, reflecting upon his childhood, wrote, "Even though from childhood I had been taught that idolatry of the nation is almost better than reverence for God and humanity, I believe I have outgrown that teaching, and it is my conviction that my countrymen will truly gain their India by fighting against the education which teaches them that a country is greater than the ideals of humanity." [9] Tagore spent the second half of his life in educational experiments at Shantiniketan attempting to stimulate young people in the creative discovery and development of themselves.

According to Tagore what went wrong in India was that she neglected the cult of Anna Brahma, which found the infinite manifested in the material world, and sought reality and value in the spiritual to the neglect of the material. Philosophically this means that Indians had taken Samkhya dualism too seriously. India's contact with the West, argued Tagore, offered her an opportunity to remedy the malady of excessive and exclusive spirituality, but unfortunately India did not distinguish "the spirit of the West" and "the Nation of the West." India, not realizing she could have the former without the latter, embraced both. By "the spirit of the West" Tagore meant the active productivity, the energetic mode of life characteristic of the West; by "the Nation of the West" he meant the entire apparatus of government which stresses equality and uniformity. The nation, he said, is like a power-loom in contrast with a handloom. Both are modes of production, but the power-loom is "relentlessly lifeless and accurate and monotonous in its production." [10] As a consequence of India's exposure to "the Nation of the West," "The present civilization of India has the constraining power of the mould. It squeezes man in the grip of rigid regulations, and its repression of individual freedom makes it only too easy for men to be forced into submission of all kinds and degrees." [11] Tagore concluded after an extensive visit to China and Japan that China had been poisoned by contact with the Nation of the West, but that Japan had been able to absorb the spirit of the West and to resist the Nation. He feared that India would not show the strength displayed by Japan, that India would adopt the ways of conflict and conquest which is the core of Western nationalism, and that India, deserting her destiny, i.e., "to raise the history of man from the muddy level of physical conflict to the higher moral attitude," [12] would seek to develop, like other nations, a civilization of power.

Tagore argued emotionally against the concept of the nation and the ideal of devotion to the nation. He warned against "the fierce self-idolatry of nation-worship." [13] His short essay entitled "The Nation" is a tirade of accusations against nationalism. The nation is "the survival of that part of man which is the least living." [14] Nations do not create, "they merely produce and destroy . . . they crowd away into a corner the living man who creates." [15] In the growth of nationalism "man has become the greatest menace to man." [16] The nation is ever watching to take advantage of the crowd mind, "this enormous power of darkness." [17] Nationalism is a thing of "gigantic vanity and selfishness." [18] But there is one ray of hope: the Age of Nationalism "is only a passing phase of civilization." [19] Tagore sometimes spoke hopefully of India becoming "a country of no nation."

Aurobindo

Aurobindo Ghose (1872–1950), the founder of the Aurobindo Ashram at Pondicherry and one of the greatest literary and philosophical figures of this century, also came to question the value of Indian nationalism, but by a vastly different route from Tagore's. Aurobindo was sent to England as a young boy with instructions that he be reared as an Englishman. The orders were that he not be allowed to make the acquaintance of any Indian or undergo any Indian influence. These orders were partially carried out during the fourteen years of his life in England, that is, between his seventh and twenty-first year, but the plans of his father to have English sons were not to be fully realized. Six months after his return to India he published a series of articles called "New Lamps for Old" on the feebleness of the activities of the Indian National Congress. The National Congress, he said, was not really national. Specifically, he charged that the Congress failed to offer a plan of action which would appeal to the distressed and ignorant masses. Already Aurobindo was planning techniques of armed rebellion, which culminated in his arrest on May 2, 1908, for complicity in a bombing at Muzaffarpur (Bihar) and incarceration in the Alipur jail for one year. During the years of his militant activity he regarded nationalism as a religion: "The movement of Nationalism in Bengal is a religion by which we are trying to realise God in the nation, in our fellow-countrymen." [20] Again, "Nationalism is an Avatar. . . . It is a divinely-appointed Shakti and must do its God-given work before it returns to the bosom of Universal Energy from which it came." [21] Nationalism was a "mission" to recover "Indian thought, Indian character, Indian perceptions, Indian energy, Indian greatness, and to solve the problems that perplex the world in an Indian spirit and from an Indian standpoint." [22] Aurobindo at this time displayed the narrow zeal characteristic of the new convert. However, the redeeming feature of Aurobindo's nationalism, even in these years of his youthful enthusiasms, was that India's existence as a free nation was not for India's sake alone, but for the world: "India must have *Svaraj* in order to live; she must have *Svaraj* in order to live for the world, not as a slave for the material and political benefit of a single purse-proud and selfish nation, but as a free people for the spiritual and intellectual benefit of the human race." [23] "Our ideal of patriotism proceeds on the basis of love and brotherhood and it looks beyond the unity of the nation and envisages the ultimate unity of mankind." [24]

During the trial Aurobindo was prophetically described by his defender, Chittaranjan Das, as "the poet of nationalism . . . the lover of humanity." His year in Alipur jail—which Aurobindo called "Alipur Ashram"—had brought about a significant change. Nationalism was now *Sanatana Dharma.* India's work was the world's work. India possessed the key to the progress of humanity. The liberation India sought was not India's liberation but the liberation of mankind. He retired to Pondicherry to spend the rest of his life working out the implications of the larger liberation. But the British were not convinced that Aurobindo had forsworn violence, and for twenty-eight years Aurobindo and his ashramites were shadowed by the police who year after year described them as "a dangerous gang of bomb-makers."

Aurobindo, like Tagore, appeared to have doubts about the nationalism of India as he watched the progress of the independence movement. He also feared that India might imitate the West in structure and miss the spirit: "Either India will be nationalised and industrialised out of all recognition and she will be no longer India or else she will be the leader in a new world-phase, aid by her example and cultural infiltration the new tendencies of the West and spiritualise the human race." [25] Finally, in his Independence Day Declaration issued on August 15, 1947, while rejoicing in the liberation of India from the British, he cautioned that the nation must be only a transition to more valuable governmental organizations: "But an outward basis is not enough; there must grow an international spirit and outlook; international forms and institutions must appear, perhaps such developments as dual or multilateral citizenship, willed interchange or voluntary fusion of cultures. Nationalism will have fulfilled itself and lost its militancy and would no longer find these things incompatible with self-preservation and the integrality of its outlook. A new spirit of oneness will take hold of the human race." [26] Thus the nationalism of Aurobindo, like the nationalism of Tagore, turned into an internationalism. Aurobindo dreamed "of individual perfection and a perfect society." He believed that a new type of man is in the making. Man is the agent of the process, the formulator of the doctrine, and the telos of all events. The end of this conscious evolution is a superman or gnostic being who is the perfect self-expression of the Absolute Spirit and the perfect medium through which Matter realizes the Absolute Spirit. The unity of mankind, which the West sees only in idea but cannot achieve because it does not possess its spirit, can be attained through India if she will but affirm the deep truths of her Vedic tradition in the involution of *Satchitananda* to Matter and in the evolution of Matter to *Satchitananda*.

Gandhi

Mohandas K. Gandhi (1869–1948) guided the Indians through a nonviolent revolution which culminated in their independence from the British. He always insisted that he was only a politician, but his followers tended to make him a saint. He became known worldwide as The Mahatma (The Great Soul). He was an activist, not a theorist. "My life is my message," he said. "I have not the qualifications for teaching my philosophy of life. I have barely qualifications for practising the philosophy I believe." [27] However, his lack of qualifications did not prevent him from talking and writing a very great deal about his philosophy. As Gunnar Myrdal has said, Gandhi "established a pattern of radicalism in talk but conservatism in action that is still very much a part of the Indian scene." [28] In the latter years of his life he was constantly asked for his opinion on a wide variety of topics. For example, Ralph Coniston of *Collier's Weekly* in an interview with Gandhi in 1945 asked what he would advocate if he were in San Francisco at the meetings at which the Charter of the United Nations was being formed. He received a typical Gandhian answer: "If I knew I would tell you but I am made differently. When I face a situation, the solution comes to me. I am not a man who sits down and thinks out problems syllogistically. I am a man of action. I react to situations intuitively. Logic comes afterwards, it does not precede the event. The moment I am at the Peace Conference, I know the right word will come. But not beforehand." [29]

Not enough attention has been given to the fact that Gandhi was a pragmatist. He said what the occasion demanded rather than what was harmonious with former statements. Hence he was often caught in denying on one occasion what he had affirmed on another, but this did not bother him. "I have never made a fetish of consistency," he wrote in his magazine, *Young India*, on September 28, 1934. Jawaharlal Nehru, who had great concern about matters of intellectual consistency, referred to him as "the paradox that is Gandhiji," [30] and his good friend, C. F. Andrews, spoke of Gandhi's "infantile confusion of thought." On one occasion Gandhi wrote, "I am not at all concerned with appearing to be consistent. In my search after Truth I have discarded many ideas and learnt many new things. . . . What I am concerned with is my readiness to obey the call of Truth, my God, from moment to moment, and, therefore, when anybody finds any inconsistency between any two writings of mine, if he has still faith in my sanity, he would do well to choose the later of the two on the same subject." [31] He often claimed that nonviolence was the one fixed guide of his life, but on August 25, 1920, he said, "I do believe that where there is a choice only between cowardice and violence, I would advise violence," and on February 16, 1922, "It is better to be charged with cowardice and weakness than to be guilty of violating our oath [of truth and nonviolence]." [32] He identified God and Truth, but he interpreted the Hindu scriptures according to his own wishes and needs. He wrote, "The stories told in the Puranas are some of them most dangerous, if we do not know their bearing on the present conditions. The *shastras* would be death-traps if we were to regulate our conduct according to every detail given in them or according to that of the characters therein described." [33]

Gandhi offered three grounds for rejection of certain passages of Hindu scriptures. (1) They are later interpolations; e.g., when he was asked if he approved of the doctrine of *varna* as given in the *Manusmriti*, he replied, "The principle is there. But the applications do not appeal to me fully. There are parts of the book which are open to grave objections. I hope that they are later interpolations." [34] (2) They are "contrary to known and accepted morality"; e.g., "The *smritis* bristle with contradictions. The only reasonable deduction to be drawn from the contradictions is that the texts that may be contrary to known and accepted morality, more especially, to the moral precepts enjoined in the *smritis* themselves, must be rejected as interpolations." [35] (3) They are in conflict with positive experience and scientific knowledge; e.g., when in an exchange of opinion regarding early marriage Gandhi was reminded that the *smritis* approved of early marriage, he replied, "But even if the texts ordering child, as opposed to early—for early marriage means marriage well before twenty-five—marriage be found to be authoritative, we must reject them in the light of positive experience and scientific knowledge." [36] These three hermeneutical devices were not what Gandhi claimed them to be. They are in fact three sorts of justifications for Gandhi's intuitions. He said, "The still small voice within you must always be the final arbiter when there is a conflict of duty." [37] His moral intuitions he regarded as superior to *shruti*: "If I discovered that the Vedas clearly showed that they claimed divine authority for Untouchability, then nothing on this earth would hold me to Hinduism. I would throw it overboard like a rotten apple." [38] The happy fact is that Gandhi's intuitions were humane, and also he had a fine feeling for the feasible. But to quote Gandhi as an authority on any line of action or thought—as his followers often did—was to forget that Gandhi was a man faithful to the truth as the truth appeared to him at a particular moment under specific conditions. He thought of himself as an orthodox Hindu, yet he interpreted scriptures and *dharmas* as he wished. His violations of the rules of his branch of the *Vaishya varna* brought a lifetime of shame and persecution upon his entire joint family. Taya Zinkin reports on a visit to Gandhi's family: "I visited Gandhi's eldest sister, Ralihat Behen, shortly before she died at over ninety. When I tried to make her talk about her brother she exploded into toothless anger and tears: Gandhi's insistence on mixing with unclean people, on being his own sweeper, and his trips over the sea, had led to the excommunication of his whole family. For Ralihat Behen this had meant a lifetime of ostracism and humiliation by the people about whom she minded: the orthodox of her own sub-caste and neighbourhood. Far from feeling proud of her brother, she stood there, doubled up by rheumatism, calling him a man so selfish that he had not cared what harm he had done to his family." [39]

Gandhi is a person about whom Hindus and non-Hindus are still arguing. The key to the understanding of Gandhi is the fact that he was first, last, and always a politician. He is often pictured as a simple, humble man—and so he was—and he was very proud of his humility! He was an extremely complicated man. Those who attempt to characterize him soon find themselves using contradictions; e.g., one author referring to his leadership of the Congress Party writes, "He brought to the task a Moderate's abhorrence of violence and willingness to arrive at compromises, together with an Extremist's passion for action and quasi-religious appeal to the masses." [40] Another author writes, "Mahatma Gandhi was no Christian, and the Christians were amazed that this should be so, for never in modern times had they seen any man tread more faithfully in the footsteps of Christ." [41] As a politician Gandhi knew the importance of maintaining a public image. His image was that of an ascetic in sandals and loincloth eating only fruits, nuts, and goat milk. But the maintenance of that image was not easy. "It takes a great deal of money to keep Bapu living in poverty!" reported Sarojini Naidu, one of his secretaries. During one period twelve men were hired to collect the simple fruits and nuts Gandhi demanded. The British discovered that the frail little man was a tough, indefatigable antagonist, and even his Hindu friends felt the lash of the lawyer tongue. When Rabindranath Tagore disagreed with a policy, Gandhi in a public address called Rammohan Roy a dwarf and attacked Rabindranath, who had recently published a volume of the poems of Kabir, by saying, "I have found it impossible to soothe suffering patients with a song from Kabir." [42]

To understand Gandhi's Hinduism one needs to note that in India during the first half of the twentieth century the Hindu intellectuals were attempting to maintain cultural identity through a period of revolutionary transition. A wide spectrum of opinions was expressed and values supported. At each end of the spectrum were groups whose values were so far apart that they became opponents: at one end were those whose desire to bring about the revolutionary transition transcended their desire to maintain cultural identity, and at the other end were those whose desire to maintain cultural identity transcended their desire to bring about the revolutionary transition. Each was a radical group—the first was radical in its demand for social, economic, and political change even at the cost of religion and traditional morality; the second was radical in its demand for the preservation of religion and traditional morality even at the cost of social, economic, and political reform. Gandhi was caught between the two radicalisms; he wanted to preserve the cultural heritage of Hinduism and he also wanted to bring about many changes. Gandhi knew that if he appealed in the name of conservatism, he would end with both radical groups coalescing in opposition to him, so he appealed to both by using sometimes the language of radical reform and sometimes the language of radical preservation.

Gandhi accepted the Hindu view of the inequality of mankind in terms of the traditional *varnas* which are determined by *karma* and which cannot be changed in an incarnation. But these classes, he said, denote duties, not privileges. If they are a hierarchy, it is a hierarchy of greater responsibilities for the welfare of everyone in the community. He tied vocation with *varnas*, and held that each person must earn his living in his family occupation, although if he wished, he could engage in another avocational activity. The most important feature of Gandhi's views on the class system was that he rejected completely the concept of Untouchability. Dr. B. R. Ambedkar, the leader of the Untouchables, pointed out in anger that all Gandhi was proposing was that the Untouchables become *Shudras,* when in fact the whole concept of *varna* was a violation of the democratic principles to which Gandhi claimed to be dedicated.

Gandhi supported cow worship on the grounds that it is the Hindu's unique contribution to the evolution of humanitarianism. It is symbolic of the oneness and sacredness of all life and a direct consequence of the Hindu assumption of transmigration. The cow, he said, has been selected to represent the entire subhuman world, and, in honoring the cow, man indicates his identity with all that live.

He held to the doctrine of *avataras,* and he worshiped Rama, although he did not consider himself a Vaishnavite. He said he was a nonsectarian Hindu. He defended images as an aid to worship. He set aside several hours each day for prayer and meditation in which he used scriptures and devotional materials from all religions. His favorite hymn was "Lead Kindly Light." Prayer he described as the effort to lose oneself in God. Prayer was one of the means by which Gandhi sought to obtain the power of "soul-force" or "Truth-force" (*satyagraha*) which alone, he believed, could induce the British to leave India. He distinguished "body-force," which is violence to get a government to change a law, from "soul-force," which is a form of law-changing in which one challenges the conscience of the governing bodies by deliberately breaking a law and accepting the penalty.

Simplicity, austerity, and nonviolence were the hallmarks of his ethical position. He wore the minimum of clothes, and that of *khadi* (homespun cloth). Throughout his life he experimented in foods, and during the last years of his life ate only fruits and nuts. Continence was the ideal for everyone, except when offspring were desired. *Ahimsa* (nonviolence) was the chief moral virtue, but it was not an absolute, for Gandhi did find occasions when violence was approved. His use of the *hartal* (strike, closing of shop, refusal to work) was in fact a form of brute force, yet Gandhi by extended reasoning fitted it into the *ahimsa* ideal. Also his fasts, which were forms of pressure on the conscience of another, he regarded as fitting expressions of *ahimsa.* In the *Harijan* for December 8, 1946, Gandhi wrote, "There are two aspects of Hinduism. There is, on the one hand, the historical Hinduism with its Untouchability, superstitious worship of stocks and stones, animal sacrifices and so on. On the other, we have the Hinduism of the *Gita,* the *Upanishads,* and Patañjali's *Yoga Sutras,* which is the acme of *Ahimsa* and oneness of all creation, pure worship of one immanent, formless, imperishable God. *Ahimsa,* which for me is the chief glory of Hinduism, has been sought to be explained away by our people as being meant for the *sannyasi* only. I do not think so. I hold that it is *the* way of life and India has to show it to the world."

Gandhi was not interested in the metaphysics of the self, but he made much of the doctrine of *svabhava* (self-sufficiency), *svadharma* (one's own religion), *svaraj* (self-rule), and *svadeshi* (one's own country). These concepts, which he found in Hinduism, were integral with his struggles for political independence. *Svabhava* was the fundamental notion of being a unique individual. Both Tagore and Gandhi rejected the Advaita conception of the illusory nature and worthlessness of the individual. Gandhi interpreted *svadharma* to mean that each person was free to worship the god of his own choosing. He welcomed people of any faith to his prayer services. *Svaraj* was the inherent right of the individual to rule himself. All tyrannies are violations of this right. He once said that the ideal government is "benign autocracy." Gandhi insisted that he held no enmity toward the British but he did toward their civilization. It is a civilization only in name, he said. *Svadeshi* was the economic principle of living by the labor of one's own hands and from the produce of one's own land. Gandhi was particularly opposed to the machine. He despised Western civilization, which he said would have everything done by machinery: "Men will not need the use of their hands and feet. They will press a button, and they will have their clothing by their side. They will press another button, and they will have their newspaper. A third, and a motor-car will be waiting for them." [43] He chose as a symbol of protest against the machine the *charkha* (spinning wheel) and tried to devote a portion of each day to spinning.

Gandhi borrowed heavily from non-Hindu sources. His anarchism he derived from his reading of Kropotkin. Socialistic ideas came to him from reading Charles Kingsley. Tolstoy's *The Kingdom of God Is Within You* gave him insights into pacifism. From Thoreau he got the notion of self-sufficiency, and also from Thoreau's "Civil Disobedience" he was strengthened in his conviction that men are obligated to violate unjust laws. Ruskin's *Unto This Last* showed him how manual labor could be the means of consolidating the educated and the uneducated. The *New Testament* gave him the figure of Jesus, whom he called "The Prince of Civil Resisters." He had such admiration for the Sermon on the Mount that he said if he were to lose his *Gita,* he could replace it without loss by the Sermon on the

Mount. He also read the *Koran* and used it in his prayer meetings. One of the finest statements of his eclecticism appeared in *Young India*, June 1, 1921: "I do not want my house to be walled in on all sides and my windows to be stuffed. I want the cultures of all lands to be blown about my house as freely as possible. But I refuse to be blown off my feet."

After Independence

When Winston Churchill, the British Prime Minister during World War II, refused to consider giving independence to India on the grounds that he had not come to that office to dismember the British Empire, he was speaking personally but not altogether historically. The British are to be credited with knowingly instilling into the minds of Indians the same longings which nourished democratic reforms in the West. Thomas Macaulay in his famous speech on Indian education in the House of Commons said that "having become instructed in European languages, they [the Indians] may, in some future age, demand European institutions," and he added that "whenever it comes, it will be the proudest day in English history." Similarly, Lionel Smith speaking before a committee of the House of Commons in 1831 said that Western education would make the Indians "feel the value of governing themselves," and therefore "the effect of imparting education will be to turn us out of the country." On August 15, 1947, the Indian people achieved independence from the British.

On January 26, 1950, the new nation adopted its Constitution. The Preamble to the Constitution sets forth the noble aspirations of the nation:

> We, the people of India, having solemnly resolved to constitute India into a sovereign democratic republic and to secure to all its citizens:
>
> JUSTICE: social, economic and political;
> LIBERTY of thought, expression, belief, faith and worship;
> EQUALITY of status and of opportunity; and to promote among them all

FRATERNITY assuring the dignity of the individual and the unity of
the nation . . .

The framers of the Constitution were heavily indebted to the
experiences of the democratic nations of the West. They were
familiar with the British documents back to Magna Carta, with the
French Declaration of the Rights of Man, and with the American
Declaration of Independence and the American Constitution. They
had read Montesquieu, Burke, and *The Federalist Papers*. But did they
take sufficiently into account their own rich and variegated tradition?
Did they exploit the two great sources of Hindu law: Vedic *shruti*
and the *dharma-shastras* (law-books)? Or did they envisage a
Western nation in the subcontinent of Asia? Ananda Coomaraswamy in an article written at the opening of the twentieth century
reflecting upon India's progress in the nineteenth century warned,
"A century of 'progress' has brought India to the stage where almost
everything of beauty and romance belongs to her past. . . . Modern
Indians are quite satisfied with an outward life that is unlovely,
unrhythmic and undisciplined. . . . Indians are destroying their
civilization as a compliment to England." [44] Tagore had advised
becoming "a country of no nation," and Aurobindo said nationalism
must be dissolved in "a new spirit of oneness." But such thoughts
were not entertained in the first flush of pride as India took her
position among the nations of the world.

India's Hindu tradition was a burden according to some of the
architects of the new democracy. While Gandhi derived strength
and vision from Hinduism, above all from the *Gita* which he called
his "dictionary of action," Jawaharlal Nehru was critical of Hinduism. He called himself an agnostic, charging all religions with
blocking change and progress: "Instead of encouraging curiosity and
thought, they have preached a philosophy of submission to nature, to
the established church, to the prevailing social order, and to
everything that is. The belief in a supernatural agency which ordains
everything has led to a certain irresponsibility on the social plane, and
emotion and sentimentality have taken the place of reasoned thought
and inquiry. Religion, though it has undoubtedly brought comfort to
innumerable human beings and stabilized society by its values, has

checked the tendency to change and progress inherent in human society." [45] "India must therefore lessen her religiosity and turn to science." [46] He added that in India "we have too much of the past about us and have ignored the present. We have to get rid of that narrowing religious outlook, that obsession with the supernatural and metaphysical speculations, that loosening of the mind's discipline in religious ceremonial and mystical emotionalism, which come in the way of our understanding ourselves and the world. . . . Some Hindus talk of going back to the Vedas; some Moslems dream of an Islamic theocracy. Idle fancies, for there is no going back to the past; there is no turning back even if this was thought desirable. There is only one-way traffic in Time." [47]

The debate over the relevance of Hinduism for Indian nationalism continues. Unlike Pakistan, which boldly proclaims herself a religious nation, India insists she is a secular nation. But Hinduism permeates the life of the people too thoroughly to allow an easy distinction between what is sacred and what is secular. Almost any act of the government can be challenged by some Hindus as infringing upon a religious custom. For example, there were angry protests in Calcutta in 1965 by Hindus who claimed that the governmental control of the sale of milk was an encroachment upon their religious right to make sandesh, a sweet regarded as essential to marriage celebrations and other Hindu ceremonies. The East India Company and the British Government often discovered they seldom could act without offending the religion of some Hindus.

Two aspects of Hinduism may be mentioned as relevant to the democratic experiment. One is the doctrine of *dharma*. The possibility of organizing a state composed of people for whom duty is the way things are done rather than an obligation one assumes under coercion is very appealing. The Hindu does his *dharma* not because he is forced to, not because he is afraid not to, not because he enjoys it, but because one's *dharma* is just what one does. The notion of not doing one's *dharma* is almost incomprehensible to the Hindu. *Dharma*-motivated people ought to make good citizens in a democracy. The other aspect of Hinduism which is important for democracy in India and in the world is what may be called humanism. A theme running throughout Hinduism is that institutions exist for the sake of man. The state is to serve the best interests of individual human beings. Somehow nations tend to lose this simple truth. Brotherhood becomes a United Nations rather than a united people. Nations become competitive rather than cooperative, and the game of nations becomes too expensive and too dangerous to play. How much longer can nations spend over half their wealth and production for the weapons of war? What is the point of wars in which everyone loses? Why wage a war which no one survives? Can the authority of nations be based on *dharma* rather than on *dandu* (coercive power)? India has raised such questions, and she has refused to enter into the cold war. She has chosen an international policy of nonalignment. This is an expression of a universal humanism or a human catholicism which has been at work in India for many hundreds of years. India out of her Hindu tradition may yet lead the nations of the world into a new form of nationalism which is more humanistic than nationalistic. Hinduism speaks for humanity against the nation. Mankind awaits the implementation of the ancient Vedic admonition:

> One and the same be your resolve, and be your minds of one accord. United be the thought of all that all may happily agree.[48]

For all Chapters

CHAPTER I

1. *Hinduism*. Madras: G. A. Natesan and Co., 1924, p. 57.

2. *The Religion of the Hindus*. Edited by Kenneth W. Morgan. New York: Ronald Press Co., 1953, p. iii.

3. *The Nature of Hinduism*. Translated by Patrick Evans. New York: Walker and Co., 1962, pp. 143–144.

4. "There are few characters more painfully unattractive than the Hinduizing Occidental." Nirad C. Chaudhuri, *The Continent of Circe*. London: Chatto and Windus, 1965, p. 91.

5. R. Antoine, "General Historical Survey" in *Religious Hinduism, A Presentation and Appraisal*. Edited by R. De Smet. Third revised edition. Allahabad: St. Paul Publications, 1968, p. 31. Thomas Berry also writes, "To give lists of Hindu beliefs or descriptions of Hindu practices without identifying the period and area in which they took place is to present a static picture of something very different from Hinduism as it has actually existed. The basic unity is the unity of a changing life process, not the unity of a fixed pattern. Even though Indian civilization was thoroughly ahistorical, even though the people were not aware of the historical significance of the changes through which their religious-spiritual traditions were passing, it remains true to say that there can be no understanding of Hinduism except that which is based on the developmental process that has been taking place in India during the whole of India's recorded and unrecorded history." *Religions of India*. New York: Bruce Publishing Co., 1971, p. 4.

6. *Caste and Outcaste*. London: J. M. Dent and Sons, 1923, pp. 74–75.

7. Richard Lannoy, *The Speaking Tree*. London: Oxford University PKress, 1971, p. 339.

8. *My Brother's Face*. London: Thornton Butterworth, 1936, p. 244.

9. B. R. Ambedkar, *What Congress and Gandhi Have Done to the Untouchables*. Bombay: Thacker and Co., 1945, p. 297.

10. *The Discovery of India*. Garden City, New York: Doubleday and Co., 1960, p. 387.

11. *Ibid.*

12. In *The Religion of the Hindus*. Edited by Kenneth W. Morgan. Part I, chap. 1.

13. Paul Tillich, *The Protestant Era*. Third impression. Chicago: University of Chicago Press, 1960, p. 57.

14. See L. K. A. Iyer, *Anthropology of the Syrian Christians*. Ernakulam, 1926, p. 218. Also J. H. Hutton, *Caste in India*. Fourth edition. London: Oxford University Press, 1963, p. 121.

15. *Asiatic Studies*, Vol. II. London: John Murray, 1899, pp. 291, 292.

16. *Philosophies of India*. Cleveland and New York: World Publishing Co., 1956, p. 50.

17. *The Nature of Hinduism*. Translated by Patrick Evans. P. 32.

18. "The Meaning of Sankhya and Yoga," *American Journal of Philology*, Vol. 45, 1924, p. 1.

19. "The Synthetic View of Vedanta" in *A. R. Wadia: Essays Presented in His Honour*. Edited by S. Radhakrishnan and others. Madras, 1954, p. 186.

20. *Self-Knowledge*. Mylapore, Madras: Sri Ramakrishna Math, 1947, p. 19.

21. *Philosophy of Hindu Sadhana*. London: Kegan Paul, Trench, Trübner and Co., 1932, p. xi.

22. *Ibid.*, p. ix.

23. "The Religio-Philosophic Culture of India" in *The Cultural Heritage of India*, Vol. I. Calcutta: The Ramakrishna Mission, 1958, p. 164.

24. *Proceedings of the 28th Indian Philosophical Congress (1953), pp. 27–28.*

25. *Facets of Indian Thought*. New York: Schocken Books, 1964, p. 32.

26. *Introduction to the Study of the Hindu Doctrines*. London: Luzac and Co., 1945, pp. 171–172.

27. *Indian Thought and Its Development*. Translated by Mrs. Charles E. B. Russell. Boston: Beacon Press, 1936, p. 1.

28. *Bulletin on the Religions of India*. Calcutta: Firma K. L. Mukhopadhyaya, 1960, p. 1. Reprinted from *Indian Antiquary*, Vol. 23.

29. "India's Problem of Problems: The Fixed Attitude," *The Aryan Path*, Vol. 14, December 1943, p. 539.

30. *Ibid.*, p. 542.

31. *The Continent of Circe*, p. 151.

32. *Manifestoes*. Translated by Richard Seaver and Helen R. Lane. Ann Arbor: University of Michigan Press, 1969, p. 123.

33. *Hindu Mysticism*. Chicago and London: Open Court Publishing Co., 1927, p. 168.

CHAPTER 2

1. *Modes of Thought*. New York: Putnam's Sons, 1958, p. 165.

2. *Indian Thought and Its Development*, p. 1.

3. *Ibid.*, pp. 1–2.

4. *Ibid.*, p. 3.

5. *Ibid.*, p. 250.

6. *Rig Veda* 1. 24. 8.

7. L. S. S. O'Malley, *Popular Hinduism*. Cambridge: Cambridge University Press, 1935, pp. 41–42.

8. *Ibid.*, pp. 171–172.

9. *The Dance of Shiva*. New York: Noonday Press, 1957, p. 4.

10. *Manhabharata* 5. 1517.

11. *Rig Veda* 1. 92. 10; 1. 164.34.

12. *Brihad-Aranyaka Upanishad* 4. 4. 22.

13. *Ibid.*, 4. 4. 6.

14. *Maitri Upanishad* 3. 2.

15. Rabindranath Tagore, *The Religion of Man*. London: George Allen and Unwin, 1931, p. 118.

16. *The Philosophy of Radhakrishnan.* Edited by Paul Schilpp. New York: Tudor Publishing Co., 1952, p. 65.

17. 4. 10. Edgerton translation.

18. *The Culture and Art of India.* London: George Allen and Unwin, 1959, p. 18.

19. *Facets of Indian Thought,* pp. 142–143.

20. *Gitanjali* 35.

21. *Indian Thought and Its Development,* p. 260.

22. 5. 42.

23. *The Quest after Perfection.* Mysore: Kavyalaya Publishers, 1952, p. 35.

24. *The Renaissance in India.* Calcutta: Arya Publishing House, 1946, p. 19.

25. *Ibid.,* p. 23.

26. 2. 3. 1, 2. Müller translation.

27. *Selections from Gandhi.* Edited by Nirmal Kuman Bose. Ahmedabad: Nirajivan Publishing House, 1948, p. 30.

28. Quoted by R. R. Diwaker in *Gandhi: A Practical Philosopher.* Bombay: Bharatiya Vidya Bhavan, 1965, p. 45.

29. 12. 300.

30. K. Damandaran, *Indian Thought: A Critical Survey.* Bombay: Asia Publishing House, 1967, p. 485.

31. "Humanism and Indian Thought," Principal Miller Lectures, University of Madras, 1935, p. 27.

32. 18. 63.

33. *Rig Veda* 1. 112. 1.

CHAPTER 3

1. *Prehistoric India.* Harmondsworth, Middlesex: Penguin Books, 1950, p. 14.

2. *Ibid.,* p. 69.

3. D. D. Kosambi, *Ancient India. A History of Its Culture and Civilization.* New York: Random House, Pantheon Books, 1965, p. 69.

4. B. Allchin and F. R. Allchin, *Birth of Indian Civilization: India and Pakistan before 500 B.C.* Harmondsworth, Middlesex: Penguin Books, 1968, p. 140.

5. K. M. Munshi, *Foundations of Indian Culture.* Bombay: Bharatiya Vidya Bhavan, 1962, p. 39.

6. Paul Masson-Oursel, Helena de Willman-Granbowski, and Philippe Stern, *Ancient India and Indian Civilization.* New York: Barnes and Noble, 1967, p. 13.

7. *Rig Veda* 1. 10. 5.

8. *Prehistoric India*, p. 200.

9. *The Speaking Tree*, p. 7.

10. *Ancient India. A History of Its Culture and Civilization*, p. 64.

11. *Prehistoric India*, p. 153.

12. *Our Oriental Heritage.* New York: Simon and Schuster, 1954, p. 397.

13. Poona: Arya-Bhushana Press, 1903.

14. *The Continent of Circe.*

15. *Geschichte der Inderschen Literature*, p. 254.

16. *Rig Veda* 1. 98. 8.

17. *Ibid.*, 2. 12. 9.

18. *Ibid.*, 2. 12. 4.

19. Macdonell translation.

CHAPTER 4

1. Cf. *Sources of Indian Tradition.* Edited by W. Theodore de Bary. New York: Columbia University Press, 1958.

2. *Hindu World*, Vol. I. London: George Allen and Unwin, 1968, p. 446.

3. Maurice Bloomfield, *The Religion of the Veda.* New York: AMS Press, 1908, p. 20.

4. *Rig Veda* 6. 6. Macdonell translation.

5. *Ibid.*, 5. 85. 7–8. Griffith translation.

6. *Atharva Veda* 6. 136. Bloomfield translation.

7. Louis Renou, *Religions of Ancient India*. London: Athlone Press, 1953, p. 12.

8. P. D. Mehta, *Early Indian Religious Thought*. London: Luzac and Co., 1956, p. 33.

9. *Rig Veda* 7. 88. 1–2. Macdonell translation.

10. *Ibid.*, 1. 84. 19. Wilson translation.

11. *Ibid.*, 5. 84. 1, 3. Macdonell translation.

12. *Ibid.*, 1. 185. 1.

13. *Ibid.*, 1. 113. 1–7.

14. *Ibid.*, 7. 88. 6–7.

15. *Ibid.*, 7. 87. 7.

16. *Ibid.*, 1. 24. 15.

17. *Ibid.*, 2. 28. 5.

18. *Ibid.*, 1. 25. 12.

19. *Ibid.*, 1. 11. 1–4, 8. Wilson translation.

20. *Ibid.*, 2. 12. 1–5. Macdonell translation.

21. *Ibid.*, 2. 33. 14–15.

22. *Ibid.*, 1. 1.

23. See R. Gordon Wasson, *Soma: Divine Mushroom of Immortality*. The Hague: Mouton, 1969.

24. *Rig Veda* 8. 48. 1, 3–6, 11. Macdonell translation.

25. *Ibid.*, 5. 83. 10. My translation.

26. *Ibid.*, 10. 129. Macdonell translation.

27. *Ibid.*, 9. 113. 10–11. Wilson translation.

28. *Ibid.*, 7. 104.

CHAPTER 5

1. S. Radhakrishnan, *Indian Philosophy*, Vol. I. New York: Macmillan Co., 1923, p. 118.

2. C. Kunhan Raja, "Vedic Culture" in *The Cultural Heritage of India*, Vol. I, p. 210.

3. *Atharva Veda* 6. 105. Macdonell translation.

4. *Ibid.*, 5. 37. 2.

5. *Ibid.*, 7. 13. 1.

6. *Ibid.*, 5. 19. 14.

7. *Ibid.*, 3. 25. 2.

8. *Ibid.*, 7. 2. 9.

9. *Ibid.*, 4. 1. 7.

10. Radhakrishnan, *Indian Philosophy*, Vol. I, p. 118.

11. Arthur A. Macdonell, *A History of Sanskrit Literature*. Delhi: Munshi Ram Manohar Lal, 1900, p. 192.

12. *Atharva Veda* 10. 7. 1–3, 22, 35. Edgerton translation with minor changes.

13. *Atharva Veda* 10. 8. 44. Edgerton translation.

14. *Ibid.*, 19. 71. 1.

15. *Ibid.*, 13. 1. 56.

16. *Ibid.*, 12. 4. 36.

17. *Ibid.*, 12. 1. 11–12.

18. *Ibid.*, 8. 1. 4. Macdonell translation.

19. J. Eggeling, *Sacred Books of the East*, Vol. XII, p. ix.

20. Quoted by R. C. Majumdar in *The Vedic Age. The History and Culture of the Indian People*, Vol. I. Bombay: Bharatiya Vidya Bhavan, 1951, p. 225.

21. *The Religion of the Veda*, p. 46.

22. *Ibid.*, p. 48.

23. *Shatapatha Brahmana* 10. 5. 2. 9.

24. Macdonell, *A History of Sanskrit Literature*, p. 208.

25. *Shatapatha Brahmana* 2. 2. 6.

26. Differences like these in the *Brahmanas* give rise to the opinion that the extant *Brahmanas* are those successful in the many disputes that arose as to the proper rituals and the correct interpretation of the rituals.

27. *Rig Veda* 10. 90. 16. Griffith translation.

28. *Atharva Veda* 9. 2. 31.

29. *Rig Veda* 1. 155. 5.

30. Franklin Edgerton, *The Beginnings of Indian Philosophy*. London: George Allen and Unwin, 1965, p. 17.

31. Renou, *Religions of Ancient India*, p. 29.

CHAPTER 6

1. *Rig Veda* 7. 103. 1, 5–10. Macdonell translation.

2. 1. 2. 7–11.

3. 1. 12. 5. Hume translation.

4. *Indian Philosophy*, Vol. I, p. 42.

5. Surendranath Dasgupta, *A History of Indian Philosophy*, Vol. I. Cambridge: Cambridge University Press, 1957, p. 42.

6. *Isha Upanishad* 9. Hume translation.

7. *Brihad-Aranyaka Upanishad* 3. 5. Hume translation.

8. *Mundaka Upanishad* 1. 1. 5.

9. Betty Heimann, *Facets of Indian Thought*, p. 17.

10. Louis Renou, *Religions of Ancient India*, p. 18.

11. C. E. M. Joad, *The Story of Indian Civilization*. London: Macmillan and Co., 1936, p. 6.

12. Robert Ernest Hume, *The Thirteen Principal Upanishads*. London: Oxford University Press, 1954, p. 2.

13. *Rig Veda* 1. 143. 7; 10. 125. 1.

14. *Ibid.*, 10. 114. 5.

15. *Ibid.*, 1. 24. 8.

16. *Brihad-Aranyaka Upanishad* 3. 9. 1.

17. *Ibid.*, 1. 4. 5, 6.

18. Hume translation.

19. *Maitri Upanishad* 6. 11. Hume translation.

20. *Maitri Upanishad* 2. 6; *Brihad-Aranyaka Upanishad* 5. 5. 3.

21. *Chandogya Upanishad* 3. 19. 1.

22. *Taittiriya Upanishad* 2. 7.

23. *Chandogya Upanishad* 1. 9. 1.

24. *Kena Upanishad* 11. Hume translation.

25. *Katha Upanishad* 2. 17.

26. *Mundaka Upanishad* 1. 1. 9.

27. *Katha Upanishad* 4. 8.

28. *Ibid.*, 5. 13.

29. *Mundaka Upanishad* 3. 2. 8–9. Hume translation.

30. *Rig Veda* 10. 16. 3. Wilson translation.

31. *Mundaka Upanishad* 3. 1. 1. Hume translation.

32. *Chandogya Upanishad* 5. 18. 1. Radhakrishnan translation.

33. *Ibid.*, 6. 1. 3. Hume translation.

34. *Mysticism East and West.* Translated by Bertha L. Bracy and Richenda C. Payne. New York: Macmillan Co., 1932, pp. 84–85.

35. *Chandogya Upanishad* 3. 12. 7; 3. 18. 1.

36. *Brihad-Aranyaka Upanishad* 2. 5. 19.

37. *Shvetashvatara Upanishad* 4. 1–10. Hume translation.

38. *Katha Upanishad* 1. 2. 5. See also *Mundaka Upanishad* 1. 2. 8 and *Maitri Upanishad* 7. 9.

39. *Brihad-Aranyaka Upanishad* 4. 3. 7; 2. 4. 14; 4. 5. 15.

40. *Ibid.*, 4. 3. 13. Hume translation.

41. *Ibid.*, 3. 2. 14.

42. *Ibid.*, 4. 4. 5.

43. *Maitri Upanishad* 3. 2.

44. 5. 40.

45. *Katha Upanishad* 3. 7. Hume translation.

46. 4. 4. 4. Hume translation.

47. *Maitri Upanishad* 1. 4. Hume translation.

48. *Brihad-Aranyaka Upanishad* 4. 4. 6.

49. *Chandogya Upanishad* 5. 10. 7. Hume translation.

50. *Katha Upanishad* 5. 7. Hume translation.

51. *Shvetashvatara Upanishad* 5. 7. Hume translation.

52. Louis Renou, *Religions of Ancient India*, p. 68.

53. *Chandogya Upanishad* 7. 2. 3.

54. *Ibid.*, 7. 26. 2.

55. *Mundaka Upanishad* 3. 2. 9.

56. *Ibid.*, 3. 2. 3.

57. *Mundaka Upanishad* 7. Hume translation.

58. *Ibid.*, 12.

59. *Mundaka Upanishad* 3. 1. 8. Radhakrishnan translation.

CHAPTER 7

1. S. Radhakrishnan and Charles A. Moore (editors), *A Source Book in Indian Philosophy*. Princeton: Princeton University Press, 1957, p. 227.

2. S. Radhakrishnan *et al.* (editors), *History of Philosophy Eastern and Western*, Vol. I. London: George Allen and Unwin, 1952, p. 133.

3. Benjamin Walker, *Hindu World*, Vol. II, p. 137.

4. From the *Sarvadarshanasamgraha*, a fourteenth-century work. Quoted by Radhakrishnan and Moore, *A Source Book in Indian Philosophy*, p. 230.

5. Quoted from the *Sarvasiddhantasamgraha* of Shankara. *Ibid.*, p. 235.

6. Quoted from an eleventh-century drama, the *Prabodha-Candrodaya*. *ibid.*, p. 248.

7. Quoted from *Sarvadarshanasamgraha*. *Ibid.*, p. 229.

CHAPTER 8

1. 18. 65–66. Prabhavananda and Isherwood translation.

2. *Rig Veda* 5. 85. 7–8. Griffith translation.

3. 5. 23.

4. *Rig Veda* 11. 90. 2.

5. Franklin Edgerton, *The Bhagavad Gita*. New York: Harper and Row, 1964, p. 167.

6. *Autobiography, The Story of My Experiments with Truth*. Ahmedabad: Navajivan Press, 1940, p. 323.

7. *Indian Thought and Its Development*, p. 191.

8. *Ancient India. A History of Its Culture and Civilization*, p. 114.

9. Sushil Kumar De in *History of Philosophy Eastern and Western*, Vol. I, p. 95.

10. *The Bhagavad Gita*, p. 128.

11. *The Bhagavad Gita*. Oxford: Clarendon Press, 1969, p. 32.

12. *The Bhagavadgita as a Philosophy of God-Realisation*. Nagpur: University of Nagpur, 1939.

13. *The Religions of India*. Boston: Ginn and Co., 1898, p. 399.

14. *The Gita: A Synthetic Interpretation*. Calcutta: Sadharan Brahmo Samaj, 1964, p. 1.

CHAPTER 9

1. *The Upanishads. The Sacred Books of the East*, Vol. XV. Oxford: Clarendon Press, 1884, p. xxxii.

2. *The Principal Upanishads*. London: George Allen and Unwin, 1953, p. 707.

3. *Shvetashvatara Upanishad* 1. 4.

4. 1. 8, 11; 2. 15; 4. 16; 5. 13; 6. 13.

5. 4. 11. All quotations from the *Shvetashvatara Upanishad* are from the Hume translation.

6. 1. 14.

7. 1. 10.

8. 4. 2.

9. 4. 2.

10. 4. 2.

11. 4. 2.

12. 3. 11.

13. 4. 19.

14. 2. 17; 3. 2, 4; 4. 12, 21, 22.

15. 3. 5, 6, 11; 4. 14, 16, 18; 5. 14.

16. 4.1.

17. 2. 17.

18. 4. 3–4.

19. 3. 3.
20. 6. 7.
21. 4. 14; 5. 13.
22. 5. 14.
23. 5. 14.
24. 3. 4.
25. 5. 5.
26. 6. 5.
27. 4. 14.
28. 3. 4; 4. 12.
29. 6. 9.
30. 6. 17.
31. 4. 15.
32. 1. 7.
33. 1. 8.
34. 1. 10.
35. 3. 1. Also 3. 2, 4; 5. 2, 4.
36. 3. 2.
37. 4. 14.
38. 4. 13.
39. 4. 13.
40. 3. 14.
41. 3. 2.
42. 5. 3.
43. 4. 20.
44. 4. 9–10.
45. 1. 14.
46. 1. 10.
47. 1. 11.
48. 4. 11.

49. 3. 20.

50. 3. 11.

51. 3. 6.

52. 4. 21–22.

53. 6. 23.

54. 6. 20.

55. *Rig Veda* 2. 33. 1. Macdonell translation.

56. *Ibid.,* 2. 33. 14.

57. Donald A. MacKenzie, *Indian Myth and Legend.* London: Gresham Publishing Co., 1910, p. 139.

CHAPTER 10

1. 4. 5; 6. 5.

2. Calcutta: Association Press, 1930, p. 8.

3. *Mahabharata* 6. 70.

4. 12. 22.

5. *Brihad-Aranyaka Upanishad* 4. 4. 6.

6. *Chandogya Upanishad* 5. 10. 7.

7. *Shvetashvatara Upanishad* 5. 7.

8. *Maitri Upanishad* 3. 2.

9. *Indian Philosophy*, Vol. I, p. 113.

10. *Ibid.*

11. *What Congress and Gandhi Have Done to the Untouchables*, p. 307.

12. *Rig Veda* 8. 48. 1, 3, 4, 6, 15.

13. 1. 174.

14. *Mahabharata* 3. 231.

15. *Shringara Shataka*, Section 23.

16. *Artha Shastra* 15. 1.

17. *Mahabharata* 12. 67.

18. *Ibid.*

19. *Ibid.,* 12. 68.

20. Arthur W. Ryder translation. Bombay: Jaico Publishing House, 1949, pp. 207–208.

21. *Ibid.*, p. 219.

22. *Mahabharata* 3. 31.

23. *The System of the Vedanta*. Chicago: Open Court Publishing Co., 1912, p. 253.

24. 2. 2. 3.

25. *Brihad-Aranyaka Upanishad* 1. 3. 28.

26. 12. 23.

27. 12. 10.

28. *Mahabharata* 12. 23.

29. See Aileen D. Ross, *The Hindu Family in Its Urban Setting*. Toronto: Toronto University Press, 1961. In this study of emotional attitudes the intensity of various relations in the Hindu family was determined as follows: mother-son, 115; brother-sister, 90; brother-brother, 75; father-son, 74; husband-wife, 16; sister-sister, 5.

30. *The Foundation of Indian Culture*. New York: The Sri Aurobindo Library, 1953, p. 130.

31. A British civil servant has made the following observation: "During my service in India my attention, aroused by a study of the village population, by experiences as Magistrate and Collector of Revenue in the United Provinces of Agra and Oudh, and by constant camping during cold-weather tours, was directed to the beliefs and ritual of the peasantry, as contrasted with that described in the official sacred books of the Brahmans. The study of the peasant religion and folklore showed that though Brahmanism had absorbed much of the beliefs of the peasantry, their religion, usages, and traditions represented a type very different from that of the priestly class, and this result was confirmed by my experience as Director of the Ethnological Survey of the Provinces." William Crooke, *Religion and Folklore of Northern India*. London: Oxford University Press, 1926, p. 5.

CHAPTER I I

1. Madhava's commentary on *Sutra* 1. 1. 4 of Badarayana's *Vedanta Sutras*.

2. *The Samkhya System*. Calcutta: YMCA Publishing House, 1949, p. 7.

3. *Ibid.*, p. 8.

4. *The Samkhya Karika of Ishwara Krishna.* London: Kegan Paul, Trench, Trübner and Co., 1890, p. v.

5. *The Secret of the Sacred Books of the Hindus.* Delhi: Bharati Research Institute, 1953, p. xliv.

6. *Samkhya Karika* 2.

7. *The Samkhya System*, p. 93.

8. *Samkhya Karika* 57.

9. *Ibid.*

10. *Indian Philosophy*, Vol. II, p. 313.

11. *Samkhya Karika* 68.

12. 2. 3. 6.

13. *Ibid.*, 5. 9. 1.

14. *Chandogya Upanishad* 8. 4. 2.

15. *Shvetashvatara Upanishad* 4. 18.

16. *Ibid.*, 2. 11.

17. *Practical Lessons in Yoga.* Lahore: Motilal Banarsi Das, 1938, p. 243. As an example of the foolishness against which Sivananda wrote, see the book, *In Search of a Yoga* by Dom Denys Rutledge (London: Routledge and Kegan Paul, 1963). Father Rutledge, after serving as a Roman Catholic missionary for many years in India, made a journey in 1959–1960 from Banaras to Rishikesh in search of a yogi who could do *siddhis* (miracles). He found none, so he concluded that there are no true yogis. I must add in fairness that such gross misunderstanding and misrepresentation of Hinduism by Roman Catholic priests is unusual. See for contrast the fine study by Jesuit scholars, *Religious Hinduism, A Presentation and Appraisal*, edited by R. De Smet. Third edition. Allahabad: St. Paul Publications, 1968.

18. *Yoga Sutras* 2. 14. Rama Prasada translation.

19. *Yoga Sutras* 2. 30.

20. *Ibid.*, 2. 32.

21. *Ibid.*, 2. 54.

22. *Ibid.*, 3. 4.

23. *Ibid.*, 3. 7.

24. *Ibid.*, 3. 10.

25. *Ibid.,* 3. 11.

26. *Ibid.,* 3. 49.

27. *Ibid.,* 4. 34.

28. *Nyaya Sutras* 1. 1. 4. S. C. Vidyabhusana translation.

29. *Ibid.,* 1. 1. 5.

30. *Ibid.*

31. *Ibid.,* 2. 1. 44.

32. *Ibid.,* 2. 1. 45.

33. *Ibid.,* 2. 1. 68.

34. *Nyaya Kusumanjali* 4. 1.

35. *Vaisheshika Sutras* 1. 3. 2. Nandalal Sinha translationl

CHAPTER 12

1. 3. 312.

2. Commentary on *Vedanta Sutras* 1. 1. 4. All selections from the commentary of Shankara on the *Vedanta Sutras* are from the George Thibaut translation. *Sacred Books of the East,* Vols. 34 and 38.

3. Commentary on *Vedanta Sutras* 1. 1. 1.

4. G. R. Malkani, *Philosophy of the Self.* Amalner: The Indian Institute of Philosophy, 1939, pp. 99–100, 105, 106, 107, 117.

5. Commentary on *Vedanta Sutras* 1. 1. 11.

6. *Brihad-Aranyaka Upanishad* 3. 8. 8. Hume translation.

7. *Chandogya Upanishad* 3. 14. 2. Hume translation.

8. Commentary on *Vedanta Sutras* 2. 1. 14.

9. Commentary on *Vedanta Sutras* 1. 4. 3.

10. *Ibid.*

11. 2. 4. 14; 4. 5. 15.

12. *Studies in Philosophy,* Vol. I. Edited by Gospinath Bhattacharyya. Calcutta: Progressive Publishers, 1956, p. 96.

13. *The Doctrine of Maya in the Philosophy of the Vedanta.* London: Luzac and Co., 1911, p. 26.

14. *Indian Philosophy,* Vol. II, p. 583.

15. *The Vedanta and Modern Thought.* London: Oxford University Press, 1928, p. 148.

16. 3. 2. 3.

17. Commentary on *Vedanta Sutras* 1. 4. 15.

18. Frithjof Schuon, *Language of the Self.* Translated by Marco Pallis and Macleod Matheson. Madras: Ganesh and Co., 1959, pp. 22–23.

19. Commentary on *Vedanta Sutras* 1. 4. 15.

CHAPTER 13

1. *The Lord of the Harvest Moon.* Bombay: Asia Publishing House, 1957, p. 5.

2. *Epic India.* Bombay: Mrs. Radhabai Atmaran Sagoon, 1907, p. 422.

3. *Indian Philosophy,* Vol. I, p. 496.

4. Charles E. Gover, *The Folk-Songs of South India.* Madras: The South India Shaiva Siddhanta Works Publishing Society, 1959, pp. 85–86.

5. Alkondavalli Govindacharya, *The Holy Lives of the Azhvars or Dravida Saints.* Mysore: G. T. A. Press, 1902, pp. 221–222.

6. R. W. Frazer, *Indian Thought Past and Present.* London: T. Fisher Unwin, 1915, p. 221.

7. *India's Religion of Grace and Christianity Compared and Contrasted.* London: Student Christian Movement, 1930, p. 22.

8. *The Vedanta-Sutras with the Commentary of Shankaracharya, Sacred Books of the East,* Vol. 34, p. cxxvi.

9. *The Vedanta-Sutras with the Commentary of Ramanuja, Sacred Books of the East,* Vol. 48, p. ix.

10. Commentary on *Vedanta Sutras* 1. 1. 1.

11. *Ibid.*

12. *Ibid.*

13. *Ibid.*

14. Commentary on *Vedanta Sutras* 2. 3. 45.

15. *Ibid.,* 1. 1. 1.

16. *Ibid.,* 1. 3. 19.

17. *Ibid.*, 1. 1. 1.

18. *Ibid.*

19. *Ibid.*

20. *Ibid.*

CHAPTER 14

1. *The Renaissance in India.* Chandernagor: Prabartak Publishing House, 1920, pp. 19, 21.

2. *Ibid.*, p. 23.

3. M. Dhavamony in *Religious Hinduism. A Presentation and Appraisal.* Third Edition. Edited by R. De Smet. Pp. 265–266.

4. Quoted by R. G. Bhandarkar, *Vaishnavism, Shaivism, and Minor Religious Systems.* Strassburg: K. J. Trübner, 1913, p. xviii.

5. All selections from the Adiyars are taken from F. Kingsbury and G. E. Phillips, *Hymns of the Tamil Shaivite Saints.* London: Oxford University Press, 1921.

6. New York: Barnes and Noble, 1962, pp. 378–379.

7. *The Tantric Tradition.* London: Rider and Co., 1965, p. 11.

CHAPTER 15

1. C. E. Sachau, *Alberuni's India*, Vol. I. London: Trübner and Co., 1910, pp. 22, 23.

2. The excellent French Indologist, Louis Renou, once wrote that "there is nothing at all in the evolution of Indian thought but both can and should be accounted for by the internal logic and inherent energy of Hinduism itself." *The Nature of Hinduism*, p. 36.

3. See N. C. Chaudhuri, *The Continent of Circe.*

4. Benjamin Walker, *Hindu World*, Vol. II, p. 100.

5. Sachau, *Alberuni's India*, Vol. I, p. 22.

6. I am well aware that my brief remarks cover without sufficient argument the delicate issue of the relations of Muslims and Hindus. Humayun Kabir has written, "The process of growth, both among the Hindus and the Muslims, for almost nine centuries was one of contact, assimilation, and synthesis. The intrusion of the new element of western influence started a

process of dissociation between the two communities, and was an inroad upon the common culture built up through a millennium." (*The Cultural Heritage of India*, Vol. IV, p. 592.) This was obviously a politic statement for an Indian Muslim to make in 1956, but he grossly exaggerated the "assimilation" and "synthesis" of Hindus and Muslims, and he fell into the understandable Indian propensity of blaming India's ills on the British. A much more accurate statement comes from R. C. Majumder: "The ultra-democratic social ideas of the Muslims, though strictly confined to their own religious community, were an object-lesson of equality and fraternity which Europe, and through her the world, learnt at a great cost only in the nineteenth century. The liberal spirit of tolerance and reverence for all religions, preached and practised by the Hindus, is still an ideal and despair of the civilized mankind. The Hindus, even with the living example of the Muslim community before their very eyes, did not relax in the least their social rigidity and inequality of men exemplified in the caste-system and untouchability. Nor did the Muslims ever moderate their zeal to destroy ruthlessly the Hindu temples and images of gods, and their attitude in this respect remained unchanged from the day when Muhammad bin Qasim set foot on the soil of India till the eighteenth century A.D. when they lost all political power. The Hindus combined catholicity in religious outlook with bigotry in social ethics, while the Muslims displayed an equal bigotry in religious ideas with catholicity in social behavior." (*The History and Culture of the Indian People: The Delhi Sultanate*. Second edition. Bombay: Bharatiya Vidya Bhavan, 1962, pp. 616–617.)

7. *Hindu World*, Vol. II, p. 102.

8. *Koran* 35. 11.

9. *Ibid.*, 50. 16.

10. *Ibid.*, 2. 109.

11. *Ibid.*, 24, 35.

12. *Ibid.*, 3. 29.

13. C. E. Abraham, "The Rise and Growth of Christianity in India" in *The Cultural Heritage of India*, Vol. IV, p. 565.

14. Page 526.

CHAPTER 16

1. Quoted from Kshitimohan Sen, "The Medieval Mystics of North India" in *The Cultural Heritage of India*, Vol. IV, p. 379.

2. All Kabir poems are from Max Arthur Macauliffe, *The Sikh Religion*. Oxford: Clarendon Press, 1909.

3. All poems of the Maharashtra *bhaktas* are from Nicol Macnicol, *Psalms of Maratha Saints*. Calcutta: Association Press, 1919.

4. *Madhya-Lila*, chap. 2. Nagendra Kumar Ray, translator, *Sri Sri Chaitanya Charitamrita*, Vol. II. Calcutta: Radharani Ashram, 1959, pp. 26–27.

5. Dinesh Chandra Sen, *The Vaishnava Literature of Mediaeval Bengal*. Calcutta: Calcutta University, 1917, p. 217.

CHAPTER 17

1. *History of Bengal*, Vol. II, p. 498. Quoted by R. C. Majumdar, *British Paramountcy and Indian Renaissance*, Part II. Bombay: Bharatiya Vidya Bhavan, 1965, p. 1.

2. Nemai Sadhan Bose, *The Indian Awakening and Bengal*. Calcutta: Firma K. L. Mukhopadhyay, 1960, p. 100.

3. Swami Nirvedananda, "Sri Ramakrishna and Spiritual Renaissance" in *The Cultural Heritage of India*, Vol. IV, p. 662.

4. "Swami Vivekananda and America," p. 19. A pamphlet prepared by the United States Information Service, New Delhi, no date.

CHAPTER 18

1. Page 728.

2. *British Paramountcy and Indian Renaissance*, Part II, p. 11.

3. *Ibid.*, pp. 14, 28–29.

4. *Hindu Culture and the Modern Age*. Annamalainagar: Annamalai University, 1956, p. 49.

5. John Strachey, *India: Its Administration and Progress*. London: Macmillan, 1888, p. 4.

6. John R. Seeley, *The Expansion of England*. London: Macmillan, 1883, p. 92.

7. *India: A Synthesis of Cultures*. Bombay: Thacker and Co., 1947.

8. C. F. Andrews, *Letters to a Friend*. London: George Allen and Unwin, 1928, p. 128.

9. *A Tagore Reader*. Edited by Amiya Chakravarty. New York: Macmillan Co., 1961, p. 200.

10. From his essay entitled "Nationalism." *Sources of Indian Tradition*, Vol. II, p. 236.

11. "The Spirit of Freedom" in *Creative Unity*. London: Macmillan and Co., 1922, p. 140.

12. From a letter to C. F. Andrews. *Letters to a Friend*, p. 239.

13. "Nationalism" in *A Tagore Reader*, p. 199.

14. "The Nation" in *Creative Unity*, p. 139.

15. *Ibid.*, p. 146.

16. *Ibid.*, p. 142.

17. *Ibid.*, p. 143.

18. *Ibid.*, p. 144.

19. *Ibid.*

20. *Speeches*, p. 24. Quoted by Sisirkumar Mitra, *The Liberator*. Delhi, Bombay, and Calcutta: Jaico Publishing House, 1954, pp. 102–103.

21. *Bande Mataram*, May 3, 1908. *The Liberator*, p. 104.

22. *Ibid.*, March 29, 1908. *The Liberator*, p. 105.

23. *Weekly Bande Mataram*, July 7, 1907. *The Liberator*, p. 106.

24. *Speeches*, p. 175. *The Liberator*, p. 109.

25. *The Foundations of Indian Culture*. New York: The Sri Aurobindo Library, 1933, pp. 14–15.

26. *The Liberator*, p. 190.

27. *Young India*, April 9, 1935. A weekly paper edited by Gandhi from 1919 to 1931.

28. *Asian Drama*, Vol. II. New York: Random House, 1968, p. 756.

29. Pyarelal, *Mahatma Gandhi: The Last Phase*, Vol. I. Ahmedabad: Navajivan Publishing House, 1956, p. 120.

30. *An Autobiography*. London: The Botley Head, 1953, p. 528.

31. *Harijan*, April 29, 1933. A weekly founded by Gandhi in 1933.

32. Louis Fischer, *The Essential Gandhi*. New York: Random House, 1962, pp. 156, 171.

33. *Hindu Dharma*. Ahmedabad: Navajivan Publishing House, 1950, p. 23.

34. *Ibid.*, p. 370.

35. *Ibid.,* p. 219.

36. *Ibid.,* p. 402.

37. *Young India*, August 4, 1920.

38. *Harijan*, January 26, 1934.

39. *Caste Today*. London: Oxford University Press, 1962, pp. 49–50.

40. *Sources of Indian Tradition*, Vol. II, p. 249.

41. R. C. Zaehner, *Hinduism.* London: Oxford University Press, 1962, p. 224.

42. *Young India*, 1919–1922, p. 674.

43. *Hind Swaraj.* Ahmedabad: Navajivan Publishing House, 1962, p. 24.

44. *The Message of the East.* Madras: Ganesh and Co., 1909, pp. 31, 33, 36.

45. *The Discovery of India.* Garden City, New York: Doubleday and Co., 1960, p. 389.

46. *Ibid.,* p. 393.

47. *Ibid.*

48. *Rig Veda* 10. 191. 4.

Selected Bibliography

CHAPTER I

Hopkins, Thomas J., *The Hindu Religious Tradition*. Encino, California, and Belmont, California: Dickenson Publishing Co., 1971.

Macnicol, Nicol, *The Living Religions of the Indian People*. London: Student Christian Movement, 1934.

Nakamura, Hagime, *Ways of Thinking of Eastern Peoples: India-China-Tibet-Japan*. Honolulu: East-West Center Press, 1964, Part I.

Renou, Louis, *The Nature of Hinduism*. Translated by Patrick Evans. New York: Walker and Co., 1962.

Renou, Louis, *Religions of Ancient India*. London: Athlone Press, 1953.

Zaehner, R. C., *Hinduism*. New York: Oxford University Press, 1966.

CHAPTER 2

De Smet, R. (editor), *Religious Hinduism. A Presentation and Appraisal*. Third edition. Allahabad: St. Paul Publications, 1968.

Mahadevan, T. M. P., *Outlines of Hinduism*. Bombay: Chetana Limited, 1956.

Organ, Troy, *The Hindu Quest for the Perfection of Man*. Athens, Ohio: Ohio University Press, 1970.

Walker, Benjamin, *Hindu World*. 2 vols. London: George Allen and Unwin, 1968.

Weber, Max, *The Religion of India*. New York: The Free Press, 1958.

CHAPTER 3

Allchin, B., and Allchin, F. R., *Birth of Indian Civilization: India and Pakistan before 500 B.C.* Harmondsworth, Middlesex: Penguin Books, 1968.

Fairservis, Walter A., Jr., *The Roots of Ancient India*. New York: Macmillan Co., 1971.

Kosambi, D. D., *Ancient India. A History of Its Culture and Civilization.* New York: Random House, Pantheon Books, 1965.

Piggott, Stuart, *Prehistoric India*. Harmondsworth, Middlesex: Penguin Books, 1950.

Raikes, Robert L., "End of the Ancient Cities of the Indus," *American Anthropologist*, Vol. 66, April 1964, pp. 284–297.

Taddei, Maurizio, *India*. Translated by James Hogarth. London: Barrie and Jenkins, 1970, chap. 1.

Wheeler, Sir Mortimer, *The Indus Civilization*. Cambridge: Cambridge University Press, 1953.

CHAPTER 4

Bhandarkar, D. R., *Some Aspects of Ancient Indian Culture*. Madras: University of Madras, 1940.

Bhargava, P. L., *India in the Vedic Age*. Lucknow: Upper India Publishing House, 1956.

Bloomfield, Maurice, *The Religion of the Veda. The Ancient Religion of India from the Rig Veda to the Upanishads*. New York and London: G. P. Putnam's Sons, 1908.

Deshmukh, P. S., *The Origin and Development of Religion in Vedic Literature*. London: Oxford University Press, 1933.

Keith, A. Berriedale, *The Religion and Philosophy of the Veda and the Upanishads*. 2 vols. Cambridge: Harvard University Press, 1925.

Oldenberg, Hermann, *Die Religion des Veda*. Berlin: W. Hertz, 1894.

Prabhavananda, Swami, *Vedic Religion and Philosophy*. Mylapore, Madras: Sri Ramakrishna Math, 1938.

CHAPTER 5

Bloomfield, Maurice, *Hymns of the Atharva-Veda*. Oxford: Clarendon Press, 1897.

Griffith, Ralph T. H., *The Hymns of the Atharva-Veda*. Banaras: E. J. Lazarus and Co., 1895.

Karambelkar, V. W., *The Atharva-Veda and the Ayur-Veda*. Nagpur: Nagpur University, 1961.

Karambelkar, V. W., *The Atharvavedic Civilisation*. Nagpur: Nagpur University, 1959.

Keith, A. B., *The Rig-Vedic Brahmanas*. Cambridge: Harvard University Press, 1920.

MacDonald, K. S., *The Brahmanas of the Vedas*. Madras: Christian Literature Society for India, 1896.

MacDonald, K. S., *The Vedic Religion*. London: Nisbet and Co., 1881.

Macdonell, A. A., *A History of Sanskrit Literature*. Delhi: Munshi Ram Manohar Lal, 1900, chaps. 7, 8.

Shende, N. J., *The Religion and Philosophy of the Atharvaveda*. Poona: Bhandarkar Oriental Research Institute, 1952.

CHAPTER 6

Deussen, Paul, *The Philosophy of the Upanishads*. Edinburgh: T. and T. Clark, 1906.

Gough, A. E., *The Philosophy of the Upanishads and Ancient Indian Metaphysics*. London: K. Paul, Trench, Trübner and Co., 1903.

Hume, Robert Ernest, *The Thirteen Principal Upanishads*. London: Oxford University Press, 1921.

Milburn, R. Gordon, *The Religious Mysticism of the Upanishads*. London: Theosophical Publishing House, 1924.

Radhakrishnan, S., *The Principal Upanishads*. London: George Allen and Unwin, 1953.

Ranade, R. D., *A Constructive Survey of Upanishadic Philosophy*. Poona: Oriental Book Agency, 1926.

CHAPTER 7

Basham, A. L., *History and Doctrines of the Ajivikas*. London: Luzac and Co., 1951.

Chattopadhyaya, D., *Lokayata: A Study in Ancient Hindu Materialism*. New Delhi: People's Publishing House, 1959.

Conze, Edward, *Buddhism, Its Essence and Development*. New York: Harper and Brothers, 1959.

Hamilton, Clarence Herbert (editor), *Buddhism, A Religion of Infinite Compassion; Selections from Buddhist Literature*. New York: Liberal Arts Press, 1952.

Humphreys, Christmas, *Buddhism*. Harmondsworth, Middlesex: Penguin Books, 1951.

Jaini, J., *Outlines of Jainism*. Cambridge: Cambridge University Press, 1916.

Keith, Arthur Berriedale, *Buddhist Philosophy in India and Ceylon*. Oxford: Clarendon Press, 1923.

Mehta, Mohan Lal, *Outlines of Jaina Philosophy*. Bangalore: Jain Mission Society, 1954.

Riepe, Dale, *The Naturalistic Tradition in Indian Thought*. Seattle: University of Washington Press, 1961.

Shastri, Dakshinaranjan, *A Short History of Indian Materialism, Sensationalism and Hedonism*. Calcutta: Calcutta Book Co., 1930.

Stevenson, Mrs. Sinclair T., *The Heart of Jainism*. London: Oxford University Press, 1915.

CHAPTER 8

Arnold, Edwin, *The Song Celestial, or Bhagavad-Gita*. Philadelphia: David McKay Co., 1934.

Bhandarkar, R. G., *Vaishnavism, Shaivism, and Minor Religious Systems*. Strassburg: K. J. Trübner, 1913.

Chitale, M. P., *Bhagavad-Gita and Hindu Dharma*. Poona: Continental Publishers, 1953.

Deutsch, Eliot, *The Bhagavad Gita*. New York: Holt, Rinehart and Winston, 1968.

Edgerton, Franklin, *The Bhagavad Gita*. New York and Evanston: Harper and Row, 1944.

Gonda, Jan, *Aspects of Early Vishnuism*. Utrecht: N. V. A. Oosthoek's Uitgevers Mij, 1954.

Prabhavananda, Swami, and Isherwood, Christopher, *The Song of God: Bhagavad-Gita*. New York: New American Library of World Literature, 1954.

Raychaudhuri, Hemchandra, *Materials for the Study of the Early History of the Vaishnava Sect*. Calcutta: University of Calcutta, 1920.

Schrader, F. O., *Introduction to the Pancaratra and the Ahirbudhnya Samhita*. Madras: The Adyar Library, 1916.

CHAPTER 9

Sastri, K. A. Nilankanta, "An Historical Sketch of Shaivism," *The Cultural History of India*, Vol. IV, pp. 63–78.

Shivapadasundaram, S., *The Shaiva School of Hinduism*. London: George Allen and Unwin, 1934.

Srinivasa Aiyangar, T. R., *Shaiva Upanishads*. Madras: The Adyar Library, 1953.

Srisa Chandra Vasu, *The Shiva Samhita. Sacred Books of the Hindus*, Vol. 15. Allahabad: The Panini Office, 1923.

Varadachari, K. C., *Aspects of Bhakti*. Mysore: University of Mysore, 1956.

CHAPTER 10

Barnell, L. D., *The Heart of Hinduism*. London: John Murray, 1924.

Basham, A. L., *The Wonder That Was India*. London: Sidgwick and Jackson, 1954.

Brahma, Nalini Kanta, *Philosophy of Hindu Sadhana*. London: Kegan Paul, Trench, Trübner and Co., 1932.

Humphreys, Christmas, *Karma and Rebirth*. London: John Murray, 1959.

Hutton, J. H., *Caste in India*. Cambridge: Cambridge University Press, 1946.

Isaacs, Harold, *India's Ex-Untouchables*. New York: John Day and Co., 1965.

Morgan, Kenneth W. (editor), *The Religion of the Hindus*. New York: Ronald Press, 1953.

Mukerjee, Radhakamal, *The Indian Scheme of Life*. Bombay: Hind Kitabs, 1951.

Radhakrishnan, S., *The Hindu View of Life*. London: George Allen and Unwin, 1927.

Schayer, Stanislaw, *Contributions to the Problem of Time in Indian Philosophy*. Cracow, 1938.

CHAPTER 11

Bhaduri, Sadananda, *Studies in Nyaya-Vaisheshika Metaphysics*. Poona: Bhandarkar Oriental Research Institute, 1947.

Chatterjee, Satis Chandra, *The Nyaya Theory of Knowledge*. Calcutta: University of Calcutta, 1950.

Dasgupta, Surendranath, *Yoga as Philosophy and Religion*. London: Kegan Paul, Trench, Trübner and Co., 1924.

Eliade, Mircea, *Yoga: Immortality and Freedom*. Translated by William R. Trask. New York: Random House, Pantheon Books, 1958.

Faddegan, Berend, *The Vaisheshika System*. Amsterdam: J. Muller, 1918.

Garbe, Richard, *Samkhya and Yoga*. Strasbourg: K. J. Trübner, 1896.

Keith, A. Berriedale, *The Karma Mimamsa*. London: Oxford University Press, 1921.

Keith, A. Berriedale, *The Samkhya System*. Calcutta: YMCA Publishing House, 1949.

Thadani, Nanikram Vasanmal, *The Mimamsa: The Sect of the Sacred Doctrines of the Hindus*. Delhi: Bharati Research Institute, 1952.

CHAPTER 12

Das, S. K., *A Study of the Vedanta*. Calcutta: University of Calcutta, 1937.

Deussen, Paul, *Outline of the Vedanta System of Philosophy According to Shankara*. Translated by J. H. Woods and C. B. Runkel. New York: The Grafton Press, 1906.

Mahadevan, T. M. P., *The Philosophy of Advaita*. London: Luzac and Co., 1938.

Sarkar, Mahendranath, *The System of Vedantic Thought and Culture*. Calcutta: University of Calcutta, 1925.

Sastri, Kokileswar, *A Realistic Interpretation of Shankara-Vedanta*. Calcutta: University of Calcutta, 1931.

Singh, Ram Pratap, *The Vedanta of Shankara*. Jaipur: Bharat Publishing House, 1949.

Urquhart, W. S., *The Vedanta and Modern Thought*. London: Oxford University Press, 1928.

CHAPTER 13

Aiyangar, S. K., *Early History of Vaishnavism in South India*. London: Oxford University Press, 1920.

Archer, William George, *The Loves of Krishna in Indian Painting and Poetry*. London: George Allen and Unwin, 1957.

Hooper, J. S. M., *Hymns of the Alvars*. Calcutta: Association Press, 1929.

Kumarappa, Bharatan, *The Hindu Conception of the Deity as Culminating in Ramanuja*. London: Luzac and Co., 1934.

Mallik, G. N., *The Philosophy of Vaishnava Religion*. Lahore: Motilal Banarsi Das, 1927.

Rajagopalachariar, T., *The Vaishnavite Reformers of India*. Madras: G. A. Natesan and Co., 1909.

Rao, T. A. Gopinath, *History of Shri Vaishnavas*. Madras: Madras University, 1923.

Shrinivasachari, P. N., *The Philosophy of Vishishtadvaita*. Madras: The Adyar Library, 1943.

CHAPTER 14

Bagchi, P. C., *Studies in the Tantras*. Calcutta: Calcutta University, 1939.

Bharati, Agehananda, *The Tantric Tradition*. London: Rider and Co., 1965.

Chakravarti, P. C., *Doctrine of Shakti in Indian Literature*. Calcutta: General Printers and Publishers, 1940.

Chatterji, J. C., *Kashmir Shaivism*. Srinagar; Jammu and Kashmir State Research Dept., 1914.

Das, Sudhendukumar, *Shakti or Divine Power*. Calcutta: Calcutta University, 1934.

Nadimath, S. C., *Handbook of Virashaivism*. Dharwar: L. E. Association, 1942.

Nallaswami Pillai, J. M., *Studies in Shaiva Siddhanta*. Madras: J. N. Ramanathan, 1911.

Narayana Aiyar, C. C., *The Origin and Early History of Shaivism in South India*. Madras: Madras University, 1936.

Payne, Ernest Alexander, *The Shaktas*. Calcutta: YMCA Publishing House, 1933.

Pillai, Tiru G. S., *Introduction and History of Shaiva Siddhanta*. Annamalainagar: Annamalai University, 1948.

Subramanian, K. R., *Origin of Shaivism and Its History in the Tamil Land*. Madras: Madras University, 1927.

CHAPTER 15

Guénon, René, *East and West*. Translated by William Massey. London: Luzac and Co., 1941.

Ikram, S. M., *Muslim Civilization in India*. Edited by Ainslie T. Embree. New York and London: Columbia University Press, 1964.

Manshardt, Clifford, *The Hindu-Muslim Problem in India*. London: George Allen and Unwin, 1936.

Mujeeb, M., *The Indian Muslims*. London: George Allen and Unwin, 1967.

O'Malley, L. S. S., *Modern India and the West: A Study of the Interaction of their Civilizations*. London: Oxford University Press, 1941.

Otto, Rudolf, *India's Religion of Grace and Christianity Compared and Contrasted*. London: Student Christian Movement, 1930.

Radhakrishnan, S., *East and West*. London: George Allen and Unwin, 1955.

Slater, T. E., *The Higher Hinduism in Relation to Christianity*. London: Eliot Stock, 1902.

Tara Chand, *The Influence of Islam on Indian Culture*. Allahabad: The Indian Press, 1936.

Ward, Barbara, *India and the West*. London: Hamish and Hamilton, 1961.

Winslow, J. C., *The Christian Approach to the Hindu*. London: Edinburgh House Press, 1958.

CHAPTER 16

Cunningham, J. D., *A History of the Sikhs*. London: Oxford University Press, 1918.

Dasgupta, B. V., *Some Aspects of Bengal Vaishnavism*. Dacca: S. N. Dasgupta, 1937.

De, Sushil Kumar, *Early History of the Vaishnava Faith and Movement*. Calcutta: General Printers and Publishers, 1942.

Fraser, J. N., and Edwards, J. F., *Life and Teachings of Tukaram*. Madras: Christian Literature Society for India, 1922.

Keay, F. E., *Kabir and His Followers*. Calcutta: Association Press, 1931.

Kennedy, Melville T., *The Chaitanya Movement*. Calcutta: Association Press, 1925.

Sen, Dinesh Chandra, *Chaitanya and His Age*. Calcutta: Calcutta University, 1922.

Singh, Khushwant, *A History of the Sikhs*. 2 vols. Princeton: Princeton University Press, 1963–1966.

Varadachari, K., *Aspects of Bhakti*. Mysore: Mysore University, 1956.

Westcott, W. H., *Kabir and the Kabir Panth*. Calcutta: Susil Gupta Ltd., 1953.

CHAPTER 17

Andrews, C. F., *The Renaissance in India*. London: Young People's Missionary Movement, 1912.

Aurobindo, *The Renaissance in India*. Calcutta: Arya Publishing House, 1946.

Besant, Annie, *Theosophy and the New Psychology*. London: Theosophical Publishing Society, 1904.

Devanandan, Paul David, "The Renaissance of Hinduism. A Survey of Hindu Religious History from 1800 to 1910." *Theology Today*, Vol. 12, pp. 189–205.

Farquhar, J. N., *Modern Religious Movements in India*. New York: Macmillan Co., 1915.

Goetz, H., *The Crisis of Indian Civilization in the Eighteenth and Nineteenth Centuries*. Calcutta: University of Calcutta, 1938.

Leonard, G. S., *A History of the Brahma Samaj from Its Rise to 1878*. Calcutta: Adi Brahmo Samaj Press, 1879.

Macnicol, Nicol, *The Making of Modern India*. London: Oxford University Press, 1924.

Morrison, John, *New Ideas in India during the Nineteenth Century*. London: Simpkin, Marshall and Co., 1906.

Rai, Lala Lajput, *The Arya Samaj*. London: Longmans, Green and Co., 1915.

Sharma, D. S., *Studies in the Renaissance of Hinduism in the Nineteenth and Twentieth Centuries*. Banaras: Banaras Hindu University, 1944.

CHAPTER 18

Archer, William, *India and the Future*. London: Hutchinson and Co., 1917.

Chakravarti, A., *Humanism and Indian Thought*. Madras: University of Madras, 1935.

Gokhale, B. G., *The Making of the Indian Nation*. Bombay: Asia Publishing House, 1958.

Harrison, Selig S., *India: The Most Dangerous Decades*. Princeton: Princeton University Press, 1960.

Lamb, Beatrice Pitney, *India, A World in Transition*. New York: Frederick A. Praeger, 1963.

Roy, Satis Chandra, *Religion and Modern India*. Calcutta: Asutosh Library, 1923.

Segel, Ronald, *The Crisis of India*. London: Johnathan Cape, 1965.

Sethna, K. D., *The Indian Spirit and the World's Future*. Pondicherry: Sri Aurobindo Ashram, 1953.

Shils, Edward A., *The Intellectual Between Tradition and Modernity: The Indian Situation*. The Hague: Mouton, 1961.

Smith, Donald E., *India as a Secular State*. Princeton: Princeton University Press, 1963.

Index

424 / INDEX